SEIDE MAISES...

GRANDFATHER'S TALES

SECTION of STOKE, COVENTRY 1940

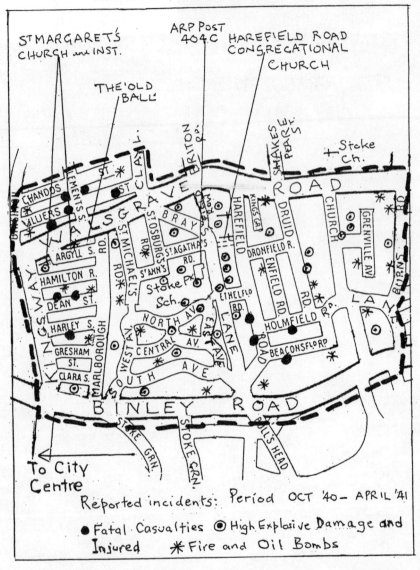

Reported incidents: Period OCT '40 – APRIL '41

● Fatal Casualties ◉ High Explosive Damage and Injured ✳ Fire and Oil Bombs

Adapted from the Operations Map of Post 404C maintained by
Warden Harry Kay

SEIDE MAISES...

GRANDFATHER'S TALES

BRIAN TAYLOR

NORMITA PRESS
LONDON

© Brian Taylor 1994

Brian Taylor is hereby identified as author of this work in accordance with Section 77 of the Copyright, Designs and Patents Act 1988

A CIP record of this book is available from the British Library

ISBN 0-9522794-0-1

First published in 1994 by
Normita Press
6 Oval Road London NW1 7EB England
and printed by
Booksprint of Bristol

TO

CHELSEA UDDO

WYLF and SID TAYLOR-JONES

HARRY and ALFIE HUDSON-TAYLOR

STEPHEN, RICHARD and VICTORIA NORMAN

ACKNOWLEDGEMENTS

The title 'Seide Maises' is a token of my thanks to all those Yiddish storytellers who in their twilight years never tired of relating their own grandfather's tales. They, with all the other grandfathers in the world, have always tried to satisfy the insatiable hunger that the question, "Grandad, what was it like in the olden days?" brings in its wake.

CONTENTS

List of Illustrations ix
Preface xiii

1. Family 1
2. Shadows of the First War 17
3. Deeper shadows of the Second 36
4. If music be the food of love 61
5. King Henry VIII School and Philip Larkin 82
6. Coventrated 96
7. Messenger boys 117
8. Training school 137
9. Girls, girls, girls 146
10. Keep fit. Take exercise. 160
11. On the Road to Berlin 179
12. Reflections 196
13. The end of the road 207
14. Demobbed 228
15. John Grierson and Documentary Film 242
16. Film Centre 260
17. A Festival of Ballet 269
18. A television debut with Jeremy Thorpe 286
19. Cool for Cats 300
20. Edward J. & Harry Lee Danziger 318
21. The May Fair Theatre 336
22. Forty Years On 351

Index 357

ILLUSTRATIONS

Between pages 48 and 49

1. The Salt Family 1917 in Manchester
2. Bandmaster Salt and the Wesley Hall Band, Ancoats.
3. Grandmother Sarah Jane Taylor 1918
4. George Taylor with his cello
5. George Taylor at his lathe 1923
6. The small crank
7. The small BLT 1926
8. Mother Ethel and BLT in Coventry town Centre 1933
9. St Margaret's Church, Walsgrave Road, Coventry 1935
10. Midland Daily Telegraph press cuttings
11. Beryl & Joyce Salt
12. Mother with Anniversary cake
13. Philip Larkin and John Stringer 1937
14. Harold Furminger with BLT in Memorial Park 1941
15. F.H.Metcalf & BLT at School Concert
16. Teenage Drama:
    Holy Trinity Church Passion Play (M. D. Telegraph)
    Laburnum Grove (KHS Archive)
17. Belgium, Easter 1939:
    Army guard in Brussels 1939
    Antwerp Cathedral 1939
18. ARP Messenger Boy 1940

Between pages 144 and 145

19. Whitley bomber at Baginton 1940(Crown Film Unit)
20. 1st XV Photograph, April 8 1941 (KHS Archive)
21. School Hall, Warwick Road, April 9 1941
22. University College, Nottingham 1942

23. D.J. White, W.B. Taylor & BLT 1942
24. Ptes. R.W. Winter & BLT 1943
25. John Stringer & BLT 1944
26. British Army Forces Centre, Hamburg 1945
27. BLT 1945
28 Captains Philip Cramner, Peter Rice and Clem Handley
29. Flt Lieut R.E. Shreeve & CCG Officer Joan Foulger
30. Spitfire pilot Harold Furminger
31. 131 Brigade Headquarters, Berlin 1945
32. Armoured vehicles of the Desert Rats 1945
33. Garden at Reich Chancellery, Berlin 1945
34 The Hitler Bunker 1945
35. Technical High School, Berlin 1945
36. Staats Opera, Berlin 1945
37. Gedachtniskirche, Berlin 1945
38. Russian War Memorial & Reichstag building 1945
39 Entrance to Olympic Stadium Berlin 1945
40. Edel von Rothe, Gisela Diege, Cyril Frankel & BLT

Between pages 240 and 241

41. Major Fred Butters & BLT in Harz Mountains 1946
42. Benn Toff (Heidersberger, Brunswick)
43. Sergiu Celibidache & the Berlin Philharmonic (HB)
44. Celia Franca & Honor Frost, Paris 1947
45. The Coronation procession from Park Lane
46. John Grierson (World Today Inc)
47. Stuart Legg (World Today Inc)
48. Sir Stephen Tallents (Crown Film Unit)
49. Sir Arthur Elton (Shell Film Unit)
50. Cyril Frankel & Peter Finch (Group 3 Films)
51. Mary Munro as Giselle (London's Festival Ballet)
52. Julian Braunsweg
53. Muriel Young, Norman Macqueen & BLT (Macqueen Films)
54. Muriel Young, Marilyn Burr & BLT (Associated-Rediffusion)
55. Harry Belafonte & BLT (Associated-Rediffusion)
56. Toni Carroll & BLT (Daily Sketch Newspapers)

Between pages 304 and 305

57. Kent Walton & BLT (Associated-Rediffusion)
58. Douglas Squires & Mavis Ascott (Associated-Rediffusion)
59. Cool for Cats (Associated-Rediffusion)
60. Mavis Traill (Daily Sketch Newspapers)
61. Douglas Squires & Pauline Innes (Associated-Rediffusion)
62. Agatha Christie & BLT (Danziger Films)
63. Stewart Granger, Cyril Frankel & BLT (Rialto Films)
64. Candlelight Room, May Fair Hotel (Danziger Films)
65. The May Fair Theatre (Danziger Films)
66. Six Characters in Search of an Author (Danziger Films)
67. Edward & Harry Danziger. (Danziger Collection)
68. William Ball (Danziger Films)
69. Norma & BLT

Unless otherwise stated, all photographs come from the Taylor collection, copyright Brian Taylor.

SEIDE MAISES...

GRANDFATHER'S TALES

PREFACE

When I started this book I had five grandchildren, now two years later there are three more, Harry, Sid and Alfie. They have entered a world where change is running apace; a new revolution under way that is sweeping all before it as it embraces the spin offs of the computer age. It has caught me in its coils too, so that what I commenced as an exercise in the written word has developed into taming the intricacies of word processors and laser printers. Thanks to the encouragement of my daughter Melanie and the loan of a 286 PC from Andy Hudson I made my first hesitating steps into Desk Top Publishing. Along the way came the enthusiastic prodding of Lawrence Titton who converted me to the faster 486 and then the help of Psychic Books publisher Carl Duncan to lead me forward onto the Aldus PageMaker.

What a journey it has been and my grateful thanks go to all who have helped me on the way. To Noel Hughes for his comments and advice on the Philip Larkin section and to others of the family of King Henry VIII School, including the tireless Jeff Vent and the *Coventry Evening Telegraph's* Keith Draper. And then especially to Harry Furminger and Rosemary Lapthorn for stirring up the thoughts of those pre-1939 days and the Bomb Happy months of the 40's.

At home my wife Norma has proved a resilient spur, aiding me in the mysteries of keyboarding, lay-out and proof reading, while cousin Jack Taylor in New Zealand, and his son Denis, have provided the basic raw material culled from family bibles and birth certificates which has given me the background to the early stories of Manchester. A final word to those others who pressed me forward when words seemed to fail: to Jack and Judy Rosenbaum, Claire Tomalin, Andrew Motion, Jacques Bonan and Jacques Nardot in Paris, and Cyril Frankel, plus the many others who in one way or another are part of grandfather's tales.

Camden Town, 1994

ONE

FAMILY

I KNEW THE day would eventually arrive when I could sit down
and look at the diary jottings I had made over the years. Maybe
I should try and put them in some sort of order, just to be tidy;
and then the other week, friends we visited told us a story about
their octogenarian father. He had fled from Russia in the First World
War and worried because his family knew nothing of their ancestry
and only a trifle of the background to his wanderings.

"What better way," he had said, "to let you all know what I
know. I'll write it down."

That day he began his task, and sometime later finished his
book. At last, his children and grandchildren realised their own
incredible inheritance. Perhaps this might have meaning for me,
too. Especially as the century I have lived through is drawing rapidly
to a close and already ten year old Chelsea, my grand-daughter, is
reminding us of the imminent arrival of the next.

"Grandie," she muses, "it will be my sixteenth birthday in
January, Two Thousand, could you and Norma try to stay alive and
come to my party?"

She has a point, and the opportunity must be grasped.

What I am loath to do is script a narrative about myself.
Diaries and memoirs have not caused me much interest, being far
too personalised to take an objective view. However, I will set out
the events of some seventy years, as a direct counterpoint, to how
they effected my friends and me, collectively.

One thing I can say, as the next millennium makes its brisk
approach, the sheer speed that things have developed since we were
born, cause the years to be unique in the history of mankind. A
review, therefore, of these tightly woven patterns should not come
amiss, before the mists of absent-mindedness obscure the clarity of

1

the truth. Wherever I look, in my early life, there is a common factor shared with the octogenarian. It so dominates those years, and was so disruptive to the normal progress of human beings, through their fifty thousand years of written history, that all other events, pale into insignificance beside it: World War One.

When hostilities terminated on November 11th 1918, those four years had changed the world. Communities, townships and villages on five continents had split and scattered, so that no amount of re-arrangement would put them back together again. Armistices and peace treaties had to make the best of things as they found them, and encourage the few survivors who returned from the battles, to establish themselves in their homes.

It was not easy to resettle in lands supposedly fit for heroes to live in, after over twenty million souls had perished. As some rejoined their shattered families, others discovered their brethren had already left. They had taken advantage of the revolution that had transformed both communications and travel, changing them into refugees, exiles or emigrants in distant foreign lands. In Britain, fifteen hundred years of history finally ended. A way of life that rested undisturbed since the days of the Roman Empire, disappeared for good.

It was before I was around, of course, but the generation that my parents represented, and those other family circles I would eventually join in marriage, were. Not one of them escaped the consequences of that conflict and each, in turn, became part of that movement of people. Some left for the colonies and the commonwealth or journeyed to the Americas. Others suffered temporary banishment to former enemy territories, as part of the Armies of Occupation. Without exception it was a time of embracing alternative cultures, and rejecting the heart lands of the past.

My father, searching for a job, had left Manchester and his parents in 1912, and with the start of the war in August 1914, stayed where he found work, in the munitions factories of Coventry. Later in 1917, he married his sweetheart to set up a home away from an existence they recognised as too narrow and restrictive. A fresh start was the crux of the idea, encouraged by the desire to expel the images of carnage the Great War symbolised. When peace came, everywhere there were active and passive participants of the struggle, who sought an alternative answer to violence and sacrifice. Before

2

1914, life had survived at a very different pace. Controlled by values that had not altered for centuries. Even before the battles began, industrial inventions, educational enlightenment and social upheaval were contributing towards a programme of reform; dates on a calendar cannot chart the real progress. Most of that was in the minds of young people as they became aware the old order was toppling and nations were arming for a conflict ahead.

To us, accustomed to such upheavals, it would seem natural that threatened families would desert their homelands for safer havens. But the result has been quite incredible. Whole ethnic groupings, who in 1914 lived behind their own distinctive national frontiers, each identified by separate racial and religious characteristics, are today so internationalised, through marriage and breeding, that their grandchildren are scarcely able to identify the origins from whence they sprung, less than ninety years ago.

The previously mentioned grand-daughter, Chelsea, illustrates this admirably. Through her veins surge a combination of English, Scots, Irish, French and Sicilian blood, making the immigrations and emigrations that such a fusion implies, richly fascinating. So, perhaps I should turn to where it began for me, to the two people who were the source of my earliest memories: my parents.

My father was born in October 1888 into a poor artisan family in Openshaw, a district of Manchester, and christened George Henry, in memory of an uncle. His father was a blacksmith, working with his brothers at a forge they owned. Around the time of the 1851 Great Exhibition the family had moved some 50 miles, from the Derbyshire villages of Bakewell, Matlock and Manifold to the developing industrial area of South Lancashire and there in 1881, John Henry Taylor had married Sarah Jane Manifold. George was their fourth child, when only one so far had survived, a daughter, Mercy, born in 1886. In the unhealthy conditions surrounding heavy engineering and mining, working and holding on placed many pressures on small family resources as each year brought an additional mouth to feed. Small wonder John and Sarah found life a heavy burden.

My mother, Ethel Salt, lived close by my father in the neighbouring district of Ardwick. She had been born the eldest, in Lancaster, where her parents resided in 1890 because of her father's white collar job on the railways. John Thomas Salt, whose friends seemed to relish using both his forenames, had married Mary Jane Langslow from North Cheshire. She came from a family of Harpers and Langslows who had lived a peaceful country existence for generations in the villages of Congleton, Alderly Hedge and Wallasey, growing their own produce and cooking and preserving the local vegetables, herbs and fruit. Shortly after the birth of my mother the Salts moved to Grey Mare Lane in Ardwick, when my grandfather became chief clerk at the main rail depot in Manchester. His position guaranteed a marginally higher standard of living than that of the Taylors.

I often heard my parents claim they met at Methodist chapel, but they also attended the local Church of England, St Jerome's, where they married. Perhaps their motives were similar to my friends and me, when some thirty years later, we varied our religious convictions to please the current girl friend's desires, or to take part in a drama club play. However, both the Taylor and the Salt families were regular church goers, in particular my grandfather Salt, who was most active in the musical life of the Wesley Hall Chapel in Ancoats, Manchester. He was the leader of the prize winning brass band and I was proud to watch him on parade at the annual Easter and Whitsun processions that were a linchpin of the traditional Northern religious festivals. He would head his perspiring musicians through the main streets of the city, followed by columns of children and adults representing the youth and congregations of the chapels and churches around Manchester. A throng of relatives and friends cheered on the young girls in white satin dresses and the boys in best Sunday suits, as they collected pennies and silver threepenny pieces for the missionary societies.

At one procession, when I was barely six, I marched alongside my grandfather resplendent in his navy and red serge uniform and gold braided cap. That day he allowed me to carry his silver topped stick, a treasure I still have with me.

I know my parents shared a love of music and their first meetings at the chapel in Grey Mare Lane, pre-dated their musical evenings at the Free Trade Hall, the Palace Theatre and the Opera House in Manchester. My mother was working in the clothing trade as a packer, while my father was a turner. On leaving school at thirteen, he signed an apprenticeship at the engineering company,

Crossley Brothers, but with the completion of his indentures his employers no longer wished to retain him as a fully fledged worker qualifying for a man's wage. Labour conditions in 1910 were very different from today. Unfairly biased in favour of the employer (particularly in agriculture where the old feudal system was still largely in place) they remained a hangover from a time when the master's word was law.

Trades unions struggled for workers' rights despite winning permission to represent the mass of the employed in this country. They were under constant attack from opponents of the 1871 Act of Parliament. This Act was the first to legalise the Unions, but in 1901 a Court judgement, during the Taff Vale case, made strikes virtually illegal. Redundancy payments, job security and the dole did not exist and no-one challenged an employer when he fired a man, however distinguished his employment.

At 21 my father was out of work, along with several thousand other young men who had completed their apprenticeships, and his only hope was the odd job picked up in an haphazard way. For an ambitious young fellow the future hardly looked appealing.

However, my mother had a close friend, Amy Howarth, whose parents owned a music shop a few miles away in Accrington, and Amy had a cousin she was about to marry who lived in Coventry. George Burroughs met my father on one of his visits to see Amy and the idea of going to Coventry took root.

The city was already an established industrial centre with a number of flourishing new factories. Motor cars, aeroplanes, pedal and auto cycles, torpedoes, sophisticated armaments and guns were rolling from the production lines. Part of the massive drive for military supremacy dominating the thoughts of the large nations. There was a load of opportunities for a skilled machine operative, only a bicycle ride distance in the South. So one Sunday my father cycled the hundred miles to see what it could offer him.

At that time he had rarely journeyed more than a few miles from Manchester. He spent his holidays in Blackpool and Southport, or if the spirit of adventure demanded it, on a short boat trip to the Isle of Man. London remained unvisited, a remote city, as unknown as Paris or Berlin. Even Coventry might indicate a long parting for young lovers. The ride took him almost twelve hours through Congleton, Stoke-on-Trent, Stone, Lichfield and Coleshill on an old

B.S.A. bicycle with a Sturmey Archer three speed gear. That bike became a reliable companion in the days ahead, as he toured around looking for a job. His first lodgings were in Harnell Lane, near by the City football ground, with an old established Coventry family, the Hewitts, who were friends of the Burroughs. My father remained close to them for the rest of his life.

Many of the problems of working in Manchester, which persuaded my father to leave, concerned its legacy of out-dated factories and equipment inherited from the first impact of the Industrial Revolution. The workshops had been set-up to take advantage of on the spot raw materials and a local need to cope with the engineering demands of the railway builders and the spinning and weaving sheds of Lancashire and Yorkshire. This in turn led to overseas markets in the British Empire, which used the convenient port of Liverpool to export pumping, hauling and lifting equipment required for their colonisation.

The huge volume of work generated meant the North was too busy to involve itself in the establishment of new industries that supported the latest inventions. Consequently, they made their home in the South of the Britain. Using green field sites and a healthy population free from the diseases caused by bad working conditions and pollution, they exploited the large numbers of agricultural labourers who had migrated to the towns to improve their standard of living.

Coventry was one of the key cities in this twentieth century development. At first my father worked at the Auto-Machinery Company, manufacturing the automatic machine tools required to produce motor cars and heavy guns. Then, as the pace of re-armament quickened to counter the threat of a major European war, he transferred to the Royal Ordnance Factory in Red Lane (a huge complex of workshops and stores that served again in the Second World War). There he helped produce the fourteen inch gun turrets for the armour plated battleships of the Royal Navy.

Although my father left his birthplace before the war began, his involvement in the manufacture of armaments ensured he was a part of the same huge universal movement of populations that had occurred in those years. Like the refugees, he required a new home and the need to adapt to a new social structure. My mother joined him at the peak of the war, in August 1917, when they married. She had planned a much earlier wedding on August 4th 1914, but the events of the preceding weeks in Eastern Europe, activated by the assassination of the Archduke Franz Ferdinand at Sarajevo, put a damper on the idea and they postponed the ceremony until later.

The family group my father had left illustrated many common influences of the time. Victorian moralities and persuasions were the basis of their solidarity. It united them, despite the pressures of living in a grim industrial city. The outside world stood largely ignored. However, with the implications of total war fully recognised, parental rule, which set the patterns of family life, almost completely broke down.

My father, the first to be affected, went to Coventry. His younger brother Ben, another trained engineer, took his wife Nellie to New Zealand, followed by sister Carrie, her husband Jack and their young son, Jack. These two families settled close to one another in Auckland and the men found a ready demand for their skills. They soon adjusted to a new life style as their adopted countries provided hope and security. Like many emigrants they never returned to their old national lands, wishing to draw a veil over all they had left. However, in a strange reversal, it is their children and grandchildren, who now try to renew links with the past, as they travel so effortlessly on business and holidays around the world.

Viewed overall, the permanency of the moves completed in the decade of the Great War is nothing short of remarkable. Where relatives split through death and destruction, time healed the losses. Where whole communities moved together, adaptation to the unknown came rapid and permanent.

In the Taylor family two children remained behind to compensate their parents for the leavers. John, badly wounded serving in the Royal Artillery in Flanders, returned to Manchester as soon as demobilisation allowed. The trauma of his war was such that he never wished to travel again, hardly even a car journey at holiday times. His sister Mercy stayed on too, with her husband Jack and daughter Nellie, living within a stone's throw of her parents' South Street home for the rest of her life, until she died at 89.

This was the pattern of one family affected by that war. Multiply it by the millions of similar ones in France, Italy, the Balkans, Russia, the Middle East and it is possible to understand the complex of peoples mixed together as they fled for security to the Americas,

Australasia, South Africa or any place prepared to take them. There was a mass of fragmented individuals sailing away from their homelands and their inheritance, to reside in distant isles, in obscure cities and unknown towns. They left behind their tribal bloodlines, their ancient customs and their native language, on a scale never witnessed earlier.

To trace this period of wandering through one's own roots is fascinating. First, the marriages and liaisons that took place between so many divergent races, whose chances of meeting previously were negligible, emphasise an extraordinary amount of to-ings and fro-ings. Then, its continuation as children born from such conjunctions proceed to raise even more exotic groupings, in yet further multiple propagation.

It is the very stuff of creation itself. A far off echo rising from a common basic element of movement and change, all centred around World War One. Naturally, the conclusions are often unequal in intensity and timing, but the overall shock result has left few untouched. It looked, in the beginning, that death on the field of battle delegated, to those remaining behind, problems of decision they seemed incapable of facing. Yet they overcame them. Intuitively, they knew their future lay either in broadening their horizons at home, or by emigrating to fresh environments across the seas.

I can review now a substantial number of divergent folk lines who have arrived into my own life's orbit through a similar chain of circumstance. My first wife, Mary Munro, came from a group formed from Munros and Bignalls, living around the base camp of their army service in Chichester, Sussex. Her ancestors, cross-fertilised by Scot and Irish regimental duties, had fought in the campaigns and conquests of centuries. They represented the formidable military expertise of the British, in spite of the Great War having taken its toll.

Grandfather Bignall died, fatally gassed on the Somme in 1916, after returning to the colours from his retirement, with thirty-five years service. A loyalty expected of the soldier families. The recall for battle meant what it said. It was a duty towards comrades and brothers in arms, for the honour of the Regiment, whatever the personal cost. In the Royal Sussex, the Bignalls served alongside the Munros. They had stood together for two hundred years. Bill Munro, my father-in-law, was not quite old enough to fight in the

8

trenches but he volunteered as the war was ending and joined the British contingent in the Rhine Army of Occupation. On parade with him was a Bignall son, George, who promptly introduced his sister, Lydia. In 1928, on the North West frontier of India, Bill married Lydia, and along came Mary, Pat, Lydia and Richard, as army postings and garrison christenings followed a pattern of Empire wanderings. Twenty-five years later I met Mary.

So we return to my grand-daughter, Chelsea. Through her inheritance we can see the widespread similarities between family migrations wherever they originated. Chelsea was born in New Orleans, one of the ports of the United States that provided an immigrant gateway to the country. Her mother, our daughter Melanie, took a rich cocktail of British Isles blood on a student holiday in 1982 and married Chelsea's father, Michael Uddo, who lived there.

His parents represented everything I have outlined. On one side was the Italian connection, Sicilians from the small fishing village of Taomina, overlooking the Straits of Messina; on the other, a family from Flanders. Each a reminder of the turbulence rocking Europe as the twentieth century unfolded. In 1917, it may have mustered merely a backwash in Sicily, as young men died on the battlefields, but a general mobilisation was in the offing and the island, which had defied invasion and exile since civilisation first reached the Mediterranean, prepared to join in.

However, what was it that ultimately sent Giuseppe Uddo ahead of his brothers and cousins to seek his fortune in another land? Could it merely be the presence of the GI's who had disembarked in Palermo when President Wilson declared war on Germany? Whatever it was, it was decisive. Within a few years, Giuseppe had built a flourishing business in New Orleans, importing tomatoes and olive oil from Sicily until his Progresso Foods were on every supermarket shelf in North America and he was a millionaire. Such could be your success if you left a war torn continent behind you.

Of course, circumstances could differ. History played a part in the disposal of luck. For instance, until the early 1900's Britain rarely considered itself menaced by Germany, with its close Hanoverian ties to Victoria and Albert. On the contrary, the real threat appeared a bear hug from Russia, ever on the alert to avenge the Crimean War and dominate Europe. Only the citizens of France and the Low Countries regarded the Boche as a serious enemy. In the war of 1870, the French had felt the rough edge of Prussian militarism and quaked as they waited on the sequel. Quarrels about frontiers, trade and overseas possessions simmered as Bismarck and his Kaiser threw their weight around intimidating the border populations.

Amongst these were Chelsea's other ancestors, the Chopins, living quietly nearby, until the stress of imminent war sent them off helter skelter for safety, also to New Orleans. Years later they formed a union in marriage with a Sicilian family, Adele Chopin and Frank Uddo, American grandparents to Chelsea, inheritor of a dozen possible citizenships.

My other daughter, Celia, also guaranteed a similar birthright for her three children. She married Paul Norman, who was an offspring of the French and Scandinavian communities in New Orleans. Paul's father was a mere half century distance from the fjords of Norway and the lakes of Sweden, and his mother a similar gap from earlier Flanders immigrants, the Thibideauxs. So Stephen, Richard and Victoria Norman qualify for a fistful of passports like so many other of today's young citizens in the Americas, Australasia and South Africa.

Yet the overwhelming fact was that in this cataclysmic upheaval a revised order of human rights developed so that the old world could never be quite the same again and the new world could start with a clean slate.

Britain was its own special case, part due to its unusual geographical location and because of its isolation as an island. Here families had inhabited the same settlements and hamlets for close on two thousand years, almost untroubled by invasions of Vikings, Romans and Normans. What they saw of such encroachments turned out to be little more than administrative inconvenience. A mere change of tax collector, as the invader himself became quickly absorbed into the life of the conquered.

Sometimes it was a handy short move into the next village as intermarriage took place, but the essential roots of my family of Salts and Taylors, remained centred around four counties Cheshire, Staffordshire, Lancashire and Derbyshire. At their peak, nothing had fundamentally altered since the centuries before Christ and they shared a stable existence unsurpassed anywhere else in Europe. Even the Armada, the French Revolution and Napoleon, upsets large enough to threaten the very foundations of world diplomacy, caused hardly a ripple. Regardless, they lived on enjoying a smug moral code and a self satisfied religious philosophy.

It was against this den of complacency that the period 1914-18 struck its most vicious blows. One million dead and two million wounded were un-erasable statistics. No family escaped dreadful pain and tragic suffering.

At the very moment of the joining of the Salts and Taylors, as my parents married on August 4th 1917 (three years after the original postponement) the Reverend Sidebotham looked up from his final blessing to see a young Post Boy advancing on my grandfather Salt. He delivered a telegram,

THE WAR OFFICE REGRETS TO INFORM YOU THAT YOUR SON RIFLEMAN JAMES SALT, IS AMONGST THOSE MISSING, BELIEVED WOUNDED ON THE WESTERN FRONT.

The wedding party stopped in its tracks. Distress swept them away to collect the facts from the police and the Regimental Headquarters.

Jim, the only surviving Salt son, had volunteered for the Manchester Regiment at 18, in 1916. On leaving school he had worked in a leading textile printing house in Oxford Street, Manchester, as a junior salesman for a while, but had enlisted with some friends. A two month stint of training, followed by a 48 hour pass; more pack drill and rifle instruction, and he was off to a reinforcement holding unit in Southern England. There he formed a platoon, in a company of local lads from Ardwick and sailed to France early in 1917. Because of the heavy casualties, he went forward, immediately, to the front line.

It was a murderous fight to face at Ypres. Mud and blood were the ingredients of trench warfare. Gun against gun, bullet against bullet and flesh ripped apart in the unceasing drama of advance and retreat. To Jim it was hell on earth as the fun of being a soldier in uniform totally evaporated. Yet somehow he survived those first days, although some of his closest mates became casualties at once, and in the odd quiet moment he wrote letters home. Come

July however, there was silence and Jim's war was over, for good. The crash and fizz of a mustard gas shell happened so swiftly, he knew neither about being knocked unconscious nor what happened to the two fellows in the bunker beside him. For days he hovered between life and death so that when he awoke he found himself evacuated, laying blind and bodily shattered in the battle casualty hospital at Netley.

It was there my father and mother saw him, covered in bandages, unable to see them and tormented by multiple deep burns, internally and externally, from the flesh eating liquid. The newly marrieds had travelled all night on the train, abandoning their celebrations, facing an air raid by Zeppelins as they changed stations in London and then gazing at the huge red brick barrack-like buildings of the Royal Victoria Military Hospital, massed alongside Southampton Water.

The hospital was teeming with hundreds upon hundreds of grievously wounded men. Boys of eighteen and nineteen with hardly a year's work experience to their name who would never work again. Men in their twenties, thirties and forties with torn faces, smashed bodies and empty gaps where their limbs should have been. Ward after ward presented a graveyard of lost hopes and forfeited careers as a devoted nursing staff rushed hither and thither trying to make the appalling seem natural, the unthinkable bearable. Yet this was only one of a score of similar institutions throughout the land where the full flower of British manhood lay wrecked.

Uncle Jim was there for weeks, hanging on to life as his shattered body tried to heal itself. Slowly he regained his sight and the use of his paralysed muscles, but when they discharged him he could no longer serve in the army and returned to Manchester to re-start his civilian job. His war was never over, not for the rest of his life. Each year afterwards he suffered the agonies of that trauma again, as the chemicals in his body shifted to the surface and suppurated into ugly ulcers on his spine and chest.

Twenty-two years later in 1939 he died, after managing a superb business career and nurturing a loving wife and family. Yet the record remained straight and true on his Death Certificate, stating:

DIED FROM WOUNDS RECEIVED IN THE BATTLE

FAMILY

OF YPRES JULY 1917.

The shock of the telegram and the journey to hospital were something my parents never forgot, for the developments in communications and travel, during the previous century, had their down side too. Despite the advantages of the speedy contact, the cold realities of the killing fields landed squarely at the family fireside, placing the tragedy of the Great War closer to home than any conflict had ever been before. A desperate ploy to level out everything that human life might represent. This terrible formula applied to my generation some twenty odd years later, when the Blitzkrieg made the Home Front the Battle Front and telecommunications retained their sad significance in moments of bitter poignancy.

Alistair Maycock, a neighbourhood friend of mine since infant days, joined the RAF for flying duties in 1941. Through our High school years, when he went to Bablake and I to the Grammar, we had kept in touch through common bands of boys and girls at tennis and local dances. With the war, his special friend, Joy Wyatt, one of the prettiest of our dancing partners, brought news of his training and postings as the conflict progressed. On gaining his wings as a pilot, they became engaged, before his embarkation for service in the Middle East. One of many couples who looked forward to the end of hostilities so that they could really start married life.

In August 1945, as VJ Day brought the whole business to a rapid end, I came home on my first leave from Germany, pleased that Hiroshima and Nagasaki had been so effective. One morning I met Joy, shopping at the local butchers, and she told me of the approaching arrival of Alistair from overseas. They planned a special licence to marry immediately. Two years apart when you were in love was penance enough and the families were preparing to rejoice.

As Saturday dawned, Joy went out with Alistair's parents to arrange the last minute details for the wedding at church and a reception to follow. Loaded with gifts and a few luxury items they had bought with a full year of unspent clothing coupons, they arrived back at the house in Harefield Road. On the front door mat lay a telegram, as expected from Alistair, to confirm his homecoming and demobilisation. Joy opened it:

THE AIR MINISTRY REGRETS TO INFORM YOU
THAT YOUR SON FLIGHT LIEUTENANT ALISTAIR
MAYCOCK HAS BEEN KILLED ON ACTIVE SERVICE.

He had flown a final trip with the relieving crew to assist them in
the take over of his duties. The aircraft failed to return.

Experiences of similar messages burned themselves into our
minds and accounted for my mother's look of anxiety whenever the
Telegram Boy visited us. Grandfather Salt was constantly aware of
the tragedy they could announce and as he helped unload the trains
of wounded that came frequently into the main line stations of
Manchester in 1917, he felt an interminable pang.

His First Aid training with the Red Cross meant he was
constantly on call, after work, to help receive the cargoes of maimed
and crippled. He remembered vividly the first time he had seen his
own son amongst the hospital beds of Netley and had a great urge
to help those who may not have parents to care for them.

Sometimes he would work all night, clearing one set of
ambulance carriages and ready to unload the next, as more and
more shattered bodies returned from Flanders. As they were close
to Liverpool, they also attended men, battered on the beaches of
Gallipoli and repatriated by converted troop ship. At those moments
he toiled as a stretcher bearer and witnessed the grateful look of
thanks soldiers from the Commonwealth countries of Australia, New
Zealand and Canada gave him as they realised they were among
their own folks again. Few imagined being shipped to a land they
thought they had left permanently when emigrating years earlier.
Or they might be sons of earlier settlers, seeing the home country
for the first time and whispering to my grandfather,

"My dad was born here and I have an aunt in London. Can
you write her I'm wounded and would like to see her."

What pictures had such lads about the birthplace of their
parents? What would those parents make of a telegram that brought
them shock news of their son lying in hospital in England, of all
places? Besides these war time miseries, as though the wounded
were not enough, my grandfather rushed out in the small hours of
one morning to aid the injured in a major train disaster. Yet
throughout his life, as if he felt a grievous debt he owed to others
for their attendance on his son, he continued to carry out such duties

even when he began to lose his sight through cataracts. His greatest concern then was he may no longer be available if they needed him in an emergency.

Such emotive personal experiences and heart searchings eventually ended the tranquillity of Victorian and Edwardian England. They provided the key to a phenomenal shake-up of consciousness. Survivors looked for fresh re-assurance away from the disorientated countries of Europe and embraced it on the far side of the globe. The bonus came in the opportunity to choose for oneself, instead of following family footsteps and being tied to the constraints of the past. From that time on, it required one lucky break. And a fortune could be there for the asking.

Perhaps the chance to choose became the most important step forward for the individual since the Reformation of the Church freed him from God. Yet all who emigrated did not necessarily have a free choice. Some, like Mauricio Glaiman, the father of my present wife, Norma, was unwittingly choosing the right to stay alive. When he forsook Poland for Argentina in 1923, he left his relatives behind in their ghetto. Born and bred into a land they claimed as their own, they chided him there was nothing to fear. Eighteen years later they were the victims of a purge so vicious, that the word 'Holocaust' was invented exclusively to describe it.

By the time World War Two had produced its own massive migrations of population, many young people were already veterans of movement from their own varied knowledge of travel and occupation gleaned through their military service. We became heirs to the relocation our predecessors had inaugurated.

My cousin, Joyce Salt, left her mother and sister, Beryl, in Blackpool as the war finished to become a war bride to her Canadian Squadron Leader, Jack Norris. They settled on the Prairies of North America. The children of the Munros from Sussex, Pat, Mary, Lydia and Richard decided to sample Australia and the United States. That movement, in turn, has prompted similar transfers in the next generation. My daughters, Melanie and Celia, from home roots in London, find partners in New Orleans, and my son, Stephen, as if defying a trend, returns to base in Sussex, at Chichester, with a Welsh Zöe Jones, and their sons, Wylf and Sid.

It is with an assuredness that these switches now take place and continue to do so. They are built on an understanding that integration has proved possible, and societies are capable of absorbing diverse skills and cultural differences. There was not quite that confidence about my father's ride on a bicycle, or the journey of his brother and sister to New Zealand so few years ago. However, that source created the watershed. In one fell swoop, out went the ancient monoliths with a breathtaking crash, as Kings and Kingdoms, laws and customs, boundaries and governments folded under the pressure. It was not without formidable cost. The old system may have floundered, but the disintegration buried the flower of a continent's manhood. The cream of our stock rotted in battlefield cemeteries. Poets, musicians, lawyers, doctors, inventors and engineers, a whole galaxy of irreplaceable talents destroyed, as each contestant hurled the pride of its menfolk against the other.

The loss was irredeemable. The effect, on the leadership of each state, was devastating. No longer enough young people remained who could chivvy for progress. Only the weak survived. Apathetic old men, who had missed the fighting, merely repeated stale and failed policies.

The peace acclaimed in 1918, in the briefest possible time, seemed threatened again. The United States pulled up short and retreated into isolationism. France, Britain and Germany capitulated behind their own frontiers to forces they were unable to control, paying false lip service to a stagnant League of Nations. A feeling of despair reigned everywhere. In swift turnabout, it seemed we were back to the beginning. Twenty years after the end of one catastrophe we were about to launch into another. So much for the platitudes that said a 'War to end Wars' as the elusive Golden Chalice of Peace failed in its come back.

At that juncture lie the tales.

TWO

SHADOWS OF THE FIRST WAR

ECAUSE I WAS born in the 1920's I grew up under some very dark shadows. Two world wars in the space of twenty years was not a good record if you happened to be around. The aftermath of one somehow got inexorably mixed up with the preparations for the next. It was difficult to avoid the conclusion that the nightmare might continue indefinitely, affording no chance for any alternative. The 'roaring twenties' may have looked fun, yet if those still alive after four years of senseless killing devised only the mildest of celebrations, what else could they be, but different. It was natural that any backlash against the stringency of a wartime society must show up as a reflex action. My parents and their friends simply opted for a less ordered life than they had previously assumed. They had to be fast about it, too.

Ten years and the whole damned business was alive again. Maybe at the start it was slow and insidious; change does not announce itself openly. However, by 1930 there was a gathering sense of doom. Even we little ones could detect that, without being able to put a finger on it. For it was a dreadful thought that our turn might be around the corner, and the subject, which our parents hated most to discuss, could be on the front doorstep again. Everything repeated before they had cleared up the mess from the previous disaster.

It was certainly something to get used to, as the Great War ended, and my parents settled into the cleaner environment of Coventry, far from the 'dark Satanic mills' of their early lives. My mother shared lodgings with my father in Swan Lane, after she

17

became his wife, with other relatives of the Hewitts, who were now firm friends of the couple.

The year they married, 1917, had seen a change in the fortunes of war. A freshly mobilised army from the United States brought its weight to bear on the battlefields. There seemed to be a smell of peace about, and my father started to look for more interesting work, away from the manufacture of Naval guns. He had taken his job at the Ordnance Works on September 22nd 1913, and almost exactly five years later on September 8th 1918 joined the Tool Room of the Armstrong Siddeley Company, where its founder, John Siddeley (later Lord Kenilworth) manufactured everything from aero-engines to motor cars. It seemed a wise choice to settle for work in fields less directly aligned to the war effort.

To complete the changeover, my parents moved from their lodgings on September 22nd 1918, to 14 St Agatha's Road in a recently developed area close by Stoke Park, at a rental of six shillings (30p) a week. In 1923, as their circumstances improved, they bought the property for two hundred pounds, financed by a mortgage from the Co-Operative Society, then the most popular lender to the working classes.

Their next door neighbours, Rueben and Hannah Smith, who left their home in Newcastle on Tyne, for similar reasons as my father, also bought their house. They paid for it with two hundred gold sovereigns, saved from long hours of overtime in the Coventry factories. They quickly regretted their action as the value of sovereigns shot up almost double, when the coins ceased to be legal tender and Britain abandoned the Gold Standard.

Despite the irregular employment patterns resulting from the seasonal nature of the motor car industry, my parents relaxed in a general feeling of prosperity that appeared around them. A regular job was the key to it. Even though he was lowly paid, my father remained in steady work, and to supplement his income he played the cello each evening in the local cinema orchestras.

He had learned to play while still a young apprentice in Manchester. Captivated by the music of the Hallé Orchestra at the Free Trade Hall, he introduced his brother, Ben, to the regular subscription night concerts. Ben then began lessons on the violin, and before long they were performing in small amateur groups. On arrival in Coventry, my father took further lessons with Herbert

Clarke in Earlsdon, at three shillings and sixpence a time. He studied the Piatti technique which Sir Granville Bantock had taught Herbert at the Birmingham Institute, and soon he deputised for his teacher at concerts and cinema performances, so that he was playing professionally, on an ad hoc basis. As films became more complex and required larger orchestras to exploit their distinctive scores, my father's talent was increasingly in demand. Only in 1929, when the talkies finally put paid to the resident cinema musicians, did he turn to teaching the cello.

Wages in war time had not been large, reflecting the generally low wage paid for manual work. Tough laws and legislation kept industrial discord in tight control, so that there was little financial advantage in being a worker rather than a soldier, and my father applied on several occasions to enlist in the Royal Engineers. Each time the factory management blocked his call-up and refused to release him, a common enough occurrence for skilled operatives.

When the war ended the general standard of living remained in the doldrums, firmly anchored by low wages and a large pool of unemployed ex-servicemen. The popular phrase in the Music Halls was 'trying to make ends meet'. This always intrigued me when I was young as I tried to understand the logic of 'hen's meat' and the pay packet my father brought home on Friday for his wife.

He never ceased to remind us how much worse things could have been if he had stayed in Manchester. Uncle John, since his army discharge had found it very difficult to make 'ends meet', working in the clapped out factories that had not been re-equipped since the days of the Industrial Revolution. They had remained busy for a short while when peace came, catching up with orders and replacements but soon things went into reverse and they laid off their employees. John considered following his brother Ben and sister Carrie to New Zealand as he heard glowing reports of their achievements, but the battlefields had drained the will from him and he did nothing about it. Yet, around him in Openshaw, many families decided to move and set out from Liverpool towards the promises of a healthier life, free from pollution, poor housing and unemployment.

It was conditions like these that caused the many problems of the depressed areas. My father's other sister, Mercy, also found it very hard going. She married Jack Brabner in 1910 and they had a daughter, Nellie. A tailoress by trade, she spent many hours, day and night, as an outworker, sewing suits and overcoats. Husband Jack, an engineer, worked at Johnson's wire works, a hard, dirty job requiring a great deal of physical effort. They lived in dreary conditions opposite a town gas production plant and beside a coal mine. A huge black slag heap towered above the whole district. A perpetual haze of smoke, soot and grime laced with a cloying, choking smell enfolded their small terrace house, mercifully blitzed to rubble in 1941 without any casualties. Behind was a tiny yard and more and more similar streets. The houses formed the standard basic unit for an industrial worker in Lancashire, complete with their two up and two down and outside loo. Nowhere was there a patch of grass or a view of blue skies, and trees and shrubs were non existent.

Whenever we visited them they looked pinch faced and grey as if, being starved of light, they had grown old ahead of their time. A similar thought struck me one bitterly cold December day, when I first saw the inhabitants of St Petersburg, lacking the warmth of the sun. However, even without a green grassed pitch, Uncle Jack was an accomplished cricketer who in his youth turned out for Lancashire. Once in his small back yard he taught me to spin a leather ball, so cunningly, a batsman could not decide which way to strike. It served me in good stead when later I played at school. Sadly, the smoky atmosphere and the working conditions took an early toll on Jack. He died in his forties, a victim of bronchitis. Mercy, on the other hand, after moving in with her daughter and family, lived to a ripe old age, following the pattern of her mother (my Grandmother Taylor) before her. You needed spunk to survive all that was thereabouts, and the female line had that in abundance.

When I visited Grandma Taylor's home in the late 1920's, it was an eye opener for a young lad from the cleaner zones of the Midland counties. The house would have changed little since she moved into a similar one close by when she married. South Street, Openshaw had not altered much at all, with its outside toilets and cold water taps in the stone flagged yards. A brown porcelain sink stood in the downstairs back room serving as a kitchen, and an oven and a hob nestled beside the coal fire grate. From there rose the rickety stairs leading to two small bedrooms, the only sleeping accommodation available for the family of seven. It was never an easy matter to cater for the birth of ten children or cope with sickness and death, which carried off five of the little ones. My grandfather was a handful on his own. Heavy drinking bouts were a regular feature, supplemented from the barrel kept permanently beside the anvil to quench the thirst of the sweating smiths. Every Saturday night, his pay packet in his hand, my grandfather leaned at the pub bar on the Ashton Old Road, until his money ran out or they refused to serve him. Yet such was his capacity, and that of his brothers, they drank all the profits of the forge, and lost the contract to shoe the horses of the Crossley Brothers' factories, with the largest stables in town. Comment enough to say, that none of the Taylor children ever let more than a thimbleful of sherry touch their lips, for the rest of their days, and then only at weddings and funerals.

Grandmother kept her head above water, supported by the odd pennies my father and his brothers earned from their paper rounds. Mercy helped, too, running errands at a penny a time after school was over at St Barnabas' Church. In the graveyard, resting beside some smaller graves of the children, grandfather was buried in 1923, the year I was born, although Sarah Jane survived until 1936. I last saw the headstone in 1939, a flat slab of grey slate, but by then acid rain and fogs had made the lettering almost indecipherable. After the Second War a new community centre replaced the old church, with the gravestones lining the outside walls; however, the school continued on its site, opposite.

At school my father was very bright. My mother also attended St Barnabas' and they shared a teacher, Miss Shirt, who taught them to read and write, but in different years. Under Miss Shirt's prompting, my father won a scholarship to Manchester Grammar School, considered somewhat of an achievement at ten. Yet although the teacher pleaded long and hard, his parents refused the offer, preferring the support of their son's earnings when he reached thirteen, and was permitted to leave school. He completed his sparse education at night school and by correspondence course, but his youth was not all hardship. In his spare time he learned to swim well in the open air pool at Ardwick Green. There, on warm summer evenings, he would splash about in the nude, larking with his friends until the local police chased them away. Then, in the spirit of a Victorian Christmas, he would collect a pot full of tips from his paper round to spend on simple family presents. A daily part of life was the knocker-up. Each morning there would be a tap on the front bedroom window to waken the family, and grandmother would see that everyone dressed as she prepared the bread and cheese sandwiches for the mid-day meal.

On dark mornings the lamplighter cycled by, to put out the gas mantle in front of their house, and the milk and bread would arrive on early delivery. Washing of bodies and clothes took place under the outside cold tap or in the scullery, where the fire heated the water; but baths were an infrequent adventure. Once when I went to see my grandmother, she told me that she sewed the children into woollen vests with a wadding waistcoat to keep them warm every winter, and as you 'never cast a clout until May was out', they stayed wrapped up whatever the weather. For herself, grandmother always wore the same long black embroidered dress that covered her from head to toe. My mother reckoned it got only a twice a year wash, May and October; but the old lady had a collection of scarves to brighten up her image whenever she went out shopping.

The Salts had a much larger house than the Taylors, at a time when renting was preferable to buying. The landlords owned many properties in Ardwick and Openshaw, and the house, at 75 Albert Street, was on a grander scale than those in the surrounding streets. It had a huge bulbous front bay window and inside the street door was a lobby with a glass door. The doorstep and window sills were of a prefabricated cement material, a kind of imitation stone, which my grandmother scrubbed and scoured weekly, with a fawn blanco block. The coloured glass in the doors was also sparkling clean despite the attempts of the atmosphere to deter such a display.

In the house there were three largish bedrooms, a dining room, front parlour, kitchen and pantry but no bathroom or internal toilet. Outside in the flagstoned back yard stood a separate brick cubby-hole, the water closet. I loved to visit it, to look at the portrait of George V pressed out on the metal door plate and play with the ten inch squares of newspaper my grandfather cut each Sunday, for toiletry use. Next to this little hideout was the fuel shed, filled with local coal from the pit beside my Aunt Mercy's house. It seemed to be a special grade of coal that spit and fizzed in the fire grate and released a tremendous heat, so that all the families swore by it and refused any alternative. The yard, hemmed in by a high wall had a wooden gate, through which it was possible to enter the alley behind.

From there I would watch the neighbours' children skipping and hop scotching, hoping they would invite me to join them.

Harry Clarke, a boy I met, had a strong local accent that fascinated me as much as mine amused him. We could never get enough of each other saying 'boo-ook' and 'buk', and 'loo-ook' and 'luk', until the day we asked him to our home, in Coventry, on a visit. It was a disaster. My parents with their Lancashire upbringing, understood him far better than me, taught in a Coventry school, and the holiday ended in tears of jealousy.

Along Albert Street was the dairy with its bare marble counter and green tiled walls, selling only milk, butter, eggs and Lancashire cheese. Grandma Salt visited it daily to collect a pint or two of creamy cool milk in a brown porcelain jug, ladled from the churn beside the shop door. When I was a little older I fetched it on my own.

In a side road, Ryland Street, stood the rather grandly titled, Manchester and Salford Wholesale Co-operative grocery store complete with sawdust on the floor, oak shelving behind the highly polished counters and a high standard of personal service. My grandmother minutely examined her purchases, one by one, as the salesman brought packets and jars from the shelves. She bought all the basics. Dried oats, beans, flour and sugar together with slices of bacon, lard and pots of jam; everything piled up with tins of sardines, salmon and corned beef. We would spend up to half an hour selecting the goods, after she rejected some and replaced others. Yet over it all, ruled an air of pure politeness, while the assistants murmured, "Yes, Mrs Salt," and "No, Mrs Salt," as if she was the Queen of England.

My parents brought me to Manchester at Easter, Whitsun and Christmas, which was invariably a special time. Then I slept in the smallest of the bedrooms, to dream on Christmas Eve of the presents I hoped to see mysteriously piled up in the morning.

The year I was five I was in high excitement as I discovered on our arrival two puppy dogs living at the house. One was black and called Nigger, the other with white blotches, was Spot. My mother's sister, Aunt Ruby and her husband, Fred Hollows, had bought them and Nigger was to stay at Albert Street. I remember that Christmas most clearly of my early years. While I sat in front of the popping coal fire, with its baking oven in full use, Grandma cooked the bread and meats we were to eat, and the two puppy dogs lay curled fast asleep on my lap. Grandfather sat opposite in his rocking chair refilling his pipe with Errinmore mixture and my mother and her sisters, Ruby and Bertha, rushed around the rooms, decorating the tree and wrapping their presents. It conveniently passed the time until my father arrived from Coventry, late on Christmas Eve.

The picture was a cosy one, emphasising the simple roots of family life. My grandfather's word was law, based on his understanding of Victorian ethics and morals digested at church and chapel. Few attempted to challenge or dismiss them. Under his watchful eye my mother and her sisters had remained at home until they married. Illicit relationships and babies out of wedlock were taboo, with nothing permitted which might disgrace the family name.

Evidence of my grandparents' success in their parental role was apparent in the furnishings of the home. Heavy velvet curtains, antimacassars, decorative 19th Century ornaments, armchairs, tables and thick carpet squares, bought and paid for, so that no debt could threaten if unemployment or ill-health intervened. Such was the influence of the Age of the Empire. What more could its citizens demand?

My mother told a story that underlines the concept. In her twenties and engaged to marry to my father, she was, nevertheless, expected indoors at eleven each evening. One Saturday night, after a trip to the theatre, she arrived home at 11.30. Grandfather was sitting up, waiting.

"Do you see that clock, lass?"

"Yes, it's on the wall."

And John Thomas Salt took off his slipper and aimed it hard at her backside. She retreated to bed without a word.

The old man was very kind to me, but then I was an only grandson he saw only twice or three times a year. We talked together a lot as he explained carefully the things I wanted to know, even though I brought up subjects his own children would have hardly dared mention, like politics, strikes and the Labour Party, topics I had heard my father discussing. He had a large library of books, mostly presented to him as Prizes for attendance at Chapel, and he was keen I should read the rather staid and chaste articles in the bound volumes of the Windsor Magazine and The Quiver.

The Salts shared a major concern with the Taylors, indeed it was a common one amongst families; the premature death of children. Both grandmothers had given birth to ten children each, five Taylors survived, four Salts. Apart from one, called Georgie, who died at the age of three, the Salts never spoke of their losses. Neither did the Taylors. My mother was the eldest born in 1890 and interspersed with the others came Jim in 1896, Ruby in 1899 and Bertha in 1903. It would seem my mother spent much of her youth bringing up the young ones but Jim was her special favourite, establishing a friendship that lasted until his death in 1939.

It was the memory of the struggles in large families and the difficulties of infant survival that coloured the attitude of my parents and their generation to the number of children they reared after they married. They had seen at first hand the constant drain on the strength of the wife, through regular child bearing, and none of my mother's friends wished to repeat the pattern.

The Great War became a ready excuse as it helped liberate them from the chore. Women's sufferance and equality had progressed rapidly in four years. Free thinking was at last combating the old adage that a wife's place was in the home. Not that it had gone too far in the 1920's, as men defended what they regarded as masculine territory. Nevertheless, reform was not far distant. My mother decided she would not have a large family and adopted the teachings of Dr Marie Stopes to support her. However, she was not so sure she should go out to work on marriage, as a career for the wedded lady was still not fashionable.

Besides the revolution in the status of women, there was another important lesson from the war. Young people no longer trusted the word of their leaders. It might seem appropriate to win elections on promises that it had been a war to end wars, but hadn't they heard that one before? What about the days of Disraeli and Gladstone and the 'Empire stands for peace'? The real message was just below the surface. 'Folk are only cannon fodder for the Generals and the Politicians', to which every family in the land bore witness.

A hundred thousand men killed in a day, at the whim of the High Command, was not so easy to forget. So why be a partner in providing the victims? A one child family, and the anti-war movement, heralded a new realism amongst ex-soldiers and civilians, in every walk of life. Nearly all my friends came from single child homes brought up by parents who had no experience of knowing what that meant. We had to grow up without a ready made playmate at our side, and no brothers and sisters to teach us self sufficiency. Of course, there were pockets where large families still persisted amongst the better-off or in Catholic groupings, but because of smaller numbers and better health care fewer children died and women felt their burdens lighten.

Amongst our neighbours and friends at least three quarters were single child families. One off children like Ruby Berry, Bernard Hewitt, Len Burroughs, John Stringer and Rosemary Fall grew up with parents who treated the idea of 'small is beautiful' as the norm. Stopping after the first birth gave them greater spending freedom to enjoy a less stringent standard of living and provide funds for further education and, previously unconsidered, foreign holidays. And in the final analysis, there was less cannon fodder on tap. A relevant point with 1939 only a breath away. Consequently, parents discouraged boys of my age from playing with the trappings of war. Guns, swords and uniforms were out, and films at the local cinema tended to neglect the glory and emphasise the torment in *All quiet on the Western Front* and *Journey's End*. At school, our teachers echoed this viewpoint. Those who had seen war service, would not talk of it and ignored the patriotism in both history and geography classes, where Empire and conquest might raise the temperature.

The stance was hardly surprising. The lurid evidence of the futility of war was all around us. Ex-soldiers, with no arms and legs begged in the streets. The two postmen who served our house had each lost a right arm and only with difficulty could hold the letters, with a wooden substitute, as they sorted the post. They regarded themselves as fortunate. At least they had a job, during a decade when unemployment was rife, especially for the maimed. Post-war recession had resulted in multiple job losses in mining and the heavy industries as local products failed to match the cheap imports from overseas. To have work was a bonus when so many still struggled against destitution and out-dated habits.

A neighbour of ours, with a family of four children, delivered coal by horse and cart. His understanding was nearly as backward as his impoverished existence portrayed. However, he was a strong Salvationist who spent the whole of Sunday in open air prayer and hymn singing. His wife, barely 22 years old, became pregnant again and seemed on the point of a mental and physical collapse. To his neighbours, who queried his ability to afford such an addition, he declared,

"God will provide!"

Two weeks later he lay dead, killed by a fall of coal from his cart. His distraught wife spent the rest of a short life in abject poverty for ever on the brink of starvation. This was a spectre to haunt the families of the time.

"There but for the grace of God,..."

they confided in each other as they thanked their lucky stars they had stopped at one child.

For the first time in my life I sensed a little of the power of the omnipotent and watched the fear of being poor haunt the eyes of my own folk.

It was into this I had been born one Monday morning at 4.20 in November 1923. My mother used to hint that I should have been one of twins but she had lost the other, and as there was a history of twin births in the family, on both sides, I suppose it was a possibility. However, a small family is what my parents opted for, and they felt satisfied it would give them the extra money to care for me. Coventry was a good place to be. They had like minded friends, either native to the city or recent settlers like themselves, sharing a similar desire to be free from areas of high unemployment and squalid living conditions. All of them felt that there was opportunity afresh in this Midland city and they could make a success in an expanding economy as it faced the realities of post-war Britain.

The house in St Agatha's Road was a two up and two downer in a terrace. Like my grandparents' homes, then, it had no bathroom and an outside lavatory, which was bitterly cold in winter. At the rear there was a long garden, backing on to the extensive grounds of a girls' high school, part of a former mansion and country house. The grounds were full of mature trees, grassy dells and a walled kitchen garden, so that looking out from our bedroom windows there was a feeling of living in the countryside. I watched the seasons unfold. Spring, when a tall cherry tree spilled its blossoms over our dividing wall. Summer ablaze with the colour of flowers and herbs in the gardens as they blocked in the bright green of the lawns the girls used for rounders and tennis. Then Autumn, as Mr Woodward, caretaker at the school, invited me along with his granddaughter, Sheila, who lived a few terrace houses from us, to watch him light the bonfires of leaves he had swept from the paths. Next, a picture of Christmas, as the trees hung heavy with snow and we heard the choir of girls' voices joining in the carols across at the school hall.

Births at home in those inter-war years were the usual practice; those in hospital a rarity. Our family practitioner was Dr Schulman who went on to steer me through childhood's illnesses and accidents. My birth was quite an event for the Salts. First borns tend to gather that extra attention, but of course, for the Taylors, already with four grandchildren, it was less noteworthy. Although it had taken my father and mother six years of married life to produce an offspring, the Salts demonstrated their joy by showering me with clothes, silver spoons, feeders, serviette rings and teething bands at my christening on January 22nd 1924, in the same Manchester church as my parents wed. They insisted that even the former vicar, the Reverend Sidebotham, now at Ribchester in the Ribble Valley (and what echoes of the Victorian novel do such names evoke?) should preside, so that we could also celebrate my Aunt Bertha's 21st birthday, from the previous week. The robe I wore on that occasion has since seen very good service. After use on my own three children, it is now in New Orleans with my three grandchildren there.

In church, where I received a middle name, Langslow, to note the maiden name of my Grandmother Salt, I behaved impeccably. It was not always the case. My father recalled the occasion he took me for an airing in my large black perambulator through the streets of Coventry. No Lady Godiva treatment was available to me and the inhabitants watched with amusement as my father had to cope with a roaring infant. Nothing he did had any effect and he abandoned the shopping and window gazing. He also ignored my demands and left me to cry and sort myself out as he walked firmly on. Two minutes from home, I fell asleep. I was not to try the same tactic with him again.

However, I spent my infancy cossetted in an enclave of parents, grandparents, aunts and uncles whenever I was on view at family gatherings. Dressed exquisitely as a page boy (part of the heritage of aunts in the tailoring trade) I attended the weddings of Uncle Jim to Clara Greenall and Aunt Ruby to Fred Hollows. The memory of such occasions is not strong, and except for one remarkable fixed picture of being pushed in a pram by my mother as she wore a skull hugging velour hat, I can remember nothing. Two or three years later and the street images are clearer with a playmate, Rosemary Fall, daughter of the local policeman who lived directly across the road.

However, I was already prone to growing emotions of a much more menacing nature. When only children find their place usurped then heaven help the consequences. Where was justice if the one and only became the one of many? How was it possible for my grandma and grand-dad, suddenly, to belong to someone else? At least that's what the green eye was telling me when I heard that my Aunt Clara with Uncle Jim had a set of twins to challenge my position. Yet not all was lost. They were girls, Joyce and Beryl, and my seniority went unchallenged.

Outside this cocoon, the world was in economic and political turmoil again. November 1923, saw the election of the first Labour Government, formed by the grace of others. The Liberal Party held a balance of power and socialism reverted to a pale shade of pink, to survive. The Unions demanded higher wages, accompanying it with the threat of strike action, but the Labour Prime Minister, Ramsey MacDonald, behaved as if he was a member of the Conservative Party. By October 1924 his authority had vanished, and he lost a vote of confidence. The ensuing election brought a heavy defeat for the socialists and in 1926, as the country drifted on towards industrial chaos, the Unions called a General Strike and Britain came to a standstill.

My father, along with nearly everyone else, stopped work, but it quickly became apparent the strikers' aims did not go far enough. They smacked of died in the wool leadership, and a lack of understanding for real reform. Soon, he and his colleagues were back at their work benches, resigning from the union and foregoing their chance to change worn out ideas. At home, as young as I was, I could feel the anxieties that gripped my father. From the daily contacts we had with our neighbours on short time, or laid off by the seasonal fluctuations of the motor industry, we could see clearly that things were wrong. Dole money was only available after a vicious means test and many friends existed on hand-outs from relatives, who in the main were little better off themselves.

The stress of running two jobs, and the general uncertainty, began to effect my father's health so that when sound films arrived to revolutionise cinema performances he seized the chance to abandon the nightly round of orchestral playing.

The strain, however, left its mark and he became very ill with pneumonia over Christmas. The pressure now showed on my mother, who worried that with the breadwinner absent from work, he was not earning. Sick pay was non-existent and my father was at an age when anything could happen. A number of his workmates had died young. All suffered from the diseases of the day, consumption, bronchitis and pleurisy, while others weakened by war wounds, became an easy target for influenza bugs. Although we could afford a doctor, medical care lacked the wonder drugs and high tech treatment that became part of the health service after World War Two. With little money to spend, many people depended on old fashioned remedies and herbal concoctions that were a practised folk lore amongst the working classes.

On a suggestion of a very old neighbour my mother bought a sheep's pelt from the butcher to try out an ancient country cure. She first boiled up the outside skin, placed it in a muslin bag, and then used it as a hot poultice to tie to the soles of my father's feet. Twenty-four hours later the pain in his lungs had gone and he was sitting up in bed, enjoying his first meal for a week. To me it could only be a miracle of mumbo-jumbo, never more compelling than when we went round to see the old woman seated by her coal fire, stirring the hot ashes with a poker and reciting recipes and treatments she swore were from the Druids.

A plus of the illness was that our next door neighbours, the Smiths, loaned us their radio set. I sat mesmerised, listening to talks and music arriving across the crackles of space, for up to now, our acquaintance with this medium was minimal. Amongst our friends only the Berrys and their daughter Ruby had this wonder at their home in Gulson Road.

They had started with a large box and dials, and an even larger black horn speaker beside it. Later they graduated to a sophisticated instrument, with its own sets of headphones, operating on short wave channels, which could pull in stations from every continent. Herbert Berry was particularly keen to show off his knowledge of the United States as he flicked around the wavebands, and listened to Country and Western music. He was an ardent fan of Cowboy singers and guitarists he had listened to during a period in the First War when he was living in Pittsburgh on secondment as an engineer. His stories of the Niagara Falls, New York and Washington came alive as we heard the accents and twangs in his sitting room. For Ruby and me, it seemed as if the whole world was at our feet. Broadcasting was true magic.

It was not until 1934 that we bought our first radio. My father was not sure that such home entertainment was acceptable for a musician, even though we had a His Master's Voice hand-wound gramophone and boxes of classical records. The days when everyone played or sang were ending, and a growing public favoured the BBC, as their programmes challenged the do it yourself musical evenings around the piano, at home. Yet the purchase of a radio, in those days, could present problems of its own. Part of the economic background we lived through.

My parents shared a fixed philosophy about money: do not fall into debt. It was a conviction their friends practised too, as they heard it preached from pulpit and altar rail every Sunday. The rules took many forms. Regular savings each week from the wage packet, stored in their individual boxes or envelopes, labelled simply Rent, Gas, Coal, or Shoes. They told their own story.

The weekly visit of the insurance agent to collect his three pence or sixpence, outlined another. On maturity, you might be lucky enough to collect the sum of five pounds to cover the funeral expenses of husband, mother, brother or sister. Perhaps also a prudent pound or two lay hidden in the Post Office or the Co-Op Bank. These small savings often helped tide over the rainy day, or paid for the treasured purchase of the year. This is where our radio set came from. But resources needed nursing, and fate left untempted. Buying an eight valve Pilot receiver with its cathode ray tube for fine tuning, and its multi waveband display panel, demanded special care. First Mr Cook, the shop owner in Gosford Street, demonstrated everything three times over. Then he promised his personal attention in fitting the outdoor aerial, before he added up the total cost to five pounds exactly.

"You'd like it on H.P. with twenty four to pay?"
And for the moment I listened dumbfounded.

"No," said my dad, firmly, "Never the never-never. I'll pay cash, now."

So the family honour, for paying on the nail, was upheld,

proving you only purchased something when you could afford it and had the money on tap.

A strict attitude towards money and family finances was evident where ever you cared to look. When I started school on my fifth birthday in 1928, I could see, at first hand, how other families had to cope. They were not all as fortunate as my friend Rosemary, from across the road, and myself. Rosemary, being some months older than I, had reported to me how much she enjoyed school. On my first day I met Miss Smith, the Headmistress, and Miss Jones, my class teacher, but it was not quite what I had expected. Rosemary was not in my class.

When my mother left I burst into tears. My classmates left me strictly alone, and remarkably, it seemed, were enjoying themselves. At break time I cottoned on, I could see Rosemary then in the playground and things were not so bad. By the end of the week I was happy and beginning to make friends. But the contact with other children had its ill effects. Suddenly measles, then the whooping cough laid me low, and I missed the rest of the Christmas Term, as Dr Schulman banished me to bed. Fortunately Rosemary caught the affliction as well, and we convalesced together, using each other as the pretend brother and sister neither of us had.

The classrooms at Stoke Council Infants School were cosy places, constructed sometime about 1870. The building lacked full central heating and fireplaces, with roaring fires, compensated for the loss in Winter. Mr Cartwright, the caretaker, replenished the coals so that we could warm our hands during the cold January and February mornings. Some of the children seemed transfixed by the dancing flames and would sit watching until the teacher chased them away. They were often the 'ragged ones', children whose clothes looked worse for wear, and came from the poorest homes.

Florrie Hooten was one of them and sat beside me in an iron framed desk. We became firm companions and she would tell me about the tumble-down houses in the court off Walsgrave Road, where she lived. Her father was out of work and they only managed a fire when he was able to scavenge enough wood from the nearby timber yard. Hence the popularity of the schoolroom flames. One of the lads from the same court made me aware of the existence of 'the boot fund', a charity sum, earmarked in Victorian times to provide footwear for needy children. Bernard arrived at school one morning without shoes or socks. Miss Smith promptly took him to her study and when he re-appeared later he wore a pair of heavy leather boots. He was proud of them and polished them each day before coming to school, a feat few of us cared to follow, and when that pair wore out he received another. Many children benefited from this generosity, especially from that row of slum houses, with their large, penniless families. My mother and Mrs Fall frequently told us how right they had been to opt for a one child home because it 'gave you a better chance' and meant you 'saved you from pleading poverty'. Fair enough reasons for them.

Mrs Fall's mother was a midwife and a strong supporter of the small family syndrome. Rosemary and I would hide behind the door when our mothers' were gossiping with the old lady in the next room. 'Getting the hot water ready,' and 'Some girls need a helping hand,' held us in wicked fascination, while references to 'pig of a husband' and 'when the trouble starts' convinced us evil was afoot. Later I realised that Midwife Campion was the supplier of some ugly grey balloons, stored in boxes of chalk dust. Rosemary and I uncovered one in a bedroom drawer and spent ages trying to blow it up. She asked if she might have some for her birthday party. Without doubt, some of the daily experiences of her grandmother had to be seen to be believed. Poverty and destitution were not a pretty sight for the squeamish.

My parents did their utmost to maintain our standard of living however disadvantaged we may have appeared to richer folk. Around the time I first attended school we had electricity connected to the house, replacing the sizzling gas mantles which lit the rooms. We also renewed some of the kitchen equipment with a white porcelain sink in place of the slim brown one, a grey enamelled gas cooker, for the black leaded one, and a gas fired wash boiler, instead of a coal heated copper. The kitchen floor was tiled and the ash path outside, previously formed from the residue of the coal fire after it was relit in the morning, covered in concrete flagstones. This was no sooner laid than I slipped on the cement and gashed a large wound in my forehead, requiring four stitches from the frequently summoned Dr Schulman.

The alterations stopped at this point; a bathroom was not added, neither was an inside toilet nor constant hot water. Amenities my parents did without until the day they died. Indeed it was a modest house like so many working class homes around us. Apart from providing the very basics of accommodation, it tended to emphasise the importance of small families with one child. The tiny rooms could cope with only a few pieces of furniture. The living room held a dining table and chairs plus a couple of upholstered arm chairs and sometimes a Singer sewing machine hidden away in a cabinet. Upstairs, in the bedrooms was the minimum: beds, a wardrobe and a chest of drawers. Yet we counted ourselves lucky because we had fitted carpets, unlike many others who made do with oilcloth or painted floorboards. At our house we kept the special things for the tiny front room, where my father tended his cellos and the gramophone, and pored over the veneered mahogany music cabinet holding all the sheet music and orchestral scores he collected. In that room he had a bulbous gas fire used during the winter when his pupils came for lessons, and an absolute menace if you placed your instrument too close to it. Many years later I had untold trouble polishing out the damage that the heat had unleashed on the delicate cello front bellies and lower ribs.

However, there were signs of a movement of sorts in the outside world. The hangover from World War One was slipping away as new political pressures cried out for attention. Just as the silent movie was making its final appearance, so there was a collapse of the financial system that had served the nations for too long. Wall Street may have started the rot, but in each country fresh forces were in charge, at all levels, and untried leaders were calling for approval from their fellow citizens. Britain's politicians called another election and formed a new government. Yet no sooner had one set of clouds vanished than more appeared on the horizon. By the close of 1929 it was anyone's guess what would happen next.

Already for me, school life was routine. I walked with Rosemary each day to our classes and most times we returned home hand in hand. Once when I did not wait for her, I was involved in a fight with Alf Timms, also living in St Agatha's Road, who gave me a bloody nose when I called him 'titch'. The action quietened my adventurous and challenging spirit for a while afterwards. But there were good things and the canvas of life was expanding. I met fresh ideas and new people, amongst them, Harold Furminger from Harefield Road, who commenced school in 1929. Our meeting blossomed into the longest male friendship I have had, through school days, wartime Britain and right to the present day. Other long term friendships have included Rosemary Fall and Bernard Hewitt, the latter continuing one his parents had with mine. And, of course, there were my Salt cousins, Joyce and Beryl, who by 1929, were just emerging as contactable human beings at last.

Then my Damascus Road arrived the instant my horizons opened to the world outside my small town beat, the moment I received the Philosophers' Stone from my teacher, Miss Jones: the gift of learning to read. The first stumbling words I mouthed as she guided me with patience and care,

'Dan is bad. Pat is sad.'

were left etched in my memory. Her successor, Miss James, caught my interest in story books and fables, as well as grounding me in spelling and writing. Such rewards brought solace and peace to the darkest and loneliest moments of being an only child. Indeed, it was an endowment to cherish, with civilisation threatened by open revolt and nationalism wreaking political chaos.

So I had crossed from babyhood to elementary school and must prepare to accept responsibility for decisions I might formulate away from the reliance on parents. They were wise enough to understand what was happening. At the age of five, while on holiday in a small seaside village in Sussex, I was able proudly to pronounce aloud to them, from the indicator board of a passing double decker bus,

"Those people are going to PRIVATE."

And they knew their offspring no longer hung on their apron strings. Their concern at protecting me from the worst excesses of their generation was no longer relevant. From now on everything must be tempered with what I might discover for myself.

THREE

DEEPER SHADOWS OF THE SECOND

WRITING UP PERSONAL details needs some correlation with known historical records to relate one event with another, but apart from a straightforward date, to show a passage of time, everything else takes on a rather different aspect than when it first appeared. For one thing, history books have the habit of becoming a writer's individual viewpoint and identify a storyline he would like us believe, while official sources, especially if they are Governmental, will scarcely state the truth if it is likely to reflect badly on the office holders in some future debate.

In all honesty, few of us have a broad and overall knowledge of the past, particularly when we are finding it difficult enough to live in the present. Consequently we tend to leave such things alone, so that we restrict ourselves to a handful of basic details. We may remember Alfred and the Cakes, Canute and the Waves and Drake's defeat of the Spanish Armada, yet from then on, Cromwell and the Commonwealth, Waterloo, Trafalgar, and Queen Victoria stand little chance. That is unless, like Robin Hood, Richard the Lion Heart and Nicholas and Alexandra, they have featured in an epic movie, or a television series.

What we need to accept is that the recording of history has always been a hit and miss affair. For centuries there was hardly any note of it at all, except for the epic poem passed on by minstrel or strolling player. In Medieval days, stories of Kings and Queens were soap opera for the peasant population, under the tutelage of a Feudal Lord. He would rather they found their entertainment there, than from the dangerous tales of Spartacus. As for the rest of the news, the special pleadings of church and state censored that and

36

avoided criticism by ruthlessly exterminating any challenger. How much can we trust, in these circumstances, the political purity of those who uncovered the story of Guy Fawkes or justified a Crusade? And if a quick profit was available by the purchase of some ex-monastic land, who would raise a fuss at their Royal suppression?

There is one certainty, the discovery of America looked very different if you chanced to be an Inca warrior, suffering at the hands of the Inquisition, who believed the truth for mankind is a product of torture and execution. However, if confusion reigned then, where is it today as State propaganda machines assess the Russian Revolution, Anti-Semitism and Apartheid? We need search no further to find the benefactors of that sort of pleading, particularly if it should make fortunes, and ruin reputations, through the newspaper headlines.

In my own case, the question is how to treat a personal story in the framework of the external events that affected me. Should the massive scale of international circumstance intrude on what is fundamentally a record, during my early years, of staying alive? Romances and abdications of Kings and Princes, the dissolution of Empires and the rise of Dictatorships is pretty grand stuff, but, on reflection, maybe the simple status of the individual in society and the creativity of the artist is more relevant. We shall see how it unfolds.

I was five when I first became interested in history after my parents had taken me for a visit to London. At the Tower and in Westminster Abbey, I felt there was more I would like to know. When the opportunity arose to talk to an inspiring local historian, J.B.Shelton, at an exhibition of Roman remains in Coventry, he invited my father and me to see the dig at nearby Baginton. Inside the fort he was excavating he described the settlers who had lived there, what they did and how they worked, and showed us pieces of mosaic, pottery and fossilised leather. Together, we traced out the earthworks and fortifications on the site and examined the heating ducts and sewers that criss-crossed the foundations. The Romans suddenly had flesh on their bones.

Straightaway, I started to plan my own exhibition and museum in my bedroom at home. Pride of place went to a sliver of rotting timber I had bought at Nelson's flagship, The Victory, the previous summer. I framed several pictures of London and the South Coast and spread on my mother's kitchen tray some foreign coins that my grandfather had inherited. Alongside these I placed a small piece of Roman mosaic and a range of highly decorated propelling pencils, made up as miniature ancient Egyptian mummies, which my Uncle Jim had brought from the Middle East after one of his sales trips for the Calico Printers Company. My father said that anything bought in Cairo was manufactured in Birmingham anyway, but I still spent hours reading the guidebooks and brochures I had accumulated. Perhaps the oak fragment I treasured so much had something to do with my choice of *The Story of Lord Nelson*, as the first book I borrowed from the local library, when I was eight. Even the taunting of an ex-Royal Navy friend of my father's, Dan Taylor, scarcely deterred me.

"Brian," he said, "if all the timber sold with the label 'From Nelson's Victory' was collected up, it would build a whole British fleet, let alone a ship. I used to sell it by the ton. So did my dad, and grandfather, before me."

But I was beyond listening or caring.

It was most likely this discovering and collecting period helped me develop an interest in current affairs. Not that I was fully conscious of the shemozzle that marked the start of the thirties, except a casual awareness of the pressures of unemployment and poverty. At Infant School, I certainly did not make the connection between the poorer children in my classroom and the pictures of hunger strikers and petitions to Downing Street, featured in the newspapers my father read.

What I sensed as abnormal were the anxious conversations that adults seemed to have, and I was conscious of the threats that concerned them, which might indicate a return to the days of 1914-18. Unfortunately, there was still stark evidence of that war in the local towns. The walking wounded were all too familiar, with many of them yet to come to terms with their terrible injuries as they yielded to middle age. There was also the sight of the conflict itself, a disturbing quantity of battle relics littering the cities and countryside. Artillery pieces, gun carriages, sea mines and ships' anchors stood beside the war memorials on village green and recreation ground. In Coventry, a monster tank on Greyfriars Green and anti-aircraft guns in every park, were as much a symbol of battle as they were of the factories that produced the deadly weapons only a short distance away. Even our homes were not sacred. Polished brass shell cases, fashioned to hold candles or bouquets, were the ornaments of sideboard and mantel-piece, and Regimental caps and tin hats hung on the hatstand in the hall. At one local aerodrome a concrete plinth indicated where the first bomb dropped by a Zeppelin had fallen close by Whitley Village. While at Radford airfield the arching hangers that had housed a Royal Flying Corps squadron, protruded derelict towards the heavens.

Still not everyone agreed to let matters rest or to swallow the inconsistency of peace represented by war. One night, in a country pub, a group of ex-servicemen decided to organise their own demonstration. They man-handled a captured German mortar from beneath the Cross of Remembrance, outside the parish church. Splash it went into the village pond and stayed there for years afterwards as a convenient water gauge with its muzzle reaching to the sky. Some trophies proved less easy to remove. They stayed around until either the scrap metal drive, in World War Two, announced their final curtain, or an air raid blasted them to Kingdom Come.

Fitting these pieces together helped me visualise the story of the times. By locating the dates of the Great War, aligned to my parent's lives, I traced their childhood to the reign of Queen Victoria. On a later visit to London they showed me Crystal Palace and when fire destroyed it a short while afterwards, the historic period back retreated backwards to the 1850's and the birth of my grandparents.

History lessons at school were adding to the picture. At Grammar School we made models of castles and drawbridges, and from the Age of the Pharaoh's, a miniature shadoof. My father fashioned some tiny water pots on his lathe and I built a replica of the Nile river bank with canvas, wire and cork chippings. It was so effective that the history master put it on display in the school museum.

School trips similarly, played a major part in the broadening of this experience. We toured castles in Kenilworth, Warwick and Maxstoke and noble mansions around the county, but I missed a journey to the Rollright Stones, considered locally as a rival to Stonehenge. The morning for that saw my body erupt in the flaming red spots of chicken pox, confining me to bed instead. I always judged it one of the mysteries of childhood, just why did illnesses catch you out when you least wanted them? Parties and outings were the sufferers, never exam week. My friends endured the same misfortunes. Len Burroughs, the son of my parent's great companions, Amy and George, more senior at school than I, forfeited a trip also because of a raging fever. That one to Oxford, I reckoned as probably the best guided tour we ever had. Organised by Shipley, our history man, it was sheer delight. He ushered us across the streets, paraded us through the colleges, cajoled us into silence in the chapels and generally saw to it that we shared his love of everything it had represented to him as a student. From then on, many of us decided that a University place was something we should not miss.

Another memorable trip was to Brussels at Easter 1939, when for the first time a school party went overseas. It was a sign of the insular nature of our lives at that stage, compared to modern practice, that only three boys in a group of forty had previously crossed the Channel. Mr Sheppard, the chemistry master, was our well-named guide. However, he was as unaware as we were, that in a space of months we would be recalling Belgium and the Belgians under very different circumstances. Almost fatalistically, in 1944, just after the liberation of Brussels, I searched out the hotel we visited, and remembered our concern that Belgium seemed so full of battlefields. After Hitler it had many more to add to the record.

That Easter we developed quite a taste for war. First we struggled and panted to reach the top of the grassy pyramid and the stone lion that overlooks the plain of Waterloo, then on to the site of World War One battles at Mons, Namur, Liége and Fort Loncin. If the others had not turned our stomachs against the very thought of soldiering, Fort Loncin could not fail. It was there, in August 1914, that the bloodiest of the battles took place. Strengthened by the Belgians to defend any sudden invasion of the Kaiser's armies, the garrison stopped the advance of the elite German troops. They fought for days, spraying the enemy, with withering bursts of artillery and machine gun fire, along the passageways and mortar emplacements. Twenty-five thousand Huns perished and all the Belgian defenders, down to the last man.

It was a salutary lesson. Young soldiers, hardly a year or two older than we were then, had sacrificed their lives in the glorification of hatred. If my parent's dead friends and my wounded uncles were anything to go by, there was no reward at that source. We had little idea as we returned to Brussels that evening what was in store for us. The implications may have already been clear enough in a year that had fostered Munich and Czechoslovakia. Right then it was easier to ignore the sound of marching jackboots from across the frontier, and the Ardennes Forest looked at peace as our coach drove by.

Not all visits were so deadly serious. High spirited young men can find diversions enough to lighten the path, if they so will it. Ominously though, even our fun seemed tainted by the black humour of a bleak future. In our hotel at the Place de Cinquantenaire (one more memorial to another Belgian battle) we were six to a room with shared washing and loo facilities at the end of the corridor. Each room, in addition, had a chamber pot, to aid any necessary evacuation in the night. In the light of day that vessel presented a disgusting sight. One morning as we awaited a summons to the latest expedition, our room-mates, Hilary Warren and Harry Green, hatched a contest. The challenge? A jumping across the beds race, consisting of a three foot leap, a step on the mattress, another three foot leap, until the circuit of the six beds was complete.

Both contestants got off to a flying start, performing the required jump and step, jump and step until they reached the fourth bed. Warren was slightly ahead but had forgotten that a full chamber pot lay on the floor between the final two hurdles. He lost the rhythm long enough to feel the force of Green's jump alongside him, and landed fairly and squarely in the utensil. He toppled heavily, engulfed in a shower of stale urine and was unable to shake the offending item from his foot. Perpetually afterwards, we knew him as Jerry, although the helmet he wore remained attached to his foot rather than where the Kaiser's forces considered most appropriate.

Throughout this period the stimulation my teachers gave to my interest in history prepared me to absorb more of the same formula. My attraction, therefore, was to anyone who might increase my understanding and when I met a particularly gifted guide I enjoyed the experience to the full.

One of these was Rev Delanoy Saberton, a curate attached to Holy Trinity Church, standing beside the cathedral, in the centre of town. We had met when he was guest preacher at St Margaret's in 1936 and I was the soloist in the anthem at Evensong. Afterwards he asked if I would agree to him seeking permission from my vicar to sing at a Charity Concert he was organising. There began a most fruitful friendship as 'Sabby' was an enthusiast for everything I had discovered was mentally satisfying; theatre, music, art, literature and the open air. He was at his best when conducting groups of young people on cycle rides around the Warwickshire countryside, showing us gems of architecture, heritage and culture. We saw the most beautiful examples of English settlements at Merevale, Temple Balsall, Compton Wynyates and Ashby St Ledgers where in the thirties the patterns of rural life were still largely untouched. Redevelopment was slow to intrude, and cottages rotted away after the villagers had departed to more profitable work in the industrial centres. Electricity and mains' water were not available and oil and candles lit the rooms, as wood fires, in an open hearth, warmed the occupants. Even in the larger towns there was much on view from Medieval times.

In Coventry, Warwick and Stratford on Avon, stood Saxon churches, Norman craft halls, Tudor alms houses and Stuart assembly rooms. These and more, Sabby carefully revealed to us as he demonstrated the development of ecclesiastic design, from perpendicular to decorative, to nineteenth century Gothic. He linked this to the nuances of religious music through chants, anthems, madrigal and cantata, and as he was a gifted organist, we would listen while he played on some of the older church instruments and one of us would hand pump the bellows. Then he would find hidden tombstones and crypts where we could translate the Latin inscriptions and trace family trees, filling our understanding of the past with illumination.

Sabby, though, was not alone in starting us wondering if this tranquil scene might survive. The cracks were surfacing in the fabric. How long might it remain without collapse? In essence we concluded, the ambition of new generations was to throw off the inheritance from the past as the influence of the far reaching Education Acts of the mid-nineteenth century was spreading into the rigid layers of our society.

It was a long drawn out process. The Right of Equality for the individual may seem a priority, but it lacked anything like a national recognition, and indeed faced the problem of a backward retreat in so many countries of the world. In Britain, despite the Suffragettes campaigns in World War One and the eventual acceptance of suffrage for women, it was anything but easy to displace a class ridden society. Both the ethics of church and state endured trapped in a web of misinformation. There was obviously much political mileage in these bitter and drawn out struggles just when I was lucky enough to find a forceful tutor, a fiery Welsh orator, as my next counsellor.

George Price was a workmate of my father and the husband of a lady who helped my mother at Church Bazaar and Sunday school. He came from Pembroke Dock where his father was a naval engineer concerned in the development of miniature submarines to combat the Kaiser's growing war fleet. 'Resurgam' was the first fruit of this venture but on its maiden voyage, with George's father aboard, it sank. Unfortunately it did not live up to its name and failed to rise again, although the crew survived.

After High school, George, too, went into the dockyard, where he served an engineering apprenticeship. At the same time he earned his spurs as an orator on worker's rights. In the hotbed of Welsh socialism, he vied for the hearts of the employees inside the Naval base, and the unemployed outside the gates. The Admiralty management did not welcome his views, and after he married Hilda in 1916, they sacked him, forcing the young couple to look for work in Coventry. He met my father at the Armstrong Siddeley factory and as they lived a matter of 200 yards from each other they would walk to and from work every day, discussing the upset world around them and the political mayhem that demanded a settlement.

The Prices had lost their only child in an infant epidemic of diphtheria, and in the disillusionment of those post war years decided against more. When I was a chorister at church I would notice them sitting with my parents as I progressed to head the choir and take on the solo soprano lines. Sometimes after evensong we would have tea and biscuits at their home in St Osburg's Road, while he captivated me with his lilting Welsh accent and radical political philosophy. I seized the opportunity when he suggested I might call on Sunday mornings to talk about the things that interested me.

It became a regular routine and my political education began in earnest. He had a vast knowledge of economic theory, and I listened to his notions, spiced with the names of Welsh public speakers he had heard lecturing before the Great War. Then, with no television or radio, the only way to pass on ideas was by direct contact with an audience so that political debate helped bring forward proposals to solve poverty and exploitation. When George was a young man, Revolution swept through the populations of Europe and he opted to rally opinion against the inevitable cycle of re-armament and war, in the hope that the awful sequence of hate and death should cease. Nevertheless, memories were short and even as we met each Sunday another conflict bore down upon us, regardless of the lessons the last one had supposedly taught.

George spoke to me of the catalysts that could set the world alight and tried to explain the part that politics played. I heard of Liberals, Conservatives, Socialists and Communists, and when I stood as the Labour Party candidate in a mock election at school, his prompting provided enough ammunition to sweep me to an overwhelming victory at the poll. One rousing summary he passed on to me held my schoolmates spellbound on the validity of the cause.

"Look you," he declared, "never in history does it happen that nations throw away the arms they have spent fortunes building up. Generals and Field Marshals don't get their promotions to do nothing. Can you believe for a minute that Hitler is equipping his air force with dive bombers and fighters and launching U-boats and pocket battleships, while we in Coventry are working flat out in the shadow factories and ordnance sheds to make guns and tanks and no-one will use them? I'm afraid, lad, you and your friends will be the ones to pay the piper. What a reflection on your dad and me. Through no desire of ours, we must manufacture the very things that destroy our own kith and kin."

No wonder the other candidates hardly registered a vote.

I also learned that deception was the real name of the game. State propaganda machines had found their feet and were setting off one faction against the other. The Berlin Olympics of 1936 saw the art at its most devastating. Promises of friendship and brotherhood revealed their false values in a sports arena dominated by racism. Distortion was the aim, distraction a means to hide the truth. It is even the same today. The intrigues of the rich and famous are readily available to divert attention from politically sensitive information. They permit the mass circulation newspapers to deliver the same daily dose of pap we listened to in the thirties. How convenient that affairs of Kings and Princes are the very stuff to anaesthetise the masses and avoid the embarrassment of facing the real issues; we have little option but to participate.

At school, we learned *Jerusalem* and *Fairest Isle* so that on Jubilee and Coronation Days we could sing a hymn of thanks to the local councillors for giving us souvenir mugs and picture books. Five shillings saw my parents and I on a rail trip to London to view the lights and decorations on the processional routes, and we joined in street party and gala as one Royal Wedding after another turned into the standard diet of BBC broadcasting.

There was no disguising it, this surface froth was merely wafer thin and the words of my mentors were patently foreboding. In the blinking of an eye, the march was on again and past failures sought revenge. Germany had swallowed a bitter pill at Versailles in 1919. The forfeiture of overseas colonies and territories in the homeland were harsh terms and the dreams of the Kaiser took a nasty knock. Yet the Wagnerian trumpets could not stay silent for long and a new leader, bearing the banner of National Socialism, already knocked at the door. Once elected, Adolf Hitler touched the soul of his people and restored their confidence.

The rest of the world scarcely raised an eyebrow. The crash on Wall Street and economic unrest were too much to handle. Germany was free to develop its own power structure guaranteeing the supremacy of the Nazis. By 1933 Hitler was Chancellor and the rest was history. Straightaway he swept aside the restrictions of the Peace Treaties and forged ahead with large scale re-armament. Soon he turned to the occupied territories and German armies marched into the Saar and the Rhineland. In quick succession Austria and Czechoslovakia fell by the wayside, as promise after promise, even Neville Chamberlain's 'scrap of paper', was not worth a jot. They were grim days indeed.

Fortunately there were some wise heads still around. Seeing the emergence of such a powerful force, despite its public relations expertise at building autobahns and racing Mercedes Benz motors, they watched the image making of a fascist dictatorship with growing fear and suspicion. *Mein Kampf* was more than merely a personal statement and Churchill in Great Britain and Roosevelt in the United States were unconvinced. Their later alliance materially altered the chances for the first time, although back in 1935, at the time I reached Grammar School, things did not look so good.

I sat the ill-reputed '11-plus' examination twice, because my month of birth permitted the anomaly. At my first attempt at ten, I qualified to attend the Central Advanced classes at Frederick Bird Boys School. Here a more pressurised curriculum than that provided at the council senior schools brought tuition in modern languages and science until the age of fifteen. This extension of the schooling period, after the age of fourteen, did not become general until the 1940's. It also acted as a very good crammer so that when in the following year I entered the Grammar School's Special written examination, as well as the local authority's 11-plus, I succeeded in passing on to the aural of each.

The interview at King Henry VIII was the most intimidating. The Headmaster, dressed in a black graduates' gown, sat in his study, accompanied by two elderly governors and two senior masters of the school. They introduced themselves, told me to read a passage of prose aloud, and then asked questions. My historical interests played in my favour as one of the staff wanted to know if I had seen a Golden Guinea, referred to in the text. My answer that there were some in the museum I had visited in Manchester, side tracked the interview into a general discussion about archaeological remains and artefacts, which led on to music and stringed instruments. The Head, A.A.C.Burton, told me that although he could award a special Governor's free place, he understood I also had qualified for a local authority scholarship and would discuss which option they would offer me. I was overjoyed, particularly as at the later interview I had scarcely walked into the room to meet another set of adjudicators before Mr Burton interrupted,

"I have seen this young man previously so I don't think it necessary for us to question him again."

That same week my parents received confirmation of my scholarship. Entering the Grammar School in September 1935 was quite an event for me. I had close friends around me; Harold Furminger and John Stringer from my earliest days at Stoke Council, Roy Lewis, a fellow chorister and son of the choirmaster at St Margaret's, and Len Burroughs, in a senior form, but a welcome reassurance if things went wrong.

The school, on the hill beside the railway station, was solid Victorian Gothic, built in 1885. The main assembly hall was wood panelled with a quota of Holbeins and van Dykes, while the wall safe displayed the original foundation document signed by merchant

John Hales and King Henry in 1545. Our form room led off the main hall and housed Form 2c, the 'c' based on surname position in the alphabet, so that we were Smiths, Taylors, Thomases and Turtons, including another Bryan Taylor. Our fatherly class teacher and maths instructor was A.B.Sale, 'The Major', who had fought in the desert alongside one of our boyhood heroes, Lawrence of Arabia, although he kept a closed lip on his experiences in those battles. Two bright First Class Oxbridge graduates, Arthur Tattersall and Ted Webb, shared teaching roles for our Latin, English and History with Nobby Hobbs for Geography, the music master, F.H.Metcalf, for General Science and a rotund F.S.Atkinson, complete with frameless eye glasses, for French.

The style of teaching from Tattersall and Webb was easy and relaxed, allowing lessons to develop into debate and discussion. As young men they were abreast of current political and social trends and brought sharp comment into our daily school work. I had constantly enjoyed questioning attitudes of mind with my friends, broadened by my conversations with George Price and Delanoy Saberton, so the classroom experience was stimulating. I suppose it was because of this my form mates encouraged me to initiate a series of newsworthy topics, just as we were about to embark on some written test. With suitable back-up from them we were able often to avoid a difficult or boring lesson and at the same time hear points of view on international affairs that amplified our own.

Arthur Tattersall was a particularly inspiring individual. Brought up in Liverpool, KHS was his first teaching post after Cambridge, and his ideas about war, the dictators and political intrigue meshed in with ours. He was chestnut haired, despite its visible thinning, tall and well built, so that on the Rugby field he was an agile front row forward, who encouraged us in games practises, by revealing some cunning strategies and offensives. In class he appeared relaxed and amiable with an encyclopaedic knowledge of German history, gathered, we were sure, from a Fraulein he visited there frequently. On the mornings he received a letter from her, before they married, we took unfair advantage as he gazed out of the window in a daydream. It gave us every opportunity to construe our Latin unseens sloppily, while his attention went elsewhere. On their marriage in 1937, she moved to Coventry, and captivated us with her flaxen hair and cool beauty whenever she attended the school functions. She told us she had no illusions about marrying an Englishman but welcomed the opportunity to be away from Germany.

It was when one or two German boys entered the school we realised something unsavoury was happening. Until then Jewish problems played no part in our isolated Midlands obscurity, and simple religious dogma taught at Sunday church, only completely confused us, with its Pharisees and Sadducees, and good and bad Samaritans. Even more remote lay the East End marches, while the Cable Street heroics of my later life friends, like Benn Toff and Jack Myers, scarcely raised a ripple. Yet the experiences of the refugees were very real indeed. Those who joined us at school were eager to assimilate into our ordinary daily existence rather than promote the sensationalism of their recent treatment in Germany. Nevertheless, we were quick to appreciate their nervousness over the blatant falsehoods of Fascist propaganda, as it became increasingly directed towards us and we took account of their obvious distress.

Strangely, a much greater impact on our everyday life occurred through the Spanish civil war. We had talked in class of Marxism and related it to our parents and their jobs in the local armaments' factories and the poverty we could see in some of the backstreets and slums of our town. The *Daily Mirror*, the *Daily Herald* and *Reynolds News* were newspapers of the left, with a wide circulation amongst young people who could read, and particularly those who regarded their jobs to be dead end occupations offering no expectations, except in time of war. With this motivation we judged the factories as an extension of the slave trade and considered our own prospects for higher education as a way of shielding us from the worst effects of capitalism.

We took to heart the teachings of our senior history master, 'Shipwreck' Shipley, as he introduced us to the ravages of the Industrial Revolution, the rise of the Trades Unions and the Reform Movement. We greedily devoured each rebellion from 1793 to 1917 as symbols of the rise of worker power and the ultimate salvation for the people of the world. What wonderful alliterative sounds we concocted from 'capitalist mill owners', 'munition manufacturers' and 'war time profiteers' as we rolled the words around our tongues at the school debating society.

On cue we grabbed, the cause of the Spanish Republicans

The Salt Family in Manchester, 1917. Back row, left to right: Ethel Taylor (BLT's mother), Ethel's brother, James Salt, George Taylor (BLT's father), Bertha Salt Ethel's sister). Front row, left to right: John Thomas Salt (Grandfather), Ruby Salt (Ethel's sister), Spot, Mary Jane Salt (Grandmother).

Grandfather Salt leads the Wesley Hall, Ancoats Brass Band at the Whit Sunday walk.

Grandmother Sarah Jane Taylor.

George Taylor and his 'cello, 1919.

George Taylor at his lathe, 1923.

Small crank turned by
George Taylor, 1948,
and shown at the Model
Engineering Exhibition.

BLT aged 3.

BLT and mother in Broadgate, Coventry.

St. Margaret's Parish Church, Walsrave Road, Coventry.

Press cuttings from the Midland Daily Telegraph.

Midland Daily Telegraph

COVENTRY   SATURDAY, JUNE 16, 1934   ONE PENNY

MUSICAL FESTIVAL

5,000 Competitors At Leamington

FINE TALENT DRAWN FROM WIDE AREA

Leamington and County Open Competitive Musical Festival, with its record entry embracing 5,000 competitors, opened to-day with a full programme of juvenile vocal and elocution contests. In the assembly rooms at the Town Hall, Mr. J. Clifford Turner adjudicated the elocution classes, and the young singers, were heard by Mr. Arnold Goldsborough. In both instances some fine talent, drawn from a wide area but mainly comprising competitors from the Leamington and Coventry districts, were in competition, calling for meritorious comment from the adjudicators.

COVENTRY BOY'S SUCCESS

An early outstanding success this morning was gained by the 11-years-old Coventry singer, Brian Taylor, in winning the boys' open solo contest. This boy, who is often heard in local concerts, caused the adjudicator to remark that he was a subtle and sophisticated singer despite his tender years.

This afternoon one of the most popu-

LATE NEWS

COVENTRY CHOIRBOY'S SUCCESS AT BLACKPOOL

At Blackpool Musical Festival Children's Day, to-day, 2,000 boys and girls from all parts of the country took part. Brian L. Taylor, Coventry, was one of three selected to sing to-night in the open solo singing class for choirboys.

A DEDDV TDACEDV

London Musical Festival Successes

The rest of this column this week devoted practically to the achieveme of young people in Coventry in th respective spheres in the music worl

Earlier in the week attention called to the success attained at

MASTER B. TAYLOR

London Musi Festival on Sa day by Mas Brian Tayl This young sin gained first p out of fifteen c petitors in open class for soloists, over although he the youngest c petitor in t class. The piece was difficult comp tion of Profes Hely-Hutch son's "The C Soldier,"

Master Taylor, who has been heard several occasions in local concerts, w warmly congratulated by the adjudi tor, Mr. Maurice D'Oisly.

For the past three years Master Tay has been a pupil of Miss Al McGowran, whose success with a nu ber of young Coventry singers over long period of years has been outsta ing. Master Taylor is solo boy in Margaret's Church Choir.

Joyce and Beryl Salt at
Cleveley, Blackpool, 1941.

BLT watches mother cut 25th. Wedding Anniversary cake, 1942.

HAROLD FURMINGER with BLT
in Coventry Memorial Park, 1941.

JOHN STRINGER and PHILIP LARKIN
at school, 1937.

KHS drama production of *Laburnum Grove*, 1939. Back row, left to right:
J.H.Thompson, H.A.Furminger, G.J.Gibson, K.J.Gavin,.
Front row, left to right: J.T.Holmes, I.W.Fraser, H.E.A.Roe, BLT, H.B.Gould.

BLT and F.H. METCALF
in School Concert, 1936

Holy Trinity Church Passion Play, 1937. Left to right: BLT, Ralph Gardiner,
Ralph Greenway, Miriam Johnson, Eileen Casson.

Antwerp Cathedral, 1939.

Army guard in Brussels, 1939.

ARP Messenger Boy, Coventry, 1940.

fighting for their lives against the Fascist thugs of Franco in Madrid, Bilbao and Guernica. The intervention by the troops of Hitler and Mussolini only solidified our faith in final victory and made the battle that more necessary. In such an atmosphere many young men copied the same path as a friend of mine from the theatrical group organised by the Reverend Saberton at Trinity Church. He was some four or five years older than I, but we had acted together in pantomime and drama and were preparing another production when suddenly he failed to appear at rehearsal. That first evening we improvised around his part and struggled along, but at the next meeting Saberton called me to one side and I added the lines to mine.

I heard later that our producer had used his church contacts to discover the missing lad's whereabouts and we surmised a scenario. Geoffrey Penn had been living at home after leaving Bablake School at sixteen. His father was a building contractor, who helped construct the scenery for our plays, and Geoff worked in the office. One afternoon he had walked off, caught a train to Euston and went on to Victoria Station. In Birmingham there was a recruiting cell for volunteers to fight in the Republican armies and they had arranged his trip. His mother received a card posted in Paris, telling her not to worry as he was travelling South on a holiday. It was the way it happened. A point of assembly at Gare d'Austerlitz, an overnight train to Cerbère on the French border and then a coach ride to enlist in the International Brigade somewhere in Northern Spain.

He had ten days training in the use of a rifle, a machine gun and a bayonet; taught to lob a grenade and light a fuse and that was it. At an isolated camp site he met other volunteers from many countries, and soon they were off to fight the Axis armies of Franco and the dive bombers of Goering.

Saberton kept our hopes alive with the occasional re-assuring statement over the subsequent three months, but we were rehearsing a new pantomime when finally Geoff showed up, haggard and exhausted. We tried to appear unconcerned and stifled our questions for another time, thinking of other young men who would never return from that same journey. Slowly the details leaked; what he endured was horrific. Shellfire and mortar fire, bombings and strafings continued day and night, as he and his comrades tried to defend the villages around Barcelona. It was a merciless battle with no quarter given, and when it ended, he escaped back to France in a fishing boat. His looks betrayed it all. At his last rehearsal I had seen him as a sparkling, bright eyed youth. Now there was neither light nor satisfaction in them any more. Whatever his own internal misery, he never explained it to us, and he extinguished all the pain when shortly after the declaration of war in September 1939, he committed suicide.

Contacts like this with the reality of conflict and anguish brought a fresh urgency to our discussions in the classroom. One day during the Munich crisis of September 1938, we attempted to sidetrack a lesson of Ed Webb on *Macbeth*. The contemporary scene offered a more urgent subject than the Middle Ages in Scotland. There came a measured reply from our teacher,

"There were many young men at school in 1914 who were as anxious as you are now to discuss an impending war. Very few survived to see Armistice Day."

That stopped any possible debate in its tracks and we returned to Banquo and the Witches with haste and respect. Sadly, Lieutenant Webb of the Royal Armoured Corps was himself a casualty of 1939-45. At the D-Day landings in Normandy he was blown to pieces in his tank. Six others, also present in the classroom that day, failed to return from war service.

The year the war began I was in the fifth form and I became more conscious that despite our talk and demonstration, there was little any of us could do to alter what seemed inevitable. The fears of my parents' generation were blatantly developing around us. The scepticism of mine rested on the knowledge that our fate was likely to be in the hands of those who had failed once already. If they could not make it work before, what trust should we place in them now?

In the months before hostilities we each acted with slightly different incentives. Certain pressures encouraged us to join the Army Cadets and Air Training Corps, but they had a whiff about them of Hitler's Youth Movements and we were unsure. We might find it easier to sit on the fence and talk instead of Peace Pledge Unions and the merits of being a 'conchie' or like one chap, we could take our convictions to the Communist Party. He, Dumbleton by name, was a great classicist who well before the usual entry age won an open exhibition to Oxford. We ragged him about his letters to the

Daily Worker and laughed at 'five year plans' and Comrade Stalin. However, we had to admit he stayed aloof to our jibes and the party line he unfurled in debate seemed far more relevant than the hard solutions of the extreme right.

Harold Furminger and I felt entitled to offer privileged comment on these matters. Our school friends indeed derided as politically motivated our contributions to the readers' letters in the *Midland Daily Telegraph*, but one evening we smuggled ourselves into the Corn Exchange assembly rooms to hear Sir Oswald Mosley launch a recruiting drive for his movement of Fascist Blackshirts. It was a sick business, not compensated by our insistence on privately calling them 'Black Blockheads'. The movement dressed its members in tight breeches with matching shirts, ties, berets and socks, and encouraged them to shout the meanest slogans they could mouth. As their leader stepped forward they yelled, 'Down with the Commies', 'Out with Jew boys', 'We march with the Axis', and stretched out their arms in a Hitler-like salute.

We thought it best to hold on tight and keep our powder dry, as we speculated on whether the odd protester would resort to using the rows of chairs as a battering ram. Discretely, strong ropes held the seating together, and a posse of bruisers ruthlessly handled any sign of disturbance. Mosley preached a nasty racist message and we felt that he emerged as a miserable, mean specimen, hardly in the same league as the bawling mesmerisers of Munich and Rome.

Far more appealing to us at the time were the Socialist word spinners: the Webbs, G.D.H.Cole, Bernard Shaw and Hannen Swaffer. When the occasion arose to hear Tom Mann (a Trade Union hero of my father's, from dock strikes and lock-outs) in a big open air meeting on the Memorial Park, we hastened there at once. Alongside him on the platform was Richard Crossman, the young Socialist candidate for Coventry, and we heeded every word as they spoke of the danger of war, of inequality and poverty and the whole gamut of left wing politics. The emotion surging through the large crowd was intoxicating and we sang the *Red Flag* and *Auld Lang Syne* until the gathering broke up late in the evening. Many years afterwards when Crossman was a rising star on the opposition benches in Parliament, I met him while I was directing *This Week* for commercial television and mentioned my schoolboy impressions of the old Trades Unionist and how I had tried to assess him in relation to Mosley. He nodded and answered,

"Tom had a noble heart without selfishness or personal desire; Mosley didn't have one. Full stop."

It was stories like these that stirred us most and made me contemplate the possibilities of a journalistic career after I left school. It could have been this interest in current affairs that provided me with the urge to try my naive talents at verse, so that in a class poetry writing competition, organised by Tattersall, I won half a crown and publication in the school magazine for a poem I called *The World*:

> *While in the paper of today,*
> *We read of doings far away,*
> *Of bloody civil war in Spain,*
> *Where many men are daily slain.*

> *While Hitler makes himself a Czar,*
> *And wants some colonies afar,*
> *The jealous French look on with fear,*
> *And call to Britain year by year.*

> *From building bridges in Malay,*
> *To fighting Moslems in Bombay,*
> *We meet our Lord in Palestine,*
> *And see his temples all divine.*

> *Now let us all to England go,*
> *And give to her what we all owe,*
> *"Oh happy life. Oh England free,*
> *All the dictators envy THEE!"*

Most probably my father's renditions of the patriotic compositions of Elgar on his cello, influenced me greatly when I wrote that. Certainly the romanticism of Empire and adventure caught my imagination, when another competition at school challenged us to write a modern novel. I made second prize, adjudicated by Ted Webb, for a version of *Treasure Island* in the classic Victorian story telling mode of Stevenson.

When I compared my experiences and opinions with my

contemporaries around Britain I met away on holiday, I found we shared similar aims and ideas. Poverty, on the one hand, and the arms race, on the other, were common ground, although we reckoned, at our age, we would have little say in the matter. On visits to my grandparents' new home in Rusholme, Manchester, where they had moved in 1933, I had a particular friend, Peter Wilson, who lived opposite. He was a year older than I was but shared similar likes and dislikes. One of our favourite pastimes was the cinema.

Along every town and city High Street, in those days, there were a whole galaxy of cinemas playing 10 a.m. performances, matinees, evenings and extra shows on Sunday. This pattern of openings, together with the practice of three day programming and old repeats on Sundays, plus a main feature, a second feature, shorts, serials and a newsreel at each screening, gave us tremendous choice, so that in the summer holidays, by virtually constant attendance, we could view hundreds of the best that Hollywood and Denham had on offer. My grandparents were never aware just how much time we spent indoors on fine mornings, afternoons and evenings, but our knowledge of the screen idols of the day was awesome. Garbo, Gayner, Faye, Davis, Harlow, Loy, Cagney, Robinson, and Ameche, we either loved or hated; Rooney, Garland, Durbin and Temple, we welcomed as long lost contemporary cousins. It was a mind blowing exercise, full of surprise and revelation as we watched from our double seats in the back row. Peter holding hands with his girlfriend, Anna, and me, holding hands with his sister, Barbara. There was nothing to beat it.

Peter attended a Boys' High School where German was on the curriculum, and when at Easter 1939 my school trip was to Belgium, his visited Germany. There was no way of avoiding the underlying tensions released by a journey of this sort, especially as many of the Manchester boys had brothers already serving as members of the armed forces' reserves. Those pre-war months weighed heavily, and the mood was not one to ignore. Peter's party recognised a similar attitude amongst other British schools who were there. It was not long, however, before they discovered the attraction of the German gun shops that sold sporting rifles, shotguns and revolvers to the many hunters' who visited the area of the Rhineland, where they were staying. Almost all of them bought pistols and automatic weapons firing blanks. Brandishing these, they engaged in mock gun battles, but the opportunity to have a live enemy, in the shape of some German school parties at the same hotel in Heidelburg was an added attraction.

Quickly they organised a series of contests in the large cellars below, with a school from Berlin as a special target. One day, for two hours, they fought like devils, firing at each other, dashing and diving between the barrels and wine racks and screaming obscenities and political slogans in a basic English and German. When their ammunition ran out, they resorted to fists and kicks, capturing hostages as the assaults ebbed and flowed. Finally, the German boys lay trussed up amongst the rubbish and the cobwebs. Only after surrendering guns, pocket knives and, in one instance, a sword, were they released. Peter confided to me that, in the rough house conditions his Lancashire friends were heir to, the Berlin Nazis were easy meat, and would never be capable of giving us genuine trouble. He was unable to test his theories for real. Peter died in a flying accident over the Yorkshire moors, a short while after he joined the RAF, in 1942.

So over the period of ten years, since the time I had first attended school to that spring and summer of 1939, sentiments and attitudes had hardened. The despair and retrospection of 1929 had lapsed, and an anti-war stance had become, not necessarily pro-war, but, most probably, passive acceptance. The authorities were not slow to make the most of the change. They underlined their disapproval of hunger marches, anti-fascist demonstrations and the peace movement by tough policing, whilst encouraging the low profile State propaganda machine to support the celebrations of Empire and Armistice Day. They mustered the full force of Establishment pomp for Royal Weddings and Funerals, so that the sound of the marching military band, the synchronisation of parading regiments of troops and horses, highlighted by the emotional appeal of mass choirs and musicians, became a handy weapon to cast scorn on conscientious objectors. I witnessed two cleverly organised sideshows dedicated to this process. The first, on our church outing from St Margaret's, when we visited the Aldershot Military Tattoo, illustrated an assortment of self interest. In fact it bordered on conspiracy between church and state to succour the status quo.

We travelled on a Saturday, by train, so that in the early

evening we could walk to the large open air arena at Rushmore where the pageant took place. When darkness fell, hundreds of powerful lanterns and floodlights lit the huge space, as units of the Army, Navy and Air Force began a stirring performance. In front of us, they recreated the battles that won the British Empire. Gordon's death at Khartoum, Clive's conquests of India, Lawrence's capture of Damascus, followed by marching and drilling, with a snatch of a Zeppelin raid, as the bombs fell around the anti-aircraft guns and searchlights. The final tableaux sounded Retreat and the Last Post, before a church service concluded with prayers and a blessing. To mankind was offered *Good Will* and *Peace on Earth*, as our parish group returned to the train, urging them to matins, the following morning at 11 a.m.

On another occasion I saw the Redcoats storming the walls of Quebec and the arrival of Captain Cook in Australia, both performed in floodlight, with fireworks, at Belle View, Manchester. What a leisure complex that was, pre-dating the Disneylands and Safari Parks by three generations. My visit there was often a holiday treat, with grandparents and aunts, and always ended when we shared a huge supper of fish and chips or Lancashire hot-pot. Displays like these showed the flag and helped colour our ideas of Britain's place in the world. They also helped us accept, without question, the bright red blotches spread over the World maps that hung in our schoolrooms. How dramatic they appeared in the Mercator projection that the draughtsmen used. It was years later I learned what a distorted picture we had seen.

I suppose Munich achieved most in concentrating our minds to the underlying truth. We sat up and took notice as a few politicians tried to alert us and some newspapers began to lift the veils. The lessons could only be sombre. The dangers of air raids, the digging of shelters, the supply of gas masks and the threat of rationing were becoming increasing realities. Arguments for peace fell lame, and some of our friends, formerly strong in their pacifist convictions, wavered. Stories from Austria and Czechoslovakia warned that Nazi methods spared neither the liberal minded nor the bright eyed student. Criticism of the Reich was not welcome from any source. Age or learning granted no excuse. Non-obedience guaranteed torture and death. As we waited and wondered it seemed the legacies of our parents' generation no longer held water, and recruitment to the part time services spurted ahead. In any case young men of nineteen and twenty must register for call-up, and by enlisting in the Territorial Army, the Royal Navy Reserve or the Auxiliary Air Force ahead of their conscription, ensured a choice of duties.

Sadly for my father and his friends it was a period of deliberation and realisation. Their hopes of world disarmament and a fulfilment of the pledges of 1914-18, as the war to end wars, lay dashed. Left in their place was the shadow factory and the munitions plant again. Maybe the world had only one plan to conjure up prosperity: re-armament. It was as if producing weapons of death remained the solitary key to lowering unemployment and banishing poverty. The march to the battlefields returned again, and nothing could stop it. Already my father's previously outspoken workmates were enrolling in the Air Raid Defence organisations, and he volunteered to firewatch at the factory. There was a popular old waltz broadcast frequently over the radio that year, Sydney Baynes' *Destiny*; we obviously had little control over ours.

A feeling of helplessness against such powerful and unidentifiable forces submerged us all. There was a sense of manipulation and of power we hardly dared think about, and like the underdogs in such contests, we retreated to areas we hoped gave consolation. For one thing my friends and I were still growing up and the desire to break away from parental authority was a prior concern. We had plenty to occupy our leisure hours: the opposite sex, ballroom dancing, the taste of beer and cigarettes, hair styles and coloured ties. Although the pressures of examinations and careers would never entirely disappear, we remembered other young men, twenty-five years before, and decided that, perhaps, with only one more peaceful summer left, we should enjoy it to the full.

Unfortunately, in Coventry, that was not necessarily an easy task in 1939. The prominent role the city was performing in supplying aircraft and armoured cars from its shadow factories, made it a boom town. In a spurt of activity, construction gangs were building on every spare piece of land. Housing estates, schools, civic offices and departmental stores were juggling for space, and the chain retailers were taking over the old city centre. Around Broadgate and Smithford Street, the heart of the town since medieval days, one after another the multiples marched in: Woolworths, Marks and Spencer, Owens, the British Home Stores and Boots. And along the new highways of Corporation Street and Trinity Street, stood a glass fronted Gas Showrooms, a Rex super cinema and a lavish re-creation of the old Hippodrome theatre, that had previously stood, for donkey's years, beside the ancient city wall and fortified gate.

There was a smell of prosperity in the air as we rode the ritzy automatic elevators and marvelled at the neon signs outside the picture palaces. Then we were ready to take our seats for the evening ration of Wurlitzer organ music and coloured lighting changes, before the main programme began. What a revolution electricity heralded, as more demand on its capacity, coaxed more and more people into the city, to work its potentials. Families came from everywhere, as they heard in Scotland, Wales and Ireland of the wages on offer. They symbolised such a fortune, when earnings, on farm and croft, were minimal, and jobs in the depressed regions at a premium. Meanwhile, to meet the calls for higher qualified personnel in research lab and technical centre, there was a steady movement of academics and scientists. Nearly all had fled from a mainland Europe, as they suffered increasing anti-Semitic persecution by the week.

This was the rub. Some recent newcomers did not share the same finer sense of community as others. From Ireland, arrived a number of IRA activists, determined to upset the applecart without further ado. In early 1939, fire-bomb letters, usually prepared with magnesium filings from the machinery processes in the shadow factories, destroyed our local mail, but there was nothing really serious until the action turned vicious.

One Friday afternoon in August, at the peak shopping hour, a bomb exploded in the centre of Broadgate. It was lying in the front pannier of an unattended butcher's bicycle and caused devastation. Public awareness of such devices was non-existent, and it caused death and serious injury to many housewife shoppers and passers-by. I was on the tennis courts, about a mile away in Gosford Park with Frank Pears, a friend from school, who asked me, "Thunder?" But as it did not look like rain we continued our game. Weeks later the police discovered a bomb factory beneath the stairs of a house in Clara Street, a stone's throw from where we had been playing. However, it was September and the tidings from Berlin and London staggered from bad to worse, so the arrest of some hostile Irishmen went hardly noticed amongst more pressing events. In the longer term, the damaged shopfronts disappeared with the rest of the city during the Nazi air raids.

I had taken School Certificate, in June that year, not knowing what might follow. When the results arrived I saw the Headmaster who told me in the event of war a possible move of the school to less threatened surroundings was under consideration. I thought my parents would prefer me to remain with them. As I had performed rather well in History, English and Mathematics but less brilliantly in French and Latin, he suggested I should try to better the results at another attempt, working on my own if the school situation remained unresolved. So I settled for that in the final run-up to hostilities.

From the moment the news of the Hitler/Stalin pact broke on August 23rd, the invasion of Poland was inevitable. Two arch enemies had become allies causing confusion on all sides. Our friends on the far left waited for the *Daily Worker* to tell them what to do, and the Mosleyites disappeared underground. On Sunday morning September 3rd, I returned home with my mother after Communion at St Margaret's Church. My father had heard on the radio that the British Government had issued an ultimatum to Germany. It was due to expire at 11, and we listened to the Prime Minister make the announcement. As he had not received a reply, we must consider ourselves at war.

Within seconds the air raid sirens started to wail and we sat indoors waiting for something to happen. The All Clear sounded shortly afterwards, so we judged it a false alarm, and went into the garden to speak to our neighbours. Fred Fall, P.C.80, who now lived on a new housing estate nearby, called to see the progress of our air raid shelter. He told us that the expertise he had acquired in the Grenadier Guards on the Western Front helped him coil and lace the puttees of his daughter's boy friend, who was mobilising with the local Territorials. Puttees always presented a problem. Were they to protect your legs when riding your horse or to keep out the trench mud squelching over the tops of your boots? Mr. Fall, as all good policeman should, had the answer. He also told us that the soldiers were assembling near the railway station ready for departure and so after lunch, when Harold Furminger appeared, I joined him on a stroll to the town centre.

In the streets there was a strange mood amongst the crowd,

as if it lacked direction. The residents of the houses were in their front gardens, exhibiting a sort of Mediterranean idleness that suited the warm sunshine, and we spoke with other pedestrians about the weather rather than the day's adventures. Yet there was an underlying frankness in the air, prematurely revealing we knew we were at a fresh beginning. The aimlessness of the false years of peace had disappeared, as we entered a new vacuum of uncertainty.

In Greyfriars Green, we saw the troops lined up with packs and rifles saying their farewells to relatives and friends. They paraded around the relics of one war, the defunct mortars and the empty howitzers, preparing their cartridges and magazines for another. Then at five o'clock there was a call to order, and they sloped arms and marched off to the station sidings. We walked home to tea.

That evening we attended evensong at the Harefield Road Congregational Chapel where the Reverend John Davies, normally a rhapsodic Welsh preacher, seemed unnaturally subdued. Tapping his glasses in his hand to emphasise the words of his sermon, he urged us to look calmly ahead with a steady faith, and then led the choir in O God our help in ages past, a hymn, which on that day must have received more performances than any other. Anti-climatic it may have been, but many a wet handkerchief lay hidden in handbag and pocket afterwards.

Of course, there were no immediate bombings, no gas attacks and no invasions, at least not in our part of Europe. Poland was too far for the bombers to fly, and too quickly conquered for the armies of France and Britain to be involved. Instead the Expeditionary Forces glowered at the enemy across the Rhine fortifications they had previously occupied in 1918. It was not surprising many of us vaguely wondered what the last twenty years had accomplished, and I sensed the regret and disappointment in my parents and relatives, who bore a double tragedy that weekend.

Five weeks earlier, my Uncle Jim had died in Manchester, leaving my two cousins, aged twelve, fatherless. His death concluded the years of suffering he had endured since the catastrophe of 1917. As we buried him in Southern Cemetery, attended by old comrades from the Manchester Regiment and his Masonic brothers, I stood next to my weeping grandfather, in his early seventies, and half blind from cataracts. His grief was inconsolable and the pain too deep to heal. Ironically, as the final hours of peace ticked away, he died on Saturday, September 2nd. My mother received the telegram that Sunday morning as we came home from church. Hence one chapter of family life ended with echoes of the past transferring themselves into the future. Just what that would hold, was anyone's guess.

FOUR

IF MUSIC BE THE FOOD OF LOVE...

IF THERE IS one thing I would choose to repeat when the moment arrives for me to be born again, if there is any choice in the matter, then it would be to live again in a musical home. I was certainly fortunate with my last conception in that it seems to have received aid from St Cecilia herself. Both my parents played the cello, my mother not so deftly as my father, and they would sit for hours in their back room by the garden, playing duets and practising scales and arpeggios. The chances are that the love they shared for music was ultimately reflected in my birth.

Melodies and rhythms were with me long before I understood what talking was about. My Aunt Bertha maintained that other children she looked after required words and stories; she pacified me with a song, or the lilting waltz beat of *Three o'clock in the morning*, which was generally the hour I woke her up if she was baby-sitting during a family trip to Manchester.

My mother recalled another night when she was out with her friend Amy Burroughs. She had left me in the care of my father and Amy's husband, George, who was also an amateur cellist. They had put me to bed and then started their music downstairs. I awoke, after a while, with a searing sore throat and being unable to speak, I tried to attract attention by banging on the floor. Naturally, the notes had their full concentration and compelled me to go down the stairs and confront my father. With their session interrupted, the cellists flapped around at a loss, and to ease my discomfort looked in the medicine cupboard for the household potions. My father grabbed a jar of vaseline, laced it with sugar and lemon, and made me swallow some. Then he sent me back to bed. When my mother returned she was furious; my father had given me scented hair pomade and not Vaseline. He did not live the episode down for months.

"Your music is more important than your child," she railed at him. "You were supposed to be looking after him, not your cello."

Although I secretly agreed with her, I had to admit his medicine had done the trick and I woke next morning free of my ailment.

The events that happened around me often seem to arise from a musical source. Visitors to the house were mainly musicians, pupils of my father or members of the orchestras he joined. Usually the call would end with a musical presentation, the debut of a recently purchased instrument or a personal composition. My father had four or five cellos in the house, bows, strings, music stands and other paraphernalia, so we were never short of the means to have a concert. Whenever my mother and I had a trip out, it became associated with my father's performance somewhere. We went to villages and parishes around the city at Alderman's Green, Wolston, Walsgrave, Bell Green and Allesley where on a Sunday afternoon a scratch orchestra appeared at church and chapel festival or village fete. Afterwards we would sit down to a country tea with home made bread, jams, scones and cakes, accompanied by prize winning tomatoes, cucumbers and lettuce, provided by the local ladies.

Other times we might watch a silent film as my father sat in the orchestral pit and the cinema manager would fill me up with lollipops and sweets. At one screening the projectionist gave me a model sailing boat used as display material for the previous week's presentation of *The Volga Boatmen*. Once, my mother told me although I do not recall it, she took me to a performance by the famous Russian ballerina, Pavlova, at the Empire Theatre, Coventry. Because her regular touring cellist was ill, my father played the cello solo in *Le Cygne*, Pavlova's most renowned role. From then on, it became my father's favourite party piece and years later as I watched Ulanova, Plisetskaya and Alicia Markova perform it with such finesse, my heart beat faster for those early memories.

When I was four we had a new toy at our house, a gramophone. I heard it arrive after I had gone to bed, and crept downstairs to find my parents opening a large packing case. Inside

I saw a 'His Master's Voice' cabinet model and I helped them set it up with winding handle, sound box and needle. Within minutes we were listening to our records. First, Caruso singing *Santa Lucia*, followed by the grand contralto tones of Dame Clara Butt. I must admit our recording of her voice tended to give it a foghorn quality, but that evening I listened anything, if it could keep me out of bed. I was a devoted fan, insisting on rewinding the machine and using it at every possible opportunity. My parents wearied of my demands and gave me a small toy version for my birthday, with its own set of black shellac records.

Using these as starters, I collected a large selection of orchestral and vocal pieces that introduced me to the classical repertoire at an early age. The Burroughs fostered my interest. Amy's father was blind, and as a young man in 1880 had trained as a piano tuner to earn a living. Soon he had his own shop in Accrington, selling and repairing pianos, and this expanded so that his sons entered the business and sold all kinds of musical instruments, gramophones and sheet music. From there we were able to buy records at a discounted price and our collection expanded into overtures, symphonies and concertos. My father cleverly managed to restrain the temptation that we should merely be listeners and we continued with the music making at home, which had been so much a part of family life in Victorian and Edwardian times.

Christmas presented a special opportunity for music when we went to Manchester. In their front parlour the Salts had a piano, set between the horsehair settee, the antimacassars and the Victorian glass ornaments. There we would congregate after dinner and bring out the instruments and music for an evening of family entertainment.

One of the relatives, George Jackson, was a church choirmaster and organist and he would accompany the songs and solos as each in turn stepped forward to perform. George had married my Aunt Clara's sister and he and his wife, Gladys, had a most attractive daughter, Joan, slightly older than me. Later, when we met at these regular get togethers, I fancied her a lot. Joan was learning the piano and she would play duets with her father. My dad, of course, had his cello, my grandfather a pipe and drum from his brass band, and my Aunt Clara and Aunt Ruby their violins. Somehow, the instrumentation was more than adequate for the space. Aunt Bertha was studying singing helped by my parents who paid for her lessons, and she had a wide stock of songs and ballads that fitted either the seasons of Christmas, Easter or Whitsun, while Aunt Clara and Uncle Jim attempted the duets from the musical comedies they had performed in amateur operatic society productions. Grandma often made her contribution with *Chopsticks* on the piano and my mother and Aunt Ruby would try a string trio with my dad. But it was he who generally had pride of place in the finale, with his favourite piece of Saint-Saens. Then grandfather would ask for the *Old Hundredth* or *Jerusalem* and we would break until the next time.

When the family home was in Albert Street, Ardwick, and I was very young, the old lady would often take me upstairs to bed when I fell asleep in her arms. However, at the age of five, after I attended school, I had a chance to do a party piece. I became the performing grandchild, speaking out clearly and confidently, with the lines of *Twinkle, twinkle, little star*. The following year it was Sir Henry Newbolt's *Admirals All*. But there was severe competition at the next gathering. My cousins, Joyce and Beryl, had started dancing lessons at the age of four and completely stole the honours with a pas de deux they had learned at theatre school. I did not like the pressure and resolved to do something about it.

For some time I had been asking my father to teach me the cello. Each Sunday morning, there was a procession of pupils into our front room for lessons. First came Donald Rollins at 10 a.m. The son of a workmate, he was highly talented and was already winning cello competitions in musical festivals. At Birmingham, he won first prize and the adjudicator, Sir Granville Bantock, arranged for him to study on a free scholarship at the celebrated Midland Institute. Unfortunately his father died suddenly and, as the only bread winner, had to seek work to help his mother.

Two young ladies followed on, Phillis Grainger and Mary Yardley, whose concentration rather depended on the state of their relationships with the current boy friends. Then colleagues from the Armstrong Siddeley, like violinist Bill Adams and his sister, Phyllis, who came for special tutoring and small ensemble playing. When my Aunt Bertha stayed with us, the performing and teaching seemed to stretch on all day. She would seek help from my father on interpretation and phrasing in her songs, and he would patiently coach her hour after hour. It was because of her I started out on the steps of my musical education.

A close neighbour of the Salts in Albert Street, was a young tenor who had been a boy soloist in the choir of Manchester Cathedral. Later he became a leading artiste at Covent Garden and on the international circuit. My aunt knew him as Tommy Thomas, but for the concert platform he became Richard Lewis, and she believed that, like him, I should have my voice trained. At work my father was friendly with the members of the Male Voice Choir, conducted by a talented musician and local Headmaster, Syd Wisdom. The group were an accomplished body of singers who had won many competitions and sang regularly on the radio. Within the choir was a versatile male voice 'barbers' quartet', the McGowran Singers, and from their leader, Harry Hall, my father sought advice. The quartet's mentor was Alice McGowran, who in those days of continuing Victorian prudery and morals was Harry's 'friend'. They waited until her mother, aged ninety, died, and they were in their fifties before they finally married. I visited her for an audition.

Alice lived in a large terrace house in Earlsdon, built during the Industrial Revolution, when the watchmakers and the weavers used their homes as a workshop. These properties had an extra upstairs floor, with a large window stretching across the front, and were then all around the city. Their driving shafts and belts often remained in place, until the bombings destroyed the vast majority of the houses. The McGowrans had moved from Ireland during one of the potato famines of the 19th century, and brought their family to Coventry. Alice first attended a convent school and received a grounding in piano and musical theory from the nuns. She had a clear singing voice and pursued her training with some eminent vocal coaches in the Midlands, until she began to conduct her own choirs and gained a reputation as a fine teacher.

Her music room, on the first floor, had a high ceiling and two tall windows, similar to the grand Victorian drawing rooms in my later homes at Regents Park Terrace and Oval Road in London. In it, amidst the dark velvet curtains, the guilt framed mirrors, bookcases and armchairs, stood the mahogany veneered upright piano where Alice sat, dusting the keys with a delicate lace handkerchief, and placing the sheet music carefully between the candelabra fixtures on each side. She was a lady at an age it was difficult to tell within a decade, yet when we first met she was probably in her mid-forties. Always heavily made up, I remember her face as lacquered, like that of a French doll of the period, with tight permed curls sitting close on her brownish bobbed hair. Generally she wore a soft silk cream blouse hanging over a dark tailored skirt, except when she dressed in a long gown, for her appearances as a concert conductor. And always, she included a mass of glass beads, ear rings, bangles and a gold Rolex watch, as well as enfolding herself in the sharpish scent of French cologne.

This was the lady I met one Saturday afternoon in October 1932. She asked me to sing a scale or two, then some sustained notes and finally a song I knew from school, *Bobby Shaftoe*.

"Yes," she said, "I think I can do something with this voice. Let him come to me on Mondays at 5.15."

My father paid out two guineas for a term of ten lessons and we left with my confidence at a peak.

The first lesson was on October 17th, a date I found strangely recurring at special points in my life. My mother took me on a Service Number 1 Corporation bus, as far as Hearsall Common. Then a short walk to Craven Street, where my mother left me to my teacher and she paced round the block, filling up the half hour. Upstairs the golden plated clock in its domed glass case was striking the quarter, and I was there until it struck the three quarters and the ring at the downstairs bell indicated the next pupil had arrived. She fingered some chords, opened a primer and demonstrated how I should sing an exercise to the sounds of *koo, koo, koo, koo, koo, oo, oh, ah*, and as I recovered from the shock that I need not sing like one of our Caruso records, the half hour flew by. The plan was that I would practise the studies with my father accompanying me on the cello, which was an easy discipline to master, so that I returned to Craven Street each week ready for further tuition. My parents thought it prudent we told no-one. Only Aunty Bertha knew, making it possible for me to avoid the jibes and comments of school chums who tended to scoff at other children studying musical instruments. Keeping mum seemed the best policy at that stage.

I had attended Sunday School at St Margaret's Church in Walsgrave Road since the age of four, as my mother taught the children there, at 10 and 2.30. It was convenient for her to be out of the house when my father's pupils arrived and he looked after the preparation of lunch between lessons. One Sunday the vicar came on a recruitment drive to collect probationers for the church choir and asked me to join. As it seemed to be both adventurous and a chance to cut away from my mother, I went to practise the following Wednesday.

I met the choirmaster and organist, 'Bunny' Lewis, who the other boys told me had acquired his nickname because his first name was Wilfred, like the cartoon strip character in the *Daily Mail*. He was chief accountant at the Singer Motor Company nearby and had a son, Roy, also in the choir. I hit off a friendship with Roy straightaway, and as they lived in Brays Lane, near my home, we would walk back from practices and services. While I was still a beginner he helped me master the intricacies of church routines and the mysteries of chants and responses and when we grew older we started to chat up the Girl Guides together.

On Fridays there was a full choir practise when the senior tenors and basses rehearsed with the boy trebles. It was an interesting insight into choral habits to hear the fruity tones and discourses of some of the elderly members, particularly regarding their priority and length of service. An ego became quickly damaged and a nose pushed out of joint if seniority remained forgotten. This extended to the boys, too. The right to lead either decani or cantori (the south side or north side of the choir) was dependant on length of service dating from the time you became a probationer. It could cause bitter rivalry and jealousies.

But the hardest lessons were in the music itself. Finding and maintaining the treble line and then the descant line if you were 'decani', was quite a feat. Under the watchful eyes of the choirmen, who stamped down hard at the least sign of misbehaviour, it required concentration and luck to ensure your place at a Saturday choral wedding where you might earn a shilling for a half hour appearance. As probationers we wore black cassocks, Eton collars and bows, without the white surplice. A special dedication service awarded this. To qualify, we must file into the seats at the end of the choir pews for three months of Sunday services, keeping our presence essentially low key.

During Advent the vicar announced the initiation of three of us for the following Sunday, and I began to prepare for the ceremony. It was not to be. Mid-week, a pneumonia virus laid me low so that I missed the event and waited until Easter to receive my surplice and a full place in the choirstalls. The illness developed its own trauma. I had a high temperature that produced hallucinations and a delirium, strangely linked to the church choir. In the trees outside my bedroom window I saw rabbits running in the branches (they were never there again) and 'Bunny' Lewis appeared to conduct me in some crazy vocal exercises.

Our neighbour Mrs. Smith, an ex-nurse, soothed my fevered brow and fed me with sweet barley water until the heat disappeared and I awaited my father's arrival from work to announce,

"I'm better now. Can I have a baked potato, please?"

I quickly recovered after that, sitting in front of the cosy coal fire my mother lit in the bedroom grate and watching the pictures in the flames as the afternoon brought an early twilight and the darkness of Winter. Luckily, I was fit enough to travel for Christmas to Manchester, although I listened more than performed at the musical evenings.

My voice training continued weekly at Miss McGowran's, supported by my father's nightly tutoring. This knitted in well with my choir rehearsals and the routine of church services on Sundays. I was singing a lot and beginning to recognise the dogma of religious worship. Listening to sermons twice on the Sabbath plus old and new testament readings, the prayers, the psalms and our choral contributions was tough meat for young lads, especially as we had hates and favourites amongst the participating clergy.

Our vicar was a nice enough man. The Reverend Jimmy Cornes. M.A. (Oxon.), M.C., said it all I suppose. Yet he failed to catch our imagination in the pulpit, and we preferred the less lightweight performances of the two curates, the Revs Bruce and Johnson. The Vicar also had a problem winning the loyalty of the ladies of the parish. They preferred to believe he had married 'for money' because he had a much older wife. She was the only daughter of a local rich industrialist, and from all accounts had been on the shelf until Jimmy had rescued her from obscurity. Her sheltered upbringing hardly equipped her for the hurly burly of church politics, and he had to face the social round himself. On the other hand he was brilliant at Armistice Day services; as the veterans lowered their British Legion flags, his voice rang out in a spine tingling performance with the words,

'At the going down of the sun and in the morning we will remember them.'

The lines, which probably formed a vivid part of his own emotional wartime experiences, weighed deeply upon him as he looked out from our memorial chapel towards the congregation, in the main body of the church.

The interior of St Margaret's was a sombre place indeed. I had first become familiar with it when my mother took me with her to place flowers on the altar which was a regular commitment for lady communicants. To a small child the building appeared massive with its large red brick columns supporting a timbered roof stretching right over the main body of the church, and its eight hundred, straight backed, hardwood chairs. Beside the chancel and the high altar, two smaller chapels led off into rather shadowy space, and when I was a chorister on the decani side, I looked down onto one of them, the Lady Chapel.

Behind our choir stalls, in a separate bay of its own, and overlooked by the church organ, stood the Remembrance altar and chapel, built and donated by a family in the parish, whose only son, Lieutenant Howells, died in the Great War. It was the most distinguished piece of the church furnishings. Beautifully carved oak screens divided it from the nave and at the side of its small altar folding panels recorded the names of the parish war dead in gold lettering. Above that hung the Union Jack and a Victorian painting of the 'Dying Crusader'. A deep blue carpet covered the floor area, illuminated from a stained glass window through which filtered a changing rainbow of light, centred on a wreath of red poppies. It held stillness and peace within it, and whenever we passed by, we invariably spoke in lower tones.

The Howells family, had also built the church and the social institute across the road, just before the Great War, and had developed a large part of Stoke. They had constructed our house in St Agatha's Road and it was because their company name, 'E.O.C.Howells Limited' appeared on the castings of cisterns, drain pipes and sewer covers in the property that I felt a certain affinity with the Remembrance Chapel. The house and church shared other similarities both in architectural style and the basic materials of red brick and blue slate. Characteristics echoed, in new buildings, throughout the Midlands, during the decade preceding 1914.

Membership of the choir introduced me to a completely fresh library of music. Masses, chants, cantatas and hymns brought volumes of sound that I relished, from harmonised Hallelujah choruses to descanted Amens that sent me home exhilarated every Sunday. Taken together with Miss McGowran's songs and the pieces I heard at home from my father and the gramophone, it embraced a stimulating audio education.

My mother was also in the act. I accompanied her to the amateur musical theatre productions when my father was in the orchestra and to many others where friends were performing. That introduced me to Gilbert and Sullivan and a whole range of shows from *The Arcadians* to the *Quaker Girl*, and the *Desert Song* to *Rose Marie*. In the Winter Season we would visit the Saturday night Celebrity Concerts held in the only auditorium in Coventry suitable for a large audience, at the Methodist Central Hall. Here many of the well-known instrumentalists and singers of the thirties appeared including Campoli, Albert Sandler, Solomon, Myra Hess, Peter Dawson, Heddle Nash, Elsie Suddaby and Janet Hamilton Smith. Janet had been a pupil of Alice McGowran before joining the soloists at Sadler's Wells Opera, and because of this contact I met her in the dressing room after the concert. For the first time I was really close to the smell of professional grease paint and powder and knew, at once, it was something I was not capable of resisting. It helped me classify my own youthful ambitions, strengthening my determination to overcome technical difficulties in my singing and trust in the voice itself.

Fortunately in the summer of 1934 an opportunity was at hand where I could get my feet wet and sing in public for the first time. Each year at Leamington Spa, about 8 miles from home, there was a musical festival that encouraged young vocalists with a competition for Boys' Solo voices. My teacher decided I should enter. I was familiar with the routine for I had watched my father's pupil, Don Rollins, win first prize there one year and had seen him appear later, playing his test piece at the prize winners' concert in the Jepson Gardens pavilion.

In the boys' vocal competition we were asked to sing *Come unto Him* from *Messiah*, and as Aunt Bertha had taken me only the previous Christmas to a complete performance by the Hallé orchestra in the Free Trade Hall, I was sure I could do well. I practised hard and Miss McGowran arranged for me to have some dry runs with various accompanists before I had to face the official Festival pianist.

Early on Saturday June 16th, my mother guided me to the Town Hall at Leamington and in the Council Chamber, after we had listened to the conclusion of the Girls' solo class, I knew it was all about to happen. There were fifteen competitors with the eldest about fourteen, and I was number six in the running order. Around us sat parents, teachers and a sprinkling of onlookers, adding to the atmosphere of the contest.

The class commenced and as I listened to the first competitor my spirits rose a little and the butterflies in my stomach ceased to fly so high. The second boy missed the vocal entry completely and had to start again, while number three forgot the words, and four went out of tune. There was a pause as number five failed to answer his call, and suddenly it was up to me. I climbed onto the rostrum, gazed out at the fifty or so serious looking adults, seated beneath the lavish gilded ceiling, and saw the adjudicator high on a stool and desk at the back. As he shuffled some papers about I wondered, for one awful moment, if it had been the best decision of my life to choose this form of torture. But Dr Thomas Armstrong seemed a kindly man, and when I learned later he was the Director of Music at Christ Church, Oxford, it probably accounted for the fact that, with so many young voices under his care, he was able to offer me a smile. It gave me an extra bit of confidence to ride over my nervousness. Then he rang the bell.

Once the piano introduction began, nothing else concerned me but the singing, and I sensed as I finished that I had managed to remember the points my teacher had emphasised. The burst of applause was flattering and my mother's wink reassuring, as I returned to my seat and sat impatiently waiting while the other boys followed. The adrenaline flowed strongly for quite a while, and as this class ended I was already beginning to think I would like to repeat it. Then Dr Armstrong came to the rostrum and addressed us. First a run down of the piece and its interpretation, leading to how each of us had fared. He said that I had a most musical style of singing and phrasing, kept well in tune and gave one of the best performances. It merited 85 marks out of 100 and a special mention at fourth place. I was very excited, along with my mother, and we rushed out to telephone my father at work, a rare thing for us to do at that time. That evening in the *Midland Daily Telegraph*, a report on the Festival carried my name as an award winner.

That was the beginning. At church, the vicar congratulated me in front of the choir, and told the organist I should sing a solo, as soon as possible. An announcement that left the normal channels of seniority a little shattered. My teacher at Stoke School, Miss Rushby, who had tended to treat me with more firmness than respect, in so far as my backside and her cane contacted each other at least once a fortnight, showed a surprising interest in my welfare that Monday. Calling me to her desk, she invited me, then and there, to sing in front of the class. And caned two other boys for grinning. My performance was even more nerve racking than the festival, although for the rest of the school year I could do no wrong and my status soared above all previous recognition.

Two Sundays later I sang my first solo in church. There began a regular duty that encompassed the whole repertoire of standard anthems, with treble solos, from Handel to Stainer and Mendelssohn to Vaughan Williams. A friend of my father, a Methodist chapel preacher, invited me to sing at a charity gala at the Paradise Congregational church and afterwards my parents joked I had sung in paradise, but they were secretly full of pride that their perseverance was bearing fruit.

That autumn I moved to Frederick Bird School where the music master, a violinist, who was in cinema orchestras with my father, quickly singled me out for the special descants in morning assembly. Because of their regularity, they helped me overcome the nervousness I had experienced when performing. I was fortunate, too, that Alice McGowran organised a series of concerts every year, with a mixed voice choir from the Singer Motor Company and a prize winning ladies' choir, which became an integral part of the musical life of the town. In these ventures she received great encouragement from the sympathetic music critic of the *Midland Daily Telegraph*, Mr Bee, known as 'Orpheus', and he attended all the regular performances she gave in front of large audiences. She asked me to sing a selection of solos that strengthened my confidence and performance techniques further, under her expert guidance and the friendly comments of Orpheus.

The following June I was at Leamington again on a Saturday morning, this time singing Schubert's beautiful arrangement of *Who is Sylvia?* in a class of twenty boy competitors. The adjudicator, Dr Percy Hall, awarded me first prize with 91 marks and said in his summing up,

'Much of the tone was splendidly placed and the intonation was impeccable. This singer has the capacity to express the song really well and the detail was always to the fore.'

That evening I sang in the prize winners' concert, at the Jepson Gardens Pavilion, in front of some thousand people. My parents, sitting with Alice McGowran and Harry Hall, watched my every move. It was intensely intoxicating to hear the applause as I finished up on stage, with the decorations of palms and flowering plants around me, and then to receive a prize from the lady Mayor. I wanted every second to stretch out to eternity as I looked across the footlights and realised that I was on to something very exciting.

The spin offs were extraordinary. At morning matins the vicar announced my achievement and publicised a solo I would sing in the anthem during evensong. I could see the Girl Guides who were on parade that day, gave me the once over. Things were looking up, and I nudged Roy Lewis to make sure he noticed the interest. Afterwards we played it very cool, reckoning we deserved a little of our own back for the times those prissy girls scarcely offered a glance in our direction.

Piggy Wheel, at Frederick Bird School, had me singing *Who is Sylvia?* in morning assembly, while he composed a special violin obbligato. This would prove the most difficult role to accommodate. How to behave normally in front of one's peers? Jealousies could boil over into black eyes, and as I was not a big chap, I did not fancy the bullyings and beatings I saw occasionally administered to small boys, by bigger ones. It demanded a delicate balancing act to treat everyone as before, although the advantage of music was that it produced a feeling of inner calm, draping a cloud of unknowing around it. This often had a tranquillising effect on those whose root reactions were violent, towards anything they did not understand. Throughout, there was a need to retain a low profile, despite the mates who took delight that your success might bring with it extra opportunities for them to capitalise on your new found popularity with the opposite sex. To keep this in perspective was difficult, when it became hindered by adults who deemed they had a special share in you. It could result in deep embarrassment, on the verge of being cringe making.

Once during open day at Frederick Bird, I weathered the full blast. Our class was on display, naturally enough, to demonstrate a music lesson, and I sang a group of solo verses within a choral piece. The class had barely started, and parents and friends crowded into the room, when I saw a lady pushing herself forward.

"Is this where Brian Taylor's singing? I'm one of his neighbours."

I prayed the ground would split open as the lad beside me sniggered. But Piggy was up to it, immediately launching into the piano introduction and rescuing the moment. Of course, there were neighbours and neighbours. The nicest were the Saywards and the Beaumonts, in nearby Burns Road, who, like my grandparents, organised musical evenings where everyone sang or played, and we ended with a bust-up supper of fish and chips.

I associate this period with many public performances, two or three times a week, so that the experience made a lasting contribution to the pattern of my life. In competitions I appeared in London, Leicester, Northampton, Blackpool and the Welsh Eisteddfod at Fishguard, each one supplying a little more confidence to my performance and teaching me how to handle different situations. I was learning heaps about presentation and what to do with my hands and feet, while the secret of not allowing technique to dominate became part of winning over an audience from the very first vocal entry. There was a great deal to learn and the constant adjustments required to achieve perfection brought its own personal satisfaction.

One of the high peaks for me was in the Boys' Open Solo competition at Blackpool, when I was twelve. I had competed the previous year and received a commendation with 9th position out of 65 entrants, but the 1936 test piece was Mendelssohn's *O, for the wings of a dove*, a section of the anthem *Hear my prayer*, from which I had performed the extended main solo at church on several occasions. In those days its popularity arose from the fine singing of the boy soprano, Ernest Lough, and the Temple Church choir, recorded in 1929. Most soloists tried to copy this interpretation. As I was confident of my technical abilities, I wanted to make it distinctive in a manner that would express my own emotions, and this I set out to do. The Salt family in Manchester had always regarded Blackpool, like so many other Lancashire people, as a personal piece of seaside, and Aunty Bertha and my grandmother joined my mother and me for the competition. I had also regularly visited the town not only with my grandparents, but also on the annual choirboys' outing from St Margaret's Church, when a few shillings pocket money gave us a day of freedom on the Golden Mile and the Pleasure Beach. It was a windy and bracing resort, very unlike the air of our inland cities, and I prepared carefully for the contest, feeling relaxed and secure.

The Musical Festival was the last event of the holiday season, immediately after the illuminations, and all the resources of the town were on full alert. The competitions were held in the Winter Gardens with its abundance of richly decorated theme halls, where the Italian and Riviera rooms, the Spanish Hall, the Grand Ballroom and the Opera House, inspired holiday makers to dream they were somewhere else, when the unreliable English weather drove them indoors. In the Spanish Hall, complete with its fake Mediterranean villas, orange trees and painted blue skies, I was amongst seventy entrants to appear before the adjudicator, that revered old gentleman of English music, Sir Richard Terry. At the end of the session I was one of four competitors selected to sing in the Finals in the Opera House that night. My rivals, two fifteen year olds who led the choir at Manchester Cathedral, and a fourteen year old Welsh boy. I was definitely in the junior age league.

That evening we assembled at the back of the stage, piled high with a mass of theatre properties, lighting equipment and scenic flats, and awaited our turn. The two Manchester entrants were chirpy and cocky, having performed in the previous year's final, but I determined to try hard and not be overawed. When I stepped out, onto the stage, it really was a moment of excitement for me. The Opera House was full and the spotlights blazed down on my lonely figure on stage. Although my best was not quite good enough, I had the satisfaction of the judges saying I had 'a voice with a lovely quality and lots of appeal in the performance', and they awarded me third prize. When I received it, a great burst of applause seemed a just compensation for my efforts, and my mother, grandmother and aunt revelled in the family triumph.

In 1935 I moved over to King Henry VIII School, where the music master, F.H. Metcalf, being a friend of Bunny Lewis, and in the way that such gentlemen have, seized eagerly upon me. At our first group music lesson he asked me to sing alone, and within days I was a soloist in the school's morning assembly. Another boy in my form, Eric Stables, who also had a powerful treble voice, joined me in a duet for the Christmas Concert held in the Sibree Hall and we formed a trio with the music master in another piece. In the summer term, because of my solo appearances at the Leamington Festival, Mr Metcalf thought Eric and I should try a duet in the Open Duet competition. Despite being the only juniors to enter in a class of adults, we won an impressive Fourth Prize. To complete the picture, the school choir entered the schools' competition for the first time too, and after a stirring interpretation of Stanford's *Devon, O Devon*, gained second prize.

The next Christmas concert, exhibited altogether more serious theatrical trappings. They dressed me as a young maiden, in blue crinoline, straw bonnet and lace parasol with a brunette wig, ringlets and heavy make-up, to sing *The Keys of Canterbury* alongside Mr Metcalf. He appeared attired in the dress suit of an 18th Century gentleman. We brought the house down and had to repeat the song again. This initiated my performance of the female lead in a series of school plays. What else was the alternative in the segregated lifestyle of a boys' school, where the piping trebles of the younger ones were ready-made to fit in with the conventions of Shakespeare's day? Thus we authenticated the classroom readings and obtained invaluable experience in the format of classical theatre.

We were fortunate that we could watch Shakespeare, in performance, at the Stratford Memorial Theatre, thirty minutes away, on our weekly Wednesday afternoon off. A compensation for attendance on Saturday mornings. Often our form masters organised the trip on a Midland Red bus, otherwise, Amy Burroughs and her son Len, would drive my mother and me, in their tiny Austin 7 car. We felt chuffed at our good fortune, in seeing so many wonderful productions for just one shilling and sixpence (7½p). Frequent theatre visits were a valuable aid to our appreciation of stage technique, from imaginative sets and costumes to great acting and direction. Sometimes it verged on the unusual, and in Birmingham, we saw Donald Wolfit as Macbeth, during the year the text formed part of our School Certificate studies. Additionally, after school hours, we attended a play reading group with scripts obtained from the British Drama League (a wonderful institution) and read, with the staff and sometimes their wives, from the wide repertoire of available modern drama. The workshop conditions we created, provided fertile ground for our acting ambitions.

Each Easter term we were able to satisfy these in the main school dramatic society production, so that with the stage experience I had gained from singing in front of audiences, I could accept the necessity of poise and purpose in performance. I discovered the importance of self observation, and greedily read Stanislavsky when Joey Kingsland, one of the school's English staff, lent me a copy. No wonder in no time at all, the whole magical world of theatre, inspired me to other things, and I became desperate to combine my singing and acting.

My meeting with Delanoy Saberton was certainly a key point in this. The solo singing, which brought our first contact, developed into a chance of participating in musical theatre. At Trinity Church he directed a group of young people from his congregation to perform a pantomime and other dramatic works throughout the year. He suggested I join his Christmas pantomime of *Sinbad the Sailor,* and under his firm but accomplished tutoring, I sang popular ballads from the Hit Parade. *It happened on the Beach at Bali-Bali, Rise and Shine* and *Glamorous Night,* with their swing and bounce, were a clear departure away from the songs and anthems I had tried before, while the accompaniment of a full live orchestra created a new dimension.

This became grander the succeeding Christmas when I played Aladdin and sang a group of solos from the musical show *Chu Chin Chow,* with its orchestrations of harps, gongs and trumpets. Yet even more fascinatingly, in these productions I discovered other attractions, too. Apart from singing love songs to several beautiful girls in the chorus, I had to manage my first kiss on stage with the leading lady, Princess Lotus Blossom.

That promised real excitement, in the days when such adventure rarely merited so attractive a reward. Naturally I fell madly in love with the Princess, some three or so years older than me, and my maturing passions increased, as rehearsals became more frequent, towards the opening performance. My good fortune was that every morning we passed each other, riding our bicycles to school as she attended the Girls' High School behind my home, and

I rode by the King's Head Hotel, where she lived with her parents. I almost fell off my bicycle when she waved, and if the day occurred that I missed her for some reason, then I spent the rest of the morning in utter misery. Even the consoling words of my friends had little effect. I carved her initials, N.C., on my school desk and wrote her name on every book cover I possessed. As I waited anxiously for the next rehearsal, I spent empty, lonely hours, until I could hold her hand and sing,

> Be sure its true,
> When you say, I love you,
> It's a sin to tell a lie,
> Millions of hearts have been broken
> Just because those words were spoken........

Although on reflection, I am sure I had it the wrong way round.

With deep melancholy, I discovered she loved someone else, one of the more senior young men in the cast, who already had a scholarship to Oxford in his pocket. However, to ease the pain there was ample compensation. In fact, for a whole week of performances, including an extra one on matinee day, I had the rights to kiss her, in front of an audience of 700 people.

None of this, fortunately, clashed with our school productions. The form masters (Webb, Tattersall, Kingsland and Liddiard) directed plays, conducted musical presentations and organised dramatic readings supported by the combined talents of T.C.Sumner, the physics master and an accomplished actor, C.B.Shore, the art teacher and a backstage Jack of all Trades, and Arnold Goldthorp, a music man and cellist. Thus the school boasted a team of high expertise and enthusiasm, and as part of our daily routine they encouraged us to run our academic work in tandem with artistic evolvement, so that like souls had the chance to enjoy the experience together.

Harold Furminger, who was also one of the captives in this training, and I, soon found that it was not difficult to fill every holiday and weekend with appearances in Passion Plays, Nativity Plays, One Act Curtain Raisers and the equivalent, that were the meat of church and youth group activities in the city. Added to this was the opening of the rebuilt Coventry Hippodrome which with its modern stage and lighting could now present large West End touring productions. Saberton insisted his group should visit the opera there, when the

Carl Rosa appeared, and in one week I saw *Bohéme*, *Trovatore*, *Butterfly* and *Traviata*, with an immediate result, that I listened for a year every Saturday afternoon to the BBC broadcasts by the Sadler's Wells Opera. I shared this sophistication, to the limit, with Furminger. We spent hours arguing the merits of the Gigli recording of *Your tiny hand is frozen* against the one, by my favourite, Webster Booth, as we wallowed in the sorrows of Violetta, Mimi, Norma and Carmen. What price the agony of reality and the consequent heart breaks, when the stage characters could say it for you?

Somehow despite the distractions I kept my own musical studies alive. Alongside my singing I started instrumental lessons on Sunday mornings with my father, while Blyth Major, the conductor, recruited me into the school orchestra.

That Christmas, in Manchester, my dad and I played cello duets, and Aunt Bertha and I sang operatic duets as George Jackson and his daughter supported us on the piano. My cousins Joyce and Beryl had their party pieces too, in song and dance, so we had need to increase the performance times to edge everyone in to the programme. My grandmother was ready for the challenge and kept the company fortified with home made cakes and meat pies, while grandfather produced his special blend of Hornimans tea for the adults. A sophisticated brewed concoction of China leaves, well laced with Scotch.

The musical tastes we shared as a family, and with our friends, tended to divert us from the political and economical cavortings of the day. It seemed fair recompense to us, so that we were able to ignore the growing international tensions and enjoy the simple delights of artistic involvement. Ordinary family joys and pleasures had a place and a meaning. Just like the moment my Aunt Bertha announced she was getting married, while she was staying with us in Coventry.

She was often a visitor, and although approaching 37, still remained a spinster. Yet our musical connections had the habit of turning up trumps. The Dan Taylors' family of Hollis Road, whom my father had met in a cinema orchestra where Dan played the oboe, had a son, Arthur, also in his late thirties and a bachelor. He and Bertha had met at some musical gathering they attended, when she was on holiday, many years before. Suddenly in 1939 he renewed the friendship and the wedding bells began to ring. There in our front room, amongst the instruments and the music stands, he asked her to marry him.

My mother was ahead of the game, and in a brace of shakes, out came the crystal wine glasses and the emergency bottle of sherry, while my father played *Lohengrin* on his finest Kennedy cello, and I recited the lines of *Twelfth Night*. Three months later they married, living first in Kingstanding, Birmingham, as proprietors of a fish and chip shop. When Arthur joined up for Army service, they decided to move close to my parents in Coventry so that Bertha could enjoy the musical scene in the city.

As the war approached I relied more on the cello than on my singing voice. When I was fourteen there had been a distinct alteration in that, which offered new musical opportunities. I had always known the transitory nature of a boy's vocal cords, since I had watched the older lads in the church choir pass into the ranks of the tenors and basses. But always, the timing was so unpredictable.

I think it was Delanoy Saberton who first realised my voice was changing as he prepared me for an exacting part in a musical drama, *The Boy Bishop*. It was composed by Sydney Nicholson, the organist at Westminster Abbey, who had based it on a ceremony from the Middle Ages when during the feast of St Nicholas', the choirboys elected a young Bishop for the day, from amongst their number in the Abbey. It was full of ceremony, culminating in the chosen boy preaching the sermon, dressed in richly embroidered vestments and copes, attended by a large procession of church dignitaries. The chance to play such a marvellous role, seemed very important to me. However, a month or so before the performance, I rehearsed with Sabby at his home and my voice trailed away. I had neither a cold, nor could think of any reason why my reliable instrument refused to work, so I faked a bout of coughing and more or less spoke the words. Afterwards he said,

"I don't think you should try to use your voice for a few days. Rest it. Perhaps I will arrange to put the performance back a little while."

Although my voice reappeared quite strongly the following day, the end was in sight.

Some weeks later at St Margaret's we were holding a special dedication service for a new set of choir stalls, carved in oak, presented by a parishioner. After the Blessing I sang the beautiful

Vaughan Williams setting of the Vesper,
> *God be in my head, and in my understanding,*
> *God be in my eyes, and in my looking,*
> *God be in my mouth, and in my speaking,*
> *God be in my heart, and in my thinking,*

and as I came to the last line,
> *God be at my end, and at my departing.*

I knew in my heart that my voice was telling me that it was now over and we had reached the end of the line.

It was a time for good-byes. I sang solo only once more in the treble mode, a Brahms' *Lullaby*, at the school concert, and then had to wait until the tenor range matured sufficiently for me to use it again.

Looking back over the final year there were some special moments I would treasure. At Easter I had again taken the solo in *Hear My Prayer* leading into *O for the wings of a dove* and had marvelled at my own pleasure in controlling the pleadings of the opening, so that they emerged into full maturity as the theme progressed. There was also a very emotional episode I shared with my father when he and his pupil, Don Rollins, gave a recital at Evensong. With Bunny Lewis at the organ, they played Sullivan's *The Lost Chord* and then gave a soaring performance of *Le Cygne*. To complete the family occasion I sang two solos, *Come unto him*, and *I waited for the Lord*. This act of worship together, marked out the whole period of seven years, from seven to fourteen, when on the one hand I said good-bye to infancy, and on the other, saw adulthood stretching out in front of me. In it was concentrated the very nature of what our lives seem to be about, and what I tried afterwards to recreate. To enjoy and share with everyone the love of people and the love of the arts.

FIVE

KING HENRY VIII SCHOOL AND PHILIP LARKIN

WE ARE THE school at the top of the hill,
That Henry the King did will,
John Hales so to found, when he got him his lands,
And his coffers with treasure did fill,...

we sang in our afternoon community singing session before trudging off to the Rugby pitches of the Memorial Park, some half mile distance from the school in Warwick Road. Boys must memorise the song by the end of their first week and by the end of the first term accept in both heart and mind that life revolved around the philosophy expressed in the verses. 'Religioni et Reipublicae' was the order of the day. A motto for all to honour, chiselled in stone, beneath the school's Coat of Arms, with its trio of falling arrows and a nodding acknowledgement to its foundation by John Hales, in 1545.

Maybe the original charter echoed the vestiges of change, wrought by the Reformation and King Henry's dissolution of the monasteries, but by the 1930's, the traditions of godliness and good learning, played a major part in the daily curriculum. There was no avoiding such a Victorian view in the pursuit of noble aims, and even fewer opportunities available for 'our courage to dim'.

Once welcomed into the way of life at the top of the hill, who would care to challenge it? So we listened to the soaring descant which our music master added from the keyboard of the old harmonium. It rose triumphantly above our heads, into the murky confines of the wooden roof beams above us, giving us no reason to doubt we were sitting in a pretty privileged position.

During those disturbed years of the Dictatorships life could pass you by altogether if you did not make a determined effort to reach the top. It was especially so in Coventry. There, should you be born on the wrong side of the tracks, you discovered the railway line marked a sharp class division, clean through the middle of the town. To the South were the 'nobs' with just about every desirable site in the district: the posh area of Earlsdon, the detached residences of Leamington Road, the mansions of Gibbet Hill, the Peace Gardens of the Memorial Park, and, most significantly, The School.

To the North stood the factories, the coal mines, the administrative centre and the shopping streets, nudged up against the two up and two down terrace houses that formed the rabbit hutch accommodation of the working classes and the destitute. Indeed, we were the school at the top of the hill, and if you attended it, you figured you were going to turn out tops, too. What is more, those poor mutts who went to Bablake, the only other decent boys' high school, were merely poor relations who paid a paltry nine pounds for their tuition, against the Grammar's twenty. Don't you check the quality by the price?

Of course, we recognised that some schools, a few miles off in Rugby and Warwick, might have grander pretensions and richer lineage; but we chose to believe our parents took their obligations much more seriously in deciding to retain their offspring at home, under a watchful eye, rather than abandon them, to board. Thus it was that decisions took shape and dies cast, for what, ultimately, life would have in store for us all.

If you happened to miss out, the alternative was dismally bleak. For one thing, your school days could end while you were still only thirteen. Theoretically, the legal leaving age was fourteen in the free schools, but if your birthday fell awkwardly you could be out in the wide world at 13 years and 8 months and off to earn your keep, boosting the family budget, at the factory gate.

Yet even this was arguable, judging from my experiences in the Forces. On all sides were young people who seemed to have skipped the system altogether, either with the connivance of their parents or a patent scheming of their own. That was precisely why, if you declared the least spark of initiative and intelligence when attending your local authority run Elementary school, you prayed your class teacher would have the patience to sort you out and help prepare you for the most testing event of your young life, the 'Eleven Plus'. A moment of truth, pregnant with unknown consequences.

As King Henry's received a Direct grant from the Board of Education, the Governors had introduced a wide range of options for admission to the school. A special place, awarded by the Coventry Education Authority, as a result of high achievement in that despised exam, could provide a complete remission of fees, plus the free supply of text books; while the Governors' Scholarship, with its own testing procedure, was another possibility to gain either a free place or a part remission of fees. Yet if your parents took the precaution of paying for you in the adjoining Preparatory Department a year or two previously, you could enter the main school as virtually an automatic right. This structure, therefore, guaranteed a trawl through the most suitable candidates, and because the Headmaster held the reins, the final selection of boys tended to fit the environment of the institution, ensuring that pupils would be from homes that aspired to middle class sentiments and ambitions. Just how Monty Burton achieved the mix was his own concern, but it effectively eliminated the chances of some 90% of my State School chums in their artisan dwellings of Stoke, lying on the wrong side of the tracks.

Of my own selection I can only speculate that a musical background, and the fortunate achievements of my treble voice, helped sway the scales away from the obvious working class upbringing I had inherited and opened the gates to a middle class future. I was not alone in this. My neighbourhood friends, Harold Furminger, Graham Parkes, John Stringer, Ron Shreeve and Charlie Townsend helped make up the 30% of pupils that scholarship boys commanded in the senior school, and when swept into the net, and dressed in the levelling garb of school uniform, no-one bothered to notice any difference.

Our fellows, on the other hand, represented a mixed bag of professional parents. The Grammar school had catered for the sons of Freemen, since its foundation, they being the ones, presumably, able to indulge in the provision, for their kith and kin, of a formal education. So around us, the whole gamut of inner city life was on display. The sons of solicitors, estate agents, medical practitioners, ministers of religion, managing directors, accountants, shop owners, gentlemen farmers and building contractors, totally emphasising that the top people upheld the image of the top school. A fact we accepted before God... and the Headmaster. It was of little significance, however, where your particular roots had flourished. Few cared or asked questions, and if, because of religious persuasion, you missed the hymn singing and prayers of the C. of E. morning assembly, then your allegiance to Popery or Judaism seldom merited a mention. In brief, once a Grammar School boy, you could not be anything but middle class.

This was certainly where I placed Philip Larkin when I met him at school. For one thing he could hardly have lived closer to the middle. His home, in Manor Road, was on the very edge of the railway line, and the view from his attic window, looked across the station, to the tower of the top school, with the Union Jack swirling resplendent from the flag pole.

His family surroundings illustrated the very essence of this lifestyle within a provincial society. Sydney Larkin, his father, was the City Treasurer with trappings distinguishing him as something conservatively exclusive in the hierarchy of municipal politics. If anything, in a city where the Member of Parliament and the elected council were of the conservative National Government, Sydney promoted the Far Right. In common with some other professional men, he inclined towards orderliness and civic planning, which in the thirties allied themselves to the prerogatives of a fascist style government and the theories of Adolf Hitler.

Philip rarely mentioned his father, mother or sister at school, following a tradition that tended to ignore such matters. Thus, he concentrated on fulfilling the spirit of the ideologies that supported the School House system. On entrance, boys joined one of three Houses; Luptons, Perrotts or Hales, where a House Master, a House Captain and a Vice-Captain could become an easy substitute for coolness in family relationships. Like many of us, Philip spent a lot of time in this convenient environment and home problems took second place.

Philip had a privileged entry to the main school from the Preparatory Department that he had attended for several years. Sydney, through his contact with the school as City Treasurer, noted the abilities of the Head, A.A.C. Burton, who brought new ideas and thinking into the organisation of the fusty old Grammar School on his appointment in 1931. Numbers were rising, academic achievements increasing, and the financial problems that had plagued the school during the tenures of the previous Headmasters, disappeared once and for all into the history books.

Sydney's formal duties involved him visiting the school on many occasions while negotiations were afoot to lease Corporation land for school playing fields and when other funding and grants were under discussion for the construction of extra facilities, including air raid shelters. There is ample evidence that Burton was a good organiser of the school's business affairs and this probably helped swing the Larkin's decision to commit their son to Warwick Road rather than Warwick School or the playing fields of Rugby, particularly as they may have feared his speech impediment and shyness could have landed him with problems at boarding school.

When I entered the Second Form in 1935, Philip was already in Upper 3 and he stayed one set ahead of me each year. As a new boy, although I already had friends like Roy Lewis in his form, I spent much of my time hob-nobbing with my own classmates. In the first year it was enough to cope with the chaps around you in daily lessons, plus the familiarisation process of pigeonholing the prefects, the senior sixth formers, Captains of Sport and the others who had a place in school activities.

Larkin, however, was unquestionably an individual, standing apart from the conglomerate mass of boys who made up a school year. Consistently, there were a number, in every form room, who gained a reputation for one thing or another, which separated them from the rest. It could be academic brilliance, prowess in sport or talent in expression, but it could play a remarkable role in a pupil's progress. Amongst contemporaries, Eric Stables and I were plucked out of the shoal because we had good voices, and immediately sung solos in morning assemblies and at the Christmas Concert. It meant a gentle ragging from the other less gifted boys, but brought a rapid acknowledgement from authority that you qualified not be treated as one of the crowd. Some achieved notice by their behaviour. A frequent appearance in detention spelt a warning to the staff that they could serve you more of the same medicine and if you had the misfortune to attract the wrath of the 'old man' himself, then you could expect trouble.

Philip's talent was obvious. His writing abilities were apparent, and his articles and poems in the school magazine, *The*

Coventrian, evoked heady praise. It was through his stake in this I first spoke to him, at length.

During my second year in Form 3x, Arthur Tattersall, our form master, set us a homework task of writing a poem and planning the production of a journal. One of the poems I came up with, *The World*, put my youthful patriotism on the line. He chose it for publication in the school magazine, and his further encouragement spurred us on to produce a form magazine. Tattersall made Ron Shreeve the editor and me the assistant, and we assembled a collection of stories, cartoons, poems and puzzles from our mates to publish a fifty copy run of *The Reporter*, for general circulation within the school. It was a difficult chore in the days before word processors and photocopiers, and Ron and I never forgot the toil of one finger typing through thirty-two pages, fifty times over.

After we had completed this marathon, Philip Larkin stopped me one day in the school yard and told me he had read my poem and also *The Reporter*. Nonchalantly he commented, "Not bad." It was not usual to have long conversations with boys in upper forms. But I accepted the compliment as genuine, particularly as he asked if I was going to submit anything for the next issue of *The Coventrian*. In retrospect he probably already had an eye on the chance to edit the magazine in the future and may have wanted to build up support. However, his interest was flattering, and when I showed him some ideas later, he suggested various alternative titles. Finally, the events of that term's Speech Day encouraged my determination to continue my writing activities further.

A week or so before the end of the school year in July 1937, we celebrated Founders' Day with a service at the Cathedral, followed by speeches and prize giving at the Methodist Central Hall. On the Saturday morning, Eric Stables and I again headed the long procession from school to the church, an honour allocated to the leading singers of the choir, and we walked close behind the Head and the Music Master, dressed grandly in their gowns and degree hoods. In customary manner a photographer from *The Midland Daily Telegraph* flashed off a picture as we trailed by the Golden Cross pub, at the far west corner of the Cathedral close.

We were a well-dressed parade, in black school blazers, house ties and caps, with our long grey flannel trousers, which some of us had only recently graduated into from junior shorts. Casual clothes were never part of our wardrobe, so divergence from a conventionally established uniform stayed unconsidered. This formality duplicated itself in the service, permitting only set hymns, prayers and lessons, chosen year after year for their worthiness and stability.

As we entered the stately, carved oak choir stalls we sang, *O, merciful and Holy*, followed by the first prayers. Next we moved to the harmonic chanting of the psalms, so that,

> *Lord who shall dwell in thy tabernacle or who shall*
> *rest upon thy Holy hill?*

became the open question. It was answered with a conviction that proclaimed the proven Victorian standards we were urged to maintain,

> *He that doeth the thing that is right and speaketh*
> *the truth from his heart.*

The Headmaster, then read the lesson, calling on us to,

> *Let us now praise famous men.*

But we doubted the maxim was for us. However we recovered sufficiently to, *Praise God in his Holiness*, carefully pointed to bring a momentary uplift to the proceedings as our voices echoed across the wide nave of the medieval building, dedicated to St Michael.

From our vantage point, we surveyed the lines of our school fellows, with their eyes glued to their service sheets. Maybe the sight of the clergy, robed in ceremonial vestments, beneath the lighted candles on the altar, was too much for them. For once, the mighty ones, even those who ruled supreme in our schoolboy hierarchy, were the meek. They only regained a little of their confidence when we launched into the crescendos of Bunyan's,

> *He who would valiant be,*
> *Gainst all disaster.*

The morning concluded with a grand finale, and the organ playing of Cathedral organist, Alan Stephenson. In rousing chords, he guided our voices to phrase the German hymn,

> *Nun danket alle Gott,*

which considering the eventual fate of the Cathedral and the school could hardly have been more dramatically ironic.

Outside there was a sigh of collective relief as we shrugged off the cloying atmosphere of holiness, and turned from Godliness, towards the afternoon celebration of Good Learning. Promptly at

2.30 p.m. we were in our appointed places at the Central Hall; the school in the large downstairs area of the auditorium, the parents and guests in the steep gallery upstairs. I led the choir in a bouncy version of *The Lover and his Lass* under the baton of F.H. Metcalf, as we sat perched high on the stage, gazing across the rows of black blazered youths below and the colourful attire of mothers and sisters above. Then came the speeches and awards, with one for Philip Larkin as a reward for his contributions to *The Coventrian*. I determined, straightaway, I would copy his success at the next Prize Day.

Philip was very helpful in the months following when I asked him for an opinion on my writing efforts. He was somewhat scathing about the comprehension and vocabulary, but the criticism did not go unheeded, and at Speech Day 1938, I received the Junior *Coventrian* prize, and Philip the Senior.

During the final days of that term, Noel (Josh) Hughes (who later roomed with Philip at St John's, Oxford) arranged for Philip to join him as an assistant editor of the school magazine. Their editor, H.E.A.Roe, was a very senior chap indeed, holding the offices of Head Boy, Captain of Rugby and Cricket and President of the Debating Society, during his fourth year in the Sixth Form. Roe dwelled lovingly on his position, making his extra long presence in the senior league an excuse to expect upper class treatment from us all. Yet, however much he tried to affirm his law by signing written orders and prosaic editorials with the initials H.E.A.R., we knew him simply as Ernie. In fact, few dared call him anything else after the severe cuffing he bestowed on a mouthy junior, who had the audacity to say, too loudly, "Here, HEAR," as the young God stepped through assembly one morning.

I didn't put a foot wrong in his presence, aided by a school drama production of Priestley's *Laburnum Grove*. Ernie played George Redfern, the staid, respectable business man, whom the police expose, in the finale, as the leader of a gang of crooks. I was his ever loving wife. I suppose my own rather theatrical outlook on things and my attachment to the drama, amused him and his crowd of hangers-on in the upper forms. They joked ceaselessly about my ability to attract the current School Captain. In the previous year's production, I had acted opposite the then reigning Senior Citizen, Stan Glover, playing a 'femme fatale', posing as a glamorous spy, while he was an Army Colonel carrying out orders to arrest me. In fairness, such roles need viewing in the perspective of a boys' school, where sweet treble voices demand dressing up in a stuffed bra and false eyelashes to maintain the status quo.

It was due to the enthusiasm of the English teachers, Tattersall, Webb and Kingsland, that a small but devoted group of boys and staff supported the extra curriculum activities of play reading, drama and theatre visits. They applied their own preoccupation with language to foster our dramatic instincts so that we had a cosy relationship of shared pursuits. Our play reading and production had a repertory system feel about it, so that we looked forward to the new characters we would create. And as we moved up through the school, other already seasoned younger entrants, replaced the boys who left.

Larkin fitted easily into this group with his literary skills and musical hobby, although his continual championing of jazz was somewhat extreme. In play presentations he fulfilled different backstage functions, and on one occasion was calling the cues from the prompt corner as we stumbled over lines at a dress rehearsal. However, his stammer was disconcerting and we ended up making wild guesses at the text, so that as far as I know, he refused to help in this way again. Yet his attendance, in and around the action, gave him ample opportunity to chase us in his function as assistant editor. He nagged us constantly for a *Coventrian* contribution and made us feel essentially guilty if he considered us slackers. In some issues, he invented a plan to fill extra page space by organising letter writing topics. Any lack of spontaneous replies, he rectified by arm twisting methods.

Probably the most successful related to sport. Josh Hughes, with tongue in cheek, set out to foment an argument. He appealed for more gym periods and a positive approach to games training. Philip's own example in the Second XV was regarded as 'latent' and thus set the scene for controversy. He and F.G.Smith (The Bishop) replied in the vein that they cared not for such proposals considering their dislike of sport, particularly Rugby Football. 'Far better', they wrote, 'to devote more time and facilities to academic learning'.

At this point Harold Furminger and I entered the discussion: we made a plea for tolerance towards those interested in alternative games rather than the school's adherence to the traditional rugger and cricket, and demanded the provision of tennis courts on the playing fields at Warwick Road.

However, it was 1939, and although Josh had taken over as editor on Ernie Roe's departure to Oxford at long last, while the dialogue continued, the war brought a partial abandonment of sport, and the curtailment of keep fit activities.

From then on, it was not difficult to find a new seriousness within the walls of our middle class environment, as everything seemed rudely shaken asunder. Call-up, military training and ARP duties entirely demolished any thought of a relaxed approach to Higher School Certificate examinations or preparations for entry to University, which had been part of the appeal of sixth form education.

A lack of suitable air raid shelters prevented us from returning to the classrooms in September, and it was not until late November that the school resumed on a five day week basis. Consequently, we shortened our holidays, telescoped our lessons, and watched the younger teaching staff enlist in the armed forces. Cultural pursuits took a beating, and time for writing almost vanished.

Sydney Larkin, who was nearing retirement, decided Philip should leave for university at the end of that school year, rather than stay to attempt the usual quest for scholarships. Financially they were likely to benefit him little, so Philip quickly obtained a place at St John's. In July 1940, he departed to Oxford with Hughes, Smith and George Dupenois, who had been School Captain that year. The summer term magazine printed the following:

> Anxious to publicise and pay our dues
> Contracted here, we, Bernard Noel Hughes
> And Philip Arthur Larkin, do desire
>
> To requite and to reward those whom we choose;
> To thank our friends, before our time expire,
> And those whom, if not our friends, we yet admire.
>
> First, our corporeal remains we give
> Unto the Science Sixth - demonstrative
> Of physical fitness - for minute dissection...

The verses held a summary of the characters who had infiltrated our school days. There was Frank Liddiard, one of the language masters, Shore, the Art man, and Kingsland, who taught English, analysed in a sparkling light verse that could scarcely conceal the savage thrust of schoolboy satire. To F.S.Atkinson, the German specialist, was bequeathed an Iron Cross, slightly bent, to complement the rimless spectacles, buttoned waistcoat and spats, that we had grown to know so well. Everything that identified him to us, as a dead ringer for a pre-war Berlin movie. The games master, 'Gymmy' Mattocks (a formidable schoolboy pun on his name, James, and gymnasium) devastatingly received the 'high jump' stands, while to classmate Bill Rider went a set of Latin cribs. So they reviewed the scenes and images we had played some part in creating, with a finality that defied further comment.

Herewith we close, with Time's apology
For the ephemeral injury,
On this 26th of July, 1940.

This comic streak was one we shared in common, unappreciated by our elders, who were anxious we should subdue it, if we were ever to become adults. Nevertheless, it was an ingredient we held in trust with our contemporaries at the Public and Grammar schools or wherever the established customs of the old British Empire remained. For us it served to counterbalance the dreadful miseries of those last years of appeasement, eternally draped in cockeyed values and pious platitudes at the altar of Mars.

The ritual never changed. It passed from one generation of boys to the next. Each break time or lunch time, on the benches of the games pavilion or with feet up on a desk in a small classroom, we would play with words. Jollying them along, shifting their meaning and implication, until a cry rang out, 'No, no, not the whip',... and thumbs turned down, in instant rejection.

Philip Larkin shone brightly when teased to reply to some line of 'witty repartee' (a phrase unhesitatingly credited to Grecian scholar, Graham Parkes). Then he stepped in, to supply the missing idiom. Sometimes we calculated the possibilities of a nickname for a fresh arrival on the staff, or an unfortunate pupil who had drawn unnecessary attention to himself. So Philip spontaneously hobbled Hilary Warren, with the picturesque, 'Jerry', after the unfortunate lad's mishap in a Brussels hotel bedroom on the school visit at Easter 1939. And he was certainly instrumental in referring to Harry Sheppard, our guide on that journey, as 'The Good'.

We judged we had a long tradition to maintain in this naming of names. It was something reaching back into the mists of the Reformation, when a Court Herald designated a coat of arms to the family of John Hales. It showed three falling arrows, based on a pun about 'a hail of arrows'. Similarly, we learned that 'Monty' Burton was only a day into his appointment as Headmaster in the early thirties, when he became inextricably linked to the men's tailoring chain store, the providers of the 'fifty bob' suits. Then, of course, there was 'Shipwreck' Shipley, 'Nobby' Hobbs, 'Squiffy' Hardy, 'Beaky' Howard, and the rest, distinctively identifying the teachers for you when you entered the second form, in unsuspecting innocence.

Boys did not necessarily merit the fame of a nickname; yet should you attract one, it might haunt you for life. Who was likely to forget the connection when it was in place? A Furminger could only be a 'smelly cheese maker' and entitled to his 'Cheese' and if your first name was Charles, how could you avoid the association with the great master of the keyboard, Charlie Kunz, who through his signature tune, *Clap your hands, here comes Charlie*, left you with the nickname, 'Claphands'. And there were 'the Dupes', 'Josh', 'Bish', 'Poik' Parkes, 'Buggy' Bright, 'Miud' Richards, 'Tubby' Fraser et al, complete with an individualised handle that labelled the goods beyond any shadow of doubt.

Philip Larkin somehow avoided the ultimate accolade. Maybe the uncrowned king of Modern Sixth humour had special immunity. The sundry attempt to saddle him with a smarting and neat reference to his father, the Civic dignitary, never succeeded, and his speech hesitancy, which in others might have attracted comment, just did not bother us enough to warrant a tag. Then, of course, the standard format, 'Pip', for the Philips of this world, was already in use for another of our fellows, 'Pip' Slater.

The months after Philip departed were quite horrifying. Whereas the first year of the war had been uneventful and peaceful, a period when we all expected the worst to happen but it never did, the second made up for it a hundred times. Night after night we lost our sleep, struggling to fulfil the duties of the ARP services and fire watching. In daylight hours at Warwick Road we recalled our adventures, side stepping school work, as we tried to grasp that not everyone was suffering to the same extent. Just a few miles distant, in Oxford and Cambridge, our friends were enjoying a comparatively undisturbed existence in their college rooms. They only journeyed home when a particular event or the report of a heavy air raid concerned their families. After the total blitz of November 1940, Larkin and Hughes hitched back to check things out and after another raid when I was returning from school and crossing the station bridge, I met up with Philip.

The Luftwaffe had been over the centre of the city again and from Warwick Road we looked down at the wreck of buildings around Greyfriars Green and into Hertford Street. Most of the shops, hotels and offices up towards Broadgate stood starkly isolated like fleshless skeletons, offering a dismal, grey picture as smoke wispily curled upwards from the ashes of the fires. There was a handful of service vehicles and pedestrians picking a path through the rubble but the town we had known was now primarily a ruin.

Philip asked how the school was faring and what we had done through the bombings. I described how 'Monty' and his team of fire watchers had helped the RAF Balloon crew, stationed on the school playing field, dowse a string of incendiaries that had fallen across the cricket pitch. He wanted to know whether the silage heap, the Head kept topped up in the garden beside the Pavilion, was intact, for we kept alive the myth that 'Monty' was developing a secret weapon from the deadly gases given off by the rotting vegetation. We prophesied no enemy would survive the smell once he released it, against an invading army. Philip told me of his own possible call-up. It was in the melting pot, although I suspected he heartily disapproved of the others of his year who were into the swing of spare time military training, alongside their appearance at lectures. Staring again at the mess in front of us, we shrugged our shoulders and said good-bye.

A short while later his parents home suffered bomb damage in a raid on the railway station, and they moved to Warwick, away from the target area.

I left school that year in July 1941, and when I next saw Philip I was in uniform, and much later, after the war, we met again when I had returned to University. By then the continuity of school friendships was over, and the adult years were upon us. The combination of military service and the bidding of farewells to our home town, proved too much for the links that former relationships had meant in pre-war years; we had scattered across the world.

Cheese Furminger is one of the few I still have a contact with, but there are so many no longer around. Some did not survive the battles, including a number of staff. Yet of all the stories of the missing, I find the saddest in that of our leader, the Headmaster, A.A.C. Burton. After influencing us to uphold the words of the School Charter of 1545, 'in the path of piety and polite learning', he failed miserably to practise the seventh commandment and fell from office. In atonement, he exiled himself to a distant part of the Commonwealth; despite the superhuman task he accomplished in holding the school together after the Blitzes on Coventry, guiding it through the post-war problems that confronted the educators of young people.

Noel Hughes, I met again in the early 1970's, when coincidentally we both turned up at a musical instrument makers' class at the College of Furniture in Commercial Road, Whitechapel. We shared a similar purpose, in a wish to exercise our hands in craftsmanship, when our working lives had dictated we were essentially literary administrators. Noel had been a publisher and journalist but, in retirement, has produced some fine violins, violas and cellos. Through him I shared anew the stories of Philip Larkin's activities and the adventures of others, as we sat mulling over the fortunes of past comrades from the school at the top of the hill.

When we look back, in the years yet to be,
And our days live again in thought.
Our work that was hard, our friends, and our foes,
The games that were fiercely fought.
God give us grace that memory be sweet,
When we dream of our boyhood's strife!
Religioni et Reipublicae
With us still to the end of life!

95

SIX

COVENTRATED

I HAVE ALWAYS been a firm supporter of the view that real war never finds its way into books. Since Julius Caesar started the vogue for 'Campaign Memoirs', writers have tried through novel, poem and play to summarise a mood which even if it arises from direct involvement cannot hope to contain all the elements of fact that such a total experience requires. It is too shattering an affair to allow more than a skin-deep impression to emerge, however brilliant the phrase or explicit the emotion. Feeling and understanding can be present, but the complete immersion that enfolds a victim or a hero in the height of a battle defies the limits of language, either spoken or recorded.

Autobiographers, novelists and narrators confront the insurmountable: the description of feelings which span every octave from boredom to exhilaration and contain the raw elements of the living and the dead. All within a spectrum of friend and foe alike. The written word merely skims the surface of an impossible task facing those who try to set the record straight.

When I describe incidents from my own limited experience, it concerns me how one separate reaction, on one night in particular, has become a cause of so much speculation. The isolation of a single factor has tended to crowd out the many more important ones that were, at the time, of more crucial relevance and as such contained greater meaning for me.

It came as a surprise to discover at interview or appointment board, when my record was under scrutiny, they invariably asked, "But were you afraid?" That question I learned to duck. Loose talk deserves loose answers, particularly as my interrogators sought to confirm only one fact. To verify on a personal level, either that I might have wet my pants, or just yelled blue murder at the S.O.B's who were dropping the bloody bombs on us.

This biased tenor of interrogation began after the raids of 1940-41, and my C. V. revealed I had lived in Coventry, as a school boy and ARP messenger. The first time occurred only weeks after the catastrophic night of November 14th, at an interview by the vice-principal of Goldsmiths' College, for a place at University. Almost as soon as I walked in to his study he said,

"You're from Coventry. Did the bombings frighten you?"

As if it had anything to do with study for a Degree and a Teaching Certificate,... unless the thirteen and fourteen year olds I aimed to teach planned to shoot me at dawn. Then there was my first company commander, a veteran of the North West Frontier, who was interviewing me at Primary Training Centre two days after my enlistment in the army,

"Were you afraid?"

As I suspected he could squash any future promotion hopes I might harbour, I opted for caution and responded in the manner I thought he would approve.

At War Office Selection Board some weeks later I had a more challenging option. The Psychiatric Panel considered my ARP and Blitz record deserved examination in so far as it could illuminate my officer potential. The rest of the candidates did not rate my chances high,

"Once with those trick cyclists," they said, "you might as well give up."

But they were not to know of my old hankering after the dramatic, and to the expected question from the Colonel, I replied like Lady Macbeth at her peak, and allowed vaulting ambition to express it all for me. Much later, in a different context if not with a dissimilar interviewer, I happened upon an ex-naval commander of a destroyer squadron, Captain Brownrigg, retired and in residence as General Manager of large commercial television contractor,

"Taylor," he asked, "were you scared?"

"Good heavens, sir, not half as petrified as I am about directing those T.V.cameras."

"You're in," he replied, "I don't understand them either."

This, of course, hardly makes it as simple as it would appear. A question that demands spotty values cannot expect even a patchy reply. Regretfully, it seeks only the thrill and not the truth. Yet what should the response be in such situations when a casual comment might create the wrong impression? For instance, how should we classify the most stirring quality of all, bravery? A query often raised by those who had not shared an experience. Yet what a multitude of possibilities hides under the definition of the word. How can you assess an incident, when by logical reasoning you conclude the hero was not brave but stark raving mad?

Take the night that three of us, Cheese, Johnny Stringer and me, with a senior air raid warden, stretched ourselves along the roadside gutter. Grimly holding on to our tin hats, we waited for the Nazi raider above, to move off somewhere else. Except he decided to leave a calling card and dropped an incendiary bomb right in our sector. It flared up and began to ignite the base of a garage door across the road. Slowly, without panic, we raised ourselves on our knees and eyed the enemy monster. The warden called out,

"Leave it alone, lads. Let it burn before you get the sand."

Thus everything, so far, was according to the best standard code of practice. A recognition of the tendency for the latest German incendiaries to burn a minute or two and then explode, on the prompting of some devilish delayed action fuse, scattering the fire (and you, if you were close enough) all over the place. Until the blitz really hotted up, and when we had our initial training sessions, the drill was to approach immediately with either sand or a fine spray of water from a stirrup pump and avoid tipping a bucket of water on it, which could be disastrous. Then, under the pressure of events, new instructions supplanted the earlier recognised drill.

So, we waited. In any case, it was most unlikely that in the short period of postponement the flames would surge out of control, and once the safety period was over we would have the fire fighting equipment to hand. Yet rarely things go to plan in battle. Our surprise was complete when a solitary figure dashed out from the front door of the house opposite, poured a bucket of water over the bomb and chased it up with a second. All attained in the instant before we could get a word of warning out of our mouths. Naturally, we dived for cover, and mentally wrote off the neighbour. But the explosion never materialised. Instead with a sizzle and a splutter, the fire and the bomb faded away.

"Idiot", we said to the chap as he surveyed his victory.

Casually, he turned tail and went back inside his house, showing the same degree of savvy with which he had approached the problem. We simply looked sheepishly at one another.

"Well, what if? Is what I'd like to know," said our warden. And we nodded in reserved judgement.

Perhaps though there was a bottom line, for we noticed each time things went right there were a hundred when they backfired. It was like the night a small group of us chatted in Brays Lane, near to our control post, while a Jerry chugged across our piece of sky. We perceived a large whitish object drifting above us in the darkness, over towards Binley Road and Gentlemans Green, yet felt uncertain exactly what it was. One chap, from the Home Guard, quickly made up his mind, and scooted off in the general direction of its fall, shouting,

"It's a bloody parachutist."

The rest of us hid behind a pile of sandbags. A minute or so later, although it seemed an hour, there was a deafening explosion and splinters whizzed by overhead. It was a parachute sure enough, but with a land mine in the harness. We never saw the fellow again, but what would the price have been if he had been right and walked back with a German on the end of a rope?

Then there was another occasion on Walsgrave Road, by Ball Hill. We had isolated a house where an unexploded bomb had drilled a neat hole through the roof prior to embedding itself in the downstairs kitchen. The family had fortuitously escaped unscathed and were sheltering in St Margaret's Institute but had with them only a small case of belongings. After an hour or so the raid died down and the bomb awaited a disposal team. The man of the house was restless, and deciding to ignore our warnings, slipped off home to rescue some personal items. He went there once, twice, and for a third visit, as each journey extended the possibility that the bomb was more likely a dud than one fitted with a delayed action fuse. Yet he had scarcely entered the doorway again, than a bang tore out our ear drums and left the house a pile of rubble. Give or take a couple of minutes, and for the sake of a few household trinkets, a family suffered the loss of a live hero.

It may be that I, and other of my friends, survived, because of a streak of self protection. Or was it plain cowardice? One more overworked word, in the emotional writings of war. I would never pretend I had anything like the guts of some of the young fighters I met later in the armed forces. They displayed neither caution nor fear, and lived to tell the tale. In those early days, it was perhaps John Stringer who best summed up our juvenile attitudes.

"Discretion is the better part of valour," he would call out, as he indulged in his favourite hobby of naming the celestial bodies in the night sky. A pastime that amused us, sitting on the fire buckets at the back of Stoke Park School, after the wailing sirens had issued their alert.

First things first, however. That Sunday in September, when war was declared, holidays had several days to run, and those of us who had decided against evacuation went to school, in small groups, for instruction. As the school lacked sufficient air raid shelters, we waited until the contractors finished the waterproofing of the trenches on the playing field. Those, and a R.A.F. Barrage Balloon squadron, severely restricted the space available for our games practice and we did not look kindly at the huge silver monster flying high over the Rugby posts.

Nevertheless, by November we were able to resume full time studies at school and together with the private tutorials in Latin and Religious History I arranged with the curate of St Margaret's, the Rev H.B.Johnson, I found myself quite busy. Entertainment and leisure activities hit severe restrictions at first, when the black out ran into some teething problems, but as tension decreased, my friends and I occupied ourselves with games of Rugby, Saturday night socials, and even visits to my Aunt Bertha's local dances in Birmingham. In these conditions, it became possible to ignore any signs of stress around us. Teachers, and some of our older friends left to join up, yet not once, in those Winter months did the sirens disturb us, except for the odd false alarm. If there was a crisis, then what crisis? Even the Prime Minister thought it was a doddle and told Parliament that Hitler had missed the bus.

I think our only admission that anything might be different, rested in the words of the popular songs. At the dance we joined in fox trot and quick step to *We're going to hang out the washing on the Siegfried line* and *Kiss me goodnight, Sergeant Major*, while under the guidance of music hall stars, Flanagan and Allen, we turned *Run, rabbit, run*, into *Run, Adolf, run*. Unfortunately though, the sighs of our partners in the last waltz as we sang *Who's taking you home tonight?* were not for us. They were for someone behind a gun in Fortress Maginot.

Of course, there was another side to the black out, depending on how you interpreted it. For young men and their girls it could be a blessing in disguise, when at sixteen the time for kissing was nigh. Not that it was a new pastime for us, even in those lost, forgotten days of sexual restriction, when a kiss was not an open invitation to bed. My initiation had come from a luscious brunette of six years old, Barbara Waters, who sat near me in a Stoke Council infants' classroom and just as soon as Miss Jones had taught us to write, sent me a love letter in the simplest format,

"I love you, Brian Taylor."

The approach was a closed book to me, so I waited until a few weeks later when a Birthday party invitation from the young lady permitted me to sample her juicy kisses under the guise of 'Postman's Knock' and 'Spinning the Plate'. Barbara was most adept at such routines. At her parties, when she was the postman, outside the door, the knock was invariably for me, and while she was spinning the plate it fell automatically at my feet.

Joining the church choir brought a considerably increase in opportunity. My friend Roy Lewis, from the heights of his eighteen months seniority, had solid experience to share in the techniques of chatting-up and picking-up after church service was over. We agreed, if female contemporaries fancied us as easy game, let them beware. Whether they were Brownies, Guides, or young ladies of the Sunday Schools and the Junior Fellowship, we faced them fair and square. Although it would be right to concede I seemed to spend an unusually long time at the chat stage.

I was already thirteen when I finally cottoned on. Then I met a beauty called Christine Wood and accepting her name as testimony, took her into the cul-de-sac, behind the church, to swop a half hour of passionate French kissing. Fortunately my cousins, Joyce and Beryl, had briefed me in the art, in a series of tutorials, when I visited them in Manchester and they tested out fresh necking and smooching procedures on me. Naturally, nothing was plain sailing. Adolescent conceits could result in embarrassing setbacks, as I discovered one evening, when a casually placed arm around the waist of a fair maiden brought an icy warning of, "Cease."

Immediately prior to the war, in the summer of 1939, this

beginner's experience was paying dividends, and we had gathered about us a varied group of boys and girls with a similar background. Most of us were at high school, enjoyed involvement in social activities like drama and dancing, and spent a fair amount of time keeping fit through sport, cycling or swimming. Socials, dances and parties reasonably required an even number basis, and we constantly recruited new faces as our contacts expanded and more bodies found themselves harnessed for a play, or for a mixed game of hockey.

The composition changed frequently. In the wake of school evacuations we lost two of our best tennis partners, Nora van Eugen and Marjorie Hammett, while general movements of a wartime population detached complete families. Everywhere, there was a re-cycling and rotating of companions. In any case, we tended to frown on long term relationships as they threatened stability within the group, while with Cheese I preferred to play the field. This meant that his partner in the 'last waltz' one week, was often mine the next, and vice versa; so we were able to compare notes and statistics by rating the kissing count or the intelligence level.

Yet never did we undertake such relationships, unless we strictly fenced them with defined limits and conventions. Nice girls were nice, and nice boys did not ask them to be otherwise. All summed up for us when, as twelve year olds we listened, in consternation, to the Headmaster announce, at assembly,

"...that certain gentlemen, no, not gentlemen,... louts, have sought to bring discredit and dishonour to this school and to themselves. They have been involved in a most sordid business and I have taken steps to expel them with immediate effect."

Try as we might, during lessons that morning, our schoolmasters remained inscrutable on the subject of the summary dismissal. It was only at break time that word spread from the prefects in the sixth, that four idiots (amongst the non-Latin students of the fifth form,... they could hardly be classicists) had attempted the un-speakable. An act carried out the previous evening at Hearsall Common, less than a mile from the school. It transpired later they took it in turns to screw a local girl, regarded as loose and easy. Afterwards, on returning home, she told her father. His telephone call to the Headmaster resulted in twelve of the best bruising whacks for each of the four, with three of them thrown out, on the spot. The fourth remained at school, because of undue influence by the others, and had erred merely as an onlooker.

The luridness and intensity of that occasion became indelibly etched in our minds. Not only because of the rather mysterious element of forbidden sex, but the fear of being reported to Monty Burton was enough to terrorise every man jack of us. I spent a totally miserable weekend, neither eating nor sleeping, because I happened to shy a snowball at a pompous looking gent one Friday evening on the way home from choir practice. My bad luck was to slip on the icy pavement, when I tried to turn and run, and he grabbed hold of my school cap.

"Grammar School boy, are you," he said, "I'll have a word with the Headmaster about this."

I suffered days of anxiety and worry until I felt safe that the threat was a bluff. Yet, if the chances of dismissal from school were judged, so finitely, by your treatment of the opposite sex, then you behaved yourself, as long as you were there. Maybe, the 'once over' looks you got from the Headmaster's young daughters whenever they passed you on their journey to school, were highly flattering. But they were most definitely out of bounds, even though you figured they might fit into a mixed group. It was how you became programmed, learning the ground rules of the day.

So within weeks of the declaration of war, we had settled back into believing that everything was almost as it was. There was no Battle of the Somme, no mustard gas and hardly a tremor in the food supply, and as some of last year's school leavers reappeared in the corridors dressed in service uniform, home on their first leave, you could sense the normalcy of it all. Those like Ernie Roe at Oxford and Len Burroughs at Reading, in their Freshmen year, wrote letters that they relished the academic life just as their predecessors had done. In class we discussed our latest interests. The Air Training Cadets, which had recruited Cheese and Ron Shreeve, the ARP stretcher bearers, where Pip Slater decided his sincerely held conchie views could suitably remain at rest, and the trumpet, which John Stringer felt best expressed the music of the spheres. For my part, there was homework, Sunday duties at church, where I assisted at Holy Communion and the demands of my post as secretary to the Junior Church Fellowship.

I judged a sure way of testing the fellowship of the young

damsels was to organise a weekly dance in the church institute, and I prevailed on Cheese to help me. Rapidly we gained a reputation for our performance as Masters of Ceremony, and found our services were in demand for dances and socials in other venues, including the Nurses' home at the Gulson Road Hospital, where Betty Seed, a friend of my mother and Aunt Bertha since their schooldays was the Sister Tutor. This brought into our orbit a fascinating range of delightful new girl friends from amongst the probationer nurses, as we learned that underneath many a starched uniform, lay hidden a passionate heart.

Equally the Christmas we shared that winter with our relatives in the North was reasonably as usual, despite the loss of my grandfather and Uncle Jim. My grandmother had moved from her home in Rusholme and was living with her daughter, Ruby Hollows and husband Fred, in Middleton, the mill town on the edge of Manchester. He was a spinner at the Warwick cotton mill, busy turning out yarn for military clothing, and she worked as a furrier, lining coats and gloves.

At the family party we sang a special song for Grandma Salt, *Little Old Lady*, made popular that season by the 'Darling of Lancashire'. Gracie Fields, in the early days of the war, had not blotted her copybook with her admirers by clearing off to America, or marrying an Italian. Other entertainers and individuals avoided similar reproaches, when deserting their homeland in time of trouble, even though their actions were no less suspect. Somehow, our Gracie's action seemed that bit more hurtful because she pretended to be at one with her old work mates in Rochdale. As it turned out, even my aunts found it too hard to swallow, despite the good work she performed at troop concerts everywhere.

If the New Year brought one special transformation I think we would claim it for our developing taste in girl friends. The stakes had risen and we had moved into a higher league. A surfeit of older girls, perhaps two or three years our senior, was making our pulses race that much faster as their absent boy friends slogged it out with the British Expeditionary Force in France, or were taught to fly with the RAF. They wholeheartedly donated themselves to us; for dancing, courting and kissing. It was a surprise to confront the extra sophistication that this older group had acquired. Mainly, I suppose, because their contacts involved work in the outside world, as opposed to life at school. Make-up, hairdressing, jewellery and clothes, despite the shortages that war time conditions had created, went into the image building designed to attract the opposite sex. This way, flirtation developed its own skills and expertise rather than a simple seeking of know-how. We wallowed in the challenge. Abruptly, we no longer savoured gym skirts with black woollen stockings, or the girl next door looks of Judy Garland and Deanna Durbin. Now our fancy turned to glamour, in the shapely style of our latest screen heroines, Betty Grable, Marlene Dietrich and Alice Faye.

Even our daily cycle rides to school took on a fresh guise, now they provided a convenient opportunity to list the secretaries, the shop assistants and the bank clerks we desired to date. Catalogued in our note books, we would name the long legged blonde, cycling to the boutique she managed, and carelessly disregarding the wind blowing her skirts hither and thither, as 'Scatterbrain'. Then there was the 'Nuffield Blondshell', someone's classy secretary at the Bofors gunplant in Gosford Street, and the Savings Bank cashier, 'the save her for us, girl'. With a touch of pathos, we included 'the Pillars of Wisdom', noted not for her intellectual acumen, but for two legs that would have done credit to the Corinthian columns of the Pantheon.

Our former heart-throbs took a beating, although they probably were never aware of it. Some, like the Princess Lotus Blossom I so desperately fell in love with when barely in my teens, threw off their tunics and velour hats and disappeared to University. Others, with the compliance of worried parents, made haste to more peaceful settings in Canada and the United States.

So we were free to enjoy the fruits of our good fortune in being able to beguile the eighteen and nineteen year old Gladys', Bettys', Nancys' and Joans', who were willing to broaden our education in a fashion that mother would not necessarily have approved. There was a problem, of course: ducking the awkward question. If you were so much of an adult, then where was your uniform? And if you were to stay silent about school, prepare yourself for an opening line from a lively local lass that began,

"D'yow werk at 'erberts?"

Which in translation, was seeking to discover if you had a reserved occupation job at Alfred Herberts, the large armaments machine-tool manufacturer in nearby Foleshill. Nevertheless, for the brief encounter, not yet to have reached the call-up age, was a bonus; guaranteeing that on the long winter nights of enforced black outs, our escort services were in heavy demand.

Then suddenly, in the early spring of 1940, the whole ball game exploded in our faces. The Germans made a rapid lunge at Denmark and Norway, taking the allied forces by surprise and after quickly over-running the two countries, turned on Holland, Belgium and France. Before I had a chance to enter the examination rooms our armies were reeling backwards through Dunkirk, and evacuating Continental Europe, while by the end of June, France had capitulated and Winston Churchill had taken over as British Prime Minister.

Luckily, I wrote my subject papers before the most damaging effects showed up and found a temporary job in the summer vacation, where I could collect some pocket money. It seemed a good idea to gain work experience in the offices of a shadow factory while I made longer term decisions on how to plan the future.

I found employment at the Baginton plant of the Armstrong Whitworth Aircraft Company, where a sweating workforce produced twin engined Whitley bombers at the rate of one a day. There they made me a Junior Planner, carrying sets of detailed parts' drawings around the assembly bays and collecting queries and problems from the supervising foremen. To meet with industrial workers in their labouring role was an interesting affair, after so many years of seeing them in their homes and in company with my father. All spent long hours on the factory floor, working overtime and weekend shifts to make good the bomber losses of the RAF. Yet, I saw it as dull and boring and concluded that such repetitive tasks were not for me, however much their dedication and loyalty to each other satisfied them.

Many nights, during July and early August, we awoke to sirens, as bombs fell on the city outskirts at Anstey and Whitley, but the factories kept going and Coventry despatched its daily quota of war weapons from the production lines. One evening, on return from Baginton, I was feeding our dog, Nigger, whom I had taken over from my grandmother. Casually glancing into the sky, I saw an unfamiliar slender fuselaged aircraft crossing rapidly overhead. It was not the usual Anson, Blenheim or Whitley and its black markings added to the hostility of the scene, so that I had a feeling this was very different. Within seconds I knew it was. From the distance came a low whistling sound and a great thudding roar. I was not sure if it was a bomb or an anti-aircraft shell, and as the noise died away, the sirens began to wail and a large pall of black smoke rose high in the sky.

I thought it was a repeat of an incident that had forced us out of deep sleep only a few weeks previously. Then a splintering crash and a series of loud bangs had disturbed the night, when a friendly RAF Hampden bomber had strayed into the local balloon barrage and fallen out of the heavens with its wings entangled in cable. It lay broken on a cricket pitch, some four hundred yards from our house; its crew battered to death on the surrounding rooftops, as they tried a last desperate parachute jump. Fred Fall, our policeman, told us you could have put what remained of them into a pint jug, and we felt sad that it had to be one of ours to prove the defences were so good. So now, maybe, we had caught one of the enemy in retribution, and when Cheese appeared a short while later we stormed off to see if we could find the wreck of the Jerry. Unfortunately, the victim was the paint shop of the Standard Motor Company, manufacturers of military vehicles. The raider had got clean away.

Coventry was an ideal target for the Luftwaffe. From vantage points on the higher ground surrounding the city you could look into the bowl, formed by the curve of the River Sherbourne, where the city centre, with narrow streets and ancient city wall, nestled close up against the three church spires of St Michael's, Holy Trinity and Christ Church. A stone's throw distant, were the Tudor buildings of St Mary's Hall and Palace Yard, jostling for space beside the Market Halls and the shops of Broadgate. These in turn, gave way to the small 17th and 18th Century workshops and residential quarters in the oldest districts of the town.

Out towards Stoke, where we lived, the land rose up from the river at Gosford Street, to the high point of Ball Hill, next to St Margaret's Church. From there we could see back across Gosford Green, the site of medieval tournaments, towards the six storey, red brick factory that housed a Bofors Gun production line, right up to the white tiled Coliseum dome of the Gaumont Palace cinema and the sandstone towers of the cathedral and the Council House.

Around the Walsgrave Road, a score of back yard sweat shops

made components for the shadow factories, and straddled the neighbourhood. Crank cases, axles, nuts, bolts, sheet metal, transfers and luminous dials, flowed daily from the sheds at the bottom of my road and the alleys of Brays Lane, and passed on to the Triumph motor cycle plant, opposite Stoke Council School. Half a mile away stood the Humber car works and the General Electric Company with their twelve thousand workers and staff. And just about everywhere else, wherever there was room, were the houses, packed with families, making up the city's population of some quarter of a million souls. It was all higgledy-piggledy, a mish mash of homes and workplaces, ripe for re-development, ripe for target practice.

As the Harvest moon started its circuit that year, we suffered a series of alarms. Sometimes in the starlight, we would troop out to the air raid shelter, other evenings we would spend hours stretched out under the dining room table as we began to sense the dangers that flew above our heads. One night the Rex Cinema in Corporation Street accepted advice from the film it was screening, *Gone with the Wind*, and did just that; but, intuitively, we adapted to periods of snatched sleep and waited for the moon to lose its fullness and make us less exposed to those prying enemy eyes.

Early in September I had decided to leave my job along with Charlie Dupenois, who had taken a similar post as I had in the Planning Department. He was the new School Captain and we figured it was time for lessons and Rugby practise to begin. My examination results had been good, requiring me to work out an educational plan that would ensure I had reasonable prospects for a career, should I survive until the end of the war. Students felt under pressure as more and more stories circulated from the occupied countries, that young people, of our age group, received short shrift from the Nazis, especially if they questioned authority. Even more to the point, the names of slightly older friends of ours, already in the forces, were appearing in the casualty lists.

Still, Harold Furminger and I had no qualms when on a mid September evening we set out to meet some friends at a pub in Bishops Street, near to the Old Grammar School. It had been a pleasantly warm day and the moon was rising brightly in the cloudless sky. Drinking time was short, with supplies tightly controlled, and after a shandy mix, to help the mild beer stretch a trifle further, we left our friends and started for home.

In the far distance the sirens began their routine wailing, and as we looked back towards the canal and along the road to Radford, we remarked on an unusual calmness and silence. Then, in the next second, there was a wild interruption. A stiff breeze sprung up from nowhere and the air began to screech around us. Three ear splitting explosions rocked everything in sight and pushed us violently towards one another, while our trousers and jackets flattened themselves against our bodies and our hair felt pressed into our faces. Stumbling and clutching, we yelled,

"Wow, let's get out of here."

We did our best to make a few paces towards Hales Street.

Now there was the unmistakable throb of German aircraft engines, and determined not to be so exposed this time we dived for cover into a doorway. But stop, what was this? An amusement arcade, of all places, complete with mirrors, glass fronted machines, display cabinets and a huge, plate glass, shop window. That was just what we needed, and not delaying to consider the alternatives we jumped like two startled rabbits and threw ourselves full length into the gutter outside covering our heads as best we could. Already the next stick of explosives was on the way down and there was a crackle as the bombs screamed above us, until they landed deeper in the town. At last, we sat up and crouched at the edge of the pavement, giggling uncontrollably and mocking our own stupidity. There, only too clearly and not ten feet away, we saw that every tiny sliver of glass in the shop windows opposite lay in heaps in the identical position we had imagined to be secure.

We ran through the streets to Gosford Green hoping we could avoid further delay. Above us the sky erupted, with a deafening howl of aircraft, bombs and gunfire as the anti-aircraft barrage took on the raiders. Behind our retreating backs, the shopping centre was ablaze, and a large cloud of dust and smoke hung over the City Football Club ground. Then, as we passed the shelters in the park, an Air Raid Warden stepped out from the shadows and suggested we took cover. We climbed down below the sandbags, underneath the corrugated iron roofing, and sat on the wooden benches lining the trench. No wonder, with so many diversions outside, the forty odd occupants, clutching their small cases and bags of personal belongings, had little cause to glance at us or interrupt their own thoughts. Yet the noise appeared somewhat deadened, and the emergency lighting functioned well enough, despite a pronounced flicker from time to time.

After about an hour, the intensity of the raid seemed to slacken, and we decided to dash for home. As I arrived, my parents were leaving the recently completed brick surface shelter in the road, while the all clear sounded, and with the evening so far advanced, we decided that we should try to sleep. In retrospect, it was not so very serious a business and our treatment of it was a fair reflection of our general attitude. At the time, we saw it little more than a story to tell our friends, which in recounting the idea of our protective instinct preferring amusement machines and glass, rather than shelter and safety, revealed us as casual and cool. Certainly, no-one had the least idea how it really added up.

Soon, as if in rebellion, we began to treat the nightly warnings as a game. If we were already in bed, we waited until the last second, to be absolutely sure that the planes were coming to us and not passing over en route to Birmingham. We began to calculate, in rather extravagant terms, that when we suffered an attack one evening, the next could be the turn of someone else.

Occasionally, the alarm system failed totally. We would wake in the midst of a dream that a bomb was whistling down, to find it really was. However, as we rarely undressed for bed, we could be downstairs and under the table, before the bomb hit the ground. Then, in October, as we rested under the table, all our back room windows fell out. Whoosh, they went,... caught in the pressure wave of an explosive landing on the girls' school behind.

Two or three nights a week, my father and I spent away from home, enlisted for fire watching duties. I reported at dusk to Warwick Road, where my steady companion was Ginger Walker, also in the sixth, and preparing to set out on a career of scientific research. We were a group of eight boys, with a master, patrolling in pairs, and designed around a two hour stint. We tried to turn the duty into fun, as we wandered along the empty corridors and classrooms. What we liked most was to climb the school tower, beside the flagpole, a forbidden area in normal times, and stare out across the darkened railway sidings into the blacked out town centre. Later we would stalk through laboratory, woodwork shop, library and art room, armed only with a torch and a bunch of keys. Sometimes we would stop and pretend that, in the shadows, the ghosts of former boys and staff had returned, and amuse ourselves acting out the chatter they had bequeathed us.

We retold the stories of Squiffy Hardy, the gangling cross eyed chemistry master, who looked in one direction and pointed in another as he called out,

"Eh you, boy, come here."

And two boys left their seats.

Then there was the base of the Shipwreck Shipley anecdotes, the historics of Room 13, creating memories of the half sticks of chalk aimed at the unfortunates who could not remember the dates of Trades Unions Acts and Reform Laws. Within the depths of the main hall we practised our greatest roles, as we stood on the platform mimicking accent and action of any who fell under our scrutiny. One night, at the lecture rostrum, spotlighted by a couple of torch beams, I portrayed my favourite character: the Headmaster. First, the removal of the mortar board, then the cough, the grimace and the pose, capped by a list of facetious school announcements. In full flow, the words froze on my lips, as Monty and his dog walked through the doorway,

"Mr. Taylor, I presume? My study 9.15 tomorrow morning."

I collected an extra firewatch duty and an essay on the *Disadvantages of free speech*.

Quickly, it was late Autumn. A Thursday, November 14th. I had played in a practice game of Rugby, with Charlie Dupenois, Graham Parkes, Ron Shreeve and others of the sixth; Nobby Hobbs, our coach and geography master, refereed. It was a fine sunny afternoon and in the changing room we all felt exhilarated by the exercise, the warm bath and a chocolate biscuit, from our ration. The evening led off with a bright milky moon in the cloudless sky as I set out with Cheese for our social get together at the Junior Church Fellowship in St Margaret's Institute. Our routine was to have a meeting with the thirty or so members and then run a dance, for a couple of hours, on the maple ballroom floor upstairs. Quick steps, fox trots and tangos from the popular song repertoire of the day, *Scatterbrain*, *Jeepers Creepers*, *Indian Summer* and *Jealousy*, soon had our feet tapping, and we felt angry at 7 o'clock, when the sirens began to wail, earlier than usual.

We heard aircraft engine sounds above the volume of our music, but it was customary to continue in such circumstances,

111

safeguarded by the black-out curtains on the windows. Minutes later, we heard one of the Home Guards from the post downstairs calling to us that a mass of flares ringed the sky, and a house, about a hundred yards to our rear, was on fire. We decided to have a short interval and as we walked down the staircase, Bryan Cox, a friend of mine from early schooldays and now a Home Guard, told me that incendiaries were falling in profusion around the district and they were having problems to cope. Cheese and I had two special partners that evening, sisters somewhat older than us, who we thought the prettiest in the group. We had flirted with them at dance dates in the previous weeks, and after walking them home, had enjoyed necking sessions of half an hour or so in their air raid shelter near Stoke Heath. Perhaps, if this spot of bother finished swiftly, we could repeat the performance. In any case, there was little point in cancelling the meeting at this juncture and we went out onto the forecourt of the Institute, at the top of Ball Hill.

It was a good vantage point. A whole area of Coventry stretched out in front of us, with the moonlight turning the rooftops into glistening pools of silver that reflected back from the windows and casements. On the tower of the Nuffield factory, we could see the barrel of a Bofors gun silhouetted against the sky, and behind, the sharp pencil pointed outline of the Cathedral spire above the stone battlements. There, only a short while previously, we had heard Johann Hoch's Chamber orchestra playing a soaring arrangement of Bach's *Jesu. Joy of man's desiring*. In the magnificent nave of the church it had been a time for quiet and reflection.

For an instant, that peace was amongst us, as a cautious stillness descended on the heavens, and the town seemed illuminated from within. But new waves of aircraft were arriving fast, and we reckoned that on such a brilliant night any pilot above would see us standing there below. So we made haste to return inside, as the telltale sound of 'bombs away' shattered the magic. Already there was a refugee family in the main hall, rescued from a blazing house off Clements Street. A warden helped to re-orientate them, with a cup of tea. At the commencement of the war the authorities decided to requisition the church institute for a variety of causes. It became a reception centre for the bombed out, a Home Guard and a Police post, a medical clearing point in the event of the destruction of a hospital, and an emergency canteen.

It was to this later activity I retired with Cheese. We joined the church caretaker, Mr Bladen, and the volunteer tea ladies, who appeared for duty, whenever the sirens dictated it, to watch over the hot water urns. Our new curate, the Rev Gerald Holbeche, who had taken over from the Rev Johnson, attended Thursday Fellowship meetings and was now busy unfolding blankets and cushions from the cupboards and organising the tables around the walls to form some temporary shelter.

Suddenly the lighting failed, and we scrambled to ignite the hurricane lamps and spare candles on standby. Yet it was obvious that events were piling up, when Bryan Cox brought news there had been a huge explosion, followed by billowing flames on the other side of Gosford Green. I hoped it had missed the electricity sub-station on Binley Road, next door to where our friends, the Hewitts, lived, although I knew Bernard was at sea on a Royal Navy corvette. Anything that concerned them could upset my mother and Nellie Hewitt's long standing Monday afternoon gossip, with home made scones, potato cakes and tea, something I sometimes shared. A disturbance in that routine would be hard to accept after twenty years of practice. I calculated, though, it would probably take more than Hitler to interfere with that.

Right now, however, was not the moment to consider awkward possibilities. There was a tremendous bang and I flung myself under the table with my dance partner, Winnie, desperately clinging to my neck. I noticed her sister, Irene, had reacted similarly with Cheese. If this could be the pleasant result, maybe things were not so bad; but a further series of crashes and crumps sounded very close indeed and flatly dismissed that theory.

During the next ten minutes everything fell in. Windows and doors flew out of their frames. The floor rocked and heaved as though the ground itself was in motion, and for certain, the bomb aimer held us in his sights. It crossed my mind that our precinct, in Stoke, had become a target for tonight. Winnie must have thought so, too, and clutched even harder around my collar as I decided, when the noise had subsided a little, to move out from the tables. Cheese had the same idea and we struggled to the front door, through the dust, to see if there had been a direct hit on the building. The Home Guard sergeant was climbing over debris at the foot of the stairs, and called out that the roof was alight and he needed water.

We helped connect a hose to a tap in the gents' toilet, and then went outside to view the damage.

The skyline right across the city was aflame and a torrid redness was overhanging the Institute. Yet there was no chance to pause too long, for already we heard another raider on his approach run. Cheese decided he would head off home to Harefield Road, some 400 yards distant. Nevertheless, as I did not fancy the air raid shelter with my mother and the neighbours, or helping my father use his extension ladder for incidents in the street, I reasoned I could be more use where I was.

Once inside again, Bryan Cox told me the fire upstairs was out and except for some glass and fallen plaster on the dance floor, there was little to see. At the back doors of the hall the wardens were admitting another bombed out family, with a dog on a lead, and Gerald Holbeche and I began to organise space under the tables for them, as well as carrying refreshment from the kitchen. Debris had buried their Anderson shelter, and their home had lost its roof. We promised to check it out later, when things settled down a bit.

It must have been after midnight before there was another lull. There was a continual stream of distressed people arriving and our Junior Fellowship members were providing stout assistance in sorting out the problems. We received more evidence that the amount of destruction was far greater than anything we had previously thought possible. An auxiliary fireman turned up to brief the Home Guard sergeant and mentioned that the street water supply had been severed and there was nothing coming out of the hoses, so they had left the fires to burn themselves out. We remembered to keep that information from the homeless families.

It was difficult to calculate the severity of the attack. With so much happening on our own doorstep, it looked as if the major thrust of the bombing must be against the local Stoke factories of the G.E.C., the Humber and the Triumph. Then as we stared towards the Nuffield building in Gosford Street, it was obvious that the fourth floor was alight there too, although it had not stopped the rooftop Bofors gun from firing spasmodically. What we did not know was that explosives had cut the mains water to the whole city, and the static emergency supplies from the canal were drained empty. Direct hits had taken a heavy toll. While I was surveying the fires from the front porch, Mr Bladen spoke to me,

"Do you think you could go across to the church and see if it's alright. I think I heard a crash from that direction, but I'm not sure and I have to help here. It's all open."

I thought it would cost me nothing to look and I walked over the road to the back of the building, beside the choir vestry.

When I pushed against the doors I could tell something was wrong. At first nothing would budge, and only by kicking hard against the bottom edges was I able to free sufficient room to clamber inside the hallway. Rubble was everywhere; I noticed the door to the choir vestry lay prised off its hinges, and cassocks and surpluses were in disarray on the floor, like a scrum of Rugby players. The High Altar to my right seemed undisturbed, although the stained glass window above hung in fragments, and the choir stalls had a thick covering of dust and plaster. I entered the main chancel that way, and as I walked onto the steps, I realised the extent of the destruction, for I could see the church had received the full force of a bomb, and the damage was serious.

It was as if the floor of the nave had erupted in an earthquake. The blast had torn apart the heating ducts set into the foundations, and ripped out the decorated ceramic tiles and wooden blocks, scattering them, at random, in unequal piles. At the west end of the building the stone baptismal font rested on its side, overhung by a cloud of dust that had formed in the alcove, rather as a shroud might appear to fashion a tent. Further up, I noticed the moonlight shining down in long relentless beams, like separate carbon arc lanterns piercing the line of windows above the main support columns. There, my attention became attracted to a higher level, as I felt a chill in the depths of my bones that caused me to pull my coat jacket closer around my body.

Up in the rafters the roof of the Memorial Chapel seemed split apart, revealing a cavernous, black wound in the structure of the building. At this point the High Explosive had burst through. Then it fell, with deadly force and energy, on the carved oak altar table, in the very heart of the place of remembrance. Nothing resisted the impact. All lay blown awry and crooked. The Flanders poppies, the laurel leaves, the craftsman gilded carvings and the wooden panels, smashed to smithereens. The oil painting of the wounded crusader and his cross had entirely disappeared, leaving a gaping, muddy hole, directly on the spot. The brave Lieutenant

Howells had died again, and we were that much poorer.

The iciness within me would not go, and I began to shiver. I rested against the choir stall, the one I sang from so many times as a boy chorister. Now I tried to hold on to the memories of the vespers and anthems that had dominated the services I had attended over the years, right to the communion of the previous Sunday morning, when I served at the altar. But that part of my life was over, finished as totally as that of the Lieutenant and his comrades.

The shock was profound; panic and fear were in charge. I wanted this battle, engulfing us tonight, to end, forthwith, and everything to return as I remembered it. I leaned limp and scared, at a loss what to do next, and my legs would not move. They no longer stood strong enough to take me anywhere, and bodily sensation deserted me. Perhaps, finally, it was the Lieutenant who took pity on me. I thought I saw the particles of dust take on a ghostly glow in the crystal light and I heard very clearly the sound of yet another bomber making its approach, and another, and another. The war was still in progress. No battle was won or lost, and the squadrons of aircraft, skimming in shallow dives across the night sky, would not frighten us. Neither would their whistling messengers of death, nor their terror tactics from Hell, destroy our will to defend our homes. Slowly I recovered. The trembling left me and I rose from my crouching position, overlooking the wreckage. By the side of the chancel, where the brass lectern with its black leather Holy Bible had been, was a heap of masonry and debris. I scrambled up, and lifted my head to gaze into the red tinged heavens, above the ruins of my favourite chapel,

"Bastards," I screamed, "You fucking bastards. Why? Why? Why?"

SEVEN

MESSENGER BOYS

ONE OF THE less violent by-products of war is the extension
of language through words and phrases, initiated and re-
adapted to describe details of the conflict, or highlights of
its progress. So we have 'Barbarian invasions', 'the Crusades' and
'the Armada', using words from older sources to represent events at
a later time. Hitler and World War Two annexed their share, too.
Evocative sounds, devised in one context, enlisted for another. Blitz,
Holocaust and Coventrated, took on subtle new meanings in the
1940's, and coloured the vocabularies of the survivors for the rest
of their lives. Further on, in the subsequent Vietnam battles, Nicholas
Tomalin's 'zapping' said just about everything his generation
thought about that conflict.

Nevertheless, on the night the word 'coventrated' entered
the dictionary, my friends and I were beyond caring about such
detail. For us, it was an unwanted phenomenon and something, in
retrospect, we would rather have done without. No air raid, ever
before, had been unleashed on a civilian target with so much ferocity
and spite, and although afterwards other raids were of mightier
weight, that one remains the forerunner of all that was to follow
at Dresden, Hiroshima and Nagasaki.

From the moment the Luftwaffe pilots crossed the French
coast, they could see ahead the inferno of the burning city, 200
miles away. They needed neither navigational aids nor electronic
beams to guide them. It was simply a case of pointing the nose
towards the flames and opening the bomb doors. On November
14th 1940, more than 500 aircraft did just that.

The Nazi Generals coined the Coventry word, shortly after
they sent their reconnaissance planes to photograph the damage.

Lord Haw Haw in his German propaganda broadcasts did the rest, by adopting the new terminology. Yet, on the early Friday morning bulletins we heard from the BBC, there was no mention of the night's specific target, only a brief description that a Midland town had suffered a bombing raid. That day, as we listened to the radio, we simply considered ourselves lucky we still had electricity to power it. With the gas and water cut off, additions to English rhetoric were furthest from our thoughts.

In the middle of the night, also, in St Margaret's Church, such niceties were not welcome. I had scrambled over the rubble to take a closer look at the shattered chapel and then edged my way to the side door where I had entered the building. There was again considerable activity above. The brief stoppage had allowed the anti-aircraft batteries to reload and adjust their fuses, so that they greeted the shallow dives of the incoming bombers with a fresh vigour. I dodged over the road to the Institute to find the Rev Holbeche, and suggested he accompany me back to the church.

We chose our moment with care. Displaying the empty confidence of battle veterans, we tried to gauge the flight paths of the aircraft and the descent of the high explosives, stoking up the fires that were engulfing the skyline. Again inside, I found the scene less emotionally disturbing than the first time, although I noticed Gerald sway visibly, as he stared at the smashed building. Years later he told me that the sight had remained indelibly etched on his mind at each Parish church he subsequently tended. His own religious philosophy and the Christian teachings had not prepared him for such an outward display of evil. Then, as we brooded there, we realised that only through the heart, and not in the mourning of material things, could it be defeated.

A little later, we left to resume our self appointed duties in the Institute. More refugee families required our aid and we sorted through blankets and spare clothing to satisfy their immediate demands, and kept the tea and dry biscuits in circulation. By 5 a.m. we felt jaded and tired. We were beyond the stage of caring what might happen to us, and it did not seem to matter any more if the raid lasted for days. Bryan Cox and I were too weary even to smile at one another. While around us, the weary firemen, policemen, Home Guards and wardens reporting the growing number of incidents in the sector, wore a resigned look of indifference etched on their grey faces. Mud and dirt seemed permanently bonded to everything we touched, and still, the Dorniers and the Heinkels were coming in a never ending stream.

Then a few minutes after 6 o'clock, quiet descended. An eerie, ghostly hush. No aircraft engines, no gun fire, no bomb whistles and no explosions, and we stood in the half light of the early morning, watching sweeping, black clouds of ash and smoke drift silently over the city. The air was moist with a slight drizzle, mixed with dark specks and brownish powder, so that we hardly appreciated that the moon had faded and dawn was on the way. The sisters Irene and Winnie Memmot, clearly worried during the initial part of the raid, had spent much of the night calmly serving tea and eking out the small amount of water stored in the kitchen boilers. Now they joined Gerald Holbeche and me, as we decided to walk to our homes along the Walsgrave Road.

It presented a vista of utter confusion. Shattered shop windows, their contents spilling out onto the pavements. Tins, bottles, packets, the merchandise of society, unwanted and unsorted, forming jumbled piles in the gutter. Black-out curtains and lace draperies hung listlessly from upper casements, empty of glass. Doors askew, roof rafters bared, lamp posts and telephone poles splintered at acute angles. Power lines trailing in festoons, trapped on broken walls, and the clinging November morning's dampness producing a wisp of vapour around the roof tops. The local poster site, at the corner of Clay Lane and Brays Lane, lay crumpled and torn, and the churned up surface of the roadway stretched on towards Briton Road. From that direction an auxiliary fire tender picked a path around the pot holes, and the firemen called to us for guidance. The driver pulled over, and they told us they had driven from Leicester, twenty miles away, in the early evening, but halted at the city boundary because there was no water in the town. With dawn they wondered if they could help.

At this point we said good-bye to each other and I started on the final lap home. In St Osburg's Road, I could see both the Stringers' and the Hammetts' houses appeared safe and as I turned into St Agatha's Road our house and the rest of the street were relatively undamaged. My pent up anxiety dissipated when I walked into our front room. At least it was normal, but at the back I saw my father boarding up the windows afresh, three days after replacement from the earlier blow-out. It was the rear of the houses that had suffered. Some chimneys lay toppled, with slates and coverings missing on the roofs. And next door, at the Smiths, the garden shed had moved about two feet and the side had a nasty slant.

As our gas cooker was not functioning, my mother knelt to prepare breakfast on the living room fire. She had banked up the coals to hold the kettle and a pot of porridge. She told me how they had gossiped with neighbours, in the street shelter, until my father rushed away to help with some incendiaries. He had spent the rest of the night keeping watch. Some of the neighbours had decided, in the fury of the falling bombs, to leave the city as soon as they could, and stay with friends in the country. My father said my mother was against that, and as he had now swept the broken glass away, he was off to work.

I have often recalled this decision of theirs. Especially when, in later years, I heard others describing why they had not departed their homelands, despite threats to them, either personally or collectively. In Germany, some released inmates from the concentration camps told me that even messages warning of imminent arrest, and evidence that other members of their family had disappeared, failed to convince them they were in danger. How could they believe that anything might happen to them, in the land of their birth?

Yet, this pattern is neither new nor different. Often those most likely to suffer, by their opposition to tyranny and repression, are the least concerned for their own safety.

Living in Coventry, I shared a similar lack of comprehension. Nothing our neighbours or friends could say made us reconsider our decision to stay put, even though another night might destroy all we had. We were stopping there, although some of our close friends, including my father's cello pupil Don Rollins and his mother, lay dead amongst the nearly 2000 killed and injured.

Life had to continue, and while my mother repaired the black-out curtains and my father left for the factory, my friend Cheese arrived on his bicycle, at the normal time of 8.30, ready for his job at the bank. I joined him, for school. It was almost impossible to cycle on the roads with the rubble and holes, so I opted to divert through Gulson Road and he struggled off in the direction of Gosford Street. It was a matter of scrambling rather than riding as so many craters gave the route the appearance of a World War One battlefield. At the top of the hill by the hospital, stretching towards the Parkside entrances of the Armstrong Siddeley, was a long line of fire pumps and rescue vehicles with the men lounging around, waiting for instructions. They had driven from all over the country, in some cases from South Wales and London, but with no water available and the communications network in disarray, there was little they could do. When I asked them about the Armstrong factory, where my father should be, they told me it did not seem badly damaged, although, like everywhere else there were no power supplies.

I passed along by the railway station that looked as if it had taken a fair amount of punishment and then on to Warwick Road hill, where I had a clear view of the main centre of the city, shrouded in smoke and mist, and badly scarred. I wondered if Cheese had made it to the National Provincial bank building that was right in the heart of Broadgate, and must surely have been hit. I turned to the school and to my surprise it looked untouched, apart from the barrage balloon on the school field that hung limp and punctured beside its tethering lorry. The Headmaster was out in the school yard as I arrived and welcomed me,

"Good morning, Taylor. Keen to come to school, I see. But it's best you return home today."

"Is everything alright, sir?"

"It seems to be, but come back on Monday. We should have sorted things out by then."

From school I pushed my bicycle into the central area of the town, skirting a cratered Greyfriars Green and up an annihilated Hertford Street, with the Telegraph building, the Empire Cinema and the General Post Office virtually gutted. Some of the surviving property, isolated amidst piles of smoking debris, was in flames, while groups of fire crews and rescue workers looked helplessly on. At the Queen's Hotel, demolition teams were attempting to sling a cable over a section of the battered building and tear it down, in the hope that it would dampen the flames. Without water the task was hopeless. In Broadgate, the bank facades had survived, although I failed to find Cheese at his, but the King's Head Hotel, the Market Hall and the shops along by Burton's, Astleys and Boots had disappeared. Over on the opposite side, Owen Owen, with the top of Cross Cheaping and the Burgess, and as far as I could see down

Smithford Street, was a smouldering heap of rubble. It was not a pretty sight and I speculated how it would affect our daily lives with the main stores and facilities blown to pieces.

The smell of burning and the choking smoke demanded I should carry my bicycle on my shoulders as I picked a way round the many obstacles. Tangled wires, broken tramway poles and burnt out cars and buses, made the going very difficult as the odd pedestrian and dismounted cyclist negotiated the narrow pathway between the fallen bricks and timber. Everyone put a brave face on things. If we should happen to recognise a familiar figure amongst the passers-by, we tried to show we were taking in our stride the worst that the Nazis had to offer. In a world of chaos, the Council House remained solidly anchored in place. Its red stone walls unleashed an air of power and strength, as some of the staff gathered on the entrance steps, with picks and shovels. But there in the block behind, it was plain to see the carved windows of the cathedral were empty, and the interior a mound of charred ruins.

Suddenly I felt tired and not inclined to investigate further. It was 10 o'clock and I noticed, along Jordan Well, that my favourite cinema, the Gaumont Palace, was intact. I quickened my step homewards and saw Johnny Stringer's dad clearing up the glass outside his ironmongers store, next door to the old chapel. It was apparent he had his problems, and we spoke only briefly of the damage around the town. Opposite, at the Nuffield factory, bearing evidence of the burning we had witnessed during the night, a policeman and an army detachment were roping off sections of gutted premises and placing warning signs at the entrances. As I moved down Gosford Street, a line of trucks in front of me emptied platoons of soldiers, with kit and equipment, into the roadway. In the next few days they became part of the action, sorting through the wreckage and standing guard at night to prevent any chance of looting and scavenging.

Once I had reached the Binley Road, I could see behind the damaged electricity sub-station, the partly demolished house of the Hewitt's, and no sign of them. Further along by Gentlemans Green, the homes of other friends, the Wyatts, the Lowes, the Rev Cornes and the van Eugens, were still whole, and apart from superficial damage looked safe. All the properties, without exception, bore evidence of the intensity of the night's activities, revealing either broken windows, dislodged roof tiles or shrapnel pitted brickwork. In the residential avenues of Stoke Park it was necessary to make wide diversions to avoid the bomb craters and the fallen fences and trees. On the roadway, behind the girls' school, about 150 yards from our house, my father's extension ladder held complete authority. It bore the sign 'UNEXPLODED BOMB', blocking off any possibility of entry.

Early that evening I met Cheese and we discussed our experiences during the day. A representative of the water company had visited his mother, and told her to boil the water she used, but as her taps were as empty as ours, it seemed a superfluous instruction. She also learned that a deep well was available in the GEC factory complex, and should we care to walk the half mile, we could fill a bucket or two. Fortunately, both his parents and mine had installed rain water tanks in their gardens, for summer watering, and by filtering and boiling, we could alleviate much of the loss. At least for as long as we denied ourselves a bath.

While we were talking, John Stringer arrived to tell us he had volunteered for ARP duties as a messenger; if it interested us, he would take us to the local Post 404C. He sounded positive enough, and not fancying another night like the previous one, we trooped off to the sandbagged stables in the forecourt of Stoke Park School. There he introduced us to the Chief Warden and his crew. Inside, it was a hive of activity, enlivened by the signalling of a yellow alert that warned the enemy were back again. We simply sat down, filled in our application forms and watched the alarm upgraded to purple. After a short interview we were kitted out with blue overalls, tin hats, heavy weight respirators and Identity Cards, barely completed as the warning changed to red and a lone plane flew overhead. Fortunately, it was not our turn again, and with little materialising, we were assigned to deliver a letter to a warden, slightly injured the preceding night.

When we returned, the other wardens were drinking tea and assessing status reports from their sectors. It emerged that many residents had quit their homes for safer zones, and this raised problems about protecting the properties if an incendiary bomb attack developed. It seemed that there were even fewer people about than at the peak holiday period in the summer, when nearly everyone moves off to the seaside, and I began to wonder if my parents' stance in sticking it out might be wrong. But I did not mention it to Cheese or Johnny. Perhaps it was best, though, that should an incendiary land on our roof, my father and I would be around to handle it.

From that night on, we embraced a new role in the war effort, as the destruction of the main services and many of our meeting places, resulted in our dances, socials and parties taking a back seat for months ahead. It would be a while until things functioned properly again. Thus each evening as darkness fell, Cheese, Johnny and I would gather to report to Post 404C. Everyone promptly named us 'The Three Musketeers' or as Johnny preferred, 'The Three Must Get Beers', and with supplies of ale on ration at the local pubs, we saw it as a proper duty to know just where our share would come from.

The boundary line fell almost directly along the Walsgrave Road, site of the Old Ball, a grim Victorian relic that had replaced some earlier coaching house; but its aura left us cold. We reckoned The Bull's Head, at the edge of our sector on the Binley Road, beside the cricket ground, much more to our taste. Here we would sit, scoffing a half pint, before walking back to our sandbagged fortress, with maybe a visit to the off-licences in Kingsway or Brays Lane. These two parallel highways together with Church Lane and Burns Road, conveniently provided the main link routes through our area. Overall the territory measured a half mile by half mile, yet every street, house and building etched itself on our minds, so that we had an encyclopaedic knowledge of the geography of the district.

In homes where there were children, we often had acquaintances within the family. Where childless couples or elderly people lived, we sketched in the relationships to build up a comprehensive picture. In our official status as Messenger Boys we had an open ticket to visit any residence to check out occupancy, particularly if we fancied introducing ourselves to a rather special female tenant. For who could argue that in the life or death situations of a raid, such information might not be vital? And in any case, our Head Warden, Mr Phipps, had given us the nod,

"Get to know your sections,"

he exhorted, and there was no need to tell us twice.

Of course, we made mistakes. Naturally, if it involves the opposite sex, who hasn't? There were two very stunning young women we had observed, living close by Harefield Road, although we had never plucked up enough courage to speak to them. They were four or five years older than us and we envied the Armed Forces boy friends who dated them regularly. Yet faint heart never won fair lady, and our newly discovered entrée to the homes of everyone led us to believe we might knock at their door to confirm the numbers for a make believe, new issue of gas masks. It was a blatant piece of nonsense but at least it offered a chance to chat up the sisters, Peggy and Mickey. Conversation was brisk, as mum sat knitting by the fire, and we left an hour or so later, well satisfied with our approaches. Another visit would be a piece of cake.

The next evening we reported to the post and as we were merely on yellow warning with Jerry busy elsewhere, we began to speculate on the possibilities of a return call. Unfortunately at that moment, Mr Brickwood, a senior warden, walked in and crossed to where we were sitting.

"About this new gas mask issue," he said. "Did my daughters give you all the information you needed?"
There was an ugly twinkle in his eye.

"I was speaking to the Head Warden, not half an hour ago, and he didn't know a thing about it. Perhaps you could tell us more? And by the way, if you want to flirt with my daughters, let me know in advance, otherwise I might be at the pub."

We were speechless.

But for once, luck was on our side and we had the last laugh. A couple of nights following, we saw Mr B. pop into the Bull's Head and we knew he'd be there a while, so we hot footed it to his home ostensibly to fetch him to the post.

"Oh no." We confirmed to Mrs B. "He's not on duty and he's wanted very urgently."

"Can't understand it," she said, "he tells me that he always goes straight there."

The girls became excellent friends, and were tickled pink that we had succeeded in tripping up their dad. On the cold nights of that Winter we had some great laughs together to lighten the tedium of waiting for a raid. Peggy announced in the Spring that she was marrying an RAF bomber pilot, but he died in action some six weeks after the wedding day. She married his Squadron Commander later, and he, too, failed to return from one of the thousand bomber raids on Germany. After that, both sisters decided the emotional strain was too much. They refused to pledge themselves to anyone until the war was over and peace was here to stay.

Very soon our deep involvement with the Post, the wardens, the families in our sector, and the daily events that surrounded them, gave us a soap opera of our own. We needed only to watch the elaborate to-ing and fro-ing of households, as some departed to less dangerous parts and others returned to be nearer either working husbands or elderly parents, to become deeply involved in a life drama that never stopped. We carefully logged vacant houses, empty shops, and abandoned sites, confident our records were bang up to date, and available in an emergency. Two full time wardens kept a regular watch over each twenty-four hour period, with days off relieved by a rota of volunteers. Mrs Foreman, one of the permanents, suitably playing the role of everyone's mum, sorted out the most complicated domestic problem if it threatened to interfere with post assignments. She had a knack of sensing when Head Quarters, at Wyken, might have a new face on duty, and hastened us out there with a message so we could judge for ourselves and flirt to our heart's content.

On such occasions the two mile walk was of small concern. Not so, however, when we felt ourselves conned by the Head Warden. There was the case when an urgent commission turned out to be the transport of a hundredweight of bird seed for his aviary of budgerigars and canaries. The Divisional Chief owned a pet food shop, and his quarterly ration of corn arrived that day. First on his list of priorities were his Senior men, and in the line of command the delivery was on our shoulders. We did not take kindly to such rank preference and our mutinous mutterings lasted for days afterwards.

At the end of our first month's service we attended a training course on First Aid, Gas Warfare and Fire Fighting, so that when the next bombs fell we were brim full of confidence. On reflection, it is strange that the Germans failed to mount an immediate follow-up to the raid in November. Another night of Blitzkrieg and there would have been precious little remaining in Coventry. There was no water, a minimum system of communications and a weary ARP service. Somewhere along the line, self assured smugness let the enemy pass up a sitting target, in the belief that the job was over and finished. So much so, that when their bombers did return, the defenders had re-grouped and were ready to take them on again.

The winter nights had now a fresh emphasis. If the three of us were clear of other fire watching duties, we would choose to meet and survey our local parish, provided the sirens had not called us already. First we would pace the twisting paths of Stoke Park, pass by the Edwardian mansions, set in their formal grounds, and move on to the terraces of St Osburg's, St Michael's, St Ann's and St Agatha's roads. Then we scrutinised the lines of two up and two downers in Marlborough Road and Kingsway. What a monotonous conglomeration of early twentieth century architecture that turned out to be. Yet perhaps, as the moon shone down, the dismal similarity vanished, and the shapes became, in our musings, the fairy castles of our fertile imaginations.

When long empty periods of air raid alerts were available for our philosophising, we would sit them out on garden walls or the benches of the Bunny Run, along the public gardens of the Binley Road. It was surprising what conjectures could interest the thoughts and fancies of young men. From reviews of the week's film releases to the latest risqué story; through a nod and wink gossip session, to the expectancy limit of the newest date. It was a fit subject for the chatter, the innuendo and the rumour. We laughed most at our own 'in' jokes, and treated with contempt any move from Jerry to interfere.

Maybe though, our best moments appeared at pun-time. Manipulating the names above the shop fronts in the Walsgrave Road; to cogitate on the factors of chance that placed a HEMMINGS (the hairdressers), alongside a GATHERUM (the chemists), next to a NEEDLERS (the cooked meat shop). Or the one we shared with Home Guard Bryan Cox, as our respective patrols crossed paths, how it was that his parents' grocery shop in Clay Lane, COX, happened to be right next door, to butcher BALLS.

Other signs promised different attractions. There was the NISBETT sweet shop, where wee Alec sat on a high stool, while his mother served us with Jelly Babies and kali. Years later Alec, and his wife Jean, in a strange twist of coincidence, moved next door but one to us, in Camden Town, as he wrote and produced multitude editions of prize-winning *Horizons*, for the BBC. Nearby at WARDS, the music shop, was an exquisite looking daughter, June. During the thrice weekly dance to Billy Monk's Band at the nearby GEC Ballroom, she partnered mature, suave, male draughtsmen from the design offices of the company. She was way ahead, far superior to our schoolboy pretensions. In those suspended hours of watching and waiting, we could only plan for our limited offensive to take place at the next dance. Maybe the excuse-me quicksteps would provide the chance. Even half a dozen twists and turns would satisfy our desires, before the partner for the evening returned to claim his prize. The darkness had the consolation of granting us a romantic dream, that we need not divulge.

At the side of WARDS was the ice cream parlour of the Italian family, PERROTTI. There too, hid a beautiful jewel, Doreen, guarded and protected in true Mediterranean style. She was, fortunately, not averse to the occasional foray when she could escape the lock and key. Yet, if we wanted repartee of a distinctly superior kind, we retired to the butcher's WHITEHOUSE, set opposite the Old Ball pub. There we sparred with the intelligent Grace, daughter of the house and sister of Jack, a slightly senior chap to us and already flying with the RAF. She kept her wits about her, and was prepared to indulge her skill whenever she returned home late in the evening from some romantic liaison. And should the skies be full of hostility, we would try to hasten her path so that she would be in safe keeping and shelter before any real wickedness descended.

Our nightly routine developed quite naturally. First, we visited 404C to collect messages and share the roll call and briefing, followed by a game of darts. Then, if there was no call to action, we might pause to catch up on studies at home before meeting in the Ball or Bull, dependent on the supply situation. On siren nights, it was a calculation of odds. A lone raider or a reconnaissance flight? A combined operation or a diversionary feint? Sometimes a single plane might hang around indefinitely, flying in circles over the city, until a night fighter arrived to chase it away. Another time, within seconds of the initial approach, there could be a ferocious assault that would have us chasing around like maniacs. In such circumstances, we felt morbidly close to a hurried departure from this world.

Once, as a Luftwaffe pilot used the hairs on our backs as a navigational aid, we stretched out, head to toe, along the gutters of St Agatha's Road. The bomber crew unloaded rack after rack of incendiaries to bounce their course amongst us. As a basket of fireflies prematurely disturbed, they whacked and thumped their landfall onto pavement and roadway, spreading ten thousand dancing sparks an inch above the ground. One harbinger of flame and burning, cracked down some five or six feet away as we lay mesmerised by the inevitability of what might happen. First it rolled, shedding its fin with a small pop. Next, it hissed and fizzed, like a coiled up snake, ready to strike, and then, in a twinkling, gushed out as if it were a Roman Candle on Bonfire Night, belching into a shimmering white blaze surrounded by a luminous blue haze.

On every side and corner the pattern repeated itself, until we recovered from our paralysed hypnosis to throw a sandbag from the pile beside the street shelter, onto each offensive intruder. Now, within seconds, we retreated to the gutter again, as another streak of fire whipped a track through the front gardens of the houses ahead of us. Manfully we tried to shield each other, huddled together in the false light, expecting any further explosion to tear us apart; waiting, waiting, and waiting.

One of us happened to glance upwards and immediately alerted the others that a member of the previous downpour was still alive and active. There lodged in the roof of the Davis house, twenty feet away in St Osburg's Road, was a nasty survivor. Mr Davis, an accountant, was the warden in charge of this section, but we could not see him, and no-one else had noticed the flare up. Cheese and I raced off for a ladder, while Johnny fetched a stirrup pump. We called for help as we ran, trundling the ladder to the front of the house. At once, I tried to clamber up the rungs, forgetting the requirement to extend it first, if it was to reach to roof level. I had to jump down, and fumbled with the extension ropes, while Cheese released the catches on the side.

Mr Davis and another helper appeared around the corner, and decided to tackle the blaze from inside the house, just as we pushed, pulled and finally heaved the ladder upwards. Johnny handed me the hose and started to pump from a bucket of water. The roof was well alight and I had a large enough bull's-eye to aim the spray, noticing that the wardens were drenching the flames from underneath. Relentlessly, more wooden rafters were catching alight with a sickening regularity, and it was hard to decide where best to direct the water. After a while I changed with Cheese and relieved Johnny at the pump. The raid was growing fiercer and the heavy crump of high explosives was replacing the swish of the incendiaries, although our ack-ack guns were making a tremendous demonstration. Yet, in the heat of the moment and the fire, there was hardly space to think about anything but the job in hand.

Gradually more help arrived and we succeeded in dampening things down, although it was proving difficult to isolate the source of the problem, stuck tight between the main timber beams. One minute the burning looked as if it would resist our efforts for ever in a light of blinding intensity, then suddenly, the very next second, there was a hiss and a splutter, and it all ended. Darkness totally enfolded us. The tension eased, and we blinked our eyes to re-adjust to the night. Everyone began talking at once. Mr Davis was in a seventh heaven, and kept patting us on the back and saying, "Well done, lads." He was even more ecstatic that we had worked on our own, without calling the auxiliary firemen, and he rushed off to Post 404C to tell the Head Warden the whole story.

Long after the war finished he never forgot that episode. When he and his schoolteacher wife had retired, he would stop me in the street, if I should be visiting my parents, and chuckle away about 'the three musketeers', and the bomb on which Hitler had written the name of DAVIS.

Tales like these were the grist of our conversation. At school, the battle to concentrate on the learning process, rather than the nocturnal activities of stretcher party, first aid crew and rescue gangs, made our daily attendance that much more important. After a night of alarms, each morning was a chance to overcome the tiredness we felt and to review the defeats and successes. Unfortunately, some days we counted only the losses, when a close friend was no longer there to join us. Then one morning there was no longer even a place to meet.

In the week before Easter, we congratulated ourselves that we had survived the sombre months after the Blitz. Unexploded bombs were de-fused, craters filled in and my father's extension ladder returned to its position, behind our terrace of houses. Throughout the district water was on tap again, shattered windows back in place and roof tiles repaired, while my mother found the food distribution, badly disrupted after the raid in November, was regaining its rationed normality. We had all felt sickened in the aftermath of that bombing. At first, lorries ferried food supplies into the city and the Women's Voluntary Services distributed them because so many shops had disappeared, but then people from outlying districts, who had remained completely untouched, either by bombs or trauma, heard of the free distributions and came into Coventry to snatch the supplies. A few days later the authorities fathomed the deception and closed down the food points. Fortunately my mother had her own reserves of iron rations, made up from gift parcels we had received from our caring relatives in New Zealand, and we survived the worst of the shortages.

School term was due to end on April 10th, the day prior to Good Friday, and my parents had prepared a trip for us to Blackpool to visit Aunt Clara and my cousins, who were living there. I had notified the Post, and Cheese and Johnny were taking over my duties, but on Tuesday evening April 8th, the sirens called us to action at 9.30 p.m. and a sharp attack developed around 10 p.m. Within an hour the pace slackened and although there were aircraft still in the vicinity, by midnight we decided it was safe to return home and try for some sleep. We were hardly inside than the bombs rained down again, and the intensity sharpened as it became apparent we were under assault from almost as many planes in formation, as we had withstood through the whole night in November.

We rushed to a series of incidents; no sooner we became involved in one than another more urgent one occurred, so that in the following three hours the scale of the raid outpaced anything we had witnessed before. There was not a moment to consider our own safekeeping, except to hug the ground when an explosion was really close by, and we went from one problem to another, trying as best we might to help wherever we could. By 3.30 a.m. there was a sight of dawn in the sky and the last raiders began to turn for their own airfields. We looked at each other, mud spattered, dirty faces, tin hats at a cocky angle and reckoned the morning would reveal the true scope of the terrible pounding the town had endured.

It certainly did just that. At 8.45 a.m., I had my bitterest shock. There as I picked my way across torn up roads and pavements, I saw from the railway bridge in Warwick Road the smoking shell of KHS. I was in no mood to rush to reach it, but as one or two other boys came along we climbed the hill together. The tower and flagpole looked safe, but the main school doors, where only the previous afternoon we had posed in shorts and jerseys for the 1st XV photograph, stood broken and dislodged. The gymnasium we had changed in, the main hall, classrooms, laboratories, workshops, were shattered, and we heard that the Head, severely wounded during World War One, was now wounded in this. Twenty or thirty of us shuffled forlornly past the battered walls of the building, stamping hopelessly on the smouldering ashes in a vain attempt to dampen the sparks and to see if anything remained. The trophies and the pictures, the desks and the books had disappeared forever, and there was nothing we could do to bring them back. A few staff arrived but no-one wanted to speak, and after I had fortunately found my own locker still intact beneath a heap of fallen masonry, I took out the books I kept there. Outside, I joined Charlie Dupenois and his brother George, on vacation from Oxford, with Graham Parkes, Miud Richards and Ron Shreeve to cycle to the Coventry and Warwickshire Hospital in the hope there might be news of Monty Burton. However, a full evacuation of patients was already under way and with it disappeared any likelihood of tracing individuals. We volunteered to clear bricks and rubble from the main drive to allow the ambulances a freer access, and afterwards, in low spirits, we decided to leave.

I rode along with Ron Shreeve, who was suffering badly from the results of a sleepless night. It had seen him pulling out dead and injured bodies from an incident in Gulson Road, near his home, where his ARP stretcher bearer party had answered a call. We passed the site of the demolished properties and felt the despair rise within us. How many more would we see in the ensuing months? How many more of our fellows would join the hundreds already killed and wounded? There seemed to be no relief to this dull repetitive pattern of death and destruction and no possibility of making sense out of the stupidity we had witnessed at first hand. What price our education, if all our learning and scholarship became as nothing, in the face of wanton destruction? What price a belief in the ultimate triumph of Divine Right if evil demanded so many hostages? And, if we were to succeed in the end, what guarantee that human frailties did not produce a bigger manifestation next time? With such imponderables to answer, we parted.

That evening at the Post, the telephone lines were down and we hastened to Divisional Headquarters to collect operational orders and swop status reports. Outward bound we checked on the safe keeping of our friends. The Hewitts, who had moved after the November raid into a replacement house in Beaconsfield Road, had heard from Bernard on his corvette in the North sea. The Maycocks and the Thackrays had contacted their sons, even though the news that Coventry had been the night's target was still not official. At the Thackray's, Catherine, one of our regular dance partners, asked if we would escort her to friends Barbara Waters, Margaret Langstone and Joan Foulger in Shakespeare Street and we diverted our journey to oblige. The girls, at least, were taking everything in their stride. They seemed much less introspective than us, although they had not seen their school disappear that day, and when we left them our gloom seemed lighter.

By 9 p.m. we were back at base, with no reports of enemy aircraft in the offing, so we chose to sleep. Fortunately, our luck held and we remained undisturbed. The following night another attack occurred, and there were several major incidents in our sector. Good Friday dawned sunny and clear, except for the wisps of smoke rising over the city, and my parents decided we would try to go to Blackpool. We surmised the railway station would be a non starter and opted for a walk along the Binley Road. Carrying the minimum of luggage, we hoped to catch a bus to Rugby or Nuneaton, where it was more likely that a train service was in operation.

As we passed through our neighbourhood streets, it was apparent that the damage was severe. The Barrage Balloons were in a bad way, hanging drunkenly on the end of their cables and my father's ladder was back in service as a guardian angel over an unexploded bomb. Few people were about, confirming the preceding evening's residential check out, when we noticed that a large number of families had taken off for the countryside. We had not walked far, when a driver stopped his car and offered us a lift to Rugby, so that within an hour we were on the train and bound for the seaside.

The next five days were happy and carefree. No bombs, no sirens, only rest and a chance of recreation. Joyce and Beryl were the ideal playmates, and we danced the hours away at the ballrooms of Blackpool and Cleveleys. Wartime dancing was a mood maker of a very special calibre. It had a characteristic of underlining the poignancy of highly emotional circumstances, wrapped up in call-ups, embarkation leaves, re-unions and departures. There is nothing quite like the hovering nature of uncertainty that the threat of death on the battlefield, produces in relationships. Combined with the sweet melody and simple lyrics of the popular songs, which became such a feature of these snatched encounters, the pressures were right there for us to feel. Vera Lynn, Bing Crosby and the other music makers of the war years knew how to play the heart strings. That Easter, after the tension of Coventry, I understood a little more of what my parents and their generation had perceived in 1914, when they named 'back home' as Blighty, and sang *Keep the home fires burning*.

Too soon, we were returning to Coventry and I was resuming my duties. There had been no subsequent alerts during the church festival of Easter, and from somewhere had developed an un-natural feeling of peacefulness. It infiltrated the demolition and repair gangs as they cleared up the mess, and we began to notice, as the days went by, we had entered a further distinctive stage in the battle. In the following weeks it was notable for undisturbed nights and the lack of any calls from fate's sirens. Unbeknown to us, of course, was the decision of Hitler to switch his forces from the West to the East; prior preparation for his invasion of Russia. The Luftwaffe, apart from a few defensive squadrons, withdrew from the battle, effectively signalling the end of the bombing blitz on the industrial heartland of Britain. We breathed freely, again.

After the holidays, I settled to carry out teaching practice at my old elementary school, Stoke Council, to meet pre-entry requirements for Goldsmiths' College, where I was due in October. This fitted the emergency plans of KHS, because no classes were possible at Warwick Road, and the Headmaster, recovered from his injuries, had arranged to take over the unused facilities at Bablake School, vacant because of evacuation to Lincoln. Regrettably, after the destruction of our text books and equipment, learning was reduced to something of a charade.

As I was busying myself with preparation for University, rather than exams, I spent long periods reading in the sunshine on the school playing fields together with others of the Sixth Form, amongst them Graham Parkes, Harry Oswin and Pete Riley. Then in the early evening, reinforced by Charlie Dupenois, Ron Shreeve and Buggy Bright, we would meet at the Golden Cross, overlooking the skeleton ruins of the Cathedral, for a weak shandy or whatever Alf, the barman, had in his delivery that day. However, once the ration had gone, it was back to messenger duties with Cheese and Johnny, and a possible discussion on what we might be able to do when the war finished.

Johnny Stringer was already a young research chemist working on the formulations that supplied the magic of nylon stockings into post-war fashion. As both a worker and a student, he was exempt from military conscription, while continuing on for a degree. The evening talks for him were a relaxation from the language of the laboratory, while for Harry Furminger and me they brought an opportunity to plan our social life, which with freedom from raids, was expanding rapidly anew.

When I left school in July, I volunteered as relief post warden, to allow the permanent staff a holiday, and kept the night watch, sleeping during the day. Apart from a sneaky reconnaissance or a premature siren, we were largely untroubled, and quickly forgot the earlier anxieties. The April raids, indeed, almost concluded my real Blitz experience. Except for the very different dimensions the Nazi secret weapons opened up later, and one or two hit and run raiders, I met nothing again that equalled the ferocity and viciousness of that year in Coventry.

Still, there was one further occasion, I recall, by when the civilian population of the city had developed a novel and relaxed attitude towards air strikes. In the summer of 1944, with the invasion of Normandy steaming ahead, the Germans mounted a series of retaliatory blows against the industrial bases supplying arms and ammunition to the Allied armies. Coventry was again in the line of fire.

I was home on embarkation leave, awaiting my turn to cross the Channel and join the British Second Army. Late one night the sirens wailed and the familiar throb of Dornier and Heinkel was back in the skies. I dressed quickly, grabbed my tin hat and outside met up with Johnny reporting to Post 404C. It was like old times as we checked in and padded off to a position on the Binley Road to observe the night sky and review the action.

On the far edges of the town the ack-ack shells were

bursting and a flare or two parachuted slowly downwards. Then, in a trice, everything changed as a thunderous roar, reverberated across the heavens. I gazed fascinated, at the most spectacular fire work display, I had ever seen, fanning out in every direction. A thousand or more flaring rockets rose in a tight box formation and exploded into millions of coloured stars high above us. The great cube of space this mobile eruption occupied, left no room at all for anything inside to survive an instant. Johnny was well briefed and pulled me into the shelter of a house porch as chunks of metal, pieces of chain, nails and rusty piping rattled amongst us.

"Better be careful, they load those rockets with whatever they can lay their hands on. Could be far worse than Jerry."

I agreed with him, as lumps of slate, chimney pots and brick streamed downwards, broken from the surrounding houses, by the falling shrapnel. Up there it was one huge conveyor belt, despatching salvo after salvo of red hot rocket casing into the night. Hell bent on annihilating every single enemy plane and in a dying flourish of glowing sparks, returning as flotsam and jetsam to earth. It was not surprising that Goering's last ditch raiders simply turned and fled back from whence they came, dragging their tails behind them. An hour later the fireworks were over and we called "Time gentlemen. Please!" with real understanding.

The tide of events moved on, and the years have become half a century. Yet while the memory of those dark nights of blitz and bombing may grow fainter, I have never failed to remember, at each recurring November 14th, that unique period of twelve hours. A whole city of over 200,000 people shared those un-nerving experiences, locked away in our secret thoughts. Fewer of us now remain, with even fewer still resident in Coventry. But wherever we are, and despite our efforts to forget, the scent of burning, death and fear remain stuck in our nostrils. I guess they always will.

EIGHT

TRAINING SCHOOL

L EAVING SCHOOL IS one thing, understanding the implications, another. Part of that understanding is to accept that the learning process has yet a long way to go; and even what is more important, to realise that education attracts more prejudice and wild criticism than just about any other topic we will ever discuss. Why should this happen? What are the reasons that make education of such paltry concern to so many parents, that they forfeit the opportunities for their sons and daughters to study beyond a very lowly level?

The result is clear cut. Britain enjoys the lowest rate of entry to advanced vocational training, compared to any of our European neighbours, or to most other industrial nations. A statistic sadly reflected at every stage in our economic progress.

Why there should be a stigma attached to learning is harder to evaluate. Unfortunately, the formula I heard in my own school days, half a century ago, remains the same today, 'Earning money is more important than earning a qualification.' So the expertise needed to foster comprehensive training programmes, which might rectify the deficiencies, lies undeveloped. Industry, commerce and government have muddled through with inadequate resources, rather than pay for the revolution required in its augmentation. The idea persists that job dexterity should be the sole yardstick. Thus, twenty years' experience conceals, in reality, twenty years' constant repetition of the same operation; learned originally in two weeks flat.

This is not what it should be about. This is neither training, education or any dreamed up slogan the politicians care to label it. Along this path lies only self-deception, cloaking the true aims of scholarship and denying everything that Sir Philip Morris, one of the most astute educationalists of our times, tried to preach and popularise,

"An educated person," he declared, "is one who can entertain himself, entertain his friends, and entertain a new idea."

If our teaching system cannot fulfil that, then it fails absolutely.

The summer of 1941, despite the turmoil in the world outside, presented me with a distinct choice. A Grammar School grounding of seven years, had served me well. Of course, there were wide gaps in what I had assimilated, many simple skills were inadequately taught, but the spirit of learning had left its mark. Monty Burton and his team had signposted the path, using techniques from a Victorian framed curriculum, to ensure that knowledge became a lifelong companion. It demanded the reward was not something to count merely in terms of pounds, shillings and pence. The stunning treasures of civilisation, which they revealed to me, were a definite bonus, compared to the meagre pickings that some of my Coventry contemporaries received. Music, art, literature and science had traded over some of their mysteries and I held the key to discover more.

For many other school leavers that summer, the future was bleak. Some had scarcely reached the age of fourteen before renouncing their scholastic ties. I had witnessed, with distress, during a period of teaching practice, they knew little of books, libraries or research, and writing and communication abilities were almost totally absent. Of course, for those elementary school leavers there was a usual catalogue of excuses for their sad plight. Evacuation, teacher call-up, air raids and bombed-out buildings, were the excuses named as condoning factors. Yet was it necessary for their family to insist, in every case, that outside the school walls, nothing else was important but a job and earning money? Where was there any concept that little more than 200 miles away lived people they had not even acquired the tools to speak to, understand or fight alongside?

True enough, my own knowledge of foreign languages was abysmal. At KHS, in common with public school traditions, we had survived on teaching methods better suited to construing Latin and Greek than any modern derivatives. Rarely did we hear an alien tongue and in class stumbled through the minimal selection of tourist phrases designed for the simplest preliminaries. Once, when the Board of Education inspectors visited the school, we found ourselves fortuitously exposed to a leading exponent of progressive language teaching. He took over from our stereotyped schoolmaster and captivated us with a true sense of accent and phrasing. In a choral speaking session of alliterative French phrases, he roared at us,

"La multitude murmur, la multitude murmur, la multitude murmur."

As we repeated it, we rejoiced in the rolling sounds, and were excited by our own corporate efforts. Unfortunately, lessons returned to their old ways, after the catalyst disappeared, and on my first visit overseas, in 1939, I was a tongue tied idiot, like all my classmates. Miraculously, when I returned to Europe, on sterner missions with the army, the pressures of examinations had brought an understanding that helped me communicate somewhat more doggedly. A situation not correspondingly shared with the majority of my comrades.

Nevertheless, disturbing as it was to observe the results of inadequate teaching, no-one sews silk purses from pigs' ears. Techniques of training the raw material may be in need of overhaul, yet if the fundamentals are not present, what hope is there of success? Home background must be an integral part of the solution, and outside enthusiasm be readily available to support the weak. Though I saw many of the problems of illiteracy during teacher training, I was desperately ill-prepared to face the repercussions I found on call-up in 1943.

During Primary Training at Budbrooke Barracks in Warwick, the other recruits were mainly from Birmingham and the Black Country. They were an under-nourished, peaky bunch, about a third of whom could neither read nor write, a fair average for intakes at this stage of the war, but despite my despair at the implications, I was able to appreciate the humour, too. It began one morning after mail call, when our first bunch of correspondence, bearing name and regimental number, arrived. One of the lads, I had scarcely noticed previously, took me aside and asked me to read aloud his letter from home. From then on, my destiny was clear. Within days I was the official platoon reader and writer, boasting a clientele of nine out of the thirty members. Nothing was sacred, letters of love,

of passion, of intimacy; always with the same stammered request,
"Please write it, as you would do it."
They called me 'The Professor', and paid me a set fee of sixpence
for writing, three pence to read, and when a soldier's wage topped
only thirty pence a day, it was handsome compensation.

Private John Ward, one of my clients, represented an even
more depressing aspect of our educational heritage. He was born
almost on my own doorstep in Stoke, Coventry, within a few days
of me, and lived close by the elementary school I had first attended
at five, where later I practised my teaching. We had never met. It
was hardly surprising, considering that in the nine full years he had
been eligible for school attendance, he had avoided all, except for a
few months. The facts intrigued me so much, that I invited him to
reveal the great deception.

He told me his parents reached the city, in a flood of
immigrant labour, from the countryside, during the First World War.
They had neither money nor resources, and because of the seasonal
nature of the motor industry, were often unemployed. Neither parent
could read or write, having somehow bypassed the reforming
Educational Acts of the late nineteenth century.

At five he missed school, probably because his parents were
not aware he should attend, and the authorities failed to catch up,
until he was almost seven. Then he went to school for a month,
until he became ill with some childhood infection. On the strength
of that and succeeding illnesses, he remained out of school for nearly
two years. When he attended school again, he was nine, at which
point he had missed completely the early learning techniques for
reading and writing. In a class of fifty, the teacher had little sympathy
for those fallen by the wayside, as in the final Junior year
preparation for the 11 plus was the priority.

School bored John and he played truant, quickly associating
with a group of similar drop-outs, who dodged the column and
avoided classes, month after month. The school attendance
inspectors were too thin on the ground either to cope with parents
who were never at home or to catch children who disappeared. The
transfer across to Senior school added only administrative confusion
to his absence. John, now thoroughly street wise in truancy, became
a lost student. He spent his days hiding from authority, often in the
local cinema. Performances commenced at 10.30 a.m. and managers

and usherettes were no match for the determined malingerer. Boys sneaked through the emergency exit doors, at the Forum on Walsgrave Road or the Scala in Gosford Street, and stayed concealed under the seats, or in the toilets, during screening after screening. They slipped out for a penny worth of chips at lunch and drifted back home for tea, never to be asked the question,

"... and what did you do at school today?"

At the age of twelve, Ward looked mature enough to pretend to be a school leaver and went to an employer who never questioned the evidence. Later he imagined he would avoid military service, too, but a brush with the law made his call-up inevitable. At least, the Army procedures pointed out to the Education Authorities, that all need not be lost. However, nine years lay wasted and the damage irrevocable. The poor chap suffered other problems, too. Amongst them, a weak bladder, which hardly endeared him to me.

On our first night in uniform we shared a tiered bunk, next to the door. Because I made an early registration at the barracks, I chose the lower cot to avoid a clamber to the upper when I wanted to sleep. Ward reported late, and was landed with the top one. Shortly after midnight, I received a wetting and awoke the platoon corporal, and the rest of the Nissen hut, with my shouts. Ward was turfed out of his blankets and forced to spend the rest of the night outside, on the steps. His bladder made a miraculous recovery straightaway. It gave no further trouble. Regrettably, reading and writing inadequacies cannot be so easily healed.

After that preliminary encounter, illiteracy became one of my concerns in the army. As the war ended and I transferred to educational duties in Germany, it was not possible to avoid the conclusion that the procedure of training young people in Britain, was completely inadequate. So with unsophisticated methods and a limited amount of time, a small contingent of Royal Army Educational Corps personnel tried to rectify years of neglect, and attempted to develop alternative skills in those forgotten by the system. I found many compensations in this work. To pass on knowledge to those who had not had comparable opportunities to study at University level, was exciting and rewarding. While to witness the awakening of new horizons and fresh concepts in others, with whom I had shared some of my most impressionable moments in the war, was as precious as anything occurring subsequently.

When I had left school, I think I soon appreciated what a distinctly different environment existed if you were lucky enough to stay on beyond fourteen. At Grammar School we remained until we were 17 or 18 years old, and could then add to the learning process at higher levels. The key was the opportunity to participate in a situation where the strivings of a group of adults, (headmaster, teachers, mentors and clerics), ensured they retained the instinctive innocence of wonderment in their young charges. Then they encouraged it to blossom and bear fruit. This example inspired me to try the same. Going on to Goldsmiths' College seemed a natural progression along this path.

Up to that time I had enjoyed my exposure to student teaching, despite the realisation that it was not easy to pass on enthusiasms to others who did not necessarily share similar motives. Obviously, not everyone would desire the same standard of fulfilment or generate the same ambition, but this did not prevent me from trying to create a response comparable to those I had discovered. I now faced the reality of equipping myself with fresh skills and techniques to make this possible.

The availability of higher layers of learning was one of the safeguards built in to the established pattern of education in Britain, guaranteeing that whatever political attitudes prevailed, there was a maintenance of the 'status quo'. Effectively, the preservation of the species demanded that even during the most unfavourable periods of history knowledge deserved protection, and a formal minimum amount, allowed to survive. This datum line marked a general acceptance level of learning, so that good times heralded a flourishing renaissance, and bad times 'ring-fenced' the basics.

In their peculiar isolation, politicians have always complained that if the expansion of scholarship developed unfettered, costs might explode in their faces. Far better to keep a lid on such social spending and let future generations pick up the tab. This became the despair of my age group after the war was over, when we watched so little being accomplished.

Today, the run down condition of a crumbling structure, confirms our worst fears, together with the promises that, again, went astray. In 1941, when my moment of decision arose to enter University, too few of my fellows were able to take advantage of what was available. Now, too many young people still remain handicapped by the same paltry finance, parental prejudice and public apathy. My good fortune was that the 'fail-safe' principle worked particularly well in the stress of war; a prize from the influential role the armies had played in the previous two hundred years. Their conquests overseas, obliged the Public Schools, the Grammar Schools and the old Universities to tailor their teaching towards providing a constant supply of leaders and administrators to rule the growing Empire. So when the Industrial Revolution added Redbrick Colleges and Polytechnics to the plans for learning, the intellectual requirements of the nation were in place, for as long as a King and Emperor survived. Not even Hitler's legions in their march across Europe could interfere with this fabric, and it remained as it was, until 1945.

It was then we really lost our nerve, neglecting to decree enough energy or finance to sustain a proper job of change for the new atomic age. As other nations surged ahead, training their youth for the future, we watched, unconcerned, from the sidelines. On the verge of the 21st century, we leave barely one third of our 16-18 year olds in full time education, as opposed to over half in other European countries; while at University level a miserable 20% are students, against 30-35% elsewhere. And this, despite the tremendous hundred fold increase in numbers of young women who take on further educational studies compared to their mothers and grandmothers.

Yet, I suppose, we must be thankful that in the darkest days of Dunkirk and the Blitz, the bottom line stood firm. The country survived, with a sufficient proportion of youthful recruits to ensure the supply of technical skills for industrial production and to maintain the structure of society. To this end, apprenticeships were available in reserved occupations, giving exemption from military service until the age of 21, while scientists, engineers and medics completed professional courses, free from the threat of call-up. Some of my Science Sixth colleagues at school found a convenient niche for their talents at institute and college. Several, like my air raid companion, John Stringer, went directly into industrial research laboratories.

In the Arts, it was possible to plan a start on courses that would eventually lead to qualifications in law, economics and teaching. I fell into this later category, and was able to commence training in a discipline that might ultimately be of value when peace came. My history master, Barry Shipley, had pointed me in the right direction. He convinced me that a university place was urgent, and registration as a student might be a valuable passport when the war was over. After World War One, the treatment of students had been generous and it seemed that again the government might support ex-service personnel.

With this in mind, I embarked on a five terms course at London University to start a B.A. Degree and obtain a Teaching Certificate. There was a further plus: the admission was conditional on undergoing military training, alongside the academic work. This consisted of three afternoon sessions every week and a fourteen day camp with the regular forces each vacation, culminating in the chance to appear before an officer selection board, after practical examinations and a short period in the ranks. It seemed a fair deal, and as a result of the raids on Coventry, I nursed a stubborn desire to be close to any final victory against the Nazis.

Financially, it was a tight affair, for wartime restrictions did not favour lavish spenders. A small Government grant, available because of the teacher training implications, and a yearly loan of £40 from the Coventry Education Committee, had to cover fees, maintenance and books, while I funded my pocket money from holiday work. The cunning of officialdom preferred it that way, ensuring only the barest minimum applied. Just sufficient for the whole apparatus to continue ticking over.

Variations on the theme of scholarships, grants and loans, encouraged other school leavers to join courses in the Arts, before call-up took effect. For male students, attendance was for four or five terms, with the promise of completing studies at a subsequent date. By these means, a portion of the nation's intellectual seed corn sought protection, and for a short while longer, avoided the inertia that contact with the military machine was likely to induce.

Yet such decisions were difficult for all of us, as in the summer of 1941 the battles seemed to stretch on for ever, and relief was far distant. Might H.G. Wells be near the truth, when we saw in his film *Things to Come*, that life could end in another Hundred Years War? Rather it was this spectre that haunted many young men and women, and consequently brought their early recruitment into the armed forces.

Armstrong Whitworth main hanger at Baginton. Final construction stages of Whitley bomber, 1940.

KHS 1st. XV photograph taken on eve of the destruction of the school, April 8, 1941. School Captain Charles Dupenois flanked to left by Ron Shreeve and to right by Graham Parkes. BLT is at left of middle row.

The School Hall on the morning of April 9, 1941.

BLT outside University College, Nottingham, 1942.

Students D.J.WHITE, BLT and W.B.TAYLOR, Nottingham, 1942.

Army recruits BLT and R.W.WINTER on a 36er from Budbrooke Barracks with Stoke Park School in background.

JOHN STRINGER and a newly commissioned BLT, 1944.

Captains PHILIP CRAMNER, PETER RICE and CLEM HANDLEY, Hamburg, 1945.

BLT, Hamburg ,1945.

The Forces Centre in Neue Raben Strasse, Hamburg, 1945.

Spitfire Pilot HAROLD FURMINGER.

Flt Lieut RON SHREEVE and CCG Officer
JOAN FOULGER with the British Forces in
Germany, 1946.

131 Brigade Headquarters, Berlin, 1945.

Berlin, 1945.

The Hitler Bunker, scene of his
last hours and cremation.

The battle scarred garden of
the Reich Chancellery.

Armoured vehicles of the Desert Rats.

Technical High School.

The damaged Staats Opera.

Berlin, 1945.

Russian War Memorial and Reichstag Building

Gedachtniskirche.

Entrance to Olympic Stadium

CYRIL FRANKEL and BLT with Ballerinas GISELA DIEGE and EDEL VON ROTHE, Berlin, 1946.

For me the compromise worked, and in October I enjoyed the chance to taste the fruits of student freedom, however restricted they might be. Right then, I had a great deal of sympathy for the reported verbal duel between Nevil Bishop, the President of the Students' Union at Goldsmiths' and an aggressive representative of senior authority, the Academic Registrar. Bishop had been studying late in the library and on departure was challenged,

"What's your limit, Mr Bishop?"

"The sky. What's yours?"

Life at that moment was like that. Only the heavens could contain it.

I left home, never to return, except for short periods of vacation or leave. My parents, and particularly my father, who 30 years earlier had cycled away from Manchester, knew what this meant to me. The first roots were severed: the break was made. Riding by bus and train to Nottingham, where the college was evacuated from its bombed-out premises in South London, seemed quite an adventure and the start of a long journey. It did not surprise me, my mother had tears in her eyes.

NINE

GIRLS, GIRLS, GIRLS...

ONE OF THE most appealing attractions of the promised student life in Nottingham was the reputation of the city as the home of the prettiest girls in Britain. How the story had arisen, I never bothered to query. If the siting of cigarette factories and hosiery mills, provided jobs for large numbers of young ladies, then who was I to complain of the purely feminist implications? Additionally, I knew enough already, from my early aspirations to sing the arias of Don José, that if I should meet my Carmen, then I should beware.

I reckoned the fame well founded, when I visited the city's leisure emporia. They contained a magnificent feast to the beholder. Nottingham seemed to be alive with places of entertainment, which, after the desolation in Coventry, made me target the theatres, the skating rinks, the dance halls and the pubs, as if I was released from a long term prison sentence. What barren land was it, less than 40 miles away, that I had lived in for so many months? Now the contrast, now the luxury. It did not take long to acclimatise.

The very first Friday night, when the college inaugural week was over, I went off to join the fun with the other new arrivals. Local brews had been around since the Crusades and Robin Hood, and we introduced ourselves to their flavours at The Salutation, the Trip to Jerusalem and The Black Boy until we judged it time to sample the music, and dance, at the Palais and the Vic. It was a dream come true. Serried ranks of unattached maidens, scarcely dented by the presence of the Polish Air Force and the Free Czech Army Brigade, lined up for quicksteps, foxtrots, glides and waltzes. The sweat rolled from our faces, and we turned to refresh our energies at the bar. We could hardly believe our further good fortune as other venues in the suburbs of Beeston and West Bridgford brought extra partners to charm, and more of our favourite popular tunes to romance them with. It required the smallest white lie to conceal our lack of an army uniform, or our insistence on catching the final trolleybus to transport us back to digs. But with everything going for us, long walks home, for the sake of a goodnight kiss, seemed an unnecessary hindrance. After all, the sea was overflowing with such a multitude of scrumptious fish, we could make our catch whenever we chose.

That was without counting the University ladies on the campus. There, the men students commanded an even greater premium. Call-up and entry conditions had done their worst. The 'thin male line' was too sparse and youthful to satisfy anywhere near the demands of drama groups, choirs, sports and social clubs, which college life expected. At the dance the pressures were greatest of all. Tuesday evening coffee dances and Saturday night hops would not function properly without us, and an intake of 60 amongst 250 females went nowhere near correcting the imbalances the war had brought to educational institutions at University level.

Imagine the pandemonium with the announcement of Gala dances and Balls. The first year women, fresh from a school sixth form, anticipating the Freshers Formal or the Christmas Masked Dance, discovered the partners already stolen by the second and third years. Experience taught that grabbing an escort at the first opportunity was the only way to succeed. And with the competition from the pretty chicks in the city outside, there was absolutely no point in looking there, to rectify the loss.

Visiting the current crop of Hollywood 'B' movies did not appease the situation either. Film story lines, simply emphasised the inequalities in the game of the sexes. Indeed, Joe E. Brown's abysmal jokes, in his spate of college musicals, underscored the male reaction of never having it so good,

"You can always tell a college man," he proclaimed, "but you can't tell him much."

Perhaps the shock of college life itself was almost too big to encompass. For me, the contrast of the pseudo Greek and Roman marbled halls and multi-shelved libraries to the blackened fire swept classrooms I had left behind at Grammar School, was a glorious revelation. The grandeur of the University College building, dedicated to Boots, its multiple chemist benefactors, and standing in splendid isolation amongst a pattern of lawns and lakes, was something to savour. No wonder, with my working class roots, I felt at home with the words of the popular music hall song, *I dreamt that I dwelt in marble halls*. Right then I knew exactly what it meant.

Although the women students had monopolised the purpose built hostels in the college grounds, the advantage was that male students could live in digs and benefit from the less strict observation of the 'home by 11' rules that the hostel matrons strictly enforced. In addition, my Mrs Blackburn in Queens Drive, Beeston, made a good substitute mum. She carried out the tasks of ironing and darning that young fellows find so difficult. Initially, along with Moggy White from Lawrence Sheriff, Rugby (a chap I had frequently met in combat on the rugger field when his school played mine) and later scientist Geoff Spooner, we revelled in the freedom of lodgings and our shared accommodation. Indeed, when Moggy finally had to pay his dues in His Majesty's Forces, the fond farewells from the family had us reaching for our handkerchiefs.

Inevitably, we slipped into the routine of term time. Morning lectures, tutorials, essays and teaching practice slotted in alongside a rota of military training, guard duties and the social whirl. The rugby club needed fifteen fit participants, the choirs needed tenors and basses, the ballet club needed danseurs, and the ladies demanded partners. I had additional commitments, too. Cello players were in short supply, and orchestra and student jazz band cried out for someone to play the bass line. As if the day (and night) did not contain too few hours, already.

That Autumn at University College, three institutions occupied the building. Goldsmiths' and the Institute of Education, evacuees from London, worked cheek by jowl alongside the permanent residents. Some lectures we shared communally, particularly in Degree subjects, and with facilities well above average for war time Britain, the arrangement worked well. Everything within was warm and well maintained, with restaurants and snack bars making the best of the rationing and although a liquor licence was not part of the scene then, local pubs were not far away. The assembly rooms were large, the stages and equipment readily available, so that Winter indoor pursuits gathered no complaints and once Summer arrived, the extensive gardens and adjoining open air swimming pool were ideal for lazing and relaxing. The women's hostels stood in the acres of woodland surrounding the University, close to the public spaces of Woolaton Park. Their isolation tended to fan speculation and gossip, but few of us prepared ourselves for the flurry, in our impressionable and fertile minds, that the whiff of scandal revealed so soon after our arrival.

One night, two young ladies ran savagely foul of senior authority. Out for dinner, with two high ranking officers of the Polish Air Force, at the Flying Horse, and a night on the town, they crept back in the early hours of the morning, making slightly too much noise as they clambered through a downstairs window of Hugh Stewart Hall. The main custodian, an elderly spinster lecturer in Hygiene, rudely awakened, caught them red handed as they clasped their passionate friends in a final embrace. Almost with the dawn (or so the story went) they departed, under escort, to the train, whisked home without a single moment to say goodbye to anyone.

Fear of pollution was the alibi, and protection of the species the justification. Yet maybe young women required a special guardianship in those days. They certainly deserved a little more luck than another inmate, similarly returning late from a romantic tryst with her beau, who raised the wrong ground floor window and stumbled into the bath, where the same elderly lecturer was practising what she preached.

I, too, became a victim on the merry-go-round of hostel escapades. In the second week of term, I was looking forward to the coming Saturday. Satisfyingly, I was to make my debut at scrum half in the college fifteen, leaving the evening earmarked for the student hop. The previous dance was lively, although I chose to adopt a low profile and watch events unfold, along with several other men of my year. The reconnaissance accomplished, plans began to hatch for the storming of female hearts the following week.

After testing the waters in the first half of the programme, I noticed the arrival of a new visitor, in the shapely form of a glamorous, blue eyed blonde. A spit image of our latest sex symbol, Veronica Lake. I went into action instantly, and swept her away for a quickstep, where I could deftly exhibit the clever chassés and turns I had learned at other ballrooms. This was familiar ground to me, and I had no intention of being outclassed. However, her coolness parried my amicable questioning as she revealed that she was a second year Nottingham student, living in Hugh Stewart Hall, who rarely engaged in college activities. When the music stopped we talked at the side of the floor, as she surprised me with her fair knowledge of Rugby football and the college teams. But fate clearly stepped my way, with the announcement that the next dance was a Ladies Invitation Waltz, allowing her little option but to ask me.

Over her shoulder, some of my Rugby Club colleagues, passed a wink of approval, and I settled in to take charge of the proceedings as we danced together for the rest of the evening. After the final waltz, she accepted my offer to escort her to hostel, and we joined the long line of couples making their way there, beside the laboratory and workshop buildings, at the rear of the main college. In the darkness of the narrow 'cut-thru' alleyway, we saw the evening's dancers stopping for a cigarette and a kiss before a final goodnight. So, taking Judy's hand firmly in mine, we entered the approaches to the Hall, and I began to speculate on my chances of similar kisses and embraces; perhaps a further meeting might be in the offing.

Nevertheless, it surprised me when instead of turning right along the path with the other students, we turned left, in the opposite direction. Now we walked along a much darker pathway, curiously devoid of any couples. I speculated on the motive. Was this subdued, icy princess, not so quiet and innocent after all? Were my wildest fantasies to be fulfilled in a spectacular romantic avowal? Would she throw me down on the nearest bench, kissing me passionately, until I consummated our love? I tried to keep my voice steady, scarcely crediting my luck as we walked straight on beyond the side of the building, housing the student quarters, towards a separate annexe hidden amongst the trees. It was bewildering and bewitching, a moment straight out of a Dorothy Lamour movie. Then, from the shadows stepped the large figure of a man, whom I could hardly mistake as anyone but the Vice-Principal of the University College.

'My God,' I thought, 'we are trespassing. We're where we shouldn't be, and I'm in for a load of trouble.'

Panic took over, and without an excuse worth repeating, I

was about to blow everything in front of the girl. Yet what was this?

"Hello, daddy," said Judy, "I'm back from the hop, now. Goodnight Brian, thanks for bringing me home."

I mumbled some appropriate reply, nodded at the V.P. and made a fast getaway. What steps had I taken, my friends wanted to know later.

"Bloody great long ones," I said, remembering the grim retribution my old headmaster was likely to wield, if we should ever be caught with one of his daughters.

Fortunately, a single swallow or a lone mistake, neither makes nor ruins a summer, and when I reviewed the episode with one of our Rugger forwards, second year man Brian Robbins, he laughed at my rawness and promised to acquaint me with the no-go areas and the no-go girls. It really was very simple and basic. Only Goldsmith women occupied Hugh Stewart (Judy was the exception) and the Nottingham University students were all at F.B. Hall, on the Beeston side of the college. With back up like this, it could barely go wrong again. During the next few weeks, I sorted it out.

One Saturday, it was kisses with Myrtle at F.B., the following a cuddle with Clarice at H.S., next a double seat in the cinema with Audrey, and more and more hops and dances with René, Norah, Kay and Barbara. By half term, I had netted ten different partners and the whole social vista was on glorious display before me. But I was heading for a fall, and sure enough it came at the Saturday hop when I met Margaret, with four weeks left, before the Christmas vacation.

Hers was an unknown face for me. In her second year, with a group of close confidants, already established in their own female hierarchy, she tended to keep away from day to day student activities. She was a stunner, long black tresses of hair with deep brown eyes, reminding me of the sensual beauties I had always adored in South American musicals. Fittingly, our first dance was a fox-trot to *Down Argentine Way*, as she engulfed me in the unfamiliar musk like perfume she wore. A fragrance I have not forgotten, yet curiously have never met again. There was an immediate mutual affinity, as if we had known each other previously. In moments we were off into a conversation that seemed to be a continuation from a distant time warp. Already it was too late. Neither Brian Robbins' shake of his head, nor another chap's wincing grimace, could divert me now.

By the close of the evening I refused to listen to anyone.

For the rest of term we were inseparable. When our individual lectures finished, we dashed madly to a pre-agreed rendezvous. We ate together, we studied together, we went everywhere together, and as the doors at Hugh Stewart Hall closed up each evening at eleven, we held on by the tips of our fingers until the framework almost sliced them off. Afternoon walks along the River Trent, singing carols in street and square as Christmas raced upon us, long drawn out coffees in Refectory; nothing would grant us all the time we needed to spend gazing into each other's eyes. Then all too suddenly, it was the Going Down Ball.

She wore an embroidered, white taffeta gown, surrounded by layer upon layer of soft lace, which might well have come from Mexico. What I knew, as she sat at my feet, while I strummed away in the college band during one of the relief sets, there was no one else quite as lovely as her. When it was our turn to dance, there was nothing I would rather do, than be her partner. Hands clasped tight, cheek to cheek in a magic embrace, how could we avoid the fatal words "I love you", spilling over into the whispered phrases that went between us? And as we moved into *Who's taking you home tonight?*, followed by *Auld lang syne*, I wanted to believe it would never end.

We kissed our last goodnights and vowed the coming weeks were an untimely separation, only made tolerable by the promise that we could resume this wonderful life next term. In retrospect I cannot calculate how I was able to pack so much activity into so few weeks, and manage to produce enough academic work to deflect my dismissal from the course. Somehow the rugby, the music, the army and a weekly Sunday visit to church had balanced the lectures and the study, and January held out new adventure, to blunt the parting.

I left early next morning for Coventry where I was to work the afternoon shift delivering Christmas mail at the Post Office. It was a sure method of raising extra pocket money and meeting up with old schoolfriends for a dollop of local neighbourhood gossip. The threat of air attack was almost zero, with the Russian battles attracting so much attention and the results of Pearl Harbour altering the geopolitics of the struggle. Even wartime shortages were not enough to prevent those of us still out of uniform, enjoying the best social action available.

My friends Harold Furminger and Ron Shreeve were awaiting their eighteenth birthdays before call up as air crew. Graham Parkes, Bright and Richards were on the verge of leaving for University to join Charlie Dupenois, Oswin, Rider and Slater. We had cause to celebrate. Fickle that we were, the vows made to Margaret, in the euphoria of a midnight ball, remained conveniently forgotten, at the G.E.C. and Rialto dance halls, and the Gulson Road Nurses Home. We considered it on the line of duty to rectify the losses of suitable young men, otherwise engaged, as the festive season traditionally hails the time for goodwill.

Despite the distractions I found time to write to Margaret and we kept the relationship alive with two or three fond letters. Mid-January and the start of the Easter term, we met again at the gate in 'cut-thru'. She had already been in residence for ten days to complete a final teaching practice for the assessments that would eventually influence her certificate grades. It was a stressful time and I sensed, when we kissed, that things might be different. Maybe it was merely the duration our lips stayed together that set the alarm bells ringing. Or was it a guilty feeling each of us shared, from broken promises so earnestly pledged just a month earlier? But we brushed the shadows aside and committed ourselves for three weeks hence, to the most prized function of the term, the Armed Services Gala Ball. It promised dancing to the music of the fabulous broadcasting dance band, the Blue Rockets, with tickets sold out since Christmas. We guessed there would be some lonely hearts at the hostels that night.

There was a series of small hiccups to our romance leading up to the big night. The first hop, Margaret had 'flu and was in bed over the weekend. The following Saturday, I arrived late from an away game at Birmingham University and she was already dancing with a Nottingham engineering student, somewhat older than me and in his Finals year. I cut in during the next excuse-me and suggested we went out for coffee. She declined, and told me she was partnering Jeff that evening, as she had met him at tea with his mother, who was Head Mistress of the school where she was on teaching practice.

"Some coincidence", pronounced team mates Ginger Gore and Cab Humphrey, from the Rugby Club, when I told them the story. Brian Robbins warned me of a similar ploy practised on him the previous year, when he was badly bruised by the same young lady. However, as I brushed my doubts aside, I felt the pangs of mistrust rising acidly in my throat. Such anxieties were new to me, and as I walked back to digs alone, I reflected on the words of the current most popular ballad,

I'm so afraid of night, 'cos I'm too romantic,
Moonlight and stars can make such a fool of me,...
Don't let me dream unless it could all come true.

Apart from that, it seemed our relationship corrected itself, and I easily convinced myself we must be in love. After all, on the home ground of D.H. Lawrence, as our literature lectures frequently reminded us, personal fate might well be linked to community circumstance. In the search for fulfilment only the individual could gauge the degree of trauma he was prepared to suffer.

Then the services dance was upon us. Routine Orders for the day required cadets to wear their best khaki, with polished brasses, as though for a passing out parade, and the excitement grew infectious as the hours went by. Stories of tears and frustrations came out of the hostels, mitigated only by the last minute arrangement of a surprise Hen Party for the girls who had not managed an invitation. The chosen ones prepared themselves, fit to kill, and arrived on the arm of their partner, ready for conquest. What more could one ask from such a battle royal?

The big sound of the R.A.O.C. Blue Rockets, volleyed around the marble columns and the crystal chandeliers of the Great Hall of the University, and the dancers in their sweeping skirts and military livery, skirmished in the beams of arc-lamps flashing across the crowded floor. The musical tone was extraordinary. A cross between Glen Miller and Tommy Dorsey, with vocalists and solo instrumentalists, far outclassing anything we had heard live before. Perhaps the palaces of Vienna were like this as Strauss played *The Blue Danube*. Certainly, when Staff Sergeant Eric Robinson, later the conductor of the BBC Concert Orchestra, coaxed a palpitating rhythm of tangos and slow waltzes from his amplified violin, our hearts felt fit to burst in sheer romanticism.

Margaret looked more beautiful than I ever imagined, and I began to slide even deeper in love with her. The atmosphere was working tricks. There was no point in resisting the total banishment of any doubt, when the engineer, Jeff, danced by, with another girl. Margaret did not bother to recognise him. The occasion was hypnotic. Bugle fanfares heralded the presence of the unit Commanding Officers, conspicuously dressed in mess gear and medals, with their ladies and Adjutants; while the buffet in the refectory, competed to outshine the gloom of war-time rationing. Wrapped in each others arms, brushing her cheek with my lips, we didn't miss a dance as the pattern of colour and movement created a spell throughout the ballroom.

The National Anthem brought the proceedings to a grand finale, and as we stood to attention for the departure of the officers, we breathed in the charged atmosphere of emotion, hoping it would not be too long before we could share such moments again. At Hugh Stewart, we kissed without speaking, and tenderly touched wrists and fingers, stretching out the remaining minutes until lock-up, as we promised to meet the following afternoon for more music at a concert by the London Philharmonic.

That weekend we floated in a mood of self-awareness we had unexpectedly stumbled into that Friday evening. She confided it was new to her. For my part the exhilaration of discovering this secret way of communicating with another soul, devoid of words, was startling.

At the concert we sat enthralled as the massive piano chords in the opening movement of the Rachmaninov No.2 (a concerto, which then was only beginning to make its romantic qualities apparent to a larger audience) swelled passionately through the hall. Instantly, the music united us in a transcending link, making the intercourse of spirits we detected between us, a totally private affair. Then the large orchestral sounds washed over our thoughts, and my own inner shadows disappeared. The fears of the air raids of the previous winter, finally lost their validity. At last the past had no arrears to claim, the future must fend for itself. It was an eternity, treasured in an instant.

So as we listened and absorbed the excitement of the performance, we felt the inner warmth of a shared experience. Perhaps, through the essence of the music, we had identified the NOW. The living pulse we should try to recognise in each second of each day, and probably the greatest contribution our relationship could offer our young lives. Effectively, that day, my virginity was breached, regardless that the physical consummation stayed unachieved with Margaret.

Such love affairs seem doomed to disappoint. Ours held too much promise in the discoveries we had made together, so that lesser meetings must fail to eclipse the journey we had shared in those weekend hours. By the time we visited the cinema, the following Thursday, with our friends Geoff Spooner and Joyce Green, we had fulfilled the contract and there was nothing left to achieve. Right then, I was too unskilled to recognise the evidence and my pride too fragile to accept the inevitable, for the final denouement was dramatic. A reminder of my unrepentant attachment to *Carmen*.

The Easter term advanced apace, and with my confidence secure, I took full opportunity of what student days had on offer. The operatic group were into a season of the 'Mikado' and I was in the orchestra. There was the weekly engagement to play bass in the dance band at the Hop, and Bob Winter and I had formed a vocal duo to perform a set of popular songs whenever anyone showed the slightest interest. Add to that the rugger and army cadet training, plus a chance of ice skating on the frozen college lake, kept my fitness at a peak; although the nag of terminal exams and the University Intermediate papers at the end of May, retained some attention on lectures and tutorials.

Somehow everything fell into place. All pushed together beside teaching practice, the Union Ball, chipping suppers at the local fish bar, and beery singalongs at the Horseshoes, as if the energies rising in the young student's blood were insatiable. But I did have a further niggle bubbling away in the background, the pressure that a virus brings when seeking to betray us. Jealousy. My maturity was still only skin deep. The wounds inflicted, could be bloody and painful.

Although we managed to see each other when our paths crossed between lectures and refectory coffee breaks brought a snatched word or two, there was no hiding that Margaret and I were struggling with our relationship. The innuendoes and rumours I heard from my friends scarcely helped. At first, I cast disillusionment aside. Yet I could not pretend that all the excuses for non-attendance at dance and social were part of academic commitment and another bout of 'flu. Often it was possible to ward off a little of the melancholy, but the poems of Donne and his metaphysical circle, which we were studying and taking to our hearts, often became a reflection of my own psychological state. How could any young man, not question his mistress when confronted with words as powerful as,

> Yet send me back my Heart and Eyes!
> That I may know and see thy lies;
> And may laugh and joy, when thou
> Art in anguish
> And doth languish
> For some one,
> That will none!
> Or prove as false as thou art now!

Maybe the solution was to ignore the snub, and enjoy the life pulsating around me. Unfortunately, that was the hardest lesson to learn.

One morning at coffee break, the story revealed an astonishing twist. Heads nodded wisely together as details of the previous night's adventures unfolded and whispers stretched to disbelieving murmurs at the crowded tables in the refectory. It went something like this. As usual, at 7 p.m., the Army Cadet and Home Guard patrol prepared for its regular stint of duty in the Armoury, except that while they assembled, an Air Raid warning had sounded, and an enemy plane had passed overhead.

The cadet sergeant in charge that night happened to be the engineering student, Jeff. He immediately reacted to the occasion by splitting his force into sections of four and allocating one of them to patrol the ammunition bunkers, keeping the rest on look-out. Then he alerted the staff officers and the other duty men. Jeff was a reliable chap, whose service and seniority had brought him the highly prized Certificate B, which would ensure rapid progress to officer training once he joined the regular forces in the summer and no-one interfered with his assessment of the situation. The alert was short, but as the sirens were a most unusual occurrence in Nottingham, the guard remained on a high level of alertness and vigilance, following through their orders to the letter.

About midnight the drama intensified. Three scared cadets rushed into the guard room rousing the off-duty patrol and garbled a tale of a skirmish and the urgent need for first aid to some injured persons. An order organised reinforcements and despatched them into the darkness, but only then was it apparent that Sergeant Jeff was missing.

Up on the wooded hillside behind Hugh Stewart Hall, moans and groans floated in the night air as a line of armed cadets swept the undergrowth with their torches. They soon found the Sergeant stretched out on the turf, blood pouring from a deep head wound; next to him, knocked out cold, was Margaret.

Minutes earlier, the patrol had passed along 'cut-thru' lane at the rear of the women's hostel on their circuit to the ammunition store. There in the stillness of the night air they heard noises coming directly from the entrance: out of bounds to all. Their colourful imaginations supplied the rest of the scenario. A German parachutist dropped from the earlier overflying enemy aircraft had made his rendezvous at the arms dump, bent on mischief. It was up to the patrol to thwart the dirty deed and without checking back or activating the usual battle drill for such an incident, they prepared to launch an assault. In they charged, bayonets fixed, arms and boots flailing; ready to sort out any S.S.Trooper who stood in their path. Jeff, in an amorous clinch with Margaret, caught the full force of a rifle butt, while she collapsed with fright and a nasty bang on the cheek. The Sergeant was not a foreign spy, he was merely engaged on his own private patrol. The difficulty was, he had chosen the wrong place and the wrong night to try it out.

Half an hour later, Jeff's head was repaired and Margaret smuggled back to her friends in hostel. With so little to be proud of, the action was quickly hushed up and forgotten amongst the other trivia of term time. Naturally, the soothsayers of the Rugby Club made sympathetic noises in my direction and at the next college hop, Bob Winter and I had an overwhelming success with *Blues in the Night*, expressing an understanding, not present previously, as we sang the soulful lyric,

My mamma dun told me. When I was in knee pants.
My mamma dun told me. Son,
A woman is two faced, will give you the glad eye,
And when that sweet talkin's done...

It was not easy to hide the hurt, and the memory was there for a long time to come. In retrospect, the fresh urgency that made me turn to study and cleanse myself from the temptations of the flesh might well have contributed to my obtaining satisfactory examination results that summer. A few days after the incident, Margaret reappeared at college, with a real shiner of an eye, and not a glimmer, from the other one, that she recognised me. It stayed that way until she left, after qualifying in her finals.

However, Jeff figured again in my life, some months later, when my turn arrived to pursue a commission at the War Office Selection Board. He was there for a second attempt after a failure at the first. Apparently his conduct report from the University cadets had not been favourable, based on the outcome of that night, and he was saddled with a dodgy rating and a poor character assessment. At personal initiative tests we were on the same team, struggling to bridge an imaginary river in an equally imaginary jungle, with merely a ten foot pole and a length of rope to aid us. His engineering studies helped us master the problem, but I heard later he failed again, and returned to unit for a further period of training. A true Sods Law, that so much could hinge on so little. Goodness knows the number of occasions he had committed a similar escapade on guard duty. How perverse that the only siren we ever heard in Nottingham, should prove such a downfall.

Later in the Army, I marvelled how the absurd seemed always to be the norm. The snatching of defeat from the wings of victory, which we described as a 'cock-up'. And then, of course, there was the final salutary thought. Might not I, if offered the same gamble and opportunity, with the beautiful Margaret as the prize, have done precisely the same? Even though, at the very moment Jeff and I faced our W.O.S.B., she had upped and married someone else, in a glorious Carmen-like gesture of real showmanship!

TEN

KEEP FIT, TAKE EXERCISE

IT MUST HAVE been reading Dunn's *Experiment with Time* that first roused my interest in recurrence and the theories of continuous repetition. Esoteric interpretations in the philosophical writings of Gurdjieff and Ouspensky came along later, but the implications of 'having seen it all before' and more devastatingly, that it might 'all have to be seen again', has brought me endless speculation.

Yet, perhaps its simplest and most instructive formulation applies to the realm of ideas. The reasoning that insists no idea is ever completely new. A rapid search, and we realise we have been there previously. Was it ten or twenty or a hundred years ago? So often, as time passes us by, it becomes clearer that today's latest fad is a hand-down from yesterday, dressed up in another suit of clothes.

I remembered this again recently, when considering the world of healthy living and keeping fit. The 'in' phrases, the 'buzz' words, can scarcely claim originality. Where have we heard before, 'Health and Beauty', 'Aerobics', 'Jogging', or the 'Dance Boom'? Was it that long ago the ancient Greeks created a Hercules, a God for the Olympics? And what price his personification of fitness? It is as well we count the occasions we have heard it already, and try not to pretend it is brand spanking new.

My father's talisman was the bicycle. Seven or eight miles a day guaranteed vitality and success, and transported him to work as part of the bargain. Everyone cycled, the butcher, the baker, the policeman, the postman. Even my choirmaster, Wilfred Lewis, a high flying accountant and company director, preferred to ride to the office on a two wheeler, rather than let a chauffeur drive him. The addicts became members of a club, biking miles each weekend in rain or shine. Our next door neighbours had relatives who arrived by tandem each pre-war Armistice Sunday from their home in Newcastle on Tyne to pay their respects at the Cyclists War Memorial near Dunsmore, along the London Road from Coventry. It counted as a round trip of over three hundred miles, in two days. Cycling that way was the magic key to well-being and the good life.

Then possibly, the atmosphere of 'dark Satanic mills' and a legacy of industrial squalor encouraged vigorous exercise and open air sport, during free hours away from work. My Uncle Fred and his brothers, Ernest and Willie, in smoke riddled Middleton, Lancashire, joined the local harriers. It was their way to escape the tuberculosis bug that haunted the cotton spinning sweat shops, although the moor lands through which they chased, equally suffered problems with pollution. Each Saturday and Sunday the Hollows' lads, despite their sagging chests and protruding rib cages, grabbed their bags of paper ribbon to lay a trail across dale and stream. Behind them stalked a hundred or more enthusiasts. Their keep fit regime was every bit as testing and ambitious as the 'burn it up' boys and girls of today; and as effective as the most rigorous diet and weight loss cult devised.

When I was of age to notice such pastimes, my mother devoted herself to the quest for a perfect body as a member of the League of Health and Beauty. Because so many families participated, the enthusiasm spread to the classrooms at school. There they dismissed the boring Drill routines of bending arms and placing hands on heads and added a 'new' subject to the time table: P.T. for Physical Training, guided by a fresh breed of teacher,... the P.T. Instructor. It was the latest fashion of the day.

Naturally, each generation must believe it has pioneered a panacea for the re-birth of Adonis and the secret of eternal youth. Yet what they undeniably produce is nothing more than a re-jig of patterns from previous systems. When Hercules began the cult of biceps statistics, little did he know what his earth bound successors would make of it.

In the 1930's, it was all down to Charles Atlas. 'Man or Mouse', the muscleman queried from the poster sites; and woe betide the ones who answered 'mouse'. Then, as the war started, we cultivated Johnnie Weismuller as our Tarzan look-a-like. That is, if you did not crave to be a true Aryan, or were a member of the Hitler Youth. By the 1980's, there was Jane Fonda and the Green Goddess, following in the footsteps of the Marilyns and the Ritas. Noticeable, because they popped up (under different names, of course) just about every ten years, right back to that arena at Olympia in 700 B.C. Give or take a little, they offered the same thing: the good old body beautiful. But despite the dressing up and the advertised message, what they failed to reveal was the true secret. The vital fact, that it was up to you, alone, to look after what the fates had willed you at birth.

However, nothing so far allows me to claim that I am an exception. I have fallen for fads and fancies as frequently as anyone else. Typically, wives and girl friends, have made their presence felt and my own close interest in 'the dance' made that inevitable. Where else will you find such devotion to the culture of fitness?

There must be a price to pay should you wish to emulate the Markovas, Dolins, Fonteyns and Massines of this world; performing and pirouetting in front of their adoring audiences, right into their sixties. Not habitually an age when we lesser mortals can still touch our toes. Then there was Mim Rambert doing a cartwheel at eighty, on stage!

But every cobbler to his own last. I had started out, both active and athletic at school. Rugby fitness required regular exercise sessions to meet the twice weekly deadline for matches on Wednesdays and Saturdays, and cricket, athletics and tennis kept the impetus charged up in the summer months. For swimming, I had an out-of-school coach, Mr Owen, a stalwart of the cup winning Coventry Water Polo Club, who in the 20's and 30's brought attention to the city, when its other sporting achievements were rare. His enthusiasm has retained my interest in that field, throughout my life. Once at University, the chance to try other disciplines improved, with facilities available for squash, badminton, hockey and Association football. While the requirement to attend physical education lectures in the gymnasium, as part of the teacher training syllabus, supplied a jargon and a science that helped performances on the sports field.

Yet, in retrospect, I can see now a much more potent driving force present than seemed apparent at the time. A task master subconsciously linked to the matter of personal survival out in the real world of those particular days. Even if student life appeared sheltered and privileged, the cold facts of war were never far away. It was impossible to avoid the tension and anxiety arising from reports of friends losing their lives on the killing fields. This was more than enough to spur us forward and make a fundamental necessity of self protection and preservation.

Personal fitness became a key issue when confronted with army discipline of the most searching kind, as preparation for the responsibility of safeguarding the lives of others in combat. It became a necessity to fulfil our optimum levels tied in to sport, recreation and good health. I still marvel at the energies of youth that bubbled forth to support an army cadet route march of ten miles in two hours, wearing full battle kit, in the morning, followed by eighty minutes of rugger in the afternoon and left enough rhythm over to permit three hours hopping at the college dance in the evening. All that, sandwiched among three journeys to digs on foot, one and a half miles distant, to eat and change clothes. I slept deeply that Saturday night.

Through all this, there were compensations that influenced our academic studies. In the midst of Blitz and Bombings education was undergoing as many changes, in its structure, as were similarly paralleled in the developments of State medicine and social welfare, described in the Beveridge Report. This new revolution, spearheaded by Churchill's government, aimed at replacing the systems that had grown outdated since their establishment in the Victorian age. It might even allow poverty, deprivation, hunger and unemployment to be banished for ever! Or until the next lot of mealy mouthed politicians could get their hands on it.

Meanwhile, the reward for the citizens of Britain, as a tribute to their tenacity in the face of Hitler, would mark the long awaited victory. Through pamphlet, lecture and film, the formulas and doctrines were circulated around factory, barracks and home, allowing everyone to feel part of the enlightened spirit of regeneration. It even appeared that education might attain a priority it had previously lacked.

At Goldsmiths' College, because of its special role in the nurturing of teachers, the staff, and thus indirectly the students, became involved with these programmes of change. Committees, working parties and research units turned to Arthur Dean, the

Warden of the college, and his colleagues, Doctors Kaye and Lewis, Beryl Paston Brown, Dolly Dymes, George Cons and Professor Schonell, amongst others, to furnish the back-up and ideas the proposed Education Act required. They aired their advanced theories during our lectures, and in teaching practices we tried to act on them. It was certainly stimulating, if not entirely successful. We often struggled to come to terms with the fact that our own school days, recently ended, did not wholeheartedly support all the methods advocated. Whatever else, the reforms initiated in that period, made a lasting contribution to the pattern of education for the next 30 years.

At the conclusion of my first year as a student, I qualified for the award of Certificate B, in the University army training corps, and in the second year moved into the advanced squad, acquiring weaponry instructor techniques. The following Christmas I was on the Yorkshire moors, with the Rifle Brigade, learning to drive a Bren Gun carrier so that on return to college Sergeant's stripes awaited me. I gave them to my current girl friend, Joyce Holt, to stitch on my uniform.

She had arrived at Goldsmiths' in the Autumn of 1942, and intrigued me with her Lancashire line of repartee. After delivering her to hostel, from the first hop of term, I held her tight in my arms to kiss her. In what I judged to be the superior tones of a Senior Male student I said,

"Not bad for a Fresher."

"A Fresher at what?..."

A reply, delivered with such a capping fizz, it convinced me not to surrender her for the rest of that college year.

Her sewing abilities had soon won us the headlines in the college weekly rag. When I gained an initial promotion to cadet Lance Corporal, she stitched in place the two stripes I had passed on to her, on one sleeve only. She had promoted me Corporal. So the headline proclaimed, in the traditional mould of undergraduate humour,

"HOLT! SAID THE LANCE CORPORAL, AS SHE TAYLORED HIM UP TWO STRIPES.

Yet her anticipation was impeccable: from that moment promotion followed promotion.

With the other men of my age group, I took Emergency Finals

in February 1943 and received notification that call-up was imminent. I had firmly decided the Army would be my choice. Piloting aeroplanes or being a sailor, did not attract me, and my relatives, in previous wars, had always opted for a soldier's kitbag. Graded A1, by the medical board, they formally asked if I wished to volunteer for underground work in the coal mines. Early in May my mobilisation notice arrived and after a college party and some fond farewells, I went to Coventry for a few days, determined to reach peak fitness so that military duties might be more trouble free.

I set myself a final task to test my fitness and one morning at nine started to walk the twenty miles to Stratford on Avon so that I could see a matinee performance of *Romeo and Juliet* in the Memorial Theatre. I barely noticed the distance and had half an hour in hand, as I sat down in the one shilling and sixpenny seats of the Upper Gallery, ready to watch my favourite romantic story unfold. For a while I could ponder on the most intriguing 'what if?' situation of all time.

Right then, I had my own personal doubts about this disturbing question. It was all too easy to speculate on the possibilities that might have occurred if Friar Lawrence's messenger had not fallen victim to events beyond his control. Or, if Romeo had arrived at Juliet's tomb a little later, after she had woken up. For the lovers, the attention of the greatest playwright in the world showed them that true love can overcome death. I had to sort it out for myself; from the beginning. Conceivably, the Gods of War would not treat me so unkindly, nor fate be so forbidding. When the final curtain fell on the drama that afternoon, the uplift I received from a stimulating performance was enough to raise my own spirits. I could almost believe that the new challenge I faced in joining the army could be as exciting as that I had enjoyed at university.

For starters, my fitness paid off instantly. The Primary Training unit at Budbrooke Barracks, Warwick, where I reported on June 17th 1943, gave me six weeks to settle in to the military routines, and the unfit condition of the rest of the recruits made my initiation that much easier.

Each day after drill and duties, they were completely knackered and fit only to collapse onto their bunks. A condition generated not only by their previous lack of activity, but by a background that had stifled their initiative and incentive.

Unfortunately the areas of Birmingham and the West Midlands, where many of my 18 and 19 year old comrades came from, were an indictment of everything that was wrong in pre-war Britain. Deprivation, that presented medical care as something only available in the last resort, through poorly funded charities. Hunger, the partner to unemployment that hit every household of the working classes. And living conditions that imprisoned nearly half the population in a slum.

This was the experience these young men had inherited, so that hardly one in three could read and write, and only one in ten ever glanced at anything more than a banner headline in the tabloids. It made the advantages I had received look very precious indeed.

Fortunately, the regimental staff at Warwick had grown used to the intakes that squeezed out these poor devils from the backstreet hovels of the Black Country, and when they found an occasional enthusiastic recruit, they responded intelligently. Our platoon sergeant offered me many tips and hints about running, when he saw I was the only one from a company of 90 men who could equal his fast pace on the twice weekly cross country race. During our first outing I was able to hold on to his heels as he put on a wicked sprint to the finishing line. Like my relatives in Lancashire, he was a keen harrier in civvy street. He had represented the county at national level, although the war had deflected him from trying for international honours, and when the Barracks sports meeting for the permanent staff approached, he suggested I represent the company in the mile, the half mile and the relays.

That was enough to secure an invitation on the day to the special tea marquee as a guest of my platoon commander, Lieutenant Bentley Tolemache, of the brewing family. In turn he helped me obtain additional firing range practise as well as a high class recommendation, when the War Office followed up my potential officer status.

For the instructors, at Primary Training Centres, managing the initiation of raw recruits, brought its own reward. It was certainly illuminating to participate in a venture with such a cross section of the male population on tap, and to observe what six weeks regulated life could do to the most unlikely conscript was a salutary lesson in health education. The hardened smokers and drinkers, whose physique was nothing short of appalling when they arrived at the depots, finished the course looking fit and healthy. A controlled diet, a set routine, regular exercise and the open air, delivered surprising results on men, born and nurtured in the squalor of the industrial heartlands.

Four weeks after my enlistment I became a Lance Corporal, allowed the freedom of the Corporals' Canteen with my half crown(15p) daily pay, and able to purchase extra snacks and drink. In one of the fortnightly intakes, Bob Winter arrived from Goldsmiths', and as I had already contacted the Rev Delanoy Saberton, an old friend of mine from youth theatre days who was the vicar at All Saints', in Warwick, I felt truly settled into army life. For me the period passed quickly enough and I was soon preparing to depart on the next stage.

At this point I think the most significant question the military machine raised in my mind was in its revelation of uncharted sets of values, which I had not previously explored. University had alerted me to differences between systems of learning, compared to those I had experienced at school. Now the confrontation was between classifications; the disparity in the treatment and living conditions of the 'other ranks' and that of the 'officers'.

Perhaps attitudes had improved since the First War between 'the gentlemen' and 'the players', but in the 1940's, a rigid class system was still perpetuated, right through the army hierarchy. Compromise, there was not. The roots remained firmly embedded and fundamental change un-delivered, contrary to the promises of the democratising War Minister, Hore-Belisha, in his pre-war reforms.

Inheritance was still the key. Birth the deciding factor. Totally upheld by the branding irons of school, university, regiment and club. These icons, no-one disputed. You either fitted, or you were out. Never the twain could meet. Yet there was a survival technique, and the better actor you were, the greater the success you achieved. All the essential ingredients, including the 'special language', the 'form' and the 'manners', could be readily imitated if you were prepared to be a willing performer and accept the code. Only very few of the true begetters were competent enough to sniff out the false, acting as watchdogs over family wealth and title. Generally, this surveillance came from the senior matriarchs, determined to retain pure traditions and prevent erosion from the other side of the blanket. They required skilful handling. Yet, on our side one fundamental fact stood out, and shook the very foundations of the whole set up. Many who claimed the upper echelons of society as a rightful heritage, had no more direct hereditary reason for being there than you or me, or anyone else, like us.

They were the 'nouveau riche', stretching back to Henry VIII's 'nouveau' in the 15th century. They had simply bought their way aboard as speculative merchants, profiting at the disbandment of the monasteries. Nothing more, nothing less. Next on the line were the 'get rich quick brigade', who through their haggling and corruption, during the prosperous years of the Slave Trade, and the machinations of the Industrial Revolution, had secured rank and estates, with the bullion. With these trappings, they legitimised their position, as did the thousands who gained their position through fraud, arms dealing and confidence trick, or whatever was fashionable at the time. They shared one common interest, that of protecting what they held, and by hook or by crook, retaining the 'status quo'. A ploy that left the establishment firmly in place.

If you felt inclined to uphold that stance, then there was nothing to stop you joining it. Once you identified the problem, native cunning took over; and in my own case, I accepted the challenge. There were, of course, many of my friends who had serious doubts about such a course of action. They preferred to remain outside the system. Though on occasion, I, too, had a deep pang of conscience that echoed into the very essence of my being.

Perhaps, it was fortunate that my origins in an industrial working background did not conceal one very real advantage I had in this contest of 'going places'. My genealogical history, through the peasant families of Salts and Taylors, was traceable right back to the Norman Conquest, or further if required. All within the confined limits of a few miles of Pennine countryside. Maybe there was not wealth or Blue Blood hidden away, but there was certainly native English purity.

Many of my friends did not enjoy this benefit and suffered through prejudice and narrow mindedness, because of their ethnic roots. Families who had settled in this country as refugees (during centuries of turmoil on the continent of Europe) still found their origins a handicap, when encountering the hard faced establishment in Britain. Total assimilation was a difficult feat to accomplish, and many agonised in pursuit of it. One friend, with this dilemma, after studying law at Oxford, was commissioned and sent as a replacement to the beach head battlefield of Anzio. There, ferocious trench warfare, reminiscent of the worst encounters of the Somme, had developed after the landings of the Allied Forces in Italy in 1943. The British, commanded by General Alexander, were trying to break out from a ring of German defences and hand to hand fighting was the order of the day.

When my friend disembarked from the troopship, he had no idea of his posting. It surprised him when he joined one of the most elite Armoured Car regiments in the Army, which because of the nature of the fighting in the enclave, was engaged in an infantry role. The other officers were mainly regular soldiers, with a sprinkling of Territorials. Nevertheless, in Companies like this, the traditions of cavalry history motivated all who served in it, and Regimental honour ruled supreme. In peace time, only personal recommendation or kinship ties could earn a place in the officers' mess, and the cliques of the Sandhurst and Staff College men could make an outsider contemplate suicide.

My friend took an instant liking to his squadron commander, in civilian life a highly educated surveyor, but he sensed the negativeness of the second in command, a pre-war officer, from an aristocratic county family. Within an hour of taking over his troop, meeting his sergeant and hearing how his predecessor died from a direct mortar hit on his slit trench, the squadron runner brought a message that he was to prepare himself for a night patrol. It was to include a sector briefing from one of the other junior subalterns.

Out in no man's land, he endured his baptism by hostile fire and his first sighting of an enemy soldier, so that when the patrol returned, he slept little of the night and stood by with his troop as dawn broke and spasmodic shelling swept the lines. That afternoon, the second in command crawled up the shallow trench system and warned my friend that the evening patrol, with a corporal and four men, would be his responsibility. They were to hide out and identify the active forward posts of the other side.

With the fall of darkness, they stole out through their own troop positions and saw a German patrol ahead, preparing to move back into its own lines. The rear man of the enemy spotted them too, and loosed off a hand grenade, forcing both groups to scatter for cover. Unfortunately the troop corporal did not move fast enough and when my friend turned his body over a few minutes later, he realised it had taken a splinter of shrapnel, clean into the temple. Un-nerved, but determined to complete the task with the patrol, he identified a mortar pit and machine gun post.

His return did not impress the second-in-command. The Captain commented that with the death of the corporal, the regiment had lost one of its most experienced and long serving N.C.O's. As if in punishment, my friend received orders to undertake the next three night's patrols, as the senior ranker told him it was to provide battle experience and help him stay alive. It did not end there. Two more nights and two more fatal casualties amongst the section, caused my friend to consider seriously the canker in the other man's mind. He was greeted with,

"Brought yourself back, have you, Jew boy? How many of our lads have you seen off now?"

With his eighth continuous patrol scheduled the following night, he felt trapped in a force of circumstance.

The situation was unenviable. If he were to mention it to anyone, it would scarcely merit comment, while, as the junior newcomer to the Regiment, he had no idea who to talk to, anyhow. In such an élite environment, it was useless to point to the fact that his religious classification named him as C. of E. (a precaution he had adopted long before his army service had reached this far) for there was no attempt to disguise the racist atmosphere. So when he reported back to the source of his problem again, he could hardly doubt that it was his life on the line. And nothing short of a miracle could save it.

The last patrol had been particularly stressful. For a long time they sheltered in a pocket of bomb holes, a hundred yards from their own lines, while an artillery barrage blew itself out. Then a pair of German snipers disturbed what should have been a clear run home and when they arrived back at the wrong re-entry point, nearly three hours later than expected, their own comrades almost shot them up.

"Lucky it wasn't me on the Bren," chided the 2 i/c. "What with using yesterday's password, and getting lost, I wouldn't have let the King of Ethiopia through!"

The young subaltern's heart reached its lowest ebb. Yet help was close at hand. Overhearing this exchange, the Squadron Commander stepped in quickly, as if he might have been aware of the hidden antagonism.

"Alright Harry," he said to his captain, "Enough of that. It wasn't easy for the Lieutenant. But I want him for other duties." Turning to my friend, he continued, "The C.O. tells me that your posting records say you speak German. We want you back at H.Q. for prisoner interrogation while the Intelligence Officer is away. You'd better get up there now."

From that moment the pressure was off and he went on to survive the battle and the war.

For the unwary such paths were difficult to stumble along. Odd ones out, or those unprepared to tow the line, could soon bring disfavour on their heads, especially if it infringed the accepted codes. Recognising these, brought their own hazards; for they could stretch back generations and vary from one established group to another. Conforming was the name of the game, and deviations only tolerated in exceptional circumstances. Fortunately, my one occasion of freakiness stood graded as excusable, permitting me to play the jester (the sole person allowed to be different) and appeal to the gallery.

At the officer selection board I had two amazing strokes of good luck. The day and a half of written tests involving intelligence, aptitude and language comprehension, were so similar to those Freddie Schonell, at Goldsmiths', had devised for us to evaluate in school examinations, that I had no trouble in attaining a high score. Indeed, one answer requested, was the same I had prepared as a model a few months earlier. Just where the borders crossed, I could merely guess, but the use of these testing techniques was in the hands of a comparatively small number of trained personnel, limiting the chances. I did discover later that an ex-Goldsmiths' man sat on the board of examining officers, but he chose not to reveal himself at the time, and I drew my own conclusions. Despite this, our information was that the written work influenced neither success nor failure, and I must assume another coincidence controlled the deciding factor.

During the personal initiative checks we had to deliver a ten minute lecture on anything we considered might interest the group, and I chose to speak about the Ballet. It was such a misunderstood subject, at the time, it never failed to raise eyebrows in the army. I produced an absolute corker of a talk, remembering all the techniques of presentation I had learned over the years, and delivered a gem to fit the occasion. Even the hard bitten commando candidates voted it the best of the day, and when I concluded with a grand pirouette, the rest of the squad burst into a round of applause. 'So much for conformity,' I thought, and signalled a silent thank you for all the student teaching practice that had gone into keeping the 'C stream' alert in the town elementary schools.

My posting was to pre-OCTU, the sweat shop of an infantry cadet's career. Our camp lay in the woods, hidden beside the chalk faced escarpment alongside the Pilgrims' Way, at Wrotham in Kent. A reminder that only a few weeks prior I had struggled with Chaucer's Road to Canterbury, in far less trying circumstances. The main function of the training brigades was to toughen up the aspiring young officer, and if he failed to expire through too much perspiring, he could count himself favoured. For six weeks it was movement at the double. A climb of 250 feet from the path at the bottom, to the top of the cliff and then down again, between each half hour lecture and demonstration, throughout the working day. When the order was given on a Monday, at live firing practice, many of the married men (over indulgent with their marital rites, in the grass on Sunday) seemed prepared to scatter their rounds of ammunition into the disappearing backsides of the sergeant instructors scaling the slippery ramparts ahead. That is, if the rest of us had not placed a restraining hand on their intentions.

Despite the route marches, battle drills, night manoeuvres and the weekly dance at the Garrison Theatre, a healthy life was on offer, as the regular rations from the cookhouse added poundage to the skinniest. The atmosphere was congenial for young men who enjoyed the open air and saw a chance of progressing in the forces, with mutual interests and similar aims. I met, also as cadets, some old Rugby playing friends; Bill Rider from KHS, Coventry, and Brian Robbins from Goldsmiths', and I learned that Moggy White, my digs companion at Nottingham, had passed through the same treadmill a couple of months previously. He found himself bungled off to finish his OCTU training at Bangalore in India, after a dramatic morning when a War Office Brigadier announced that the complete cadet company must 'volunteer', on the spot, for service in the Far East. No questions answered, and no options available. The Army could be like that sometimes. This threat hung darkly over our heads when we heard that the same Brigadier was about to address us. The resulting parade revealed he was, this time, seeking only genuine volunteers, with no married men accepted, however great their enthusiasm. I felt it was something a single one could miss too.

Soon it was over, and we were despatched on a seven day driving course with fifteen hundredweight trucks and Norton motorcycles. And a useful ploy it turned out to be, permanently excusing us from having to complete a civilian driving test! Then, after a short leave, we went to the seaside at Heysham Towers by Morecambe Bay for four months of officer training.

163 O.C.T.U., was housed in a holiday camp, except the campers' chalets were our barrack rooms and the Happy Redcoats, our instructors. A back up staff undertook all the chores, for inside the camp was a prisoner of war compound, manned by Italians captured in the Desert. With food cooked and served in a manner, not to be put to shame in the best Pasta restaurants of Rome and Venice, we reckoned it a fair arrangement. We arrived on October 17th 1943, decked out in sparkling white linen flashes, adorning our forage caps and epaulettes. The only cloud on the horizon threatening to stem from the splendidly moustachioed Regimental Sergeant Major, as he called us to attention, looked us over from top to tail, and spat out,

"Officer cadets,... genteeelmen. Yer think yer muvver would be proud of yer now,... sirs? And especially yoo, cadet,... sir. Don't move, sir!! I know I must be 'urting yer, 'cos I'm standing on yer 'air. I wan' it cut. Terday!"

On the whole fortune treated me well. Morecambe was certainly not the end of the world, and my platoon officer, Captain Ravensdale, was an ex-Goldsmiths' man. Naturally as cadets, we needed something to make us suffer a little or it could not be Army life. Quickly we hung a Sword of Damocles over our own heads, raising our susceptible anxieties on the chances of an R.T.U., the sentence of 'Returned to Unit'. It was a rare occurrence, except in the most blatant cases, where in the field a Courts Martial might result, and generally there was only a slight danger of missing the final commissioning ceremony. However, the threat served a purpose and made us aware it was all up to us. What better way than that the army should follow the codes we had obeyed at school and University? Simply put, if you disregarded the boundaries, then the final reckoning might prove a disaster area. One seasoned cadet, back from fighting against Rommel where he had won a D.S.M., summed it up completely for me,

"Keep your profile low, laddie. Speak after you are spoken to,... and don't volunteer for the front rank."
Wise words in a familiar British style, if you wanted to prosper, and survive at the same time.

During night exercises, in the depths of Winter, when out on the bleak Lancashire moors, there had to be a great deal of give and take. The order to shave, in a freezing cold waterfall, needed the gift of psychological persuasion to guarantee acceptance. On the other hand, our basically pliant spirits and the supply of a steady stream of hot food, fortified our bodies against the worst excesses and scares. Within my platoon there were some extremely brave and clear headed soldiers. Their personal fitness far outdid anything I hoped to achieve, and their ability to re-act quickly in tense situations, bore tribute to their survival through the toughest battle campaigns. It was their example that taught many of us how to behave in difficult circumstances.

There was the time we were advancing as a platoon through the heather, when the 25 pounder Field Artillery failed to raise their supporting fire at the appointed moment and exploding shells and shrapnel caught us full blast, as the barrage crashed all around. Without so much as a shout or the alteration of his pace, one of our more experienced companions calmly guided us to safety along a ditch, when the rest of us were thinking only of throwing down our weapons and running. Such second nature reaction averted panic and confusion.

On another occasion, a section of six of us were in charge of the mortars, and failed to recognise that in our target range an attacking platoon was far in advance of its agreed position. The two explosive rounds we had lobbed away were descending rapidly towards the front men and we could only watch helplessly. One dropped close to the more forward group, but failed to explode, without them noticing, and the other dropped fortuitously short, behind them, in a harmless explosion. Meanwhile, they engaged in their favourite sport; sniping at sheep grazing on the distant landscape. A use of live ammunition frowned on by the authorities, who then had to pay off the farmers at five pounds a carcass above the market value. We sat tight, not absolutely sure anyone had observed our blunder, and not prepared to own up unreservedly. But our section leader for the day had no trouble in reaching his own conclusions,

"What you don't know, you can't miss," he quipped. "Forget it. That lot wouldn't notice if they were run over by a tank."

And the tension evaporated as we ran on to the next objective.

Off duty we shared other common activities. Within our ranks there was a general love of theatre, contributed by a number of actors, musicians, writers and designers, amongst them John Singer, later to write highly successful light comedy shows for the BBC and Merlin Thomas, Professor of English Literature at Oxford. Together, we were able to present a commendable Christmas entertainment to the garrison.

We named our pantomime *Everything in the Window*, and performed it in the camp theatre, which had housed the Holiday makers cabaret turns in more peaceful days. The venue that December prompted us to consider just how long it would be until such reminders would be returned to their primary function. Just then, and after Christmas leave with our families, it seemed that progress, on the road to victory, was painfully slow.

At this stage my own progress remained anchored strongly, in my own physical well-being; a fact without which I could not have completed the course. In only the second week at OCTU, a serious setback threatened me. Selected to play for the unit Rugby team against an RAF XV at Blackpool, I intended, after the match, to snatch a short 24 hour leave for a visit to my cousins, Joyce and Beryl. Unfortunately, they visited me in hospital, where I ended up for X-Rays after falling awkwardly during the game, and receiving a nasty whack on my foot. I remained under observation, much to the delight of the other stricken patients, who greeted the appearance of my cousins with a rousing chorus of wolf whistles. The Doctors released me four days later to return to my unit. Although this excused me drills for a while, as a week of field training approached, I had to force my heavy army issue boots onto a badly swollen foot.

It was there, on the moors at Abbeystead, at the evacuated shooting lodge of Lord Sefton, I valued the spirit of true comradeship. The other cadets, realising I had a serious problem, nursed me through the marches and assault courses, so that I could concentrate on protecting my injury and avoid attracting the attention of the supervising officers. It was a faultless show of team spirit and I can never overlook the loyalty of the men in my own section who contrived I had the lightest loads to carry and the easier physical tasks to fulfil.

The sympathy that we showed towards one another was something we developed from the close alliances we built up in these highly charged sessions of activity. It is something, often unfairly dismissed, in the carping criticisms that decry the value of public service, and in particular, the armed services. The real implications of not merely being concerned with looking after oneself in relationship to others, but also of caring for others (as a reward in itself) is a lesson which I have never forgotten from those war years.

At another Battle Camp, we also had an example of this ethic of camaraderie and mutual support. An older man, formerly a Grenadier Guards' sergeant, and in civilian life a policeman from Manchester, accidentally set off the trigger on his rifle, loaded with a blank cartridge. The explosion made a ghastly mess of his left hand, which at the time had been resting on the barrel, but one of our group, experienced in the art of helping wounded comrades in the North African campaign, had a field dressing in place and the rifle hidden, before the Staff Instructors had realised that something might be amiss. For weeks, we bathed and tended that hand and kept mum, until any possibility of a Court of Enquiry about a self inflicted wound had disappeared. Only when a particularly officious orderly became involved in our passing-out medical examinations, was anything out of the ordinary noticed. By then, our mission was rock solid, with no final conclusions ever reached, and the cadet graduated as a Second Lieutenant.

Unquestionably, my own fair health record had an important bearing on my ability to carry on, despite the injury to my foot. The natural impetus this generated took me through to the final parade on February 12th 1944, my commissioning into The Worcestershire Regiment, and a posting to the Initial Training Wing at Norton Barracks, Worcester. My good fortune was that this assignment did not propel me into joining a battalion already on active service overseas. Instead of reporting to an Adjutant in the quiet Vale of Evesham, I might have sailed away on the high seas, bound for the battlefields of Italy or the Far East, alongside a number of my ex-cadet colleagues.

Once I was at the Barracks, the pressures were off completely. It was comparatively easy to adapt to the life of an Instructor and pass on the military subject matter I had absorbed in my training. Unlike Goldsmiths', I had no-one looking over my shoulder for assessment purposes. The functions of company administration and Regimental duties became a routine. Pay parades, battalion drill, firing range control, live grenade practice and Defending Officer at Courts Martials constituted a familiar curriculum, with their own language and technical know-how. It was neither better nor worse than a well-run school, University Department, film unit or business organisation, varying in efficiency, as it depended on the quality of personnel charged with its operation.

At Worcester we had the advantage of a location in one of the more delightful English counties, surrounded by orchards, hills and meadows, forming a gem of rural lifestyles. I was also able to enjoy a feast of sporting activity, with tennis, football and swimming, available on a daily basis as part of our training routines.

One morning, however, when playing a set of tennis with the medical officer, he noticed I was limping and asked me along to the surgery for an investigation. He insisted I had X-rays for a bad swelling and diagnosis revealed I had received a hair line fracture of the foot, which during the healing process had deposited a hard lump of calcium around the injury. This had restricted the movement, weakening the muscles and tissues, so that the arch had dropped. Eventually, after a distinct amount of Army red tape, a Court of Enquiry adjudicated a medical downgrading. Subsequently, on demobilisation, they classed me as disabled, and nearly 50 years after that, decided I merited a War Pension!

Over the years, I have suffered discomfort, with the need to beware in the selection of shoes. In 1954, the blind osteopath Bill

Tapp, who was a wizard with similar injuries on dancers' feet, managed to make it more comfortable to bear, and keeping fit became part of the treatment. Indeed, my first marriage to a ballet dancer meant I had a constant prod to do so, for I doubt if anyone could live with a ballerina and not have a little of the daily routine of class work-outs rub off in their direction.

For me, right now, taking exercise and keeping fit has become part of the business of living, although I do not believe I take the instant remedies very seriously any more, especially when I see another fad hit the tabloid headlines and advertising columns. It serves to remind me we have all been there before.

ELEVEN

THE ROAD TO BERLIN

FAR TOO OFTEN, when momentous historical events are breaking around our heads, we become so wrapped up in our own inner thoughts, we fail to recognise the significance.

During my teen age years, with preparations for war and then the conflict itself causing untold havoc, the desire to opt out of the implications was always tantalisingly present. Thereby the drama, hidden below the surface, was conveniently ignored.

It was probably for this reason that the fabric of some war time stories, which in recent years have made such startling headlines, passed unnoticed. Action was there in abundance with the Blitzes and the Battles, ensuring that newspapers, films and broadcasts were never short of a story. After a while, the biased propaganda reports grew transparently thin, and it became a matter of ruminating in a sheltered backwater until it was your turn to face the reality.

Such naiveté encouraged a laziness of mind, which overlooked the political implications of Lease Lend, or the tragedy behind the Holocaust. For me, it was certainly more comfortable to remain unaware that Churchill might well have sacrificed Coventry to keep the secret that his intelligence services had captured the German cipher codes. Ignorance can be bliss, especially when the bombs are raining down. Like the Roman soldiers guarding Hadrian's Wall, when the barbarians invaded Northern Europe, few knew where the real threat was developing and even less cared about the longer term historical implications.

When Rudolf Hess, Hitler's closest confidant, parachuted into Scotland and the Japanese attacked Pearl Harbour, apart from a cursory remark to my friends I felt nothing unique about the events. Indeed, if we accepted food rationing together with clothing

179

coupons and the black-out, then who would expect us to increase our motivation on something more remote. Such circumstances made the consideration of revenge an academic reaction rather than a deeply held emotional conviction. If the war had developed differently and Britain compelled to capitulate in 1940, then my contemporaries and I might have illustrated another story. The chances are we would already have disappeared anyway. As students we would have offered little sympathy to the conquerors, and certainly would have obtained short shrift from them.

However, by the end of the war, it became a reality I could grasp. Millions were dead or missing for no other reason than the Nazis had decreed it; revealed in all the sordidness and bestiality of pure hate. Here was a final reckoning, beyond any fabrications that had distorted the truth on our own side. When we entered Germany, the sheer weight of wickedness revealed, united us all in a desire to close this chapter of history, as soon as possible, lest it corrupted the rest of our lives. For me at least, there was no longer an option to remain indifferent or uncommitted.

At the time I joined my unit at Norton Barracks as a Second Lieutenant in February 1944, life was still a 'bit of a game'. In the atmosphere of the officers' mess an inescapable nostalgia for the nineteen thirties hung heavily in the air. The routine of an Infantry Depot Headquarters seemed steeped in the traditions of pre-war days. Colonel Gabb, the Commanding Officer, displayed a distinct ambience of India and the great days of the Raj, as he attended the weekly Dinner Night and, surrounded by the Regimental silver, passed the port to his company commanders. The Victorian red brick barrack blocks added to the illusion; their archways and iron staircases encircled the parade ground and the cricket field.

In the centre stood the main fortress gate, surmounted by a stone tower and a whitewashed pole. There flew the colours of the Worcestershire Regiment. Each morning the Duty Officer, with his Guard, raised the flag and sounded Reveille; then at the stroke of ten p.m., lowered it again to the trumpet calls of the Last Post and Lights Out. Inside the Adjutants Room, beneath the tower, freshly commissioned subalterns made their first introductions on arrival. Tightly clutching their copy of *Notes for the Guidance of Young Officers*, they halted and saluted for their orders.

Emphasising the message of the *Notes*, Captain Wass warned

them 'to avoid the instances of laxness in discipline and behaviour, which had such a deplorable effect on the efficiency of units during the 1914-18 war, especially towards the close.' He cautioned that it was up to them, in their new appointment, to realise that 'the tone of the Regiment in these matters is set by the officers, and filters down to the latest recruit with amazing speed.' Then, with a cursory dismissal, the new man found himself released to discover everything for himself. Only then could he see, pushed almost out of sight, the true purpose. Behind the old facade lay the orderly rows of Nissen huts, hastily constructed in 1939, to house the intakes of 'hostilities only' recruits, together with the cook houses, stores and offices to make it operational.

We were a mixed bag at the depot. The senior training staff consisted of a group of older men, many who had served in the First War, with a sprinkling of younger officers who had returned wounded from overseas. Yet the largest section had newly received their commissions, like me, and awaited a posting to a fighting battalion. We juniors, with a ready rapport between us, made friends easily. Anything on offer, we accepted. Living on a day to day basis, we came to regard Norton Barracks as an interlude before the battle. We reckoned the senior members of the mess were inclined to voice their moans by a comparison to peace time soldiering. Maybe after all, it was no bad thing to make the best of a slice of life we would, no doubt, have missed in peace time.

Nevertheless, we were still distant from real suffering, and untouched by the personal disasters that were part of the daily scene in the occupied countries. So as we joined the reserve of young men awaiting the call of General Montgomery to charge into a Second Front across France, there were few misgivings. Why, in our youthful enthusiasm, should we not sweep all before us? Why should we not join hands with a victorious Russian Army in Berlin?

Monty was our shining hero as he marshalled us to our role as warriors, and we prepared ourselves for sacrifice. It was what our training had been about. Nothing more, nothing less. Now, as the large divisions began to assemble for the coming battle, it was an even bet that the laws of supply and demand would require our fit and willing bodies to substitute for any losses in combat.

In 1944 there were two great areas of conflict, Europe and the Far East. Since Dunkirk, four years earlier, the Western side of mainland Europe had seen few allied troops, except for the odd sea borne reconnaissance raid. Then in 1943, after throwing the Italians and Germans out of North Africa, the combined United States and British forces landed in Southern Italy, capturing Sicily and severing the Axis supply lines. This largely developed into a holding operation, while the main invasion geared up through France and Germany, with the Russians attacking on the Eastern side. It was a master plan, carefully co-ordinated under the combined agreement of Churchill, Roosevelt and Stalin, to finish off Hitler and all he stood for.

Away in the Far East, the efforts to combat the Japanese on equal terms was proving a wearying process. The Americans fought island by island through the Pacific, involved in sea battles whenever the Japanese navy crossed their sights, and the British, after preventing a sweeping breakthrough in India, confronted the enemy in a vicious slogging match through Burma and Malaya. There was no disguising that this theatre of war was only of remote concern to us back in Britain. Our priorities seemed much easier to define.

At Worcester we heard enough gossip and saw enough movement around us to realise that the time for D-Day was rapidly approaching. Reports from Russia confirmed the Communist forces pushing the Germans backwards into Central Europe and the Balkans, as the Nazis retreated from their earlier objectives of Moscow and Leningrad.

During the months before the Invasion the tension increased as postings of specialist officers and other ranks reached a peak between the barracks and some newly formed, highly secret, units. There was, also, a distinct tightening of security as we shepherded our freshly trained infantrymen to under strength battalions in the South of England. Leave was cancelled, phone calls monitored and a wild rumour circulated that Monty was visiting the training camps to change the staff, if they were not up to scratch. We embellished the story with that of the unfortunate subaltern who failed to salute the pennant on the General's battle wagon, rattling by in some remote part of the country. Screeching to a halt, the Commander-in-Chief leapt from his vehicle and cashiered the guilty man on the spot. Or so the report went!

False alarms disturbed us throughout the Spring and early Summer, until finally Tuesday, June 6th crowned the result of the preparations. We heard the news that the Grand Design was under way as we sat down for breakfast, and spent the rest of the day betting on how soon our turn would come. Yet, two weeks later nothing had altered, although one of the Worcester battalions had battled onto the Normandy beaches, and some of the young men we had trained in our camp were casualties. By August several wounded were back in the depot to speculate on their return to the battle, as they displayed red raw scars, missing finger tips and damaged feet. One of our fellows, Russell Robinson, who had been with us until a week or two before the Channel crossing, had lost a section of his hand from an exploding mortar shell, and wondered how he would cope later with his interrupted studies in dentistry.

I went on stand-by for embarkation first in July and again in August, but my C.V. as a qualified teacher suddenly caught up and earmarked me for special education duties, not specified, with the Second Army in France. It signified a lull while I was despatched on two courses; first to a catering officers' teach-in at Chester, and then an educational and current affairs session at Harlech Castle in North Wales.

It was hard to believe such a sudden change in priorities, but as both courses were mixed, the female company did much to enliven the nature of the instruction. And who was to question why? Escapades were all that more appealing when the accomplice was of the opposite sex. At Worcester, where there was a large A.T.S. contingent, I discovered uniform had a peculiar ability to make the beautiful even more attractive. Subalterns and commanders were as exciting and frivolous beneath the formal khaki service dress as they were when you called them Madelaine, Peggy, Joan or Joyce, although the fancy free stance of a military liaison had to adapt to army rules and respect the class implications.

One morning, another lieutenant, Benny Goodman, and me, found our activities sadly curtailed when summoned to Adjutant's Orders to explain our presence in the A.T.S. Sergeants' Mess the previous evening. As far as it concerned us, the occasion was entirely innocent. We had been out with the two most attractive sergeants on the base for dinner, and to attend an Elgar concert in Worcester Cathedral. Erudite stuff, indeed. Apparently, though, it was not satisfactory that one of our companions had been a close friend of Goodman's sister at Oxford, and a regular visitor to his home.

While the other was in Army Education, with common ground between us. In future, discipline demanded, A.T.S. other ranks, whatever the relationship, were strictly out of bounds. And that included casual partners at the weekly Regimental dance. However, we were not to be out manoeuvred and soon we met them off limits from the camp, after they had changed into civilian clothes. An arrangement that continued without restriction for many months.

I am not sure, however, what result might have ensued, were we reported again. To judge from the case of the subaltern who announced one morning that he was engaged to the dazzling blonde A.T.S. waitress in our mess, it could have spelt that, like him, we would be posted away before nightfall on Embarkation leave.

No doubt our spirits were high, and our youthful exuberance made light of problems, despite the disturbing stories that filtered back when the Germans started their V1 and V2 bombing attacks. As the armies advanced, liberating France and Belgium, we read, at last without censorship, some of the tragedies and horrors from the years of occupation. If you bothered to look carefully, you might notice the world was slowly shifting gear, taking into account the debts that cried out for repayment.

Once the short delay was over, I joined the trek into Europe. After yet another embarkation leave in Coventry, during which I performed the role of Best Man at Trinity Church for Bernard and Betty Hewitt's wedding (he also on leave as a Naval Lieutenant bound for the Far East, on the Battleship Anson) I was off by Dakota to Belgium. Right on cue, my first billet was back in Brussels, almost exactly at the same spot I had lodged in Cinquantenaire, with the school trip in 1939.

Over five years little had altered, except the city was shaking itself out of the torpor that the Gestapo had bequeathed. The enemy were still very close. Their Christmas offensive through the Ardennes, awakening memories for me of the Fort near Liege and the slaughterhouse battles of the previous war, that had involved my uncles. Yet as the push fizzled out, it was clear the next big assault would be ours. We would sweep into Germany, with a mass invasion over the Rhine, and on to Berlin. Maybe we could reach it ahead of the Russians. Our present front line stood poised near Arnhem. There, a slightly premature parachute drop by the Sixth Airborne division in September, had resulted in a bloody battle until a relief column from the Second Army ferried them back across the river. In this section of flat farmland, from Nijmegan, Eindhoven and Weisel in Holland, to the Belgian garrison town of Leopoldsburg, I took up my duties.

The amount of re-organisation that was happening in the liberated territory as the civilian population recovered from years of oppression, was quite extraordinary. The relief that the years of nightmare were over at last was apparent everywhere, as each town and village junked its yoke of Nazism, and spontaneously feted the Allied armies. We were overwhelmed with invitations to parties and dinners from the citizens in daily contact with us, and although supposedly we should not accept their hospitality, because of the food shortages and rationing, it was difficult to refuse their offers of friendship. At one festive meal I attended, when billeted on the Joos family in Louvain, the only words I could utter were, 'Je suis plein', and I was incapable of bothering which way they interpreted it!

The specialist role allocated to me in Education tactics was part of the master battle plan that Montgomery had prepared for his 21st Army Group. He had foreseen a massive anti-climax occurring as soon as the fighting ceased in Europe, until either demobilisation or a switch of armies to the Far East became practical. In the meantime, whatever the long term decision, boredom could develop through a lack of purpose, as battle weary troops grew restive in idleness. Apparently Monty had witnessed a similar vacuum at the Armistice in 1918, and he hoped his foresight would control such a debacle again.

For a few weeks I watched the preparations for the coming River crossing from Divisional level, as I linked up with units in their battle stations, while they underwent training for the final assault. I cannot forget one such session when the Engineers had skilfully erected a pontoon bridge over a wide section of river, similar to conditions they expected on the Rhine. Then, they monitored it, as columns of troops and vehicles maintained a rigid spacing, to keep the weight evenly balanced between the pontoons, before reaching the opposite bank. It was evident that transport must proceed slowly, with all extra loads removed before the crossing. However, one Guards subaltern in charge of a troop of heavy tanks, disregarded the instructions and despatched a huge transporter, loaded with its tank, over the narrow bridge. For the first fifty yards, until the mid point of the river, it looked good; then slowly, with sublime dignity, the decking twisted over and deposited the double load into the water. The pontoons rolled back, regaining their original line-up, while the driver and his Corporal swam hard for the bank. The young officer looked on, scarcely able to comprehend what had occurred, but assured of a roasting in his mess tent that evening.

Early in March, I found myself withdrawn from lecturing at the various battalion headquarters, and placed in charge of a five man mobile unit; three Education instructor sergeants, a driver and a heavy truck. Our orders were to follow the advance troops closely, and wherever there was a hold-up or rallying point, establish a base to cope with the dissemination of news and information. From there we would provide a link with the release of Allied prisoners of war, who were expecting freedom, as German territory fell into our hands. Before joining the advancing forces again, we had to secure a centre for operations so that the rear troops had a meeting place for study and leisure when their job of guarding the captured areas began. We were to be self contained and fend for ourselves, contacting local army commanders, as we drove ahead to requisition whatever we needed from German civilian authorities through the local town Burgomeisters.

The three sergeants had been chosen to complement each other. Sergeant Thomas, a schoolmaster in civvy street, spoke fluent German; Sergeant Castle was a handicrafts' specialist, whose knowledge of 'Do It Yourself' gave him a key role in our quest for suitable premises; and there was Sergeant Benn, a high flying intellectual from the London School of Economics. Benn fascinated me. He kept us alert with his economic and social theories and provided a mine of information from his own background roots, of what the war was overwhelmingly about,... Judaism and race hatred.

Our driver, Sam, was also a useful chap; he boasted a host of more unusual skills, from poaching to scavenging, although on our initial day's drive on the German side of the Rhine the map, and the frequent diversions, completely baffled him. As we progressed from roadblock to roadblock, for almost half a day,

Bocholt seemed to get no nearer than a constant 40 kms.

"Well, at least I'm keeping up with the bloody place," he kept muttering to himself.

Saturday, March 24th 1945, had dawned cloudless and bright as we stood watching the sky, alive with hundreds of aircraft and gliders. They glistened silver like, in the sunlight, as the rays reflected off the perspex cockpits and observation domes and the throb of straining engines filled the heavens. We realised we were on the final leg of the European war, and little could stop us now. In the distance the sound of heavy artillery fire marked the launch of the bridgeheads over the river, just as above one of the gliders broke its tow rope and dived down from its tug plane. It banked at right angles to the general flow, descended slowly towards a meadow close by, and as it skidded across the grass, we made a path towards it. A Corporal and Sergeant climbed out and shouted,

"Which is the road to Wesel? Our anchor's adrift, and we've a 15 hundredweight inside we need to get up to the lads."

"It's straight ahead," we said, "would you like a cup of tea?"

"No thanks," they replied, "Berlin's calling."

And with no more ado, they unloaded the vehicle from the plywood and plastic 'whale' and drove off like bats out of Hell.

Our own departure followed quickly, and my first view of Germany was a satisfying one indeed. Once across the pontoons we were in a desert of rubble and demolished buildings. Successive Allied raids, and an intensive artillery bombardment had made the bridgehead a shambles as we gingerly picked our path along a white taped route leading through a former main street. There was barely an eight feet gap in the fallen ruins, and returning traffic circulated around another pontoon, some half mile away. No civilians appeared anywhere, and the Military police guided us in convoy as we thudded into the potholes, with our loads of supplies bumping and shifting in the back of the vehicle. 'If only,' I mused, 'I could show the wardens at Post 404C this lot. At least they'd know we had returned a visiting card for the one left with us in November 1940.'

We met the same sight in every village and town. Devastation and destruction. Until I began to wonder about my motives, so complacent and pleased I felt. However, it was not without cost. We could not miss the thick groups of wayside graves, marked either by an upturned rifle with a helmet on top, or by a simple wooden

187

cross of two sticks. Many of the mounds looked hastily dug, so that occasionally limbs or torn uniform rested outside the piled-up earth and mud, while at the verge British and German signs warned, 'Achtung Minen'. We could only hope that a puncture would not force us off the narrow road , into the perils at the side. To sustain the flow of moving transport, the police bulldozed away a breakdown, instantly.

At intervals there was evidence of the ferocity of the attack and the defence. First we saw our casualties, buried hastily in a row. Next, a burned out tank or armoured car. Then an up-ended German 88 mm anti-tank gun, and more graves, until a mile or so further on the pattern repeated.

Major diversions were everywhere. Debris had closed the roads, and our Engineers were replacing the blown-up bridges, with portable Bailey structures. At these points, it was a giddy ride as the Traffic Controllers waved us daringly around the obstacles. But it was some time before we saw the first civilians or even a bunch of Wehrmacht prisoners. Then the anger of years boiled up inside and I yelled, 'Serve you right, you bastards.' Yet it was hardly likely, in all the noise, they would have heard, much less understood, what I was saying. I opted to leave them in their misery.

As the day wore on we halted beside a cluster of shattered farm cottages, where a platoon of infantry were brewing tea. We joined them to eat our ration pack. A family walked up, ragged and bewildered, scrambling over the wreckage which a few days previously must have been their home. They seemed little different to those I had seen similarly confused in France and Belgium, and certainly reminded me of the survivors in Walsgrave Road, Coventry, as they knocked out the broken glass from their window frames, that morning after the Blitz. Reaction to distress produces a common denominator in moments of fear, and as the old German grandfather (the only male in the group) turned tearfully towards the women and children, it was as if I was re-living those nights of counselling in St Margaret's Institute, with the homeless arriving at the door, carrying what little they had left, in a tattered bag.

At dusk, we pulled into Bocholt. By then, malice had almost left me. We searched for space to park the truck and Sergeant Thomas called to a passing civilian for directions. Yet he seemed more concerned to hurry off before the curfew fell, and could not indicate a landmark in the rubble that might help us through the chaos. Later I ate supper with an R.A.S.C. Transport company, who had temporarily occupied the only surviving hotel in the town centre and we talked of the disintegration of German ambitions. Somehow, their gossip of the cock-ups and disasters on our side, did not match the confidence we heard in the news bulletins. They had toiled across the miles, starting at the break out from Tobruk in the desert, nearly three years earlier. Perhaps there was an excuse for their battle fatigue.

"If it makes you feel better," they said to me. "This is their home and it's up to them to tidy up the mess."

Perhaps that was right, for unadulterated revenge is not as sweet as it looks. Already, this war had been going on for a Hell of a time, too long.

I discussed my Educational Centres with the Major in charge of the transport unit, and he suggested a recce of the local technical high school, standing deserted since the capture of the town. It was a well equipped building for over a thousand students, with lecture rooms, a library, assembly hall and laboratories as well as stocks of teaching materials, paper, paints and timber. It was ideal for our purpose and I moved the sergeants in straightaway to prepare for an early opening. However, the main field of action had already moved on, and when I contacted the Chief Education Officer, Colonel Gunner, at Headquarters, he told me to hold everything until he could visit us the next day.

There was plenty to amuse us. Sergeant Thomas flushed out the school caretaker, who lived on a smallholding within the school grounds. He owned a cow, some chickens and pigs, and in exchange for a tablet of soap, we dined, that evening, on fresh eggs, ham and German sausage. We also consumed a large amount of Schnapps, which I had located in a distillery next door. Conveniently, I requisitioned a barrel on the spot, signing a chit for the warehouse keeper to show I was removing it for analysis. He looked relieved I did not burn the place down, for there was a rumour British officers reacted that way, if disobeyed.

Some of the houses and properties left standing were roughly looted by our troops as they advanced, but they had not made a real job of it, like the Russians in Berlin. After the sufferings in Eastern Europe, the Russians had far more to recoup. For all that, some of our side did well, too. A commando officer travelling home on the leave boat, some months later, showed me a dazzling display of jewellery and precious stones he had unloaded from various bank vaults. In civilian life he was in the trade, and knew exactly where and what to look for. I later met a sergeant interpreter in Berlin, who had fled the city from Nazi persecution in 1936, and on his return used his knowledge to profitable effect. He held a portfolio of title deeds to blocks of properties in Kurfustendam, the most prestigious address in town, each one certified in his name and suitably endorsed. He purchased them for a song in the disorganised days of June 1945, when the battle was over, and the three Allied powers had barely begun their occupation.

Despite all there was to keep us busy there was a continual reminder of the problems surfacing amongst the local population. A defeat on the scale now engulfing the Germans, could only produce an atmosphere of despair and hopelessness. Normal civilised values had disappeared. Life had lost meaning and purpose as the lies of Goebbel's propaganda had proved false and worthless. At that moment, the Allied forces which he had described as impotent, were breaking down the inner gates of the Reich and storming its streets and doorsteps.

We found the contrasts perplexing enough. One moment we would hear of a bitter battle fought out a few miles up the road by a Nazi Youth Battalion of 13 year old boys, sitting behind their machine guns and firing in maniac delight as our troops advanced towards them. They ceased only when their bodies lay riddled with bullets and they could no longer move. And then the next minute, witness a group of German women chased by a handful of Russian ex-prisoners and displaced persons, released the previous evening from the nearby prison camp. Who were we to interfere? Battle drills for such a situation were not in any army curriculum.

The arrival of Colonel Gunner brought fresh orders to move to another location at Emsdetton, earmarked as a staging post. The town was full of British and Canadian ex-prisoners waiting for the local airfield to become operational, to fly them home. Our educational and advice services were in immediate demand. Another officer of the Colonel's staff had already settled on a small departmental store in the high street, for our Forces Centre, and after introducing me to the British Town Major, left me to my own devices. The arrangement worked well. The Major passed me on to the local Burgermeister with instructions I could requisition any equipment and supplies I wanted, with an interpreter to guide me around.

Chairs, tables, desks, drawing boards, carpets, curtains and lighting went into the back of our three ton truck as we journeyed from factory and warehouse to unload at our base. When something was not available I commissioned a local craftsman to supply it, while the three sergeants decorated, furnished and made the premises habitable. Even the German girl who helped us with the language, entered the spirit of the mad rush to open and organised a gang of hausfrau cleaners to tidy up our rubbish and whisk away the waste. Only one small hiccup interrupted our 48 hours of preparation. When I visited the Rathaus a second time, two British officers and a squad of Military Police were arresting the Burgermeister.

"The most dangerous Nazi in the area," confided the Intelligence Corps Captain. "Solely responsible for putting the finger on thousands of Jews. He ruled this district under direct command of the S.S. in Berlin."

"Oh well," I said, "he spoke very good English."

The department store we converted was typical of the general drapery cum furniture shop standing in every small town of the thirties. It was a sort of watered down, Central European version, of Marshall and Snelgrove in Oxford Street, or Bobbies in Leamington Spa. There you might buy your household goods, have your hair cut or take tea at the Palm Court, surrounded by a grand staircase and balconied galleries. We decided to exploit all these inbuilt facilities again, converting the main front entrance and staircase to form a concert and lecture hall, and changing the galleries into a library with pictorial exhibitions. We grouped the classrooms, handicraft studios, a laboratory and private study closets around the salons, while the prim and formal cafe became a snack bar. Sam, the driver, was in charge of that. Sergeant Castle worked wonders with the decor, using coloured panels and indoor plants to brighten up the interior and Sergeant Benn brought an old disused fountain he found stacked in the cellar, back into working order.

We had a further stroke of luck. An Educational Corps sergeant arrived in a Jeep, saluted me warily and announced he was on a mission from the Colonel. Apparently the previous day he had received a tip off, about a huge warehouse on the outskirts of a neighbouring town, which was the main regional store for Deutsches Gramophon, the largest record producing company in Germany. He uncovered a vast selection of brand new discs, ranging from the classics to the popular music catalogue. More than enough for the British army, three times over. He had a massive collection outside for us, a windfall of a bonus. It was a mint record miscellany of symphonies, overtures, operas, and concertos. Each one, performed by leading European orchestras and soloists during the previous 40 years. It would form a source of supply for our nightly recorded concerts, for the foreseeable future. While the sergeant told his story, I began to look a little more closely at him,

"Excuse me Sergeant, did you say your name was Goldthorp?"

"That's right,... sir. And the last time we met, I taught you music at school in Coventry!"

We all shared the joke and as I had liberated a case of local wine only that morning, we opened a bottle on the spot to celebrate the re-union.

The centre was a runaway success. There was a queue, over a hundred yards long, before we opened the doors to let in the first of the R.A.F. ex-prisoners. It was an emotional moment for them, wearing odd pieces of clothing, collected during their days in the camps, to supplement the torn remains of the uniforms they had worn, when shot down. A few were prisoners for over five years, and they now looked at books, newspapers and magazines they had not seen since they flew from their airfields in England.

Our resources were immediately under pressure. Classes in art and handicrafts went on strict ration, and Sergeant Thomas' language lessons were on a rote basis of teaching that defied all the education theorists. My musical appreciation concerts stretched on long after their advertised finishing time, as I tried to satisfy requests for encores, so that when we opened the second day I was already taking action to requisition the premises next door.

Colonel Gunner and the H.Q. staff looked flabbergasted at our achievement, and they immediately encouraged me to hand over the operation. They suggested I move on to repeat the triumph at other towns along the main battle route. First we earmarked

Luneburg, where shortly the surrender terms would be negotiated and then, on its capture, Hamburg. At this stage, the British Second Army attack was developing into a mighty 'swanning' movement across the countryside, delayed only temporarily by spasmodic enemy resistance, as the leading columns swung towards the Baltic Sea.

At the end of April there was only mopping up left. We recognised that the European war was over, and with the announcement, on May 1st, of Hitler's suicide, it seemed that nothing else could shock us. Yet I was told as a young boy, that only when the penny finally dropped, would I know the truth in my heart. The last weeks of the war proved the point for me, and although the denouement was dramatically swift when my own vacuum of innocence collapsed, the ultimate reality of the moment found me completely unprepared. The break through came with my journey into the heathlands of Germany. A surprise encounter with events I had scarcely bothered to acknowledge previously, turned my deepest passions inside out. I came face to face with a crime of such magnitude that I can still, after nearly fifty years, scarcely credit it.

The day after the Colonel's visit to Emsdetton, I set out on a recce towards Luneburg and Hamburg. The plan and procedure would be roughly the same as we had practised; choosing the location, requisitioning the supplies and reproducing another education centre. As I went ahead, the team would make a hand-over to relief personnel arriving from the U.K. and then join me, ready for the opening.

We drove along for a while, skirting Osnabruch and Hanover, avoiding diversions and delays by using the principal military route as little as possible and sticking to minor roads. Even on these, the flow of refugees and displaced persons could not be dodged. Some tried to hitch a lift from us, others stood dazed on the verges, watching silently; part of the walking dispossessed, of every race, who were crossing and criss-crossing the entire continent in those break up days.

Suddenly, a vast new group of people, carrying hand luggage and blankets, forced us to a halt. Yet in a spooky way, they seemed more organised and alert than others we had passed that morning. We waited as they surged down the road, like a flock of unguarded sheep, and asked where they were heading. They had walked from the next village and were angry at their fate. Apparently British troops had forced them from their homes, and deprived them of their possessions. Everything snatched away to provide help for 'das kriminals'. Seeing we had nothing to offer, they moved off in a huge block, splitting up around the sides of our truck.

Intrigued, we drove along carefully, until ahead we caught up with a couple of War Correspondents in a Jeep. They asked for directions to the 'Belsen Camp', as unfamiliar a name to them at that moment as it was to us. We had no idea that my decision to go along with them for the ride, could be so traumatic.

We need not have worried about finding the camp. Only a short distance down the road and the smell guided us. The sweet, sickly stench was something I have never forgotten. We stopped at an unimposing entrance with its guard room by the side, and just gawped through the barbed wire fence, at the sight in front of us. It was both incomprehensible and indescribable in its sheer weight of horror. Nothing I can write touches on the monstrosity of that place and although our forces had liberated the camp some days earlier, there was too much foulness behind the fence, ever to be eradicated. Let it be said I have no desire to bear witness to the memories of those nightmares again. Especially as others have described them so movingly.

We left after a short visit, paying our respects to the dead and dying, and when I was able to obtain some photographic records of the tragedy, from the relief workers there, I determined to use them, in a special way, on returning to our base at Emsdetton.

The story of Belsen and the crimes at the other places of shame, are well documented in the archives, in far nobler language than I could ever repeat, but one small incident reveals the agony of hoping to reach for an understanding. One of the villagers we had seen on the road, eventually returned to live in his home, some half a mile from the gates of the camp.

His conscience was presumably clear and untroubled as he explained to a group of us, much later, when the site had become a memorial, that his neighbours knew nothing of the events. Indeed, as far as it concerned him, it was the place that Hitler detained the most violent of European criminals, whose own state prisons could not safely house them. He dismissed as absurd that train loads of victims travelled nightly to the local station, and marched past their curtained windows, on the way to extermination. No-one heard the sound of children's cries or their parents' voices in the columns guarded by the S.S. I told the man I did not believe him. But, I suppose, anyone can believe anything if it suits their brief and they choose to ignore the truth.

On the evening we returned to Emsdetton, I mounted the photographs I had collected on large wooden display boards and with Sergeant Thomas to translate, we wrote a narrative of the Holocaust and the victims of the Nazis. Next morning the Garrison Commander organised a detachment of riflemen to marshall the citizens from their homes and herd them in long lines, to visit the exhibition. We did not relax our task until we were sure everyone had read the message and viewed the pictures. When we left, our replacement team opted for a permanent display, with constant up-dates, as the news of atrocities and war crimes came to light. We copied the presentation wherever we had an opportunity, and hoped our efforts would bear some fruit eventually.

Belsen was not a fleeting incident of revenge, committed in the heat of battle or an isolated episode for subsequent absolution. It marked the wickedest and vilest assault on man, this world has ever seen; a villainy against the most sacred thing of all: human life. Yet if the eye is blind and the mind shuttered, there can be no comprehension of that.

"British propaganda and fakes," sneered those hundreds of ordinary people we paraded in that small West German town, as they turned away at the end of the line. I turned away, too, mourning for mankind.

TWELVE

REFLECTIONS

WHATEVER WE CARE to speculate about freedom of choice there is in fact very little we can do about the most fundamental milestones of our lives: when, where and to whom we are born, and when and how we die. We may be lucky or unfortunate, with no chance to roll the dice a second time, and in so far as mum and dad are in the reckoning, the lottery they entered was the most risky undertaking they embarked on together. On reflection, perhaps my parents and I struck a reasonable enough bargain. I never wished for a change, and I hope when they died they shared that view. I tried not to disappoint them.

It might all be a game, except we have to make do with what we receive, rather than what we would choose. Riches or poverty, strength or weakness; that's our lot. But if we receive the gift of 'love', then scarcely anything else is of importance.

That was my inheritance, caring parents, and the finest Fairy Godmother could not have rewarded me more. They showed me how to enjoy life, despite surrounding miseries and woes. Granted the advantages of liberal thinking and sympathetic understanding, they led me along paths of learning, discovered by my ancestors living in their settlements during hundreds of years. Their philosophy had ultimately accepted change and development, permitting them to survive, where others failed, and prolong the family line.

My parents had accepted this challenge, too, shifting their home away from the tribal roots which could no longer support them, and adapting to new influences to survive. So it transpired my father's aim was clear and concise towards me,

"I don't want you to tie yourself to working in munition factories all your life," he stipulated. "Make construction not destruction your motto. Go out and seek what peace has on offer."

Supported by this objective it was ironic that my own self realisation occurred through war, not peace, and I discovered truth in the midst of armed conflict.

In the weeks after Belsen and the consequent disintegration of the Nazi war machine, I needed time to assimilate the stark fact that the love I had learned to bear towards others was not necessarily a universal commitment. For some the sacredness of human life did not exist. Evil was an allowable expense; it allowed a seemingly civilised nation to condone an outrage of a scale never previously imagined. Millions of Europeans approved the misuse of power and authority for almost fifteen years without one serious attempt to stop it, or even to protest seriously about it. Just what sort of society might this be?

We must accept that if nations are to survive, there must be controls on the individual. Yet in Germany, the tragedy occurred by creating excuses for wilful action, and blaming the requirements of government, as more important than anything else. In any case, restrictions on the actions of citizens can either be oppressive or humane, but if, in the pursuit of political power, the State orders it, those constraints can become dictatorial in operation. Then, with the aid of bureaucracy, propaganda and terror, liberty for the individual ceases.

In Britain we have been fortunate, except in the few years of Cromwell, in avoiding this kind of State interference. Perhaps we were able to retain enough of our communal conscience to prevent the fostering of such an abuse. In whatever way it happened, it favoured us, so that our traditions and our undisturbed occupation of the island since 1066, fostered a real sense of justice. In broad terms (despite a host of inequalities) parents, teachers and leaders, have consistently supported a respect for basic liberty. A freedom built on the words of Moses and the Sermon on the Mount, supported by Roman Law and Contract, bound together in an orderliness aspiring to moral rectitude and personal emancipation.

In May 1945, this was the lesson I absorbed. Nations rise or fall by their re-action to fundamental right and wrong, just as easily as the individual. Their peoples have an option: to choose a moral path to follow, because a national conscience operates towards either good or evil. After the debacle of the First War and the attendant financial collapse of the world economies, opportunities seemed evenly stacked, permitting the qualities of each nation to emerge in a natural pattern. For Britain the choice supported a democratic solution. In Germany and the U.S.S.R., the answer allowed the formation of a single tyrannical party state. By their own admission, they sacrificed personal independence to the uncontrollable demands of a central despotic government.

The evolution dominating our lives is the choice to be free. That qualifies decisions about ourselves and our place in society. The balance we achieve develops a sense of identity, self respect and inner calm,... our own autonomy. This, I believe, was the outstanding difference between the police state of the Nazis, and our British way of life. How much the barrier of the English Channel aided this unique isolation from others, is an open question. It certainly played an integral part in helping us conform to the reasonable demands of our society, while protecting our personal identities and individual sovereignty.

A clandestine process of suppressing this individuality, was where Bismarck and the Kaisers had their greatest success, as they re-unified Germany during the late 19th century. A one state, national identity was the sole criterion for all their policies; only partially subjugated by the defeat in the First War. Then Hitler bequeathed it and exploited it, with his 'Deutschland über alles' doctrines. Under the Nazis, opposition and personal identity were squeezed out, by torture and fear, wherever they appeared.

What better practise of enforcing state conformity than by the introduction of a secret police force and encouraging the young to turn informer on parents and friends? Could there be anywhere in history a more unedifying threat to family stability? It took a resolute spirit to defy that, particularly as the victims may previously have cast aside the very essence of their own self respect, by accepting uniformity.

This was the crux of the reason for the horrors of Belsen and Auschwitz. No individual in the Reich stood up to be counted. Maybe there were some, a select few, so small in number, their fate became an example to discourage the others. For the majority, what the national State decreed, was indelible law. Never challenged, never altered, despite the hardship and suffering it might unleash on the rest of mankind.

Seeing these people in 1945, I found it hard to grasp that amongst them not one was capable of supplying a rallying point the others could support. Amidst a galaxy of wrongdoing, and with the evidence so clear, why was the 'blind eye' conceded, as a weapon for the oppressors? Those who failed to challenge such knavery must always remain 'the poor in spirit'.

I had many conversations with Germans of all persuasions and class, when we policed their lands in occupation. They had little realisation of the magnitude of the personality change they had undergone during the days of the Third Reich, and offered only one answer to the question,

"Did you know?"

"IT WAS ORDERS. WE WERE AFRAID."

In the turmoil and upset spawned by the end of the war, that reply became an easy cop-out. Yet was it remotely possible, that fear for personal safety was sufficient, to pardon such cowardice? Was it feasible that lies, false loyalties and controls could have so lethal an effect, on plain common sense?

I cannot conceive how anyone, from my background or that of my school friends, could have proved so lacking in backbone and caved in so readily. What would the teachings, culled as infants at our mother's knee, have symbolised then?

Imagine if the confrontation had faced Spitfire pilot Harold Furminger, Wing Commander Shreeve or Captain Bill Rider? No doubts there. The comradeship of the Rugby field and the classroom had supplied them with a fierce resistance to what was wrong, and a defiant vigour to frustrate evil. That schoolboy training was plainly observable in the brave actions of daring young men like Major Frank Gilbert, awarded the Military Cross on the battlefield by General Montgomery; and Captain George Dupenois, who dashed ahead at Arnhem, with a Piat mortar, to protect his platoon from a Tiger tank, and standing square on, blew it to Kingdom come. Where could deeds of this calibre spring from, if not from the heart and an assured freedom of spirit? We gave short shrift to political philosophies that demanded a capitulation of our fundamental principles. Our rejection of the weasel words from the tempters of the 1930's gave us the strength to defeat them in 1945.

Nevertheless, the lessons of one generation do not automatically insure that failure never repeats itself. Nothing guarantees that historical interpretations stay trustworthy for ever. Brain washing is a fact of life and even the most alert are vulnerable. I heard many times, from my schoolmasters, that there was no warranty for truth in what the newspapers published. How more relevant is that warning today? Conglomerate and international ownership of the press, the journals, satellite television and the radio waves is surely intimidating; and when combined with instant replay, public relations front men and psychological persuaders, it requires superhuman vigilance to retain a cool perspective. In such a melee of opinion makers, the lessons of history remain ignored, without shame.

Only recently we have witnessed another traumatised nation, behave in exactly the same manner as the Germans under Hitler. Argentina, during the Rule of the Generals, became a carbon copy of the Nazi example. Disappearing people, torture, summary execution and concentration camps were the State weapons against individual freedom. The whole gamut, master minded by S.S. Bully Boys, who had escaped from their collapsing edifice during the final days of the war. On the nod of Peron and the connivance of the authorities they had taken up secret residence, around Buenos Aires. Then, from their hide outs, they guided their willing sponsors in the operation of a Military Dictatorship.

False evidence, midnight searches and informers were the patterns of suppression, leaving the population paralysed by fear. Loathe to oppose the Regime. After the horror was finally defeated in the aftermath of the Falklands conflict excuses and answers abounded,

"It was orders. We were afraid."

This despite the testimony that children of friends and neighbours lay murdered at Police Headquarters. Each one solely condemned on accusations of supposed political affiliations, or student liberalism. In hospitals and clinics pregnant women suffered torture with their new born babies snatched away for sale to the highest bidder. Even today hundreds of mothers make a weekly pilgrimage to the Pink Palace (the setting of the Evita legend) in the hope that they will at last hear the truth about the slaughter of relatives and companions. Of course, there were rich rewards for staying silent. There always are. Business prospered as party officials enjoyed even higher standards of living. Yet how could it be so easy for those whose parents had only a short while previously, suffered the horrors of persecution in Europe, now permit its repetition in their adopted home? Sadly this example does not stand alone amongst other national states in the world.

You either have backbone or you don't, and grudges cannot continue sealed for ever. But I retain a conviction that my friends and I would not surrender one iota to despotic dictatorship, whatever it cared to throw at us. The values, instilled a lifetime ago, always endure.

Such values become the positive markers of behaviour, assisting in the recognition of good from evil and of violent actions from peaceful harmonies. Murder, rape and robbery can never be right. When they attract political virtue, as under a dictatorship, it is for us to find the courage to condemn, whatever threats of excommunication and disapproval arise from those prepared to condone their practice. In Germany it was a lack of moral fibre that precluded the rejection of evil. What can any minority (and the Nazi Party was no more) attain if the majority revolts and refuses to participate? It is not the initial conquest of territory that produces the problems, it is in the follow-up efforts of policing it where the resistance arises. That is the message the world is slowly learning today. For there is no dignity in the support of terror tactics wherever they reign.

The reasons for the failure of courage may be open to speculation. Yet I believe that our upbringing in Britain is sound and true, whatever statistics of crime and violence try to prove otherwise. The early training we receive in marshalling an inner discipline to govern ourselves is fundamental while a semblance of the structures of a family society remain. In school the teachings still underline the balance of self assertion, within the general welfare of the community, making it possible to enhance an ability to develop meaningful relations with others, and to take pride in what we do. It can be a rewarding experience in itself as we tread a delicate path around the snares that seek to entrap us. For instance, take one small aspect of the learning process and how in my childhood it moulded an attitude of mind that when it must adapt to changed situations, it never rejected the primary model.

'Thou shalt not steal' was amongst my earliest memories of right and wrong. Hardly a difficult idea to absorb with a policeman living opposite representing the law, and my parents emphasising the retribution, if commandments were ignored. It was not all bad and sometimes droll and comic, but there was no possibility of overlooking the stark memorials around us that testified to the rewards of blatant transgression.

Victorian prisons in all their dismal severity were plainly visible in each large city and town. Strangeways Jail in Manchester was close to where my grandparents lived and on the Binley Road, near my home in Coventry, stood an ugly set of common law stocks, where not so long ago the petty criminals served their sentences. If you were a glutton for real punishment the massive Tower of London might be pressed into service, as it was for the kilted Army Lieutenant, Baillie Stewart, held there in the thirties on a charge of High Treason. I listened engrossed to such tales as Police Constable Fall related them with full authority to my playmate Rosemary and me as we walked along beside him on patrol. However, my father's story of his brother John left me in no doubt which side I was on, even though the humour seemed black, rather than cautionary.

My Uncle John found little to comfort him on his first exposure to enemy fire in 1916, when he and his comrades entered the trenches of the Somme. Red eyed from lack of sleep, permanently hungry with the paucity of the rations, and scared so much by the sheer Hell of it all, his bowels seized up for days on end. This was no mean feat for a Taylor. A family of regular habits, renowned in South Street, Openshaw, because of father John's custom to stand them in line, six in number, each morning at 6 a.m. to await their turn on the seat of the outside loo. When conduct of such regular protocol was under danger of disappearing in the stress of the battlefield, it is hardly astonishing that John felt tempted to ignore another of his father's iron rules

He was fascinated by the gold watches, silver cigarette cases and diamond rings his more combat seasoned comrades displayed as trophies captured from the enemy (or rather, robbed from the corpses littering and decaying in No Man's Land). So one night he and two friends prepared for a foray to see what they might find.

Slipping below the wire and across the mud, in the hundred yards of shell holes that divided the British and German lines, he dived into a large crater for cover, when a star shell unexpectedly illuminated the surrounding area. He buried his head in his hands and let his eyes grow accustomed to the gloom as he realised his two comrades were no longer with him. But he was not alone. Ten feet away a German infantryman sat astride a large pool of water, with his helmet cocked at an angle. John froze in terror, but as the soldier did not seem to notice him, he took a more measured look and realised the eyes were unblinking and the breathing stilled. He also noticed the large gold wristlet watch nestling beneath a field-grey jacket sleeve. A real prize, if ever there was one. The temptation was too overwhelming for the raw Lancashire lad and his controls fell apart. Swooping over the corpse he began to loosen the watch strap.

However, a reckoning was at hand. As the buckle yielded the body sat bolt upright in a spasmodic muscular movement, and at the same moment, with a heart rending sigh, released a pocket of air trapped in the lifeless lungs. It was simply too much. John dropped the trophy, shinned over the crest of the hole and made a wild dash to his own trenches, more scared and terrified than he could ever remember. In compensation his bowels reacted as though grandfather was right outside the lavatory door knocking and shouting that his time was up. It certainly was as far as incidents like that were concerned. A few weeks later, on the same sector, he lay gassed and badly wounded, never again to test his conscience in such unusual conditions. The story remained a model for the rest of the family to take note and obey.

Yet where would we be without temptation? Possible transgressions were frequently present when junior elementary school boys, in a bid for recognition by their senior peers, encouraged the fellow traveller to participate in trickery, and relieve the local shopkeeper of sweets and goodies. It looked so easy with a back turned, or a counter left unattended. I resisted that. However, in my first term as an undergraduate wariness was not enough.

While buying a tobacco pouch at Woolworths, and with the assistant's attention distracted as I paid, another student pocketed a briar pipe and walked away. Outside, when he showed me the stolen goods, I became so overcome with feelings of guilt I returned to the store to pay for it.

Halos so bright would have a short endorsement these days. Life styles have changed, and deceit seems to colour behaviour instead of honesty. Where is the border line now? Is it transgressed when expense claims adjust figures always upwards? Or where does company entertainment cease and private pleasures take over? Perhaps an Italian society demands that Customs Duties, Income Tax and corruption are fair game if everyone participates, but fraud and confidence trickstery seem the accepted road to riches in every major economic environment. Likewise there is the question of mitigating circumstances. Is black necessarily eternally jet black? Can it sometimes be dark grey?

I am not sure where this placed my moral smugness, when at Worcester in 1944 I acted as Defending Officer for a young soldier charged with stealing. He was in a load of trouble, not only the robbery indictment, but one for attempting to avoid an overseas posting and another for serious damage to War Office property. It was the latter that gave me most cause to question the proceedings very closely, because I was at a loss to understand 'serious' concerning a single broken window. It might just happen that the other charges displayed embellishment too. I felt I needed every assistance after my previous effort in defending an erring soldier for desertion, brought him a six months spell in gaol.

This time I went to interview the prisoner in the cells and discovered that it was not as straightforward as the prosecution might have us believe. Behind his arrest was a truly human interest story that should have made the pages of the novelettes.

The lad had married a few days before his call up, some eight months before, to a young lady whose brothers had been his childhood friends. They had not had a close relationship until his mobilisation was imminent and then it had been a whirlwind romance ending at the altar. During training the couple had met frequently (Worcester being a short train journey from their parents' homes in Birmingham) and they had been happy together, but after a posting to one of the holding battalions listed him for overseas service, the marriage began to go awry. On embarkation leave he became worried she might be two timing, but when challenged she denied it, and the rest of the time slipped by without more ado. Back at the Regiment, and within three days of embarking for the Middle East, a well meaning friend wrote to say the wife was 'at it again'. Upset and angry at what he considered to be her infidelity he stewed on the information for twenty-four hours so that on the evening of the unit's departure for the troopship climbed through the window of the A.T.S. hairdressing salon, and took an electric dryer and a curling set. At dawn the Military Police searched the quarters of the departing personnel and as two sergeants approached his kit bag he admitted the theft and was arrested immediately.

A Courts Martial was now in the offing and while he was in close confinement I examined the story, and decided that he might be victim of an unfortunate chain of circumstances. Anxious at the report of his wife's disloyalty he feared that once on the troopship the problems would multiply and the marriage disintegrate. By delaying his journey he might have a chance to save the relationship, although on security grounds he could not communicate with his wife, and she, unaware, believed he was already at sea.

I consulted the Welfare Officer and the Padre, and reckoning I had a fair knowledge of the evils of stealing, believed I could successfully defend the lad, while we sorted out the young couple's marital problems. Representatives of the social services visited the girl and soon assessed that she was innocent of the allegations. They decided it might well be that jealousy from her brothers was a root cause of the upset. She was eager to see her husband again to relieve his distress, and as the trial was now close we prepared to go ahead on a 'Not Guilty' plea.

The court proceedings inspired me enough to explain dramatically that stealing must imply a permanent desire to deprive the owner of possession. This young soldier had no such intentions. His temporary retention of the articles had merely provided a method of drawing attention to his personal crisis, so when challenged he had identified himself immediately as the guilty person. I convinced the tribunal, and they dismissed the charge as mistaken, recommending the soldier's release. That afternoon we sent him on compassionate leave. On his return, ready for embarkation, he sought me out to offer the couple's sincere thanks. He told me of their reconciliation, and of a baby on the way. What more could Mills and Boon demand?

In the maze of conflicting causes wronged minorities and injured egotism the differential of what might be right and might not be wrong is increasingly difficult to perceive. The catastrophes and strife of modern living force the pronouncing of moral judgements, under intense pressure. Yesterday's wisdom sounds hollow set in today's materialistic values, and integrity and honesty climb a slippery slope. In such circumstances what do we claim for those whose image represents law and order, yet whose actions spell out deceit and turmoil?

When I was in Berlin, a senior army Colonel, commander of the Military Police, called at our mess one Sunday morning. He threatened a Courts Martial, with a prison sentence, to any officer he caught 'flogging twenty cigarettes around the Reichstag.' The following Sabbath he was himself resting in jail, charged with major conspiracy to defraud, involving other prominent military personnel, throughout the British Zone. At his trial the intrigue revealed villas in North Africa and olive groves in Italy, profitably swopped for Army stores and equipment.

Another long serving Brigadier declared at his Courts Martial that the Corps Commander had accepted gifts of black silk pyjamas, looted from an ex-Nazi warehouse. This old boy network implicated the Royal Navy in shipping stolen Mercedes from Hamburg to Hull, and the RAF flying duty free wines and spirits for illicit sale on the street stalls of London.

Sorting out the ethics of such Black Market deals, when the local rank and file sell their bodies for food or a cigarette, is not the simplest test of good and evil, nor does it necessarily present us with the reality of man's inhumanity to man. Pascal wrote, 'the worst thing of all is when man begins to fear the truth, lest it denounces him'. In that cry, is the fear of those who might condemn themselves. The final anguished whimper of the guilty, framing the words,

'I didn't know it was happening. It did not concern me,' or the ultimate plea of the wicked,

'IT WAS ORDERS.'

It was this threshold of understanding I faced in April 1945. In my rejection of the excuses for the Belsens of this world, I felt a unity with everything I had inherited from my upbringing in a free country. I saluted the love and example of those who had handed me this birthright.

THIRTEEN

THE END OF THE ROAD

WHEN I LOOK back at old diaries, theatre programmes and travel itineraries from the days I spent with the Forces in Occupied Europe, I can only marvel at the wide variety of opportunities available there. At that time I was working in education and had a deep interest in the arts, the two spheres the army establishment avoided a commitment, unless it suited them. The traditional reaction was invariably the same, summed up in the Drill Sergeant's comments to a recruit he was bashing into shape,

"If you've long 'air, laddie, then yer must be an hartist."

Indeed you may just as well have declared yourself queer, if you wanted less respect at a Selection Board, and the suspicions that arose on the brow of even the most liberal commanders, with the mention of the word 'education', had to be seen to be believed. Nevertheless, by May 1945, it was orders: orders from above, in the shape of Monty himself, which altered the ball game. What was 'out' was now 'in', and education had come of age. So the word of the peach and roses complexioned 'teaching wallah' was a command, to be acted upon immediately, with no questions asked.

I sampled a little of this enhanced position when I first arrived in 21 Army Group, with the fighting still in full array. The advance across the Rhine hastened the transformation. Fresh priorities were in hand, and decisions made about four million ex-service personnel, men and women, to be thrown shortly onto the job market in civvy street. This time round there was to be no mass or hasty demobilisation and an equitable release scheme, 'in situ', organised to prevent the swamping of the available facilities.

Everyone in the Navy, Army and Air Force had a demob number, based on age and length of service, providing a rough notion of when their turn would come. Special cases called for special treatment. Those called up when students had priority to return to their classes. Tradesmen and anyone professionally qualified, in short supply on the labour market, had convenient jobs waiting for them. I fell between two stools: a Class B release as a schoolteacher, or one as a returning student. Persuasion, however, from an Education Corps Brigadier, persuaded me to opt for normal demob while staying to help the retraining plans of the Rhine Army. The arm twisting brought a promotion to Captain, and a handsome uplift in my pay and allowances.

As the fighting ceased I was in the middle of my assignment to open a group of Forces Centres. With the announcement of the plans I recognised their value, as focal points for an enormous range of educational and leisure activities, to service the troop concentrations in the Garrison Towns, which were there to police post-war Germany. The background of school and university had influenced my thinking, and wartime discussions with actors and musicians, indicated the advantages of opening combined Theatre and Arts centres, when peace came. The possibilities for such enterprises had challenged our points of view, as we saw the results of a cultural revolution, foreshadowed in the work of the Council for the Encouragement of Music and the Arts (C.E.M.A.) and E.N.S.A., during the darkest period of the battles.

Already our efforts in occupied Germany were proving highly successful, as we provided a 'clinic of learning' coupled with the arts. Now we settled in to the life of occupation troops. Live music recitals supplanted our gramophone record concerts, and we presented touring soloists sponsored from the U.K., besides forming our own groups for choral music and orchestral performances. In some of the service units we located talented personnel and other enthusiasts prepared to lecture on everything from Russian to calculus. If a particular skill or segment of knowledge was not available locally (and we rapidly took advantage of German specialist instructors) we arranged to import experts from colleges at home.

On one occasion we persuaded Sir Lewis Casson, who was touring in a production of Shakespeare with his wife, Dame Sybil Thorndike, to talk about George Bernard Shaw. He spoke non-stop for over two hours, and held a large audience captive to his reminiscences of their work together at the Malvern Festivals.

THE END OF THE ROAD

Whatever we needed, we located and put to use. We requisitioned a kiln for our pottery studio, hired repair facilities for our musical instruments, and when we presented a drama workshop we called on the Royal Engineers to build a theatre stage. Two weeks after the armistice ceremony at Luneburg Heath, I began to operate from a requisitioned Students' Union building in Hamburg, close by the Alster Lake and opposite the Atlantic Hotel. It met all the requirements and established a blue print for the whole operation. Art and music studios, lecture halls, a library, a cinema and small theatre, workshops, quiet rooms and refreshment bars.

From there we organised a series of courses to train and guide others. We helped them short circuit red tape and lethargy, supplying an alternative means to relieve the boredom that waiting for demob could so easily evoke. Often it was a matter of drawing on neighbouring resources, as in our own case, the nearby studios of the British Forces Radio Network. I reported to the Chief Education Officer at Rhine Army as follows:

'The Forces Centre choir conducted by Captain Trevor Harvey (a former BBC Men's Chorus conductor and musicologist) broadcasts weekly on BFN for all the Religious services. A programme of sea shanties will be broadcast from the Centre, in the near future. Already many of the artists, who have given Sunday recitals at the Centre, Capt Philip Cramner (concert pianist), Cpl Eric Lawson (a violinist from the Manchester Hallé Orchestra), Gunner Evan John (a Welsh tenor in the Royal Artillery), have been booked for another series of solo broadcasts from the Centre.'

The music and concert projects received a great boost, with the help of Captain Howard Hartog, a talented London impresario and music critic, who arranged concerts by a number of German soloists, including Theo Hermann, Walter Ludwig and Josef Metternich from the Hamburg and Berlin Opera Houses. Tapping into this wealth of European culture, as the war drew to its close in the Far East, was an exciting business. The air was alive again with thoughts of civilian life and preparing for tomorrow. Careers, opportunities and training were the buzz words, and our clientele in the British Army of Occupation could scarcely get enough of it. The drudgery of five years demanded a fair reward, and although the presence of war criminals, refugees and displaced persons formed a constant reminder of all we had endured, a 'fix' of culture guaranteed a revival for flagging spirits.

There was no shortage of choice. The Hamburg Philharmonic Orchestra, tours of the Old Vic with Richardson and Olivier, Sadler's Wells ballet with Fonteyn and Helpman, and at the other end of the scale, circuses and cabarets with Lili Marlene in person. Then, as the old sweats amongst us set out to return to civvy street, we discovered another dish on the menu,... leave.

At the end of July I was off on my first, via a 24 hour train journey to Calais, along a rail track under repair after its battering by the Allied bombers. In dingy and worn out carriages, some without windows and seats, we laughed and chatted across half of shattered Europe, listening to the news that the electorate had shamelessly rejected Winston Churchill and voted a Labour Government to power.

We saw it as a major shift, reflecting the mood for change, sweeping through the generation involved directly in the war. It made us more determined than ever to end the inactivity and excuses of the thirties. We reckoned a radical programme of reform would support the ideas and goals we had thrashed out in our Army Bureau of Current Affairs sessions (ABCA for short) and discussed endlessly in the mess. Then as I arrived in Coventry, the atomic bomb fell on Japan, the fighting stopped and the war was over at last.

Straightaway I met an old school friend, also on leave. Ron Shreeve, with a set of Pilot's Wings and a commission, was back from training in Canada, where a succession of conversion courses in the preceding twelve months had reflected the ebb and flow of the battle fronts. Finally he had trained for air traffic control duties and was shortly off to Germany on a posting. Ron had firmly decided on his future. He enjoyed the camaraderie of the services that gave him a higher standard of living than he could expect at home, and he was preparing to sign on as a regular officer. It was a wise decision for him. He quickly reached the rank of Wing Commander to find the security he sought.

Another friend, Geoff Spooner from Goldsmiths' College, had managed to complete a science degree before his call up to the army. Now he expected an early release to teach in London, where staff shortages were showing up in the State schools. It looked as if the policy for the absorption of forces' personnel again, into civilian life, was planning out as promised. Perhaps everything might be just as fruitful and progressive?

I returned to Hamburg in a converted cruise liner, and heard of my posting to Berlin. I was to join one of the specially formed military groupings making up the pompously titled, Grand Imperial Strategic Reserve, which included 131 Lorried Infantry Brigade, part of 7th Armoured Division, The Desert Rats. They had recently taken part in the Victory Parade with United States, Russian and French troops through the streets of the captured capital and now augmented the garrison of the British Sector. The four Allied powers had the responsibility of sorting out the disarray the surrender had unleashed, and in a joint committee of their senior commanders attended to the daily problems of government.

The Desert Rats were certainly the most elite fighting division of the British Army in 1945. They had spearheaded the drive against Rommel and his Panzers from Egypt, across North Africa, Sicily, Italy and finally through North West Europe. Berlin was the end of the road. A welcome relief where the battle stained officers and men tried to forget the horrors they had witnessed. Brigade Headquarters consisted, in the main, of a group of Londoners. The officers were largely City territorials, and the batmen and drivers, almost to a man, former Cockney newspaper sellers. In the succeeding years I have often reminisced about those days when buying my daily paper on a West End street corner. One thing is certain, our mess displayed a feast of medals and honours far outshining anything I had ever seen before.

Brigadier Gordon had won a D.S.O. and Bar, the second in command a Military Cross and a mention in despatches, each liaison officer held at least one decoration or oak leaves, and even the Mess Corporal wore the ribbon of the D.S.M. They were a wild bunch, dressed each morning for breakfast in threadbare battle dress jackets, corduroy trousers, suede desert boots and crumpled peak caps. A breakfast that always became a special occasion. The moment to open half a dozen bottles of champagne captured from the S.S. at a Chateau near Epernay. They grabbed the lot from the cellars, and shifted it in a fleet of trucks, right along the road to Berlin.

"The place was crammed full," said the Brigadier. "Just waiting for us to choose our Marque."

Most certainly they had done a good job, and that Winter we did ours, by drinking it all.

Stationed in Berlin was a curious experience, especially if compared to the other European capitals I had visited in previous months. This is where it began six years previously: then, a few weeks ago, climaxed so disastrously, for all the perpetrators. Shortly after I arrived, Jimmy Quirke, one of the Liaison Officers, gave me some initial sightings and a run down. Decorated in the Desert and again in Normandy, he subjected me to a hair raising ride in his Jeep. Skidding and slithering over the rubble strewn streets, he pointed out the Russian lines, the concrete Bunker in which Hitler died and where to send my batman for Black Market trophies. A few days later he left the army to seek peace in a monastic order, having satisfied himself that only prayer and humility might mitigate the sufferings he had witnessed.

Our Brigade buildings were in the Charlottenburg district, close by the Funkturm Radio tower, where the Autobahn to Hanover began. A short distance away lay Kurfurstendam, badly assaulted and plundered, and behind our boundaries, the wooded parkland estates of the Grunewald: a much less damaged part of the city. A large block of up-market detached houses and villas were at our disposal, including a sports club and a six hundred seat theatre, re-named 'The Jerboa', as a tribute to the Desert Rat. The officers' mess and bar occupied a large house, with a separate one for offices, and another for the Education Centre. This had formerly been the home of a sculptor and contained large studios, workshops and storerooms. I was never able to find out about the original owners, although some of the cleaning staff we employed had worked there in Nazi days. Captain Peter Carter, my predecessor, had selected the building with an eye to the variety of teaching functions we were likely to provide for the troops. On demobilisation, Peter became Headmaster of one of Britain's first purpose built comprehensive schools in Hertfordshire. He had made an excellent choice in Berlin.

I shared my living quarters with one of the technical arm officers, and we made full use of the four bedroom, four bathroom villa, behind the main mess. Our camp commandant had organised the local labour well. A profusion of services was to hand, from laundry to boot repairing, with a tailor for our shirts and uniforms, and a first class chef, from one of the leading pre-war Berlin restaurants, in charge of the food.

Brigadier Gordon elected me mess secretary and on his insistence I drove off along the autobahn, through the Russian zone, to Denmark. There I loaded a large truck with gourmet food and drink, fresh from the farms and dairies, all un-rationed in that country and available in quantity. After the years of meanness and a miserable supply of victuals, it was an Aladdin's Cave of edible delights. I collected thirty grand blue cheeses, forty pounds of smoked fish, stuffed eels, sides of bacon, legs of ham, fresh chickens and game, cases of eggs, butter and cream cheese, supplemented by jars of fruits, crystallised berries and rich syrupy jam. We had seen nothing like it ever before. And after bartering our Scotch whisky for Russian caviar, we had a feasting over Christmas we will never forget.

After that, the autobahn route became a regular journey for me. Starting a few yards from our billets, it stretched out from the city towards the British occupation zone, then on to Hanover and the Ruhr. It consisted of two, three lane concrete carriageways, curving across flyovers, junctions and underpasses, through the sandy plain and pine forests that edged up to the highway. It gave a smooth fast ride, not imitated in Britain until 15 years later with the opening of the M1. However, travelling in the Russian sector became permanently tinged with a feeling of insecurity. The unexpected developed into a general normalcy, and most journeys added another story to our repertoire.

Once we sat paralysed in our Jeep when a huge five foot wheel surged towards us. It crossed the centre reservation of the autobahn, after breaking free from the axle of a monster truck, pulling three trailers. Fortunately, in the final second, it swerved into the ditch, and we breathed again.

More often Russian soldiers stopped us to barter vodka, or a looted artefact, for cigarettes. At this time, only a few months after the end of hostilities, we faced a great deal of propaganda pressure from the Germans we met. They insisted the British and the Americans had fought on the wrong side, and that communism was the real enemy. In the midst of War Crimes Trials and the unveiling of the hypocritical racial doctrines, this did not go down particularly well with many of us. But there were increasing numbers of our allies who seemed prepared to sympathise with the scheming. For some, it became an accepted sport to scoff at the intelligence level of the Russian troops. They pointed to the mad Moguls, claiming they washed their hands in the loo pan and flushed the dirt away. Also, they berated the Siberian guardsmen for wearing armfuls of wrist watches that stayed unwound, until they could find someone who knew how to start them ticking again.

There was no question though, that the Russians, treated their occupation duties much more seriously than we did. At the very least they made the Germans suffer for their arrogance. Piecemeal, they dismantled engineering plant, machine tools and generating stations, and shipped them to Moscow. We, on the other hand, hastened to refurbish bomb damaged production lines, even at the expense of importing scarce replacements and spares from a ravaged Britain. At Wolfsburg, our R.E.M.E. technicians struggled to bring the Volkswagon factory on stream again, while British purchases rejuvenated Rollei camera plants and Solingen cutlery manufacturing. Yet a few miles distant, in East Berlin, the Russians were carting off the automatic telephone system to replace the ransacked lines of Stalingrad.

One day I witnessed an example of the fear that the Red Army soldiers could generate in their former enemies. A group of Wehrmacht prisoners was marching, under guard, along the autobahn, some 20 miles from Berlin. I was helping the driver of our Jeep mend a puncture, when suddenly a prisoner broke file and dashed into the trees beyond the curb of the road. For a moment there was pandemonium amongst the others as they muttered, weighing their chances for a mass escape.

The Russian officer quickly re-gained control and sent two of the escort to chase the fugitive. Soon they reappeared frog-marching their prisoner to the feet of the officer. He drew his pistol and in one sweeping movement, shot the German through the head. Quiet descended immediately, and the prisoners huddled together, disturbed about what might happen next. The officer replaced the gun in its holster, kicked the corpse to the side of the road, and motioned his men to start the grey uniformed prisoners moving again. They passed by, at the double, and when the officer drew level, he smiled at us and nodded a greeting.

Nonchalantly, we continued to replace the wheel. On our return that evening the corpse had gone, and although I made a short report of the affair, the powers above chose to handle it like so many similar incidents with a standard acknowledgement, 'We have our reasons: they have theirs'. And in a climate of suspicion, fostered by friend and foe alike, anything could happen.

Perhaps there was a certain logic behind the Russian attitude. Even today, in Moscow, it is not difficult to understand. Twenty-three million dead, and half a country devastated by the scorched earth policy of Hitler, takes a lot to forget or forgive. A memorial, six kilometres from the heart of the Kremlin, marks the spot the armies of the Reich finally halted. It brings the whole business into stark perspective. At least, the polished pink marble Hitler had sent from Berlin to decorate his dream of a Reichskanzlei in Red Square, became building material for the reconstruction of Moscow after the war.

The bitterness, therefore, that surfaced in those days of 1945, needed little prompting, and favours to the ex-enemy were few and far between. Nevertheless I am sure the Russians would not have shown the same eagerness as one of our senior officers revealed on giving me instructions to deliver a German interpreter back home, when we no longer required his services in Berlin.

As the war was ending, Professor Zenkel lectured on English literature at Gottingen University, while the Desert Rats swept by clearing up odd pockets of resistance. The Brigade Headquarters recruited him instantly to ease their move to Berlin, and when I arrived, he taught advanced German in our Educational Centre. As his usefulness dwindled, he wished to rejoin his family, and the responsibility became mine. Half way along the 100 mile autobahn journey to the frontier post at Helmstedt, which marked the border of the British and Russian zones, stood an army staging post, commanded by an old friend from OCTU days at Morecambe. I stopped to ask his advice, as I wished to check if the German civilian, hidden in the back of the truck, could be safely smuggled through the check point. He told me there had been a recent change over of Russian personnel, and they seemed greedier than the last bunch. I may now require a whole carton of cigarettes rather than a packet. Definitely an up-lift in price.

At the border on the Russian side, the inspection was much more detailed than I had experienced previously, and I had to wait my turn in a small queue of vehicles. When one of the guards started to untie our securing straps at the back of the lorry, I reckoned the moment had come for action. My driver was already creating a fuss about the delay and I walked to the rear hoping the Professor would keep quiet. However, the carton was enough; in fact, too much. As the soldier accepted the gift he signalled me to wait, and I was the one to feel panicky. Then he slipped his hand into the inside of his jacket, handed me a packet of Russian tobacco, and waved us through.

Our only other problem was in Brunswick, when I met Benn Toff for the first time. I decided to stop there for refreshment at the forces' Welfare canteen, where I supposed some tea might fortify my passenger, under the covers. Benn, a great cuddly bear of a man, was in charge of the J.H.C., which he ran on behalf of a Jewish charity organisation, and although I was to meet him under far improved circumstances several months later, he now stepped in front of me as I made an exit with the refreshments.

"Excuse me, nothing to go outside. It might get into the wrong hands."

"Like who?"

"Germans."

Fully realising the irony of the occasion, I walked over to an empty table in the refreshment bar, and consumed the double ration myself. Several hours later we were in Gottingen, and after a tearful re-union between the Professor and his family, I left to return to Berlin.

Occasionally, at special receptions in their zone, we met up with our Russian opposite numbers. Obviously chosen for their impeccable command of English, they were invariably courteous and knowledgeable about the arts and culture, as well as having a prodigious appetite for caviar and vodka. It was quite a feat to remain standing upright at these parties, but the quality of the alcohol and the roe, was such that it was rare to have a hangover the next day.

Sometimes, when the roster brought a night as Duty officer, the guard patrol might alert you to a bewildered Russian soldier straying into our lines. We would telephone their sector, and a liaison officer would arrive to escort the culprit back. While giving him a drink in the mess, we would ask the fate of the young soldier on his return. The gesture was invariably the same. Two fingers forming a pistol to the head, and 'Phut'. A summary trial for what must often have been a simple case of getting lost: save in Berlin, where there was never any mercy.

Such was this city which reeked to its pores of everything immoral the Nazis symbolised. It smelled of hate and death. Near our billets was the Olympic Stadium, scene of the games in 1936, where racial prejudice almost ruled supreme, and Hitler refused to honour the victory of the coloured American Jesse Owens. As we took a Sunday morning walk around the sports arenas and swimming pool, its architecture, in Wagnerian operatic style, bore all the hallmarks of rallies and brain washings.

It was the same at the Chancellery in the Eastern zone. The facings of pink and fawn travertine around the Corinthian columns and statues (or what remained of them, after the invading armies had taken a swipe) bore all the hallmarks of a UFA Film production. While the Brandenburg Gate, rising in isolation, amongst the huge piles of rubble and abandoned armoured vehicles, stood awaiting its next performance. Then, to cap even that, alongside the very heart of Government, next to the fire charred Reichstag, a Russian War Memorial, sombrely out shining the gaudiness of the Nazi shrines, and all resplendent in bright, finely chiselled marble.

The memories were everywhere. Wait until the twilight and the spectres of Sally Bowles and her motley crew would pass you by, stumbling on the side walks as they dodged the broken paving stones and twisted relics of the battle. They crept into shell splintered doorways to occupy tiny one roomed apartments, re-fashioned to house as many occupants as possible: a left over of the large mansion flats that had dominated the central districts. In that bitter Winter of 1945, they wore every stitch of clothing they possessed, to ward off the chill in their fuel starved quarters, and eked out a meal from the barest, frugal rations. Life was hard amongst the frozen dust and icy debris that covered the ruins, all that remained from the era they tried to forget. Mein Kampf awarded no consolation prizes.

However, when we visited our officers' clubs, hastily redecorated and furnished to welcome their victorious guests, it was as if we had taken a step backwards. At the Embassy, the Blue and White, and the Country Club, we dined and drank each evening amidst the pillars and velvet drapes that had decorated the luxury restaurants and grand residences, in the hey day of the Third Reich. Served by uniformed flunkies, we picked at the hors d'oeuvres and cocktails which only a few months earlier had graced the menus of the S.S. and Wehrmacht, at the same bar.

Of course, the American Clubs were choicer, with a one-upmanship we could not wait to sample. Their food supplies far outclassed anything issued to us, through normal channels. Even in the heat of the battle the G.I. was so well fed, that if we had the chance, we opted for their ration packs rather than our own. In Berlin the luxury treatment stretched to fresh strawberries, blueberries and raspberries, supported by lashings of mouth watering ice creams and fruit juice. And with the freezing cold outside, it proved enough to make the memories of banqueting Nazis very small beer indeed.

Yet reality was never far away. Down the road, behind the Reichstag building, rested the grim truth. The wildest lottery in the biggest Black Market of Europe, where family jewels fetched a quarter of coffee beans, and heirlooms and works of art, a carton of cigarettes. Nothing was sacred. Everything had a price. From Senior Service to Woodbines, from Mazawattee tea to Nestles condensed milk, and should you care to produce a tablet of Palmolive or Lux, then your evening included all the schnapps you drank and a pretty girl to hold your hand, at the Lesbian cabarets in the off-limits cellars of the Tabasco, the Royal and the Monte Carlo.

Still there was one shortage more acute than anything else. Male company. Speak to a housewife and her husband was 'kriegsgefangen' or 'tot', with the chances, nine times out of ten, he was in 'Russland'. So in dance hall, bar and cafe, sat the lonely frauleins. Chatting together, dancing together, huddled together in their fur collared coats, muffs and ear warmers as the wind outside swept the flakes of falling snow across the wasted city. No wonder our Medical Officer's main concern was to ensure that no-one left the camp enclosure before showing his pack of condoms to the Duty Corporal at the barrier. To take a soldier to your bed might resolve the difference between survival and starvation. If such encounters led to an unwanted pregnancy, then abortion was speedily available, on the slightest hint it might be Russian rape.

Supplementing the rich supply of beleaguered ladies of the night, was the decision by the occupying powers to promote Berlin as the centre of operations for the neutralisation of Germany. A bevy of attractive partners from the A.T.S., the W.R.N.S., and the

W.A.A.F., were matched by counterparts from the United States, Russia and France, all toiling away in Control Commissions, War Crimes Investigations and Four Power Conferences.

After five years of masculine isolation on the battlefields, the officers of 131 Brigade found it almost too much, too suddenly. The slog across the desert sands, the swanning over the Italian hillsides and the trudging in the Flanders mud might have finished for good, but as they idled away the months to demob, many a hardened campaigner fell victim, either to the wiles of the female Berliners or the sophistication of the bilingual lady administrators.

Our camp commandant disappeared completely two weeks prior to his release. Gone, it was rumoured, with the beautiful blond German secretary in the Brigade office. He re-appeared, some days after his departure was due, a shadow of his usual self. Nevertheless, the old boy network worked at its most efficient and arranged an extension of his service days, so that he had no cause to confront wife and family commitments at home, for quite a while. Another of our Staff Majors decided that reverting to his old job of junior insurance clerk in the City, hardly took into account his two hero medals. So he settled for a post as Colonel in the Control Commission, alongside a stunning Senior Commander of the A.T.S. who had stolen his heart. He wrote to his wife in Epping, whom he had seen for two weeks in the previous five years, that he needed,... space.

As the crash and crack of broken romances and marriages built up around us, I thanked my lucky stars it was not a problem I had to face, even though my brow might not be as sun-tanned as the others. A fact brought to my attention by my old crony Harold Furminger, who on my adoption by the Desert Rats, while he was sweating out the sun, in shorts, at an air base in the Sahara, quipped, 'Get your knees brown'.

Boredom was proving a problem; 131 Brigade's altered life style demanded a range of modified responses. They did not necessarily produce a natural fit, or even attempt to identify the problems of the years of peace which might lie ahead. A little of what it felt like was revealed in the following item, conveyed from hand to hand, throughout the Headquarters in those Winter months of 1945:

FORM OF DAILY SERVICE FOR USE IN THE BERLIN AREA.

LET US PRAY:

O Lord, who has promised that when two or three are gathered together out of thy sight, Thou wilt grant their requisitions. Fulfil now Oh Lord, the desire in our hearts for ever increasing departments, and grant that we Thy servants, having directed all our efforts to creating a job for ourselves, may remain in thy pending basket for ever. AMEN.

> *Our area which art in Berlin,*
> *Notorious be our Name,*
> *Our forms be filled in,*
> *Our will be done in Berlin,*
> *As it is not in the Desert Rats,*
> *Give us this day our daily proformas,*
> *And cancel our indents,*
> *As fast as we can submit them,*
> *Lead us not into efficiency,*
> *But increase the chaos,*
> *For ours is the YMCA, the NAAFI, and the ENSA,*
> *For information and delayed action. AMEN.*

O Lord grant that this day we come to no decisions. Neither run into any kind of responsibility. But that all our doings may be ordered to establish new and quite unwarranted regulations. For ever and ever, AMEN.

> *HYMN*
>
> *O Thou who seest all things below,*
> *Grant that thy servants may go slow,*
> *Impress our minds to make no plan,*
> *But pass the BABY when we can.*
>
> *And when the tempter seems to give,*
> *Us feelings of initiative,*
> *And when we're failing to go slow,*
> *Chastise us with a GRO.*

Mid war and tumult, fire and storms,
Strengthen us we pray with forms,
Thus will thy servants ever be,
A flock of perfect sheep for Thee. AMEN.

ADDRESS........ CCL. (Couldn't care less)
SECOND HYMN.... Too much trouble.
BLESSING
    May the grace of Indecision, the suppression of enterprise and the blessings of Idleness be amongst us and remain with us now and always.

That Christmas, however, there were faint stirrings of revival in Berlin. It was barely six months since the Russian tanks and artillery had fought, through strasse and platz, with such desperate ferocity, yet life was rising out of the rubble. Music, theatre, and cabaret, the things the city believed it did best in the world, were making a comeback, despite dripping roofs and dank derelict cellars. The Berlin Philharmonic Orchestra, the Deutsches Opera, and Willi Schaeffers Revues were struggling to make themselves heard again, de-Nazifying their programmes and their personnel, and convening in the ruins of their previous buildings.

Already damaged theatres and opera houses, throughout Germany, gained the highest priority for repairs, even ahead of homes. It clearly underlined the importance of cultural traditions to the defeated people. In the British sector, a large rambling cavern of a theatre, less bombed than the others and close to the Brandenburg Gate, restored its pre-Hitler name, the Theatre des Westens, and housed what everyone regarded as the premier opera company in the city. The Russians had the destroyed Staats Opera in their zone, and were hastening to remodel it on Kirov and Bolshoi lines, but it was not yet in operation. So the Stadtische Opera in Kant Street, made the first genuine attempt to split from the Nazi era and the staple diet of Wagner.

The new Intendant, Michael Bohnen, turned to composers either banned or ignored, and performed their work with a strong group of singers and a newly assembled orchestra. In addition, he recruited some of the old German dancers from Diaghilev days, amongst them Tatiana Gvsosky and Jens Keith, to create a classical ballet group. All this, and the unrivalled facilities of traditional craft workshops for scenery construction and painting, gave a real boost to the musical life of the Berliners. For me it was a revelation, brought up as I was to watch opera from touring companies whose scenic flats shook themselves to pieces whenever an actor closed a door. At last, I saw Grand Opera as the Europeans had nurtured it.

The Berlin Philharmonic also performed at the Theatre des Westens. Re-formed and housed by the Americans in their zone of administration, it had suffered a series of catastrophic problems. The blood letting, to purge the orchestra of its quislings and informers, was not pleasant. Musicians who had lost their jobs through a refusal to accept the party line, settled many old scores against pro-Hitler sympathisers. Even more upsetting, was the sudden loss of the new conductor, some three months after his appointment by the American authorities. One evening, after rehearsal, he was mysteriously shot and killed at a check point by U.S.guards. The resulting turmoil unfortunately multiplied, as a considerable number of U.S.Army officers tried to practise their amateur conducting skills on a 'real bunch of musicians'. However, although it looked as if there would be no-one around to satisfy not only the musicianship, but the security and political hurdles, a young Rumanian, washed high and dry by the tide of war, was lecturing on advanced conducting techniques at the music Conservatoire.

His credentials were in order, and thus Sergiu Celibidache, found himself given the chance to show what he could do. He seized it with both hands and within a short while had won over even the doubters amongst the conservative musicians in the orchestra. I went to his first concert in the British sector in October 1945, and the excitement of his performance and the sheer brilliance of his interpretations seemed pure genius to me. I could hardly wait for the next concert, and the next, as a thrilling experience in my own musical development began. Travelling between the venues where the orchestra performed twice or three times a week, made it a simple task to cover all the performances.

Celibidache refused to commit himself and the orchestra to more engagements, insisting on the importance of proper rehearsal and study for each concert. By demanding such standards he did not necessarily enamour himself to promoters and impresarios with their commercial instincts to the fore, but his methods won acclaim from his players and adulation from his audiences. In later years, after critics in London, Paris, Rome and New York had praised his talent, he collected a wide and devoted following, maintaining his insistence on adequate preparation, without which he refused to consider an engagement.

There was a further bonus for me: one of the Signal officers at Brigade, also a keen fan of the ballet, arranged for us to visit the Gvsosky/Keith company in rehearsal at the Stadtische Ballet, as well as see the opera presentations. That Winter, too, there were ENSA tours of the Sadler's Wells Ballet and the Ballet Rambert and each night we would bring the dancers back to our mess, after the performance. In time honoured fashion, the dashing officer blades seized on the chance to flatter and impress the young ladies of the Corps de Ballet. The champagne corks popped, the bubbly flowed into the dancing slippers, and we tangoed and fox-trotted until the chimes of the small hours reminded us of military duties and morning reveille. At these parties I met Sally Gilmour and Walter Gore, of the Ballet Rambert, and Celia Franca and Gillian Lynn, of Sadler's Wells, all of whom I later re-met in civvy street.

However, despite such interruptions, I maintained the daily routine of educational lectures and courses. Strictly to order, as students and staff settled into a peace time army, we were awash with regimentation and special procedures. Luckily, the compensation came from the large amount of free time, available to us. We were fortunate that within our boundaries was a well-equipped sports club, originally part of the residential estate, containing tennis courts, swimming pools, squash, badminton and indoor gymnasiums, complete with instructors and maintenance staff. In the pattern of Berlin living, during the freezing Winter months, we flooded the open tennis courts to provide first rate skating facilities. Each afternoon, hundreds of us learned to skate and dance on ice, until our muscles could take no more of it.

Helga, one of our teachers, was also a solo cabaret artiste. Some evenings, I would watch her perform at one of the dingy, underground clubs that Berlin had made so famous. A few still survived in the same premises that Christopher Isherwood had frequented in the thirties, and attempted in satirical sketch and scornful verse, to joust with the political personalities of the day.

Often the music was piano and drums, but other times a scratch band of six or eight players would entertain us, belting out the rhythms for all they were worth.

Yet, behind the coloured spotlights, the microphones and the tat, there existed another world, a world where the puny tables at the edge of the minuscule dance floors became the trading place for a host of wheelings and dealings, eclipsing the fantasy on stage. Inside the darkened walls the past seemed scarcely different: it wore a look of sordid reincarnation, a grubbiness stretching back to Blackshirt and Brownshirt, as the roads of war weary Europe brought an endless supply of cosmopolitan peoples to the gates of the city.

Some were ex-prisoners, returning from the remotest of frontiers. Others, the remnants of vanquished races and persecuted minorities, exhausted in the slave camps of death. And the rest neither cared nor knew where they came from, as long as for a moment they stayed undisturbed. Maybe the future would deliver promise, hope or aspiration. However, right now, branded as the flotsam and jetsam of civilisation, nothing mattered more than preserving the energy that could offer them a breathing space. Regretfully, the bargains and hagglings they forged between themselves could not overcome the breakdown we had witnessed. A rupture so shattering, between the haves and the have nots, that it split the world into two massive camps, divided by an iron curtain, and called it capitalism and communism. That state of the art survived for another forty years.

In the time warp of events that Berlin represented in those immediate post war months, it was not surprising that so many tried to hold on to memories of better days. For the middle aged and elderly it was bleak and uncompromising. Precious little to celebrate, bar the fact of being alive. A way of life had disappeared and there was nothing to replace it. Thousands of jobs went missing, former sinecures of the Nazi rule. Pensions, subsidies and largesse swept away: the old and retired concealing what few possessions they had hidden when the Russians wrecked their homes. Others scrabbled daily through piles of junk and rubble, hoping that something from their past might show up again.

For me, everything that portrayed that awful picture of Berlin lay summed up in a meeting I had on returning to the city in May 1946, just twelve months after the war ended. I was on a visit with another officer, Major Cyril Frankel, to negotiate a concert tour of the Berlin Philharmonic, conducted by Sergiu Celibidache.

After organising the contracts and itinerary, we had a further small task to carry out. There were friends of ours in London and Paris, who before the commencement of hostilities in 1939 were involved in secret negotiations, through the United States and British Governments, to rescue prominent Jewish writers and artistes from persecution, in the Hitler occupied territories. Then, they had received considerable help from a German emissary's wife, who, they had discovered, was now living in Berlin, under straitened circumstances. They asked us to deliver a parcel of food and medicines, although it was not possible to alert her to the visit. Unaware of what to expect, we searched out one of the storied apartment blocks still left in the central district of the city, close to Kurfustendamn. Bricks and debris stood piled on either side of the main doorway and in the gloomy, dark, front hall there were signs of the battle waged outside. On a tattered notice board, amongst a scribbled list, we recognised the name of the Baroness, and turned down the stairs to the basement.

Her door was beside the unused lift shaft, covered by a heavy metal plate, more suited to a bank vault than a home. It looked forbidding and, as we rang the bell push, we doubted if anyone would hear. Suddenly there was an eye at a tiny hole in the centre of the door, and a female voice demanded who we were.

"Two British officers," we answered. "Friends."
And then realised the irony of the statement.

A shuffling went on, followed by footsteps, and the door slowly opened on a length of chain, as a lined wizened face looked us up and down. An old housekeeper, in tattered and dusty clothes, waved us forward, to enter a long corridor lined from floor to ceiling with shelves of books and documents. In the half light we stumbled forward over scattered files and boxes. At the far end, another door led to a large room, with tall casements overlooking the garden area of the surrounding flats. It was in a rough state out there, reflecting the fighting that had damaged the exterior of the buildings, but in the sitting room was an obvious attempt at order, amongst a scene of chaos.

At least things were roughly gathered in piles. Baroque gilded pieces of furniture in one corner, small delicate tables in another, and the gold framed paintings of generations of Prussian Generals, rested against the far wall. Sadly the dusty velvet curtains were only half attached to their heavy brass rods and two crystal chandeliers hung menacingly over a lacquered dining table and chairs. It appeared that the contents of a vast mansion were all there, crammed together, leaving just enough space for the mistress to sit silhouetted against the light from the window.

"Come in," she said, in impeccable English, as we tried to adjust focus to our surroundings, "Do tell me all about your fascinating selves. And why you are here."

While Cyril explained our mission and gave her the parcels we had brought, I noticed the grandiose delight she enjoyed as she heard the messages from her friends. Someone had remembered her, and woe betide those who tried to take the moment from her. Birthrights warranted acknowledgement. She savoured hers to the full.

"Oh yes, how kind of dear Lotte and the Rothschilds. Are they well? We used to have such fun together. Are they back in Paris, or New York? Well, perhaps next time they will come to see me themselves. And you, young men,... where are you from? A handsome young Major and his Captain,... you must be having the time of your lives."

We told of our visit to Berlin and the purpose of our meeting with the orchestra.

"I must say," she said, "their string tone, these days, is unfortunately not what it was when Herbert was watching over it. But then everything changes, does it not? And you tell me you are stationed in Brunswick. Have you met the Hanover boys? The Princes? You know poor Bunny does miss his Wimbledon every year. Such a pity. And always a wonderful partner. You must spend a weekend with them. They'll adore you. I was there a few weeks ago. I'd go more often, but crossing the border without letting the Russians know you are there, is such a frightful bore."

Tea was obviously not on the agenda, and it was already dusk outside, so we made our excuses and bade our farewells.

"Do call again," she cooed, "whenever you're passing."

We stumbled into the street, with the darkness crowding around us and walked to the Jeep. It was only then we spoke of the experience,

"Makes you wonder how we finally made Berlin," said Cyril. "Hardly necessary it required all that disruption, don't you think?"

"Yes," I nodded, "we must have missed something on the way."

Yet, as we drove by the ruins of Gedachtniskirche and up the Unten den Linden, we could faintly hear the sound of the rebuilt machine that was already starting to drive the Germans along again. The sound that was recognised in the latest joke to pass round our mess,

"Dankeschon,... Bitteschon,... Dankeschon,... Bitteschon."

As it told the story of the workers on the building site. There they toiled, night and day, transferring bricks from hand to hand, to unload a ceaseless flow of lorry trailers. Five years later they had overtaken the British trade in exports. Another ten and they were among the three richest nations in the world. The conquerors and the conquered, the heroes and the weak, must one day stop to marvel why it is that sacrifice scarcely leaves a mark on the shifting sands of time.

FOURTEEN

DEMOBBED

I LEFT BERLIN with 131 Brigade in March 1946, and a month later received a posting to Headquarters 5 Division, in Brunswick. There, I joined Major Fred Butters, who had been my supervisor at 7th Armoured, and was now the Senior Staff Education officer, so the change over was smooth and friendly. With my departure from Berlin THE WAR finally ended for me, and from this point my thoughts became focused on a re-entry into civilian life. I realised a large chunk of time had gone for ever, and as I was too young and immature, in pre-war days, for any work experience, it was an unknown factor in my life.

Of course, there were many ex-servicemen from the First War prepared to offer advice on how they had survived their demob in the twenties, but comparisons were difficult. For instance, casualties in the Second War were far less than anything they suffered, and although I had lost some dozen or so companions from school, church choir and university, it was nothing to equate with the maimed and lame I saw on the streets during my childhood. In this respect the lasting memory of my parents was of death on the distant foreign battlefield: mine, the bombing and destruction of the habitat of my birth, so that there was no longer a place to return. Like many of my contemporaries, this became an important element in the process of deciding what to do next.

My posting to Brunswick came, therefore, at an opportune moment when I needed to examine the challenges that lay ahead, and I was fortunate in that it turned out to be one of the most pleasant.

Two new acquaintances played a large part in this and not only helped in the transition but became long term friends and comrades. One of these has since died, but recollections remain fondly in my thoughts. I met Captain Benn Toff when I first passed through Brunswick in 1945 to deliver a German professor to his university home town. Then, his characteristic approach to the moral problems we all faced in dealing with the German population impressed me so much, that eventually on my arrival at 5 Division, I knew I had found a kindred spirit when we discovered a common delight in sharing a love of music and the arts.

There was a further bonus. Within 48 hours of presenting myself at Officers' Mess C, I met Major Cyril Frankel; an enthusiast, intensely dedicated to the arts, who since the war has made a mammoth contribution to a vast number of imaginative ventures. Life reveals few true soul mates. I have been lucky that I have had a fair share: Harold Furminger, from my earliest days, Mary Munro as my first wife and Norma Glaiman as my second, plus Benn Toff and Cyril Frankel. Each has played a distinctive role in the unfolding of my destiny, from youth to maturity, helping me enjoy and appreciate the joy of living. Yet, those days of 1946 and 1947 when the big issue of changing from war to peace was in its embryo stage, were possibly the most exciting period of all. The electricity we sparked off in each other made our triumvirate a very special relationship indeed.

Benn was an extraordinary person. Whenever he was with you, his presence transmitted a sense of fun and well being. He was a large chap, rounded and tall, with black wavy hair and penetrating brown eyes. On leaving school he had taken a job in the theatre, starting as a call boy at the London Palladium. His sharp responses and hard work soon promoted him to assistant stage manager for the variety shows and pantomimes, and within a year he was stage manager.

It was a tough profession to succeed in, demanding responsibility of the highest order and blame for the slightest shortcoming. Shoulders craved extra broadness to bear the backbitings of artists, and an armoured steeliness to meet the standards of perfect lighting, sound and performance. Always the motto must be 'Check' and 'Double Check'; and if the scenery pulleys were working at the five minute call before the curtain rose, make sure to check again, one minute later. On one occasion, when he was touring with the spectacular musical of the thirties *White Horse*

Inn, he forgot his golden rule. He failed to check that his assistant had pressed the switch to produce the ice on the ski run for Act 2. Five minutes later the boys and girls of the chorus fell flat on their faces as they tried to skate on stage; by the third act he was fired.

For a while he became stage director to Billy Cotton and his Band. As they travelled the garrison theatres and battlefronts in the early months of the war, he learned to increase the sound speakers a notch or two to drown the noise of the Blitz. When theatre tours permitted, he patrolled the blacked out streets of Holborn and Camden Town, as a reserve policeman, before helping to establish Welfare and Social centres for the forces overseas. In 1944 he joined the Jewish Hospitality Committee, following up behind the advancing troops of the British Liberation Armies, and arrived in Brunswick a few hours after its capture. Straightaway he requisitioned the bomb damaged Lorenz Hotel, in the centre of the town.

In better days, the hotel had housed Hitler and his entourage on their trips to the Harz Mountains, and Benn's first piece of remodelling was to convert the Fuhrer's permanently reserved bedroom suite into a Jewish Synagogue. The deposed madam owner, a 70 year old wizened dragon, sat in the downstairs reception area, clicking her knitting needles and ordering around the German lackeys who were working for the occupation forces. One morning the Military Police arrived in Jeeps and armoured cars to arrest the old woman, and as our liaison officer pointed out, butter had melted in her mouth. She, in Hun like efficiency, had revealed to the S.S. all the Jews in the district and committed them to Belsen, a few miles up the road. Better safe than sorry.

The JHC, whatever our rank or duties, became a second home. The canteen, the bars, the rest rooms and the library were perpetually full and when Cyril, Benn and I decided to institute a series of concerts in the old restaurant and ballroom, it was standing room only. It seemed an appropriate alliance as Cyril's introduction to me, in the mess, was through music. He was listening to Rachmaninov's *Second Piano Concerto* on the radiogram, after Fred Butters had brought me there on my arrival at the Headquarters, and we began to chat about the recording, as it was not the usual sounds heard at lunch time in the army. We had mutual interests in the ballet and the arts, and he told me of his wartime visits to the

Gertrud Kraus ballet in Palestine, while his unit was resting there, and trips to the opera houses in Naples and Rome, during the break-out from Anzio. He had fought in the Italian campaign and at the furious battle of Monte Cassino with a reconnaissance regiment, before crossing into Southern France and North West Europe to join the 2nd Army. Recently he had taken charge of the Welfare Services at Division Headquarters, and was keen to make live entertainment available to the troops in the area.

His story was fascinating. He had gone to Oxford early in the war, and with another student, Anne Cloake, formed the University Ballet Club. He invited a string of personalities to lecture, including Marie Rambert and Ninette de Valois, and produced programmes of new ballets, amongst them Walter Gore's *Bartlemas Fair* and *Confessional*. This later work, danced originally by Sally Gilmour as the tormented heroine of Browning's poem, was remarkable in that the music of Sibelius accompanied the spoken word. So successful was the debut that Marie Rambert asked to adopt it for her company repertoire, and it features in their programmes today. I had seen it several times in CEMA and ENSA tours during the war, most recently when the company had visited the Jerboa Theatre in Berlin, and reckoned it revealed an unusual combination of talents. It was therefore no surprise that Cyril's aim was to create his own Ballet Company in London, after demob.

He had also edited and published a dance magazine, *Arabesque*, while at Oxford, that continued in production, so he contributed articles from overseas while serving in the forces. This had given him a large number of contacts in the theatre. Together with the practical stage experience that Benn Toff brought, there was a natural desire for the three of us to spark off some fresh theatrical adventure. However, one principle remained uppermost we all agreed on: anything we presented must be capable of supporting itself, as funding from army sources was almost invisible. If we required cash, the returns must cover the large costs that artistic endeavour involves. There is, without question, a risk in promoting the arts; it is an element of the lottery. Yet, with the end of a decade of hate and destruction, what better time to tackle it?

We were lucky. Cyril discovered that a famous Central European circus was idling time away in Winter quarters, a few miles from Brunswick. In the turmoil of post war collapse there was no allocation of oil for its generators and transport, nor fodder for the animals. He seized the opportunity and impressed on our commander, Major General Gregson-Ellis, to make fuel supplies, stores and spare parts available, so that circus performances might provide an uplift to troop morale. The General warmed to the idea immediately, and within days Circus Barum was back on the road. For the war wearied and demob happy soldiers it was a childhood dream come true, watching a breathtaking circus again, with trapeze artists, clowns, performing horses and high wire acts. At the grand opening premiere in the multi-coloured Big Top, repaired impeccably with parachute silk and balloon fabric, the local German Burgomeister appeared and asked for Major Frankel.

"Sir, would it just be possible for my people to come too?"

They cobbled a deal on the spot. A Germans only paying audience in the morning: British troops free, each evening. All the profits to 5 Division. It was a bonanza and a life line for our cultural events.

As the money rolled in from the fun of the circus ring and the fair, it went to pay for rehearsals, for music scores and soloists at the symphony concerts, chamber recitals, opera and ballet performances. Through our education network we arranged illustrated lectures, briefing recitals and exhibitions so that the audience had no need to start their musical appreciation from scratch, and Cyril published a weekly newspaper to publicise everything we had on offer. It brought an abundance of travel and organisation as we visited cities in Germany and Denmark to enlist orchestras, conductors and soloists, while Benn stayed strategically at base, in charge of presentation. This allowed each event to have its own special theme and decor, as we revelled in our new role of Impresarios.

In Berlin, we persuaded Sergiu Celibidache and the rejuvenated Berlin Philharmonic Orchestra to make their first post war tour. From Copenhagen, we booked the beautiful pianist Elvi Hendricksen, and from Hamburg, the Beethoven specialist, Ferry Gebhardt. They were to perform in a week of what we reminiscently called 'The Promenade Concerts of the British Army', with four orchestras, six conductors, twenty soloists and a choir.

Trevor Harvey, whom I had met at the Forces Radio Station just as the war ended, arranged to broadcast some of the concerts.

Captain Michael Frostick, another army friend, and married to a ballerina of the Danish Royal Ballet, helped with the Copenhagen contingent. And in London, Kay Ambrose, the balletomane writer and illustrator of many books, fixed for us to use the score of Benjamin Britten's *Serenade for Tenor, Horn and Strings*, in its German premiere.

Our venue was the Garrison Theatre at Wolfenbuttel, formerly the Lessing Theatre, named after the 18th Century philosopher. It had a classical styled three tiered auditorium, with 900 seats, which had taken over some important functions in the neighbourhood, after bombing destroyed the Brunswick Opera House. The concerts were a resounding success, listened to by capacity audiences, including many newly arrived wives from Britain, who were joining their husbands in married families' accommodation. Few of them had contemplated when they left home that a soldier's lifestyle, in an occupying army, combined such a variety of facilities.

There was, too, a certain personal satisfaction in the event. We were able to foster a real sense of musical enjoyment amongst Celibidache and his players. Convinced that artists deserved the best of working conditions, we provided extra rations and first class hotels for everyone, and in repayment were rewarded with some magnificent interpretations that seemed to shake off the post war blues. The performance of *Fetes*, from the Debussy *Nocturnes*, was so massive and astonishing, when the brass and strings rose in crescendo to the finale, that the whole audience stood up and cheered, and refused to leave their seats until the orchestra repeated it. Benn Toff, of course, with his eye on theatrical magic, first presented a heavily perfumed display of lilies and roses to the soloist Elvi Hendricksen, and then eclipsed it all by crowning Sergiu with a crimson-ribboned, laurel wreath.

It proved an absorbing experiment; particularly as our finances showed a surprising profit, independent of the cash flow from the Barum Circus, still touring fruitfully in the British Zone. The winter season of events that followed, benefited from the additional subsidies as concert and cultural seminar proved they could attract large audiences, if the right ingredients were in place.

Perhaps it signposted a way for the developments in the arts unfolding, in Britain, as ENSA broke up, and the new Arts Council took over the work of CEMA. Unfortunately, no-one paid attention to the provision of entertainment in its broadest sense. I have never understood the urge to compartmentalise this huge field of opportunity, classifying the arts as educational, and everything else as pop culture. Why should one not subsidise the other? Why should football stadiums and opera houses remain so far apart? More intensive use of one form must enhance the overall effect of the other. Pavarotti concerts and Bejart ballets are the very stuff of large audiences entertained in large arenas. Such a use, alongside the weekly sports fixture, could result in better facilities and more finance for the superdomes and indoor arenas. And what about utilising the exhibition space beneath the tiered seating to display the unseen collections of painting and sculpture, hidden in the cellars of the Tate and the National Gallery?

Unfortunately under army rules, nothing lasts for long. As happy as our duties had turned out to be, civilian life was beckoning and demobilisation could not go unheeded. Cyril was the first to go, and as Benn and I turned away from waving him good-bye, we were down to two, in Rhine Army terms, for anything we wished to present. However, we had other hopes riding on Cyril. He seemed determined to promote his plan to form a Ballet Company and what better time than when changing a uniform for civilian clothes? Even here, the army had developed its own last laugh. It provided all you might require. That is, if you cared to model a tweed suit, a striped shirt, a cotton tie and a pair of stiff, brown shoes.

Benn's Cockney-Jewish upbringing delivered a story for every occasion. With a father who had been a tram conductor, and two brothers with a line in sharp repartee, it was no wonder that when Cyril's demob flight became airborne, he should say,

"I just hope he hasn't to work too hard, like those poor tarts on V.E.night. You know what one said to the other, as they passed on the stairs to the fifth floor attic they shared for work? 'I've been up these bleeding stairs 45 times tonight.' And the other replied, 'Your poor feet'."

A few nights earlier, during a farewell party to Cyril, given by the Circus Barum, he related the following story.

"The fat lady in the circus has had a bit of a problem recently, and went complaining to Herr Barum about her lack of a sex life.

She threatened, if something was not done about it fast, she would refuse to sign her next contract. The boss got hold of the strong man, who much against his will, was prevailed on to see the fat lady in her caravan, after the show. There she was waiting for him, stretched out in her birthday suit on the bed. The strong man looked at the quivering mountain of flesh for several minutes and as she asked impatiently what he was waiting for, he sighed and said, 'For Christ's sake, Maggie, fart, and give me a clue'."

Perhaps though, the story he told, and we still update to suit the occasion, was first recounted after an evening at the ballet. During the performance, unfortunately, one of the ballerinas had broken the shoulder strap of her tutu. There revealed, for everyone to admire, were her bosoms, in their creamy nakedness.

Benn later went on to describe how a friend of his, a waiter at a Lyons Corner House (the Hard Rock Cafes of the day) had decided the time had arrived to better his position. Therefore he applied for a vacancy at the up-market Claridge's Restaurant, in Mayfair. The maitre d' was loath to involve himself in such a risk, pointing out that he thought the candidate, with only a Lyons training, could scarcely cope with the distinguished clientele of a luxury hotel. Then as no-one else applied for the position, he felt persuaded to give the waiter a chance, resolving to keep an eye on the fellow. That evening the new man did well. He served the soup, the main course, and prepared for the sweet. Giving a nod and a wink to his superior, he placed a bowl of strawberries and cream in front of a lady guest. Unfortunately, she leaned a little too far forward, and from the low cut dress she wore, out popped a bosom. Without turning a hair, our hero scooped it up in his hand, guided it back in place and sidled over to the manager,

'How about that? Lyons training for you.'
But the maitre d', unabashed, replied,
'At Claridge's, you always use a warm spoon.'

With such a companion around it was not difficult to enjoy life at its full zest. I produced and directed plays, organised concerts and recitals and had no time for boredom. In one thriller, *Uncle Harry* by Thomas Jobb, Benn built a large motorised revolving stage on its own tracks, so that our scene changes could be cinematic and fast. For another play, we showed the Blisses menage in Noel Coward's *Hay Fever*, as a two storey villa with rooms that disappeared before your eyes: a trick Benn and I had devised with the opera construction workshops at the theatre, but an essential piece of the know-how he had acquired from his experience at Drury Lane, in the Ivor Novello spectaculars of the thirties.

Fortunately, my senior officer Fred Butters, was also a keen supporter of the theatre, and when his wife arrived in married quarters they spent a great deal of their free time, assisting our wardrobe and properties departments, as well as appearing in roles in the productions. His interest encouraged our Divisional education duties to accent the importance of self help activities and our staff of Sergeant Instructors lectured on the practicalities of these efforts. It was a busy period of invigilating examinations, supplying teaching materials and advising on career opportunities, so that reports from friends in civvy street, made conditions at home sound far less cheerful than we were enjoying.

We heard from Cyril that things were not easy in London that Winter of 1946, particularly if it crossed your mind to start a ballet company. Although he had collected a large number of dancers and choreographers, like Celia Franca, Wally Gore, Sally Gilmour, Frank Staff, Leonid Massine and Kurt Joos, to work in the Ballet Frankel, they had contracts with other companies, until firm bookings and a tour were in place. This hinged, on the basic factor: the availability of sufficient finance. The administrators, stage and design staff were also on hand and supplying a great deal of input, but the final go ahead was still not forthcoming. We had often discussed the sources of sponsorship and the framework that would generate a regular cash flow for the building of sets, making of costumes, rehearsals and the paraphernalia of pre-performance and it seemed that some finance would be available from members of Cyril's family. Amongst these were cousins Denis and Gerald Frankel, involved in the project, since Oxford days.

The master plan was to buy a large property in St. John's Wood, London, gut it to form ballet studios, and build a complex of classrooms for a theatre school to support the dance company. This educational function specifically appealed to me and for a while things developed promisingly. Cyril had a close friendship with Marie Rambert and she suggested an amalgamation of his projected company with hers, while Sir Thomas Beecham and the Royal Philharmonic Orchestra were keen to provide the music. A number of theatre managements had shown interest, amongst them Jack Hylton, Bernard Delfont and John Christie at Glyndebourne, while Lady Cunard and Baroness Ravensdale offered their support in raising funds.

Benn Toff and I engineered many excuses to absent ourselves on a 48 hour pass from Brunswick. Because we knew the Ministry of Defence director, engaged on unravelling a secret Nazi rocket project at a former German air base nearby, we used the daily liaison flight to Camberley in Surrey as a rapid means of transport. So we kept abreast of the new productions in the London theatres, which were flourishing in the post war atmosphere. In those Winter trips we saw Hermione Gingold and Henry Kendall in *Sweetest and Lowest* (the final revue of that series and maybe the funniest) the mad, loveable Crazy Gang at the Victoria Palace, and Ralph Richardson and Alec Guinness in *Cyrano* and *An Inspector Calls:* all wonderful, stimulating entertainment. While we also managed the first night of the Sadler's Wells Ballet, at the re-opened Covent Garden Opera House, now delightfully converted back to its original purpose, after a wartime role as a Dance Hall.

Yet each time we visited, we saw the problems that were facing our demobbed friends: the liberal dowsing of cold water on bright young men, whose dreams clashed with the established hierarchies. For the holders of the reins, emerging undamaged from their shelters back in London, it was a question of re-emphasising occupation rights, demanding obedience and giving nothing away. Parental authoritarianism also raised its head. Where family businesses and stock had prospered in the climate of war time controls, siblings, released from service overseas, found themselves brutally delegated to menial duties, as if their journeys had never happened.

Gerald Frankel, discharged from the RAF at the same time as Cyril, was the first to succumb. Home front pressures dictated that young ladies must no longer suffer cavalier routines of here today, on leave, and tomorrow off on embarkation. Fathers and mothers extracted honourable intentions from both parties and talk of a future in theatre hardly smacked of firm financial prospects. So Gerald earmarked his cash for solid business undertakings, a house and a wife. All around him, a similar fate provided evidence from his friends,... security and a family base.

Each time I reappeared in those months of early 1947, someone else fell hostage. The swash bucklers of '39-'45 were no more. Back they were, where they started: in the bank, in the insurance office, cosily tucked up, in front of the fire with the missis. Of course, there were still the strugglers against the tide, and they had their moments of success. But others had to start from scratch, as they landed on their home shores with fresh personal commitments taken aboard in foreign lands.

One friend of mine, after service in the East, returned accompanied by an Indian wife; a sort of surprise for mum in her provincial world in Rugby. I lost track on how he handled the subsequent arrival of the whole of the bride's family, when the crumbling British Empire forced them to leave their roots.

Michael Frostick, back from Denmark, was in trouble, too. His glamorous dancer wife, expecting a leading role in the Ballet Frankel, instead was living in cold, fuel starved digs during a bitter London winter. Totally remote from the glitz and glitter she had, until recently, enjoyed in Copenhagen. It failed to last, and Michael eked out the remainder of his gratuity, alone.

In the initial enthusiasm of lifting the ballet company off the ground, we tended to ignore problems that might warrant examination, if things did not plan out as we hoped. However, battle drill training had emphasised the importance of the alternative line of attack should the original target stay blocked. Show business optimism we might have in plenty, yet we knew of the perils of artistic adventure. As time passed by, with financial headaches unsolved, it was fortunate that most of the dancers were able to pursue their day to day commitments without interruption.

Benn Toff was of a similar mould. When he left Brunswick, in 1947, he quickly re-established himself in the theatre and recording business again, on a part time basis, providing him the means to spend his spare hours, each day, on the dance project.

But it became apparent that financial difficulties could spell delay, particularly as we determined to start only with full funding. So the opening was postponed and debacle avoided. Temporarily, Cyril returned to Oxford and re-commenced his long interrupted law studies, supported by the special grant to ex-servicemen. He joined the hundreds of others in a similar predicament, all sharing the common bond of war-interrupted studentship. The reversion was not a straightforward metamorphosis. It soon revealed the unrealities that the tight structure of service life had imposed. In forming a shelter, part of a huge state supported edifice, it was only relevant within its own ambit of creation: to fight wars. Civilian life required a different structure, a framework that springs from the individual. Primarily, it demanded, that back at University, the learning process must begin with a period of adjustment.

Many discovered this transition difficult and regretted the alterations to lifestyles involved. It was not only that some fellow students had just left school, and were almost a generation distant, it was in the attitude of those who had remained behind. Meeting teachers, at lecture and tutorials, who had spent an era behind closed walls, missing the war, and were unaware the way the world had changed outside, meant a realignment of the teacher/pupil relationship. Adding to the confusion, in that world outside, were bank managers, officials, landladies and the rest, who had not changed either. A whole stratum of civilised folk, oblivious to the private anguish of Alamein, the River Kwai, or Belsen, expecting the returnees to see both rhyme and reason in studies, last considered, five years previously.

The places of learning had scarcely adjusted either. The changes were in us: everyone that much older and life stained. Ideals we once chased, looked faded and forgotten; studies and research required digesting, unsupported by frivolous pastimes, as each spoke of their previous terms at college as 'in my time'. Schoolboys did not match up to comrades; verging on thirty was already late for trainees, and unity of purpose appeared somewhat old fashioned. So it was that security became a password, and risks accepted only at peril. Cyril wrote to me of these unexpected consequences and their effect on the people around him. It made me determined to try to avoid the pitfalls.

In my final weeks I became a student again, by attending the Forces Educational College at Gottingen University. Freed of military duty, it brought a taste of peace, to read once more in the library, attend seminars and to indulge in a few college theatricals. Decision time was approaching. I did not wish to extend my army service further, despite a late appeal from the Educational Brigadier offering promotion and a regular commission. No doubt there would be disappointments after the uniform rested in the wardrobe. Then quickly, as I uncovered the small print behind the administration of further education grants, I felt the chill hand of bureaucracy. Although there was a possibility of a place at Oxford and another at University College, London, a stereotyped letter informed me, my only option was to return to Goldsmiths', where I had already been a student. It was not the end of the world, and the promise of six terms in London could hardly be bad, particularly with the cash backing of three months' paid, demob leave, and a war gratuity of £90. So that is what it had to be.

Although I was almost twenty-four, I could count on a slight nod of satisfaction, in that, so far I had avoided permanent attachments. Initial aims to remain single were still intact, despite my involvement in two serious romances. One, an intriguing brunette, Trudie, was an actress in our Drama Company at 5 Division and a relief worker in the Displaced Persons camps. Shame that she decided her work was more important to her than love, and left for Israel to organise the hand over from the British.

The other came from my youth in Coventry, and stirred deeply felt passions from the past when I met her again, during a leave from Germany. Nora, with the ravishing blonde hair and fair skin inherited from Dutch ancestors, had previously been a schoolgirl tennis partner and almost made me lose my resolve. Though I was lucky to survive the syndrome that had struck a large percentage of my released comrades. Now they discovered those wartime promises, sealed with wedding bells, meant that relationships could be too easily cobbled together, under the influence of embarkation leaves and enforced partings. In this atmosphere, I began to regard my preference for further studies as the chance to adjust to a post war environment.

My Coventry contacts from schooldays, also realised, as I did, that a return to their hometown seemed thwarted by a lack of facilities, as a result of the bombings. On demob they, too, were deciding either on University places, or movement away; although our purely private reasons were not necessarily applicable to other ex-service personnel, who were planning where next to seek adventure. There were a number of possibilities to hand. Schemes in commonwealth countries, like the Ground Nuts plan, and the exploitation of oil reserves in the Middle East needed engineers and administrators, while wartime training, particularly in flying,

Major FRED BUTTERS and
BLT in Harz mountains, 1946.

BENN TOFF on stage.

SERGIU CELIBIDACHE and the BERLIN PHILHARMONIC , 1946.

HONOR FROST and CELIA FRANCA planning their ballet *Khadra*, Paris, 1947

The Coronation procession from Park Lane, 1953.

STUART LEGG.

JOHN GRIERSON.

Sir STEPHEN TALLENTS.

Sir ARTHUR ELTON.

CYRIL FRANKEL and
PETER FINCH on location.

MARY MUNRO as Giselle.

JULIAN BRAUNSWEG in San Sebastian, 1955.

10.0 THE SCIENTIST REPLIES

A programme in which viewers' questions are answered by a panel of scientists.

Tonight's Panel :

Sir Harold Spencer Jones, F.R.S.
Professor Sir Alexander Todd, F.R.S.
Professor H. S. W. Massey, F.R.S.
Professor P. B. Medawar, F.R.S.

Chairman : Jeremy Thorpe
Scientific Adviser : Norman Macqueen
Directed by Brian Taylor.

The Radio Show, 1957: MURIEL YOUNG, NORMAN MACQUEEN and BLT.

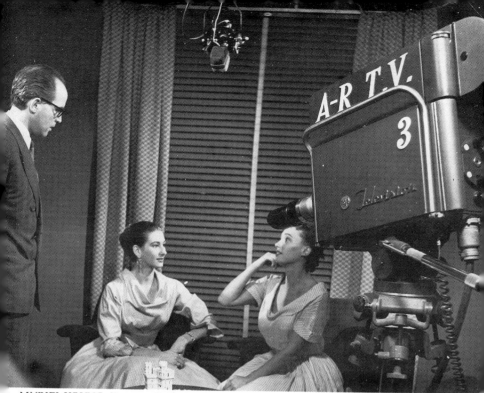

MURIEL YOUNG discusses Ballerina MARILYN BURR's appearance on *Kingsway Corner* with BLT.

BLT in a hot moment with HARRY BELAFONTE on *Cool for Cats*.

Vocalist TONI CARROLL prepares her debut on *Cool for Cats*.

which had taken many young men to Canada, the United States and South Africa, gave an encouraging reason for some to try a stint in diverse locations. Additionally there was a huge demand for help of all kinds, from the aid agencies working in the battle devastated lands of Europe and the Far East. Into these areas of opportunity, many friends now found a special niche.

Cyril Frankel pursued his ideas for as long as possible from Oxford. However, hopes of a ballet company began to fade, and with parental pressure suggesting a lawyer's brief, he chose, instead, to find a temporary niche in theatre and film. Final commitments were slow in arriving and more time needed to make the big decision, but after so many years of little else than pulling a trigger, it was barely surprising.

It was interesting to compare what was happening to those, not involved in the services, for one reason or another. Perhaps it was all a matter of freedom of choice. It is unlikely that Philip Larkin would have turned aside from poetry, whatever the climate of peace or war; and equally, after university, would have probably always chosen librarianship. Others, by-passing the forces on leaving school, elected for the path of science and journeyed along that avenue into research or higher scholarship, just as they would have done in normal times. Len Burroughs became the Director of Long Ashton Agricultural Research Laboratory, Don Walker advanced the studies of liver fluke in sheep, and John Gloster emerged to be a leading Professor of Ophthalmology.

Similarly, ballerina Celia Franca had never swerved from her total commitment to dance since the age of nine, and neither wartime privations nor the demise of the Ballet Frankel, could stop her achieving what she determined to do. That she did most admirably, by leaving London behind her and founding the universally acclaimed National Ballet of Canada. It emphasised her instinctive ability to be in the right place at the right moment, plus sufficient self-confidence to wait patiently for fate to unwind.

So my choice was obvious, and on a day in September 1947, I returned to the University and its books, if not wholly to its ideas.

FIFTEEN

JOHN GRIERSON AND THE DOCUMENTARY FILM

GOING BACK TO Goldsmiths' seemed a wise enough decision at first, but after a few weeks I began to have my doubts.

It was a grey period of our history, bedevilled by a bitterly cold winter, power shortages, transport breakdowns and an air of frustration. It was as if everyone suffered from the same hangover of duress, distinguished by miseries of unheated buildings, empty bomb sites and neglected public services. Even the colours around us were a grim reminder of the battlefields. Drab sweaty yellows, shit browns, vomit greens and depressed purple that sought to re-echo the army khakis and the air force blues we had lived with for so long. Every wall and floor surface became a reminder of the decoration in barrack room and billet, and in a hopeless jumble we recalled constantly what we had been. It looked as though we could not cast out the past, wearing the odd piece of service kit with our demob suits: a forage cap, a collarless War Department shirt, a Naval donkey jacket and a webbing haversack to pack our National loaf sandwiches and Spam for lunch. And girl friends had their uniform too, a home produced leather hand bag, a re-cycled woolly sweater and a parachute silk blouse. No wonder we all displayed the same faded features; we had, as a nation, become familiarised to the smell of boiled cabbage, the taste of defrosted cod and a one bar electric fire.

As my first term ended I commenced a teaching assessment to check if my five year old Certificate was in need of an upgrade. Everything I wanted to avoid, I had to confront. A blitzed damaged school in South London, flapping tar paper to cover empty window frames, dripping ceilings whenever it rained, and a central heating system, splattering and hissing, yet never surrendering one degree of heat into the classrooms. The staff were fraught and humourless, past the age to seek a better post and unnaturally young to retire. In mercy someone should have placed them out to grass, to masticate on their faded ideals and devastated egos. Two weeks of hearing their moans about the routine, the equipment and why they had missed a call-up, was enough to have me scurrying back to my tutor in revolt.

I won my case and abandoned any thoughts of a career as a schoolmaster. Yet, for some of my fellow students it was part of the deal. If you were to accept and be accepted into the old routine, then a chunk of compromise was the sole rule of the game. On the other hand, should you desire fresh horizons, then you were on your own. Our little group of ballet enthusiasts had found this out to our cost; there was no easy option while the time bomb from yesterday still ticked over, as strongly as ever,... the Establishment. Nothing had changed that; neither in the higher echelons of society, nor in the lower. It could be argued its autonomy was even more deeply entrenched than before.

One thing is certain, the English Establishment is unique in its control of all the commanding heights of life. There is nowhere that is free from the cartel formed by the official and orthodox forces of politics, religion and culture. Because no other nation has anything quite like it, it almost represents a bonus. The assemblies of Royalty, Church, County and State combine, with a harmony that overcomes understanding, yet speaks for the kingdom in gathering any divergent voice there may be, so that eventually they will join the chorus too. Altogether it moulds the liberalising spirit in our parliamentary lottery, and smoothes out everything to form a great unity, with the smallest of differences, which typify the English character. In the end the whig becomes the tory, the socialist becomes conservative and the rebel of yesteryear, the hero of today. So it is that the whole complicated shooting match eats its own tail.

Over the centuries it has received its challengers, from Bunyan to Shaw, Wat Tyler to Nye Bevan, but in the end it wins you over, often with the flattery of social bribery and a place in the House of Lords, which makes every other corrupt system dull and flat footed in comparison.

In cultural affairs, the passionate heart of any nation, Britain has come to operate as tight a control of the creative forces as any authoritarian regime. So from the Roundheads and the Puritans, the Roman Catholics and the Non-Conformists, it has embraced them all, whether poets or politicians, disclosing its greatest strength and showing a unity of purpose that its most dangerous enemies are unable to match.

Importantly, this exists in far more than one lonely aspect of our complicated society. It spreads itself into every corner of our lives. It is just as difficult for a young person to break through the closed-shop controls of a Trades Union, as it is for the un-initiated to enter the Royal Enclosure at Ascot. Only the appropriate membership and admission procedures grant the key to any peculiar old boy network, whether it is medicine, Lloyds or the police force. Without the necessary introduction, the benefits of belonging and taking part remain closed for ever. I had manoeuvred skilfully around one of the mightiest upholders of this masonry, the Armed Forces. As I had become adept at playing the game, so I had progressed, right to the moment of giving it all up. My acceptance of the half colonel's pip and crown, as I was about to leave, could have ensured a pleasant ride for life. Now, by rejecting the offer, I faced the tests and obstacles that starting out on a different career demanded, for admittance through its restricted gateway.

What was clear was the glimpse of the Educational Establishment I contacted on my return to Goldsmiths' no longer appealed to me as it had done five years before. I felt more attracted towards the areas of public entertainment, which had opened up for me in the closing months of my war service. Unfortunately, the momentum of the ballet project was dying, and the educational role I had considered within its framework was not going to happen. However, I had received a seductive taste of professional theatre and it was towards this I began to move. As it turned out, like so many other things in life, as the door to one venture closed, another began to open.

Obviously, Cyril Frankel had felt the collapse of his plans much more keenly than I had, and, at Oxford, had realised that further progress on a path to qualify as a lawyer would leave him with a basketful of unachieved desires. As I picked up my books that autumn, he left his at Oriel College, to try his luck in the film industry. To start earning a place from scratch in this complex animal was as notoriously difficult as gaining entry to the orthodox professions, although the Catch 22 position stayed clearly set out from the word go,... no job without a Union Card,... no Union Card without a job. A straightforward proposition, if ever there was one, of defining the rules of the game. There were, however, a few slender threads of possibility, which, with perseverance, might be made to work.

Cyril took the most menial chore available, kept mum, and bided his time until he paid the piper. He worked as a messenger boy cum tea lad in the sweat shops of the film world, the processing laboratories. It was no easy sinecure. Carrying cans of film, slopping out the chemical developing baths, tidying up when everyone else had finished. It required a lot of guts to swallow an impeccable war record, a staff appointment as a major, an Honours Degree at Oxford and a family flat in Park Lane. And this might have proved his undoing, when his disguise almost gave way with a chance meeting in a lift. As he carried a load of film cans up to the pre-view theatre, a friend of his sister, the secretary of a high powered cinema executive, was on her way there, too. Recognising him from her visits to his home, she said,

"Oh hello, Cyril, what on earth are you doing here?"
Sharp as a flash, Cyril replied,

"Cyril? I'm not Cyril. I'm Denis, his cousin. Everyone mixes us up."

The young lady turned away, deeply puzzled, and never mentioned the encounter again, even though she met him at family dinner the following Friday. Six months later with the object achieved, the path was open to film production, and he received his Association of Cine Technicians membership card.

It was because of his job in films I, too, considered the possibilities of a career, and when one evening he invited me to Union Headquarters in Soho Square for a lecture by Dr John Grierson, it seemed a fascinating prospect.

Grierson was an impressive speaker, a live wire of a man, clear in his aims about the value of film and determined to pursue them through thick and thin. His pioneering work in Documentary in Britain would on its own be enough to guarantee his fame in the history books, while his extraordinary energy in founding the

National Film Board in Canada and his leadership at International Film Associates in New York and at UNRRA, made him a powerful advocate in the world of motion pictures. Wherever he spoke, his penetrating analysis of his subject matter, be it film, journalism or politics, made the listener sit up and think, as he examined each fundamental truth and exposed it in a fresh light.

In an hour and a half of lecture I became captivated. His concept of social observation through film, and his appraisal of the power of the medium for teaching and influencing people, made a strong impression on me. Here was a picture of the world I had been seeking. A commitment to a purpose that marshalled its audience from the broadest of spectrums and brought new ideas and learning to everyone.

I remembered the films I preferred had echoed this feeling of searching for truth, through a documentary approach. British films from the thirties, John Clements in *South Riding*, Ralph Richardson in *Night of the Fire;* the Hollywood efforts of the forties, *Boomerang*, *Gentlemen's Agreement* and *Call Northside 777*, as well as the many straight documentary features I had seen at school or in the local cinema, *Night Mail*, *Fires were Started*, *Desert Victory*, and *The March of Time*, had always left me with a desire to see more. On the other hand, using films as a teaching aid in school classroom and Army educational lecture had been part of the techniques I had employed.

I realised Grierson was expressing views I shared, but had not been able to formulate. He was touching on aspects of education and entertainment I accepted as the root of all I planned to do. His words remain etched in my mind.

"The solution is straight and simple, and in an educational world that has come perversely to worship indecision, and feel honoured in unbelief, I hope I shall be forgiven my certainty. Go and ask men to mobilise themselves for the destruction of greed and selfishness. And mean it. Ask them to forget their personal dreams and pleasures and deny themselves for the obligation of economic anarchy and disorder all over the world. And mean it. Mean it so much that men will know that no power on earth will stop you in your tracks. Mean it so much that people will know that, as far as human fallibility allows, the age of selfish interest is over and done with. Make it your religion: which is to say, make it your bond with the people. I haven't a doubt that they

will accept the new loyalties and the new attitudes of sacrifice and effort without a qualm or a question. And I haven't a doubt whatever that they will march with you till the skies open and the future is born."

Powerful stuff, indeed. I left the first encounter that night determined one way or another to make a closer acquaintance with this inspiring man.

Good fortune went with me, and I have one of my tutors at Goldsmiths' to thank for that. When I had returned to college on demob, I knew that the absent years had altered my priorities, even before I tried a stint of teaching. In these circumstances theoretical educational discourses had little point for me, despite the authority of Arthur Dean, the Warden, who delivered them. Mathematics, which I had once enjoyed, also did nothing for me any more, and I wanted to spend my time pursuing subjects I felt to be more relevant to my needs. Beryl Paston Brown, later created Dame for her contributions to English language, was far more to my taste as we explored Shakespeare and the early playwrights, while the music unit of Betty Barnard and Lesley Orrey and the Geography Department with George Cons and Gladys Hickman, catered much more for what I wanted to do. It was to George Cons, who when not at college produced teaching films for Gaumont British, that I spoke about Grierson's talk. His immediate response was,

"Why not invite him to lecture here? I know him well; from the days I researched for the G.P.O. film unit in Blackheath."

An invitation went out, dates agreed, and the 16mm projector placed in my charge, should it be required for film excerpts. Again, I listened spell-bound to a talk on the power of documentary film. Afterwards, George Cons asked me out for a drink and a sandwich with Grierson, along with another ex-service student, Mick Vickers, who had been at Norton Barracks Worcester with me and was also a film and theatre fan. We retired to the Rosemary Branch, a pub nearby, and the captivation continued. Grierson was a kindly man and brought us frequently into the conversation soliciting our opinions on student life, film and politics. He realised we shared an experience (for he, too, had been an ex-forces' student, when he returned to Glasgow University after three years in Naval minesweepers, during World War One) and he asked what ideas we had for our future. To one of his questions, "What are you good at?": I replied, "Taking risks." This seemed to interest him, and when the evening ended he suggested I contact him after my studies finished in a couple of terms. I was ready to take him at his word.

Naturally I was overjoyed as George Cons predicted an exciting outlook, and I awaited a speedy end to Finals. Grierson kept his word, seeing me again and sketching out the possibilities, so that I began, post haste, to clarify the start line through a series of interviews. First, I met Donald Taylor, a senior producer in charge of Crown Film Unit, and he advised me about the union position. It was difficult at Crown. Union stewards acted by the book and did not encourage the employment of non-union members, however bright they were. So I next came face to face with one of the labour organisers at Union headquarters. There he duly administered the cold douche of establishment practice.

"Why didn't you join the industry when you left school? You must have chosen to go to University rather than take a job. What a pity, you could have avoided the army if you'd got your ticket when you were fifteen. And then you wouldn't have a problem."

There was no profit in arguing against that, and it seemed as if I would have to try for entry, as Cyril had done, through the laboratories, unless I could qualify as a script writer. Grierson had a better idea: why not apply directly to the Films Division of the Central Office of Information, where he was the Controller of Government films? There, trade union rules were small beer, when set against the Civil Service regulations of appointment by merit. What is more, the regulations granted a wide discretionary authority for specialist knowledge and wartime experience. I could be part of the Production team, whose record for absorbing unusual talents was apparent in its employees: Denis Forman, afterwards Head of Granada Television, Helen de Mouilpied, a premier producer of documentaries and Philip Mackie, the playwright, were all on the staff.

The COI, then, was the vehicle used to provide the information services for Government Departments. Headed by Sir Robert Fraser, a former newspaper editor, who later became the first Director General of the Independent Television Authority, it had played a leading role in combating the propaganda pouring out of Goebbels' word factories in the war years. Its new commitment was to win the peace. In the Films division, many of the technicians had worked with Grierson in the pre-war expansion of the documentary movement at the Empire Marketing Board and the G.P.O. Niven McNicoll, the Senior Administrator, had developed a series of films with him for the Empire Exhibition in Glasgow in the mid-thirties. Jimmy Davidson, in charge of film printing and perpetually setting his jacket on fire whenever he put his smouldering pipe in his pocket, was the cameraman on Grierson's debut film *Drifters*. Charlie Dand and John Maddison in the Distribution Department had taken their first posts on the same unit.

It was as if the entire history of documentary was on display, illustrating a book by the chronicler of it all, Forsyth Hardy, himself a film information officer in the Scottish Office. Attached to the COI was Crown Film Unit, which employed even more of the original writers, directors and producers. Stuart Legg, one of the earliest recruits, had joined Grierson from Cambridge and went to Canada with him, where they won a number of Academy Awards for hard hitting news films, which competed with the *'The March of Time'* series. In 1948, he had returned from North America to produce films about Government economic policies. These productions, sponsored by the Economic Information Unit, came under the supervision of another veteran of Government public relations, Clem Leslie. Also at Crown were John Taylor, Max Anderson, Leon Clore, Philip Leacock and Ken Cameron, each attracted to the industry through contact with Grierson. Additionally, under this state umbrella, Humphrey Jennings, Alex Shaw, Donald Alexander and Harry Watt, made independent films, using cameramen, editors and writers who had learned their trade in the British Documentary movement. It was a rich seam of experienced people.

After graduation, then a Civil Service Board and finding somewhere to live, I started work at seven pounds, six shillings a week in October 1949. The Headquarters of the COI was Norgeby House in Baker Street, sporting a distinctive white stone facade, built in the thirties, while at the rear were a number of red brick blocks of flats facing onto York Street, Crawford Street and Dorset Street. During the war some of the flats served as Government Offices, others as 'safe houses' for spies, refugees and political escapees, with yet more harbouring the fustiness and mystery of escape committees, secret air drops and guerrilla briefings. Gradually these activities had given place to the home and overseas activities of the information services, including the film researchers and crews of Stuart Legg's unit. I worked in the front offices of Norgeby House with six or seven production control officers, accommodated in typical Whitehall fashion, surrounded by Ministry of Works furnishings, as befitted our lowly ranking.

This hardly disguised the oddness of the set-up, caught, it seemed, in a time warp, where the business of enemies, of subterfuge and propaganda continued undisturbed by any peace settlement. The titles proclaimed Pensions, Health, Agriculture and Trade, but for the occupants behind the desks it was as if they were fighting a cloak and dagger war with the Atom Bomb, while transferring their coded messages to friends they kept on the 'other side'. It did not surprise me, when years later, criminal proceedings revealed that some of them were doing just that. In a world where goodies and baddies hid under the aliases of communist and capitalist operators, it required little sacrifice for some high ranking officials to change allegiance and join the other side.

Yet, besides the background material for a spy movie, there were other activities occurring around us. The Festival of Britain was on the front burner. All complete, with a chance to display the latest industrial products, the concepts of designers and architects in re-building the bomb damaged cities, and the spin-offs from the invention of the jet engine and the development of nuclear fission.

This was the raw material from which Grierson created his philosophy of film making: 'I look on cinema as a pulpit, and use it as a propagandist'. Film was there to sell the goods British factories produced, to sell the benefits of a Welfare State, and to sell the meaning of Government by democracy, in a world emerging from a period of darkness. No politician or Ministerial Department could afford to muff the challenge. What had been the start of a revolution in the 1920's, when Sir Stephen Tallents wrote the formulas for the public dissemination of Government information, in his book *The Projection of Britain*, some 25 years later had developed into a thriving industry, with its personnel flooding into every area of media presentation.

My colleagues in the Production Office shared a similar background. We were mainly ex-forces, interested in films, journalism and public relations, so it was easy to settle into the style of the job, with snatched lunches at the Beehive pub, almost a part of the main building, and an evening drink further up Baker Street, at the Volunteer. As one of the women controlling officers was leaving to have a baby, I inherited her portfolio of film projects in various stages of production. I found that one of them, about children at play, for the Ministry of Health, was causing some headaches. The subject concerned a great deal of the material I had heard in psychology lectures at Goldsmiths'. This, plus the practical experience I had gained from teaching, gave me a fair insight into the film's brief. Fortunately, in a series of meetings and viewings of the rough cut, I was able to balance the differences of opinion that were causing friction between the sponsors and the film director. It helped me establish an accepted position within the department very quickly, and the Health Ministry invited me to oversee their next group of subjects.

Learning the expertise of film became that much more readily absorbed. With the vast archives of the Central Film Library available for viewing at the small private cinemas in the basement of Norgeby House, I thrived on the opportunity to widen my knowledge of the media from sources all over the world.

Other projects came my way, from the Festival of Britain, the Scottish Office and from Legg's news documentary unit. Now he supervised the production of a ten minute reel entitled *World in Action*, for cinema release every month. He and Grierson had used this name for a series they had produced in New York, after the end of the war, and had recommended it to Clem Leslie, the Treasury's publicity man.

It seemed a good idea to use the format to present the post war economic and social problems that plagued the Government, during its attempts to reorganise the country. Presenting such topics in a lively and entertaining manner is not everyone's meat, and subjects as diverse as 'The Balance of Payments', 'Full Employment' and 'Changes in Work Practices' do not naturally provide the most thrilling of stories.

However Legg's impressive writing abilities (Grierson said Legg should be writing leaders at *The Times*) demanded great imagination to translate dull statistics (regarded by the Treasury as essential) into a presentable script. One of his commentaries, written at that time for the series, seems to have been used in every Government handout in the ensuing 40 years,

'Britain', wrote Legg in 1949, 'is on the way up. Breasting the road to recovery, busier than she has ever been before.'

How often have we heard that one?

The great thing for me, was being swept along, as part of the team, concerned in the battle for the ear of the electorate. When we had screenings or script conferences at Beaconsfield Studios, the technical headquarters of Crown Films, I took a car from the general vehicle pool to drive Grierson there, together with Legg, Clem Leslie or Sir Robert Fraser. I listened to their continuing debate on the political aspects of the information game, which despite the lethargy of the sponsoring process in supplying cash and resolution, somehow muddled through.

Often, late in the evening, I would return with Grierson to Le Petit Club Francais for a meal of Quiche Lorraine and French Fries, and he would talk about film and his own personal devotion to spreading ideas far and wide. He forced me to think hard, as he fired questions that demanded instant answers, in his desire to enrich the brotherhood of man and set fresh goals for its accomplishment. He longed to find the spirit of adventure he had shared in the early days of the Empire Marketing Board and the G.P.O. film units, because he reckoned the unity of direction they had achieved, placed them above the vanity and jealousy of the individual.

The French Club was a valuable recreational release from a working life in documentary film. Olwen Vaughan, the owner, was as much a part of the club, as it was of her. In her late forties, tall and with blondish wavy hair, she was a cross between Edith Evans, Arletty and Good Queen Bess, although Judi Dench came close to her in a portrayal on television.

The domain she had established in the early years of the war was in a terrace of ramshackle Georgian houses at the side of St James' Place. She ruled it with a rod of iron. When it opened, because of her own half French upbringing, she attracted the Free French officers of De Gaulle's staff from their Headquarters around the corner. Also, there was a sizeable contingent of the Documentary film movement who came along in support of Olwen's devotion to the movies and her stewardship of the London Film Society with its successor, the New London Film Society.

To help her organise the society, she had enrolled an ad hoc committee of management consisting of Grierson, Paul Rotha,

Peter Noble, Sid Cole, Rodney Ackland, Dilys Powell and Elizabeth Bowen, and Grierson insisted, when I joined the COI, that I became the assistant secretary and treasurer. It was certainly a prize position to hold and gave me a wonderful opportunity to view the feature films she collected for the Sunday afternoon screenings at the Scala Cinema in Charlotte Street (rebuilt as the first Headquarters of Channel 4 Television).

She had the rare knack of unearthing films which others believed lost or destroyed, and persuading producers to show their new productions at the society before release in the cinemas. Through her friends, Iris Barry at the Museum of Modern Art in New York, and Henri Langlois at the Cinemathéque in Paris, she had invaluable contacts in the movie making business, guaranteeing programmes of outstanding interest.

On many occasions at Heathrow I awaited the arrival of a print on a trans-Atlantic flight, early on a Sunday morning, for screening that afternoon at 3 p.m. Yet her magic hardly ever failed, and then she would produce another enticing masterpiece out of the hat, which would have the London film critics scurrying to the performance to make sure they did not miss it.

Grierson treated her with great respect. 'There's no-one like Olwen for putting the spice into a visit to the movies' he would say, and compare her brilliance in setting up a scoop to the rather dull and leaden attempts of the programme makers at the British Film Institute. But the lady waged a personalised vendetta against the red tape of the institute of those days: a hangover from the period she worked there, and they had overlooked her for promotion, when bureaucracy intervened. In later years, when Grierson presented his own unique film programme on television, *This Wonderful World*, he assigned Olwen the task of researching his material, and she rewarded him with some miraculous gems of movie making.

Olwen's sister, Dorothea, was a skilled accountant and looked after the financial side of the Club and the Film Society. She had married TV personality, Magnus Pike, and we sat down once a fortnight in St James' to sort out the problems of running the Sunday performances. One evening, after we had finished our planning, Grierson asked me across to his table in the dining room, to meet Robert Flaherty. He was in London to lecture on his recent film,

Louisiana Story, and had kept a close relationship with Grierson since 1933, when he had made *Industrial Britain* at the Empire Marketing Board and later *Man of Aran*. He was a cult figure every documentary film man worth his salt tried to emulate; a messenger and story teller who used the camera to communicate his interpretation of everyday life. This was the crux that Grierson and he, from their respective Scots and Irish backgrounds, never ceased arguing upon, yet each deeply respected the other with a friendship of love and comradeship. I was captivated by the great hulk of this white haired, crinkly faced character, who tried in his films to reconcile the impact that machines imposed on man, whether in the Arctic, the South Seas or the oil fields. It turned out to be an exciting evening as Grierson described the problems he was facing in the sponsorship fields.

"We no longer have the raw enthusiasm of the early days. The Civil Servants want too much of the cake and won't give us the raisins and candied peel to mix the recipe."

Flaherty waited a moment,

"You were never a patient fellow, J.G., and time heals everything. Maybe you should stick to the production end, like me, and let these younger men fight the sponsorship battles."

And turning to me, he said,

"I reckon you boys have to carry on where we are leaving off. From what I see of the challenges ahead, they are like nothing we ever thought of."

When he died a few months later, Olwen arranged a memorial programme of excerpts from his films, which clearly identified his personal thumb print on all he did. It showed his reactions to the struggles a film maker must overcome in presenting his philosophies in the medium he has chosen, and how his statements, about man's quest to live within the confines of the natural world, are for ever relevant. Through his own efforts he emphasised the very basis of creation, leaving a legacy everyone can share.

Still behind the film and show business facade of Olwen's club, there was another, more secret world. Something I stumbled on during my spasmodic off-duty visits, when it seemed the darker side of sustaining the bonhomie of club life proved too much for her and she disappeared to her flat above the bar and restaurant.

Her alcoholic capacity was nothing short of phenomenal. Unfortunately, brandy and gin by the case, and packs of cigarettes by the score, did not relieve the despair of giving pearls to others and receiving glass beads in return.

If I discovered her unavailable, I would wait three or four days, until the pressures of the next film society programme required her attention, apart from something I could do. On one such occurrence I ventured up the stairs, beyond her dividing door, defying the rigid instructions to her staff that no matter what, she was to remain undisturbed. The flat looked deserted, empty bottles lay strewn over the floor and a sickly choking smell of stubbed out butt ends and spilt booze wreaked through the rooms. She was not around. The bed unmade, the cotton cover, pillows and blankets piled in a crumpled heap. Then, as I looked at a stretched out sheet, it moved enough to cause me to mutter,

"Olwen?"

"She's gone away," answered a voice, unmistakably that of the lady.

"Away?"

"Yes, away. Right away from all those bloody stupid questions you want to ask me."

I certainly did have some questions, but in situations like that it is wiser not to press them. Yet later, you wonder, when the tide has advanced on you that little bit more, why you could be so utterly dim to refuse such a cry for help.

But that was Olwen, and that was Le Petit Club Francais. During a similar binge she took pity on an introvert photographer who frequented the bar, and married him. On the wedding night, his bridegroom's gift was to walk off to a nearby hotel with a sailor, one of the guests. For documentary drama, you could hardly cap it. It was the stuff and essence of the place. Every frame of picture to tell a story. Not fiction but fact. A special magic, that Grierson and Flaherty used to illustrate their message, and Rodney Ackland revealed in his plays.

There could be no doubt. There was charisma. From Ashton, the white jacketed barman, who dropped off to sleep as he served you, to Sasha the cat, whose independent streak guided him around the whole of St James', including the Royal Houses and Palaces. And with such a stage setting, what price the actors? The tête à têtes were a gossip diarists dream. Ken Tynan and Jill Bennett, Alan Rawsthorne and Marion Leigh, Pat Dolin and John Gilpin, in twosome corner tables. The hoi polloi of Balcon's Ealing Studios. The glamour of the lady documentarists, Margaret Thomson, Kit Jebb and Bessie Bond. The musicals, the ballet, the painters and the drunks,... nothing was missing, except the cameras.

My course seemed set enough in documentary film and as I was really beginning to enjoy it, Cyril Frankel also moved across from Highbury Studios, into the same environment. He worked for a while as a unit manager at Crown and was soon directing the monthly news documentaries for Stuart Legg. This brought us in contact again, something neither of us had thought a possibility a few months before. It was like being in the army once more, although in a Civil Service context there were more restrictions. However, our previous experiences of red tape and who and who not to trifle with, bore fruit. We sussed out the staff who based their power on always saying "No", from those who stretched the rules. Just like the services, a thorough knowledge of what the regulations and memoranda implied was an essential acquirement if you wished to succeed.

One of the films that concerned us both, was about the fisheries' research laboratory in Aberdeen, where Cyril had directed an accomplished 30 minute version of *Explorers of the Depths*. The subject was particularly close to Grierson's heart, too, because of *Drifters*, and he sent Cyril and me off to Edinburgh for a Saturday screening to the Scottish Departments. In setting up our arrangements we were not happy about Civil Service guidelines that permitted only a frugal level of accommodation, because of our lowly official status. Additionally, we frowned on the necessity to work during the weekend, without reward or overtime payment. At the very least, our tastes, cultivated in the officers' clubs and hotels of Germany, France and Denmark, had come to expect a fair amount of sophistication, and we did not relish the bed and breakfast boarding houses our employment categories rated. Come what may, we determined to stay at the best hotel, The Caledonian, in the heart of the city.

The tide of events, fortunately, played into our hands. Before departure we telephoned two or three of the smaller hotels but found them already fully booked. On enquiring from Angus Ross, a Rugby playing colleague of mine of Scots descent, we learned that Saturday was Calcutta Cup Day, as important in Scotland as the New Year and Robbie Burns Night. We made our decision and reserved two of the best suites at the Caledonian Hotel. We had an excellent two days of food and lodging. Returning from the trip we presented our accounts, totally outside the standard limits, to the Allowances and Subsistence Officer.

"Can't pay this," he sniffed. "It's not within your status, and you're not eligible. Back to you, to pay yourself."

"Oh," I replied. "Not what I understand of Para 23, subsection C, Page 104, of the Directory."

"Doesn't apply. Has to be war, civil disobedience, or Act of God. Nothing like that happened in Edinburgh this last weekend."

"No? Not an occasion when every hotel, boarding house, caravan and tent was in Scottish occupation? Have you ever tried booking a room when it's International Day at Murrayfield?"

"Oh, the Rugby match. I'll need to confirm what you say." And two hours later, he paid us out in full.

Although *Explorers of the Depths*, and many other of our theatrical releases were popular with cinema audiences, a change was evident in the permanent set up of Government film making for this type of audience.

The system began in 1940, when a shortage of films for general distribution gave the documentary movement a showcase for its 'real life' features, produced under Government sponsorship. Large paying audiences saw, *Target for Tonight*, *Desert Victory*, *The Way Ahead* and *Western Approaches*, as well as short information films about digging for victory, health problems and food rationing. Once a month a topical factual film appeared. It lasted up to 15 minutes, and was viewed in over 3000 cinemas, without charge to the exhibitors. Most importantly, it gave the Government a perfect display case for its information policies. In their early days I had watched these monthly films at my local cinemas and through them became aware of Crown Film Unit and the documentary approach to subjects. Humphrey Jennings' emotive pictures of the Coventry Blitz, *Heart of Britain*, especially impressed me, in the way it revealed a poetic appreciation of the horrors surrounding the air raids. However, with memories of the war receding, attitudes were changing, and cinema owners saw no good reason why they should screen Government propaganda without payment. Particularly, as in all other circumstances, they charged for advertising space. This, they emphasised, should apply to boring political messages.

For a long time, Legg, Grierson and Fraser had fought to suppress these, arguing with the sponsoring departments about the content of publicity statements. They sought constantly for a formula to allow entertainment values a priority, divorced from the tedium of bureaucratic exhortation. Stuart summed up the general feeling, in a memorandum at the time,

'Monthly release. What a God awful title. Menstruation implies dreary inevitability, not lively enterprise.'

There was no disguising the fact that the gradual disappearance of films that originally found their inspiration in the basic themes of national life, as Grierson and Flaherty intended, seemed to confirm that the medium was losing its power to persuade and losing sight of its aim to project Britain.

Certainly Grierson was becoming disillusioned. His efforts to promote international subjects as a distinct government programme of film making, examining the aspects of world wide trading, the implications of communications and the acceptance of humanist responsibilities, reflected his ideas that 'the peace' had its own battles to fight. Yet the awareness of famine, the acute wastage of resources and global pollution remained low down in a list of priorities. He could only cast scorn at those who refused to admit their importance, in the early post war years. Nevertheless, despite the struggles, he took pains to encourage young people like me.

One morning, in his office, he told me he had lectured the previous evening in Coventry. He had telephoned my parents to tell them of his visit and that he knew me. They had arranged immediately to meet him at the Central Hall, and afterwards he spoke to them. He wanted me to know that I had their support in what I was doing to establish a career, and he asked me to tell them how touched he had been that they had come to see him. I know my parents never forgot the meeting.

Grierson's caring attitude towards members of his units was something special. The young men he had taken under his wing in the thirties, Arthur Elton, Basil Wright, Jack Holmes and Edgar Anstey, always stayed loyal to him and the ideal he stood for, through every change of sponsorship and location. He was proud of their success and fostered their contributions to the overall popularity of the movement. He even served as an efficient broker in lover's trysts, and married off two radiant Canadian researchers who had worked for him at the Film Board, to Arthur Elton and Edgar Anstey. While his brother-in-law, John Taylor (on his wife Margaret's side) who had assisted Flaherty on Arran, he encouraged to marry film star, Barbara Mullen. His caring and influence stretched right through the work ethic, so that if you believed something sincerely enough in the job you were doing, then he would support you, whatever flak came in your direction.

I watched this happen frequently. Never more admirably than when he defended one of his Group 3 productions, *Man of Africa*, directed by Cyril Frankel. Despite the bitter hostility of Sir Michael Balcon, who wanted it thrown in the dustbin because it featured coloured actors, he insisted on its screening, and introduced it at Film Festivals throughout the world.

But the sands were running out in this beach-head of documentary film. A new Conservative Government had proposals for dismembering the mighty edifice of sponsored film, considered, in their manifesto, to be the height of socialist meddling. Unfortunately, the spur that the war had given to such enterprises had largely vanished, to be replaced, in Grierson's words,

'By a godly number of dull wits and fat backsides in complacent and utterly ugly mediocrity.'

He fashioned an exit for himself by moving to a fresh venture at Group 3 Films, where he reckoned there might be a 're-dedication to basic documentary terms in an organisation along classical commercial lines'. There he would have some access to government funding, helped by the experienced features' producer, John Baxter, and chosen for his ability to assemble viable film projects at low cost. Together, they launched an organised company, with its own distribution network, which 'would be willing, in loyalty and discipline, to give documentary a purpose again. And work and plan and fight for it'. The films they produced bore this stamp, and became an important part of British film history in the 1950's.

SIXTEEN

FILM CENTRE

SHORTLY AFTER Grierson left the COI, Stuart Legg decided to go, too. The bitter in-fighting that had developed no longer appealed to him, and as he had a readily available alternative, he decided to move. Film Centre played a similar role for commercial and industrial sponsors as the COI had done for Government Departments and Legg joined Sir Arthur Elton on the Board, with Grierson as part time Chairman. He became quickly involved into several projects and when a few months later, as the rug disappeared from under the feet of Crown Film Unit and the COI's Film Division in a series of economy cuts, he suggested I follow him.

At the offices in Tottenham Court Road I met Sinclair Roade, George Seager and Peter Brinson, each working for a different group of clients: amongst them, Shell, the Iraq Petroleum Company, B.O.A.C., English Electric, Marshall Aid, and the Australian Government. Initially, I supervised a number of industrial productivity films and lectured on film techniques with Peter Brinson, at various training courses. It suited my background, keeping me in touch with my early mentors as well as making a good new friend in George Seager. I introduced him to Rugby and Squash and in return he saw I became thoroughly acquainted with the tastiest restaurants and learned to distinguish the flavours of well-brewed beer, mingled with the sophistication of vintage cognac.

Stuart Legg was working on a project for the Australian Government and he asked me to help. We organised a London based unit, staffed by ex-pats from Australia, to edit and dub thousands of feet of colour film, shot on location, during the Queen's first ever visit. As the necessary processing facilities did not then exist outside

Europe and America, we arranged to fly all the footage to London, and complete the two hour film here. The tour was extensive, journeying over vast areas of the continent, some of it very thinly populated. The Australian Film Board wanted to show the vistas and beauty of the landscape and what went on there, possibly encouraging more emigrants to try it for themselves. It was an ideal subject for such a theme, full of unusual viewpoints, which could lift it out of the rut of a simple travelogue, and place it alongside other colour features like *The Coronation* and *The Conquest of Everest*.

Stanley Hawes, the Film Board's chief, came to London to supervise the production and as he had been one of Grierson's original recruits at the Empire Marketing Board, he already knew Stuart well. At our first meeting he sketched out the story line, describing the background to the visit through geographical location, historical reference and social culture. Then, by using Australian commentators, actors, and musicians we would give it a smell of the distant Commonwealth continent. It turned out that Stuart and I were the only members of the unit who had never seen the country.

It was a wonderful challenge. The exposed film negative arrived at Heathrow after a flight half way round the world, was ferried across the Bath Road to the Technicolor Laboratories (positioned almost on the airport runway) processed and printed, so that within 24 hours of shooting we screened the rushes in colour, and reported the quality back to the camera crews in Australia. In the days before video tape and satellite transmissions, it was some feat. The editors in our cutting rooms built up the sections of film as we received advance coverage before the Queen arrived, and later added the shots of her actual visit to show the opening of the Canberra Parliament, the parades of schoolchildren, and various festivals and galas connected with the tour.

During the filming the Australian National Symphony Orchestra recorded music tracks in Sydney, and sound engineers covered choral singing and welcome addresses at the State functions, so that with the Australian conductor, Sir Charles Mackerras and his musicians in London, we added linking melodies into the dubbed sound track of the completed rough cut. Nothing quite like it had been tried before in colour, because of the intricacies of location filming and the difficulties associated with the laboratory processing; but we handled the organisation and editing with great finesse, allowing Stuart to tidy it all up in the final rewrite. At one of the commentary recording sessions we hit our most taxing assignment.

We were employing Australian actors resident in London from the BBC, the theatre and films to cover both dubbed voices and the commentary lines in the script. Amongst these was Peter Finch who knew Stanley Hawes, and was keen to record for us. I had heard a few of the problems of working with Peter from Cyril Frankel, who had recently directed him in a splendid script of Wolf Mankowitz, *Make Me an Offer*, for Grierson at Group 3. At that time Cyril and I shared a flat in St Johns' Wood, and often the phone would ring in the middle of the night, usually after 4 a.m., as an inebriated Peter asked the time of his studio call. Sometimes his wife, Tamara, telephoned, enquiring if we knew where he was or alternatively, that he was home, but flat out, drunk. Cyril had many problems shooting around his absences from the studio, but he always tried to make up for his lapses and was very apologetic about the binges.

It did not surprise me, therefore, when he failed to arrive, one Saturday morning, at our recording studios for a voice-over session. I phoned his home, and yes, he was on his way. Things might not be too bad. Stanley and I had flasks of black coffee and orange juice standing by in case of need, yet when he finally appeared, full of contriteness, he seemed ready to go ahead. It was when we began the recording that I realised we had a difficult task in front of us. The slurred words and the S's were impossible to handle, and the more we strained to correct mistakes, the worse it became. After several attempts, Peter stood up and said,

"I'm sorry Stanley. Let's forget it, and you can forget my fee. I was naughty last night, met too many old friends."

When he left we sat around trying to decide what to do. Should we try for another day? Forget the whole thing? Stuart came up with an idea. One of his former Crown editors was a master at altering recorded dialogue; eliminating fluffs and stutters and shifting pieces of the track around from one take to another. In fact, after he had tampered with a speech, you could never believe a word! Anyway, we invited Ralph Sheldon along and within a couple of days he had sorted it out, cutting the S's back to their starting point, speeding up the slurs and replacing the hesitations, so that Finch seemed to speak, more or less, normally. After adding some background music, I am sure not a soul was any the wiser.

Within a few days of the Queen waving 'Good-bye' in Sydney, we had the final cut ready, dubbed, titled and in the laboratories for printing. The following week a thousand copies of the film were out on release in Britain and Australia and we had a grand Royal Gala opening at the Odeon in Leicester Square. Screenings went on all over the world, and Government officials I met in later years always considered the film one of the reasons their immigration policies were so successful. Even some of my family who left for Australia in the sixties with a £10 one way ticket, reckoned it had woken in them the possibilities of making a fresh start there.

By 1953, I was still not a member of the Union, although I found no disadvantages in that position. Certainly, I was already carrying out duties, which according to the Rule Book required a ticket, and there was no doubt that George Seager, Peter Brinson and I were working in areas that were strictly out of bounds. Yet, on the other hand, we were performing assignments of research, script writing, editing and producing in a highly professional way, and no-one challenged our authority. Only once did someone try to take me down a peg or two in front of some important sponsors, and I felt I had to be bitchy in response. A sound supervisor at an orchestral recording session crossed swords,

"Isn't it the first time you've been to a gathering like this, Brian," he enquired cockily.

"As a matter of fact, when I was in the army in Berlin, I did it frequently with Celibidache and the Philharmonic. You were back here in civvies during the war, weren't you?"

He didn't answer.

That apart, the mystique of Union membership caused no problems and George, Peter and I were more than a little surprised when a union organiser approached us to join, with an explanation that he thought it was due time we regularised the situation. Odder things have happened, I suppose. The Union quickly processed our formal applications, and accepted us as full members. We figured that after the many film production initiations we had suffered in the last few years, we were round pegs in round holes anyway. The pity was that as late entrants to the profession, we had met such a preliminary barrage of union regulations that scarcely did anything to take account of the experience we had collected, simply by being that much older (and wiser) when we were ready to start work. Unfortunately, as far as I can see, this position is still prevalent in many walks of life today, despite determined attempts to rectify it. Once again, the Establishment raises its troublesome head.

I felt, however, my apprenticeship was finally over when Sir Arthur Elton called me to his office at our new headquarters in Conduit Street, to ask if I would work as his editorial assistant on a film commissioned by the BBC about Grierson and the British Documentary movement. The idea came from Paul Rotha, Head of BBC Television Documentaries, who had been a successful film maker himself, responsible for a large output of factual films like *World of Plenty* for the United Nations, and *The City Speaks* for the Manchester Corporation. He was also a devoted film historian and had written many reference books with Sinclair Roade of Film Centre; so with the 25th anniversary of *Drifters* due shortly, it seemed a good opportunity to review the progress.

Arthur was the ideal producer for the venture. An original member of the E.M.B. film unit, he had worked as a writer, director and producer with the main groups at the G.P.O., Shell Film Unit and the Ministry of Information, so that few films of the period had escaped his notice. Our first action was to trace copies of the old films and arrange a screening. Unearthing some of the very early ones, especially if they came from overseas, was a formidable chore, and I set to work ferreting out library contacts and delving into old catalogues.

My previous searches in the Central Film Library, with Mrs Hackford at the COI, now proved well spent, but many productions existed only as negatives and reprinting copies needed a clearance from the original owners and sponsors. This is where the network of former colleagues Grierson had built up over the years was particularly useful, and soon we had hunted down *Song of Ceylon*, *Housing Problems* and *North Sea* from the early thirties, and *London Can Take It* and *Diary for Timothy* from the war years.

Our storyline was straightforward enough. It started in 1927, when Grierson had taken his ideas along to Sir Stephen Tallents. Tallents was the secretary of the Empire Marketing Board and had been appointed to promote a scheme publicising Britain and her products to the world, as well as encouraging trade with Empire countries. The Board saw the significance of documentary film subjects to do just that, and gave strong support to the objectives. In a short time Grierson was influencing a wide range of film making, from teaching and education to scientific and research projects, as well as developing fields of study, based on the techniques of Flaherty and Eisenstein. Young people trained at his units and journalists wrote about his achievements as he filmed the excitement and drama that unfolded around the daily jobs of ordinary folk working in the fields, in factories and in the fishing fleets. Huge audiences had viewed each production, either in the commercial cinema, or in a previously untapped area of non-theatrical outlets, serviced by 16mm projectors at schools, workplaces and community centres.

Grierson's energy and drive were astonishing. He was a catalyst to sponsors, producers and distributors alike, stretching imaginations, seeking fresh interpretations and encouraging all around him to break free of the traditional modes of thinking. Always it was a new experience to work with him, and it was this sense of adventure we sought to capture in our programme for the BBC. We decided to use extracts from a selection of films, covered by a commentary from Grierson, culminating in a discussion with Tallents, about the possible way ahead.

One of the problems with film shot in the silent days when Grierson's experiments first began, was that cameras cranked at 18 frames per second. Once talkies came along with Al Johnson and the *Jazz Singer* in 1929, the speed increased to 24 frames per second, to help produce a better sound quality. Although it is possible to stretch the old silent films, allowing the addition of sound at the optimum speed, it is both expensive and time consuming. However, Grierson was ahead of his contemporaries. Shortly before he shot *Drifters*, he was in the United States and became aware of the startling changes that sound recording would bring to movie making. So, despite the budget only covering the silent film costs, he shot his story of the North Sea fishermen at 24 frames a second, and 25 years later we exploited his foresight by adding a recorded track.

Each evening, I met Arthur in the film cutting rooms at Shell-Mex House, in the Strand, to further our researches and the assembly of the programme. One evening Basil Wright came along to discuss sequences from *Song of Ceylon* and *Night Mail*, another evening Edgar Anstey and Jack Holmes assessed my re-editing of *Housing Problems*, and after a cable from Cavalcanti, then working in South America, Arthur selected sections of *Pett and Pott*, to salute the varied talents Grierson had marshalled around him. He had employed a youthful Benjamin Britten to compose music, W.H.Auden for scripts and poems, Flaherty and Cavalcanti to direct with a score of others who went on to make noteworthy contributions in the artistic world. This we wished to illustrate.

Working with Arthur brought its own self rewarding experience. A large figure of a man, with a bristling ginger beard, he could have stood in for Charles Laughton playing King Henry VIII, and his sharp intellectual wit made him a congenial companion. We would clock-off from the cutting rooms each evening at 8.30, walk to Simpsons in the Strand for dinner, and after Roast Beef and Yorkshire, followed by meringue glacé and brandy, Arthur would dust the crumbs from his beard, wave me to settle the bill, and return for a further two or three hour stint at the editola. By this stage I was usually flaked out, but he would urge me to journey home with him by taxi to Haverstock Hill in Hampstead, so that his wife, Margaret Ann, could serve coffee and proffer comments from her years with Grierson in Canada. Then, still flush with energy, he would settle for a session of carpentry, building cupboards and shelves for his books in the house they had recently bought.

The following evening at five, the procedure would begin again. Sometimes we would have Paul Rotha and Stephen McCormack from the BBC, or one or two of the older documentary boys along for a meal, and then the tales and reminiscing would extend until the restaurant closed. More than likely, we would need to rush off and add something we had heard in conversation during dinner to the final assembly. It never ceased to have its high spots.

Towards the close of our work, Grierson became a nightly visitor. He would mercilessly tease Arthur about the seriousness he was devoting to the project, and said he had always reckoned he could have improved on *Drifters*. One evening he banished Arthur from the cutting room,

"Come on, Brian, let's get into that fishing boat sequence. It's far too long and boring for television. They want action, not Arthur's sentimentalities."

And he junked shot after shot as repetitious, and concentrated on the foaming waves, the toppling baskets of herring and the swinging nets. Skilfully, he matched it to a recording of Mendelssohn's *Hebrides* overture, which he had originally chosen for the pit orchestral accompaniment in the silent days, and sliced a six minute section down to two.

Afterwards he suggested a drink at the Norfolk Hotel, his pied à terre in London when he was away from his home at Calne. His feature productions, at Group 3, were attracting attention for their documentary style approach, particularly a mining disaster story, *The Brave Don't Cry,* based on a tragedy at the Knockshinnock pit; and another, *Devil on Horseback,* featuring 16 year old Jeremy Spenser as boy jockey, Lester Pigott. His *Man of Africa* contained everything he had proposed about introducing film to the Commonwealth countries to promote a fuller understanding of how other people and races coped with their problems, and he spoke of his excitement about this aspect of his film making. Yet, even more so, he felt that our television project was a signal that new things were in the offing,

"You know, that programme we worked on this evening, in only one viewing on the BBC, will probably be seen by more people than have watched *Song of Ceylon* in 25 years. That's power for you; it's a revolution. Every documentary film maker of today should fight to use it. You are lucky chaps to have that chance."

I sensed his message. Maybe it was time to look afresh at the viewers. This new audience, emerging all over the globe, demanded entertainment at the flick of a switch. Maybe, the sort of information we had passed on through cinemas and 16mm screenings was more appropriate for television. We finished our pints of beer and walked across to Paddington Station to get a feel of the nightscape.

"I love this place," he said, "it's the heart of things around here. Just look and you can see the world parade before you. It has the guts of all we called the Industrial Revolution. A mix of peoples and places to make it function. It's the story we told in *Night Mail.* But the old steam engines have been replaced by the diesel, and soon we will welcome the arrival of the electrics. Those are the ones we must get aboard. The electrics and the television sets. That's where it's bound to happen."

He was right, of course. There was nothing to stop the onward march of the cathode ray tubes, the satellites and the cables. Grierson's original horizons were under threat, about to vanish. Yet he was aware of the pioneering role he had played and wanted to be there in future developments, too. His later television presentations and *This Wonderful World* programme, which was peculiar to him, showed his mastery of the techniques of communication, and his understanding of what made audiences tick.

As the assignment ended, I also reached a decision on what I would like to do next. On the day of the transmission there was a final duty to undertake, checking the programme ready for the telecine machines. I re-measured each reel and totalled up the footage to ensure we did not exceed the scheduled length of one hour. Consternation stared us in the face, somehow we had 200 feet too much material, an over-run of 2 minutes.

After the hours on the cutting bench, we had already sacrificed so many of our favourite sequences, and it looked as if we must junk another. Fortunately, Stephen McCormack knew his television backwards, and came to our rescue. For BBC broadcasts, the film projection speed is 25 frames per second, to suit the demands of the power supply and picture quality. Our cinema calculations at 24 frames per second did not apply. So we had 45 seconds to spare, with no fade out worries to hinder us. Later that year Stephen left the BBC for an appointment in one of the ITV commercial stations shortly to open in London. He asked if I would like to join him and direct some of the live programmes. It turned out to be an offer I could not refuse.

SEVENTEEN

A FESTIVAL OF BALLET

THERE WAS NEVER much doubt that once I became hooked on 'the ballet', it would sustain me for the rest of my life. It was something I discovered myself and because no-one bullied me into it, the initial magic remained untarnished. The discovery also came at an age that was in its own way important, too. I was fourteen years old, one of those special numbers like seven, twenty-one and seventy, tied to the ancient law of octaves, which I find play their own mystical games within our life cycle. In 1937, I certainly believed I was ready for new things to happen to me and on a certain Wednesday afternoon, they did just that.

Our weekly half day free from school, given in lieu of Saturday morning attendances, were our own, if the school Rugby or cricket teams did not demand support. Sometimes my mother and I would go to a cinema matinee performance, or if our friends, the Burroughs, offered to drive us, we would visit the Memorial Theatre at Stratford. Len Burroughs was in the Sixth form and when our mothers decided a trip to see Alicia Markova and Anton Dolin was what they would like to do, we both wondered what we were letting ourselves in for. We need not have worried. From the moment I heard the opening chords of *Les Sylphides* I reckoned this was going to be something quite different. It was, and that afternoon, Len Burroughs and I made a hasty revision of everything we had previously thought the ballet to be about.

Years later, I spoke to Markova and Dolin, about this initiation and they told me how many other of my contemporaries had succumbed in similar circumstances. For them it was a happy appreciation of the efforts they had put in to the pioneering work of the thirties, alongside Ninette de Valois and Marie Rambert. I was fortunate to continue much of my own adventure into the world of dance by observing these two artistes in performance and off stage, during the immediate post war years, when they worked in close association with my friend Benn Toff.

Benn had re-established his theatrical career after demobilisation, when I returned to University. He formed a partnership with Julian Braunsweg, a Polish impresario living in London, who had a myriad of connections with dance in Europe, and was presenting a variety of overseas companies on their first post war appearances in Britain. Before the battles had effectively closed off such activity in 1939, Braunsweg had managed tours of Pavlova, Nijinski and Woizikovsky and produced Baronova and Massine in a musical play *Bullet in the Ballet*. His verbal idiosyncrasies echoed those of some of Hollywood's most talkworthy stars, like Carmen Miranda, who would say,

'A block off the old chip,' or,

'Six of one and a dozen of the other.'

Julian would pick up the telephone and announce to a surprised caller,

'Who am I?' and when introduced, would reply,

'I am very pleased to meet me.'

Nevertheless, his contacts were impeccable and his expertise of the world opera house circuit, acquired in the anti-Semitic rumblings of the thirties, were invaluable when he booked protracted tours for artistes and companies. Benn's involvement was directly in production. He assumed responsibility for staging, lighting and programming, so that he was both director and manager and over a period of a couple of years helped to introduce Ram Gopal, the Indian dancer and his troupe, Ana Esmeralda and her Flamenco dancers and the Grande Ballet of the Marquis de Cuevas. But his real command of stage wizardry showed up in his presentation of the small company headed by Markova and Dolin, a tour billed as the first major appearance of the two stars since their return from war-time engagements in America.

To avoid the small venues and the run down theatres in the provinces, he organised the construction of a large portable stage with full theatre lighting and settings for visits to the largest halls, pavilions and auditoriums in the country. Such an innovation for the performance of ballet was unique because the established companies of Sadler's Wells, Rambert and the International Ballet, demanded fixed prosceniums and orchestral pits as furnished in conventional theatre buildings. Both Julian and Benn were scornful of this line of approach, and with their audacious ideas brought ballet to sections of the population previously starved of such entertainment.

The venture proved so successful and the tour a money spinner, that they were soon under pressure to extend their commitments to the European opera houses in Monte Carlo, Madrid, Venice and Naples. In 1950, despite the ghastly failures of other ballet gambles, they decided to risk all in one glorious effort and announced the formation of a new large classical ballet company, to be led by Markova and Dolin. It was to have an array of International stars, a corps de ballet and orchestra of one hundred artistes and present established classics alongside a programme of new choreography.

Where Julian uncovered the finance is an intriguing mystery of the theatre; yet he did just that. Although not for the first time or the last, his wife's family jewels and heirlooms, brought out from Poland in 1939, under the eyes of the Nazis, were handed over to a friendly pawnbroker, as security for the money he borrowed on loan.

This enlarged group, emerging from the dancers and musicians already touring the provinces, established themselves very quickly. Through Benn I was able to watch their progress at first hand, and took part in the briefings and planning with Dr Braunsweg, who asked Cyril Frankel and me to advise on public relations and advertising. We watched the superb work that Alicia Markova contributed by performing all the main ballerina roles in the company repertoire, and the support given by Pat Dolin in organising the practical side of auditioning, supervising classes and dancing at least once and sometimes twice nightly. Under this devoted guardianship, the company grew into a splendidly co-ordinated unit, ready to make a major contribution to the arts.

One of Dolin's great roles was Prince Albrecht to Markova's Giselle, in a production he had directed in many countries. He decided to re-work the version again with costumes and settings by the painter Hugh Stevenson, who had designed an earlier interpretation for the Ballet Rambert. Dolin believed this would emphasise his indebtedness to classical traditions, while complementing the newly commissioned pieces in the company repertoire by Frederick Ashton, Michael Charnley and David Lichine.

In London the debut took place at the Stoll Theatre, close to the Aldwych, which Sir Oswald Stoll had built as an opera house forty years before. Since demolished, and replaced by an ugly office block, the decor was in the grand style of golden Baroque plasterwork and red velvet, forming an appropriate backcloth for such an occasion. There the new group, named Festival Ballet (in a celebratory nod towards the impending Festival of Britain of 1951) opened a fresh era in British dance. The dancers were a world wide mix. Massine, Danilova and Riabouchinska representing the best of the Diaghilev and the de Basil Russians, Chauviré from Paris, Oleg Briansky from Brussels, John Gilpin and Belinda Wright from Britain's Ballet Rambert, all adding support to the established partnership of Markova and Dolin. In such a gathering artistic temperament was not lacking and the display of some fiery emotions needed skilful handling by Benn Toff and Julian Braunsweg, so that each evening's performance remained on a level footing. Maybe the petty jealousies and individual conceits that rose, as fast as boiling milk, when hair brushes and pointe shoes flew across the dressing rooms, had something to do with the birth, on stage, of some exciting theatrical highlights. Whatever it was, the company was a success and attracted increasing audiences.

Some evenings after a performance, Benn, the Doctor and his wife Vera, asked Cyril and me to join them for dinner. Always the conversation was about work in hand. Revived productions of the classics, a particular guest artiste or the gossip of the dancers, but Benn never failed to keep the atmosphere twinkling along with his comments and his latest stories. One time while Julian enlarged on the problems of a series of ice shows in London, based on such tales as Cinderella, Dick Whittington and Carmen, Benn remarked he had heard that Julian was planning to present *The Desert Song*, on cold oilcloth. On another occasion, when he was asked about his family, Benn replied,

"I have two brothers: one has his jacket off, I was bent off, and the other was tossed off."

But he could also be devastating at your expense. As I said goodbye at the stage door, after introducing him to my most recent girl friend who had come along to a performance with me, he called after us,

"Brian, I nearly forgot. Your wife rang earlier and asked me to tell you to be especially quiet when you go in the house tonight, so as not to wake the children."

Benn's biggest challenge came some twelve months after the company had made its initial start. Programmes were popular, the critics impressed and box office takings more than covering costs, but a London base remained far from settled, as the Stoll Theatre committed itself to a long running musical and became unavailable for a ballet season.

However the management of the Royal Festival Hall stepped in with an offer. Their brand new hall, constructed for large scale orchestral concerts and opened on the South Bank of the Thames for the 1951 Festival, had an awkward gap in its summer programming. Mainly because Britain's premier orchestras were regularly engaged in the summer round of Promenade Concerts at the Royal Albert Hall. A similar competitive group of performances would not be viable and the problem was to find alternative entertainment. Unfortunately, the architects' brief for the building had not included provision for theatrical presentations, so a stage production would require extra facilities.

It was a great chance for Benn. Capitalising on his experience of touring with the ballet he conceived the idea of pre-fabricating a stage with a proscenium arch and orchestral pit, including all the mechanics and wiring, capable of presenting complete productions from the repertoire. As it was impractical to fit a rigid fire curtain into the framework of the building (demanded by the Fire Authorities in purpose made theatres) he satisfied the regulations by using an inherently fire proof material (noile silk, imported from the continent) for the scenery and backcloths. Settings were painted directly onto it, and curtains and hangings dyed to matching colours. The bonus was that this stage system could be set up, or struck, in less than 24 hours, so that there was a minimum loss of revenue and a ballet season could begin shortly after the end of a series of orchestral concerts.

At that time it was a fresh approach to the problem of such multi-purpose use, and Benn's ingenious solution received a deserved ovation. Cyril and I could not miss the opportunity to send Benn a Greetings Telegram on the first night of the season:

'CONGRATULATIONS ON YOUR BIGGEST ERECTION TO DATE.'

From this venue, Festival Ballet ran a summer season of six weeks, followed by another at Christmas. For audiences it was a distinct treat. Attracted by the sweeping lines and general comfort of the building, incorporating the best of post war design and materials, the viewer had unrestricted sight lines to the stage and sat in an air conditioned atmosphere. It provided a sharp contrast to the poor and out-dated conditions in most London theatres, and was the key to the success of the venture.

One of the many triumphs for the company was Dolin's production of *Giselle*. Although he introduced a string of international ballerinas to dance the leading role, the supreme honours always stayed with Alicia Markova. Benn dubbed her performance days 'G Day', as Alicia prepared herself in a long established routine of morning class, a restful afternoon and a careful thinking through of the implications of the action and the character. As essential as this was for her, it was often too much for the volatile tempered Dolin, who scorned such a discipline before his appearances. Yet, whoever they were, he partnered each ballerina with astounding expertise; rehearsing, encouraging and supporting them to a sensitive understanding of his artistic requirements. Chauviré, Krassovska, Riabouchinska, Danilova, Marchand, Sonia Arova and Toumanova, as well as some of Marie Rambert's soloists, including Sally Gilmour, Paula Hinton and Belinda Wright, were amongst the many dancers I saw perform with him.

In three years, from the wings or front of house, I watched over a hundred performances so that I came to regard this story of love and betrayal, with the same deep feelings I had when watching Shakespeare's play *Romeo and Juliet*. For me there are few more moving emotional levels than those that arise from watching great artistes perform their special roles. Ulanova as Juliet, Callas as Norma, Olivier as Othello and Richardson as Cyrano, have all left their mark on me, but Dolin's production of Giselle became an enrichment I will always remember.

I was also fortunate that another friend, Michael Frostick, was the Press Officer at Covent Garden. After a sticky time when he was first demobbed, he had succeeded keeping the ballet well within his sights and held a managerial position at the Opera House. Through him I was able to see many of the performances there. Again, Giselle was a firm favourite, most often with Margot Fonteyn in the Ashton production, but other ballerinas appeared from time to time and I was able to compare the interpretations between the companies. Although Fonteyn was unique in her own inimitable way, I preferred the Dolin version with the illuminating moments of extraordinary drama he created between the principal characters. No doubt his long association with Markova had alerted him to the peak emotional points in the romanticism of the Adam music, so that he was able to contrast the combination of the rustic and noble elements of Act 1 with the ethereal fragility of Act 2. So the tensions mounted right to the climax, and the final tragedy became that much more mesmeric.

I first watched Mary Munro dance Giselle in a Ballet Rambert production at Finsbury Park open air theatre, one summer evening in 1952. The weather had been particularly fine that week and I chose a performance in the moonlight, rather than one stuffed away in an enclosed space. Despite the diversions accompanying such rural occasions; aircraft overhead, traffic roar and games in the park, the quality of her performance shone through the barriers. The great ballerinas may bring their exclusive technical professionalism to the role, and in the preceding twelve months I had not missed a single one, yet hers was an interpretation that brought a refreshing innocence to the story.

The events in this production, played out by a tiny ensemble of young dancers, who although lacking the panache of more experienced performers in the grander company presentations, nevertheless riveted the attention of the audience, as if revealing the tragedy for the first time. It was enchanting and something Marie Rambert was constantly conjuring up from her casts. That evening some of the other gems of her repertoire were on show too, and like all the hard working members of Mim's companies, Mary danced in each item on the programme. Even though the group was small there was no-one who lacked enthusiasm or devotion. As the final orchestral notes died away into the night, I left with a refreshing insight of ballet and Giselle in particular, impressed on me by the musical and dramatic ability of this young artiste.

It was some time later, in January 1954, after I had seen her on stage at several performances, that I met Mary at a party. My recollections of the first performance I had seen her dance had a lot to do with our striking up an immediate rapport, and soon, as meeting followed meeting, we forged a liaison that had us talking of romance, marriage and the future. There were complications (could there be otherwise?) but we relaxed for things to sort themselves out, while she continued her dance career and I worked in films.

Being a Rambert ballerina was no bed of roses. Constantly out on tour in the provinces, existing out of a suitcase and sleeping in digs or the company bus, with Madame's eagle eye staring piercingly at you through rehearsal and performance, was about par for the course. I became deeply concerned about the under nourishment the dancers subscribed to so willingly. Cigarettes, coffee and biscuits were the orders of the day, and religiously maintained week after week. Fragility may be the fashion for a ghostly Giselle, but eight or nine shows a week and attendant rehearsals plus morning classes and the odd Sunday television appearance, necessitated stamina and strength. I tried to be present each Saturday at the final performance whether in Chester, Carlisle, Eastbourne or some other Arts Council rendezvous, then whisk her away to London for proper food and a day of rest, to recharge the aching limbs.

When one of the tours brought Mary to the Kingston Empire, I arranged to take my friends John and Susan Allison with Michael Frostick to see a performance of *Giselle*. Michael had recently moved to Festival Ballet to take over their Public Relations. He was also European representative for the American music and ballet impresario, Sol Hurok, and as Benn and the Doctor achieved further successes with their company, they received an invitation to tour North America under Hurok's management, later in the year.

Mary was outstanding that evening and excelled herself in the role. Although Mim, in her most torturous vein, had waited until after the afternoon matinee performance before telling her she could dance the part that evening. It was part of the Rambert style: being mean to keep them keen, which the dancers accepted as a way of life. In a similar vein she continually pleaded poverty in front of her company, and kept even her longest serving soloists on a pittance of ten pounds a week, confined to working weeks only. For the rest of a contract, as much as three months each year, her dancers existed on the dole, or the generosity of parents, husbands and friends. But there was not a member amongst them who would have chosen otherwise,

"It's an honour," they repeated, "just to be under the eye of Madame."

At the final curtain we went backstage and saw Mary listening to Madame's comments on her performance.

"You were very good, darling," she said, as she noticed our approach, "I've always believed you were not just a dramatic dancer."

Then, when she judged us out of earshot, delivered the devastating coup de grâce she always kept up her sleeve for her stars,

"What a pity in Act 1 you smiled so much and showed those unfortunate ugly teeth of yours."

Mary accepted it bravely enough as she had learned to do over the five years she had danced with the company. It renewed further a determination that the first thing she would organise, if she left Mim, would be cosmetic dentistry. Yet, while she stayed, there would never be enough cash for that.

For me it was a new experience to have a girl friend I could see regularly on stage. It proved a fair counterbalance to the film medium, where audience reaction only arises after the creative process is complete. The theatre provides the immediate response with moods and emotions translated instantly between the stage and the gathered assembly, so that the artiste reacts, during the performance, in the most subtle ways.

Mary had a wide variety of fascinating roles, but she revealed her dramatic abilities most outstandingly in *Winter Night*, a work choreographed by Walter Gore to Rachmaninov's *Second Piano Concerto*. The story was very personal to Gore in his love for two ballerinas, Sally Gilmore and Paula Hinton. It described a man's impassioned upheaval at being in love with contrasting women, and his desperate but futile attempt to hurt neither. Mary played the first and later scorned mistress, and built the part into such intense tragic heights that the press acclaimed her as 'one of Britain's really great dramatic dancers'. On the other hand, she had a brilliantly sharp comic sense, appearing in short humorous sketches for Frank Staff's *Peter and the Wolf*, John Cranko's *Theme and Variations* and Jack Carter's *Life and Death of Lola Montez*. She was certainly highly talented and devoted to the dance: a rare combination noticed by the critics and encouraged, particularly by Peter Williams, the editor of *Dance and Dancers*, and the revered Cyril Beaumont in *The Dancing Times*.

During the following months our relationship grew closer and after we had taken a short holiday in Belgium with dress designers Irene and Eric Wild, she appeared at the next Rambert class, wearing an eternity ring of marquisettes I had given her. Mim lifted up the finger, looked at it closely and announced,

"Mary has got engaged. This time with diamonds."

Shortly afterwards, however, disaster struck, and the future looked alarming and uncertain. Working on a shoe string budget, as Rambert dancers realised, meant that the bare necessities of life missed out. On tour, the company bus was often the only luxury, carting cast and settings from one isolated community theatre to the next in the bleakest of conditions. Always the show must go on strictly to schedule, if the cash was to be there to pay the weekly wage bill. And this was a problem in itself. Low pay meant a desperate fight to economise on food and warmth, to leave enough money to buy make-up, tights and practise shoes, not provided out of company funds. Then the nagging worry, the perpetual fear of confessing to injury or illness, in case it brought a non-appearance and a cut in salary.

It was not easy when Mary became the victim of one of the management's petty economies. Sadly, it left her isolated and without recompense as she desperately tried to contribute to the philosophy of show business. One day, shortly before the evening audiences were due to arrive at the theatre, Noreen, another of the company's leading dancers, finally listened to her colleagues and sought medical help for a high fever, with a red raw rash that had plagued her for days. She received an emergency admittance to the isolation ward at the local hospital, after diagnosis of a vicious strain of the chicken pox virus, and the doctor rang the theatre to warn of the danger of a contagious infection. But tradition dies hard: the show must go on and Mary replaced her sick friend, wearing the only costumes in the wardrobe, the same ones Noreen had worn all week. With an extra rehearsal called half an hour before curtain up, there was no time to fumigate any suspect fabrics and no time to consider the consequences.

Within days, but fortunately at the weekend when Mary was in London, she surrendered to a similar virus, suffering a searing temperature and puss filled spots. She was quite seriously ill for days, without a word of sympathy or the weekly payment due from the company management. So, mournfully disillusioned, I took her away to the seaside to speed her recovery.

On my return to work at Film Centre, George Seager suggested we went out to lunch with Mary at our favourite restaurant, Père Auguste in Gerrard Street. The owner was Colonel Nigel Dugdale, an old friend and the senior PR man at the War Office, who allowed the flamboyant manager, Auguste, to place a distinctive mark upon the French menu. Over champagne and salmon we tried to figure out a plan for the convalescing dancer. Our colleague at Film Centre, Peter Brinson, a devoted balletomane, had contacts with the Covent Garden companies through his friend Peggy van Praagh, and there seemed a possibility that Sadler's Wells might be an interested in Mary joining them. Then, of course, there was a chance something could happen at Festival Ballet, through Benn Toff and Michael Frostick.

It was Michael who came up with a proposal; one that smacked of show business opportunism and underlined his flare as a publicist. Anyone remotely connected to entertainment, at some time or another, finds a certain fascination with a 'star is born' situation. We all knew and loved *42nd Street,* believing it could happen repeatedly, as it did to Janet Gaynor, Judy Garland and Barbra Streisand. In that transformation of the ugly duckling to Swan Princess, we witness the realisation of a fairy story scenario. A couple of days after our lunch, Michael telephoned.

"What is Mary doing?"

"What is her position with Rambert?"

"Might she be fit to dance in an emergency?"

As we discussed each question a plan emerged. Festival Ballet required a burst of publicity to coincide with the announcement that Sol Hurok was to tour the company for six months in North America. Sol wanted names and newsworthy stories to guarantee advance ticket sales, and although box office stars Toumanova and Danilova were guest artistes, and Igor

Stravinsky was emerging from retirement to conduct *Petrouchka*, there must be an accent on youth. In the current season at the Royal Festival Hall, Toumanova was to appear as Giselle in a few days' time. That very morning she had injured her foot, and Michael's idea was to replace her with a young unknown dancer. Dolin would partner the replacement, and the news story released as 'a star is born'. Sol Hurok liked the angle, and as he had seen Mary in a solo role on television a few months before, he urged Michael to win maximum exposure for the switch.

The first hurdle was to unlock Mary's position with Rambert. The management had treated her most shabbily during her illness, and she had not heard from them at all, so we asked Cyril Frankel (relying on his legal training) to compose a letter enabling her to resign from her contract, on grounds of company negligence. John Allison, a general practitioner and close friend, outlined the medical reasons in a separate document and we sat back to await the fireworks.

In the meantime Mary had met Dolin. She charmed him with her enthusiasm and he immediately started to rehearse her in the most delicate points of his choreography. After a short while he reported to Benn and Julian that she would make a wonderful Giselle. Instead of appearing just once, he decided to dance with her for three of the planned four appearances; a special compliment from Dolin, who normally insisted on dancing for the press night performance only. Then he spent many hours tutoring her into the role.

The following evening the waters became somewhat rougher. Madame had received Mary's letter and telephoned her. What was Mary trying to do, she moaned?

"You know the problems we have with our wardrobe, darling. We are so poor. How can we afford the luxury of extra costumes? And where do we find the money for you to be ill?"

It was the old, pleading poverty line, trotted out to suit the occasion. However, for once, Mary answered back and said she no longer wanted to dance with the company. Mim became very angry.

"I will sue you. You can't break your contract with me, just because you are ill and because you send me a legal letter. Who is behind all this, advising you against me? I just don't know who you know."

Unless she had second sight, which some swore she had, she was not to guess I was sitting right next to Mary listening to every word on the extension. Mary gave nothing away and I sensed that Madame put the phone down feeling perplexed, as well she might. I spoke to Michael about the conversation and he decided to ask Dolin to intervene. Pat would call Mim to tell her of the difficulty over Toumanova and suggest Mary might take over. He could point out the reflected glory that would boost the Rambert tradition, underlining its undisputed fame as the nursery of British ballet. Next morning Madame telephoned Mary again.

"I've some wonderful news for you, darling. I've persuaded my dear friend Pat Dolin to give you a marvellous chance. He's going to partner you in *Giselle* in place of poor Tamara. What about that? And he's asked me to come and help you at the dress rehearsal."

Mary went off that morning much happier than I had seen her for weeks. With the pieces in place the design could unfold. Michael leaked his first story. A short item, to catch the morning papers that Toumanova had an injured foot and was unlikely to dance for a few days. Then on the day of the performance a press release for the evening editions,

'Tamara Toumanova, the £500 a week ballerina, will not be able to make her guest night appearance at the Royal Festival Hall tonight. She has sprained her ankle. The title role in *Giselle*, in which she was to appear, will be danced by Mary Munro, of the Ballet Rambert.

Miss Munro, 23, slight and dark-haired, is one of Marie Rambert's leading dancers. Her Giselle has been highly praised. Tonight gives Miss Munro the biggest opportunity of her career.'

That was it. Hard news is scarce in the dog days of August and there was little else that day to get excited about. The photographers and the interviewers arrived in haste at the South Bank stage door, as Benn, Michael and the Doctor waited to speak to them. The new star was a hot story.

Yet unaware of the fuss she had stirred up, Mary worked

away in the final dress rehearsal, prompted by Marie Rambert and Tamara Toumanova, and partnered by Dolin. There was an air of pregnant anticipation. Some of the other dancers had trained with Mary over the years, and some of the men, like John Gilpin, had partnered her at the Rambert. So, although as on all similar occasions, there were tinges of regret from those who wished that good fortune had shone on them, everyone determined to make the evening a success.

I had been busy, too. Mary's personal wardrobe was sparse, reflecting the hard life of a touring dancer on a low salary, and it scarcely fitted the image we hoped to unveil. Another friend, Irene Wild, was the answer. A talented costume designer, she had workrooms which supplied Harrod's and Liberty's, and we sketched out what would be the minimum requirements. She would certainly need a stunning dress for after the performance, as Pat Dolin had asked her to accompany him to the Savoy for dinner while the expected Press calls and photo sessions would demand changes for indoor and outdoor wear. Late in the afternoon of the debut we delivered a complete new wardrobe, all pressed and ready for the evening.

It was a great triumph. Mary carried off her part in fine style, so that the audience warmed instantly to her performance even though momentarily expressing dismay when Dolin stepped before the curtain, dressed as Albrecht, and announced to the packed Hall that Toumanova would not appear.

"But," he continued, "I have brought for you tonight a young dancer. And with the help of her teacher, Marie Rambert, I am sure you will acclaim her a new star of British ballet. Ladies and gentlemen,... Mary Munro."

There was no doubt that in the first act she was nervous, but her freshness overcame any technical problem and with Dolin playing a sympathetic and caring partner, she sailed through the role, bringing a poignancy to the mad scene, seldom seen previously on the London stage. In Act 2, her dramatic talent was distinctive, so that the final denouement and farewell to Albrecht as dawn filters into the woodland glen, left the audience enraptured by the emotional tension of what they had seen. For a moment there was silence, then the applause burst out and cheers brought curtain call after curtain call. It was an evening to treasure, and Michael Frostick was certain of his headlines.

'FOR A NEW GISELLE, A DREAM COMES TRUE', wrote William Hickey in the *Daily Express*.
'THE NEW STAR', proclaimed the *Daily Sketch*.
'A DANCE TO STARDOM', signalled the *Evening News*.

The story was front page news with pictures and interviews. The *Daily Mail* followed through with further comment and photographs:

> 'It was hail and farewell day for two stars of the ballet. Miss Mary Munro, who triumphed on Monday night as Giselle at London's Royal Festival Hall goes out shopping, while Miss Moira Shearer gave her last performance in a dancing role as Titania in a *Midsummer Night's Dream*.'

and then added:

> 'Miss Mary Munro, who danced to fame as Giselle on Monday night, will go on a 26 week tour of America and Canada as a soloist with the London Festival Ballet Company.
> This will give her a commencing salary of about £20 per week,... double her present salary with the Ballet Rambert Company, who have agreed to release her.'

With such reviews and publicity, it was no wonder that the Royal Festival Hall sold out for each of Mary's performances. At the third appearance John Gilpin partnered her, but Dolin stepped back for the final evening. That night the stage overflowed with a huge display of flowers as more and more bouquets showered upon the new star during the curtain calls. Afterwards we had to hire a taxi to take one load, while I drove the rest away in a car I had borrowed for the evening. Hurok was well pleased with the notices and flew to London to be at the last performance. Afterwards Julian, Vera, Pat, Benn, Mary and I went out to dinner with him. As the press had wind of the celebration, I had to show a low profile as a mere escort to Mary to support the role she had adopted in front of the reporters. It made a better story that she had no time for boy friends, in pursuing the hard working life of a dancer.

In any case, Mary remained tied to the coils of a teenage marriage she had entered into with another member of the Rambert Company. This had ended disastrously a few weeks later, but had not yet been into the courts because of the poor financial state of each of them. Then, divorces were difficult to obtain and complications about 'the grounds for separation', the 'decree nisi' and the Queen's Proctor, made the procedure hazardous and lengthy. It had also some unfortunate repercussions.

My cousin Joyce Norris in Canada, at my bidding, saw a performance of the ballet and met Mary afterwards. Later she saw a review in the local paper containing a reference to Mary's married state, of which Joyce was unaware. She wrote a puzzled letter to me declaring, 'I thought you said she was your girl friend, but the paper says she is married!' And in the more puritanical age my parents and relatives still enjoyed in the fifties, such a suggestion was heavily frowned upon.

However the omens were favourable. After her London success, Mary took daily class with Festival Ballet to learn their repertoire, and towards the end of September prepared for departure from Southampton to the United States. She would be away a long time; six months. And although Benn promised to be back before then, I felt sad as I waved Mary and the company good-bye at Waterloo Station. If our relationship could survive this we conjectured on the prospect of marriage in mid 1955, after her divorce.

Certainly the events of that summer were memorable, and there was a cosy feeling that so many of my friends were part of the whole adventure. It was comforting to know that fact was just as romantic and exciting as fiction, and the old formulas for the rise of a young star still read like a fairy story. I found myself using the same theme a short time later when directing a musical play on television, written by Hazel Adair, for Millicent Martin and Peter Gilmore. In our *Rush Hour* series, a tale of the young unknown actress making good, echoed the magic that is behind the grease paint and heartaches of the world of entertainment. For me, that magic started in earnest, when as a youth of fourteen summers, I saw Markova and Dolin at Stratford, and met the spell of the ballet, head on.

EIGHTEEN

A TELEVISION DEBUT WITH JEREMY THORPE

ONE OF MY lucky breaks was to discover when I was quite young, that a useful trait in my character was in accepting change tolerantly. That is on the basis there is little you can do about it, anyway, unless you have Luddite tendencies. The clichés have never been more readily available,... 'everything must end eventually',... 'life is not a rehearsal', and the like, so in the style of Confucius, when 'rape is inevitable, lay back and enjoy it'.

Those of us, with the good fortune to be optimists, have invariably swallowed everything as it comes, allowing the revolution to sweep over us and then buckling down to the new, with hardly a cursory nod. Essentially that's why we are here now, simply because our forebears survived the massacres and the plagues of the last 50,000 years. That alone should be enough to make the pessimists stew on the 'what is', rather than pretend about the 'might have beens'. It is a question of looking at things differently. Accepting that change does not necessarily mean neglecting the past, and is a suitable method to transfer energy away from regret, towards exploration. The development of the self arises solely from the will to opt for an active experience. Without that, we cannot claim our inheritance, or any purpose for living.

The year 1955, confronted me with a root change again. I was looking forward to the thrill of an adventurous way ahead supported by various prospects on offer. The odd circumstance was that I would have to adjust on two facets, because the future demanded both a career and an emotional showdown. It demanded

286

a fair amount of tricky balancing; a vocational advancement did not deeply perturb me. So far, I had felt movement along this line a natural one, as I moved from schooldays to army service and then back into the civilian marketplace. The adjustment to situations and places had been reasonably smooth and I had no cause to think I could not cope in this direction.

My career was progressing satisfactorily. I enjoyed film-making. I enjoyed the job and the stimulation. There was scope for a great deal of self expression, within the confines of working to other people's briefs, but I was pursuing also the possibilities of gaining the freedom to initiate my own creative ambitions. Certainly in documentary film my colleagues shared similar aims and we had the advantage of a common purpose as well as a desire to succeed in our craft. Our ability to meet the technical challenges brought us closer together in seeking solutions, for my friends tended, like me, to be late arrivals in the industry. We did well and gained a confidence in our achievements that augured a bright future. It was this confidence I took with me when transferring across to television, and I saw no reason why I should have any hang ups from my lack of specific expertise in that media.

The ultimate encounter was hardly overpowering. Once we defined the format and deciphered the boundaries, the elements for transmitting a live television show were clearly recognisable in the mechanics that made up the direction of a film or the presentation of a play in the theatre. In a nutshell, it was not unlike driving a complicated vehicle or flying an aeroplane, requiring instant decisions and responsible action.

When Stephen McCormack asked me to join him at Associated Rediffusion, one of the companies granted a licence to operate in commercial television in 1955, the formalities were straightforward enough. My interview was in a manner I had come to associate with the Forces, but then as the management team consisted almost exclusively of senior ranks from the Royal Navy and the Army, it was a fair compromise. Captain Brownrigg, the managing director, had commanded a squadron of destroyers in the Mediterranean and seemed far more interested in the record of my Army Commander in 1945, than what I knew about broadcasting. Nevertheless, lower down the echelons the expertise was firmly in place, with ex-BBC Television personnel like

McCormack, Lloyd-Williams and Michael Westmore as programme supervisors and Michael Yates, who had led the BBC Design Department, backed up by first rate camera and sound crews, headed by John Hamilton and Vic Gardiner, straight out of Lime Grove and Alexandra Palace studios. I soon had a letter of appointment in my pocket and a date to start a Producers course at the training base in Kensington, attached to a salary that made it very worth while.

As this happened in my working arrangements, it was convenient that in my emotional life developments were in hand, too. Initially, as I was an only child, I had felt a certain sense of isolation when meeting other people, as most only children do, but the war years ended that, and I generally felt confident about relationships. This in itself was a small boost when I came to tackle the other change in my pattern of life, the test of marriage, and the trial of sharing with someone on a permanent basis.

Getting married never disappeared entirely out of discussions between parents and children in the days of the forties and fifties. Weddings were part of the deal, comparable to starting school, finding a job and standing on your own two feet. It was always there and we did not forget it. Gossip at home was about family relationships and having babies: a sort of ritual soul washing. My mother and her married friends had no other aspiration but to see their children comfortably settled in domesticity, just as previously their mothers had followed a similar dictum. It was the respectable thing to do, and you became aware that you, too, must comply without fail. In such a climate of opinion divorce and separation were out of bounds. Adultery, wife beatings and promiscuousness lacked corroboration, however much you were conscious they went on. And, as young lads with sharp eyes and ears, that facade was not an impregnable fortress.

By the age of six (and one year into infants' school) it was apparent that little girls were not the same as little boys and the process of learning what it was all about, depended on the gang you mixed with. That our parents should believe that purity went hand in hand with their specific silence on such topics, was beyond our understanding. It proved no bar to our enquiries. In fact, they need have looked no further than their own brood to see how the small lasses in our mixed classes showed an amazing skill at composing the most startling suggestions in their love letters. Or they might have questioned the naming of our young friends as 'Jigger' Turrell and 'Finger' Ryan, when neither could dance nor play the guitar. However, the gap between information and action was where the real chasm occurred. Little girls may have been protected from carnal desires by the careful supervision of their parents, but they gleaned enough in their innocence. It armed them with the knowledge they had something more precious to sell than little boys; and the sale price included a wedding ring.

Nevertheless, mothers and fathers sheltered behind this wall of silence right up to the time of betrothal. We all know of the number of cases amongst our friends, where years of married unhappiness have been the direct result of this lack of understanding. It left them vulnerable and naive, even to their wedding night. Somehow I got by. My friends and I found time alongside our football, Jumbo Leo and Fivestones to speculate on where we came from and how. The mysteries of the subject may not have been completely solved, but we could manage.

There were books we passed on to each other in the Public Library, Graham Greene's *Stamboul Train* and Chaucer's randy *Canterbury Tales*. So, by the time we entered grammar school, we were well versed in finding the erotic classical painting or the partially nude pictures, in the *Health and Strength* magazines. Yet the adult conspiracy to keep us from the facts, spread even to our schoolmasters. They saw no requirement to explain the awkward sexual references in the texts we read.

Then we discovered, one day, that the 'Good' Sheppard, our chemistry master, who tutored the sixth form in biology, was very straightforward about the topic of reproduction. It was an easy affair to sidetrack him during one of our School Certificate year lessons, and he delivered an explicit sex lecture that fully answered our queries. Even the difficult ones like Siamese Twins, abortion and contraception, he dealt with in a clear fashion and was prepared to continue his instruction as further points arose later on. Perhaps because he was a handsome bachelor, who openly walked arm in arm with many a pretty lass, he was more in tune with our wishes to extend the school curriculum into previously unmentionable areas. It certainly relieved his colleagues of any responsibility. However, for us, it was a breakthrough. For the first time, we felt a robust and natural respect towards the opposite sex. Quite where this left our parents, I am not sure, but we might have benefited considerably if their attitude had been more matter of fact.

When my turn arrived to test out these theories on family sex education, I wonder if I was any more successful. I tried to answer the more difficult points as they arose, but if I was preaching to the converted, as I suspect I might have been, then I deserved the reaction I had from my son, home from school on his final half term holiday. After a subdued knock on his bedroom door, I entered to take a morning cup of tea. He was asleep and the blinds were down, but he was not sleeping alone. Two heads rested on the pillow, the extra one, blonde and female. He awoke before I could exit, summed up the situation and said,

"Dad meet Marion........Marion, my father."

I proposed another cup of tea, and made a hurried departure. Later that day when his companion had left, I indicated my interest.

"Stephen," I confided, "you must be careful,... diseases and viruses. All around us. I hope you take some suitable protection."

"Come off it, dad," he snapped back, "Marion is a nurse at Edgware General. She's qualified, you know."

For what? I wondered; but kept my peace.

My own entry into the sexual Olympics occurred when I was free of home and at University. While the growing attitude of relaxation, towards such taboos, was part of the change the war encouraged. By the time I left the army the barriers were down. There was no going back to the stuffiness of the thirties, although the marriage ceremony was still demanding its hostages. My age group soon enlisted in the ranks, despite their protestations it would never happen to them, and the norms of our parents' generation found a breathing space to re-establish themselves alongside the new world order. It was not to last for long as the Beatles and the pill called it quits.

Thus I kept my bachelor status until 1955, entirely as a result of not wanting to settle before I salvaged the lost years of secondment to the army in a stable work environment. When I was finally confident, I married Mary Munro at the British Embassy in Madrid, while she was on a June tour with Festival Ballet and I was kicking my heels, waiting the moment to join television. So I managed the changes in one grand leap.

The television training course was at the old Viking Film Studios and the Granville Theatre in Fulham, under the supervision of another ex-BBC man, David Boisseau. A thorough professional, with an unflappable calm, he smartly had a whole bunch of us up and running. He prepared us to enter the heady atmosphere of live programming, in the days when fluffs and break downs appeared instantly on the viewer's screen, without any intervention of pre-recordings and clever editing.

The new intake came from a variety of backgrounds. Cyril Coke from feature films, Philip Saville from acting, Joan Kemp-Welch from theatre directing, Dick Lester from radio, Hazel Adair from writing *Mrs Dale's Diary*, along with a mixed bag of journalists, photographers, stage people and the like. But the BBC monopoly was a tight one and there were few technicians available outside the stranglehold of Broadcasting House. This had distinct advantages, for the instructors were from a common source, providing a certain unity to the images on the screen, and giving the technical language a basic identity. Soon we were talking about gen-locks, strobing, image orthicons and avo-meters as though we had known their mysteries all our lives. Although the thought of sitting in a tiny control gallery to direct a crew of 30 or 40 individuals (who had not met each other until four weeks previously and had to entertain an audience of some millions of viewers nightly) was not for the faint of heart.

As the course wound down, Stephen McCormack asked me to look after a science programme, brought to the company by Norman Macqueen. It was his idea to have a question and answer session on scientific topics, departing radically from the BBC's formal approach to science, built on long boring lectures. Norman had a vast experience of filming special technical processes in slow motion and time lapse photography, and he reckoned that film clips, visual aids and laboratory experiments could illuminate scientific facts. Together we developed a half hour slot around a panel of distinguished scientists replying to viewers' requests. We aimed to present the information in entertaining terms, and sought out the most photogenic and amusing boffins from the Universities and Research Laboratories throughout the country. There was Sir Peter Medawar, the Head of Biology at University College, London,

Professor Wynn Jones from Newcastle, Professors Massey and Blackett from London, Sir Alexander Todd from Cambridge, Sir Harold Spencer Jones, the Astronomer Royal, Dr Farqueson from the Met Office, and Sir Edward Bullard FRS, as well as a number of distinguished Harley Street surgeons, psychiatrists and consultants, who rapidly established such a rapport with the audience that the press began to ask,

'Why hasn't the BBC got a programme like this?'

There was, though, a major difficulty. Although we tested a number of candidates, from actors to science correspondents, including Norman Macqueen, they lacked the sparkle we were looking for. What we needed was a down to earth approach, which would not frighten off the viewers by an overdose of scientific waffle. With the immediate opening of the commercial television stations, it was a general problem. So many new programmes were searching for anchormen and presenters, and the BBC had locked away their Dimblebys and Michelmores in exclusive contracts. But one morning, while I was checking out the lists of applications the company had received from potential interviewers and announcers, I happened upon a Mr Jeremy Thorpe, '... interested,' he wrote, 'in politics, law and sundry subjects,' who offered, '... to enliven a debate or a programme with spirited comment.'

He had recently performed well as the losing Liberal candidate for Barnstable, at the General Election in May of that year, and was now nursing the seat ready for another try. When I rang his number he was away in North Devon, but his enthusiasm was such that he telephoned within the hour and arrived some three hours later in my small bull-pen office at Rediffusion.

I liked him instantly. There was no mistaking the talent. It was there in abundance. Charm, wit, the gift to listen, reason and contribute a considered statement, all coupled with a raffish handsomeness that a few years before would have seen him in the cockpit of a Spitfire or astride the turret of a Churchill tank. He had appeared only briefly on television previously, connected with his duties for the Liberal party; yet I had no hesitation in plunging him into the deep end, as Chairman of *The Scientist Replies*, in a mock transmission the following day. His performance fully justified my confidence. He handled the rehearsals and the test impeccably and I could scarcely wait for our first programme to show him off with the scientists. He hit the bullseye immediately. And the *Evening News* was not the only newspaper to note we had something quite unusual:

'Jeremy Thorpe in *The Scientist Replies*, is a young man amongst his learned elders. He has an extraordinary but not in the least irritating self-assurance and he is wisely content to signpost the discussion with his questions and then leave the experts to get on with it without interruption. One gets the impression the scientists are at their ease.'

With the series under way, Jeremy became proficient at balancing queries ranging from black holes and nuclear physics to the growth of an embryo and virgin birth with delicacy and style. When we dealt with the topic 'What is life?' in a single programme, he kept the explanations clear of becoming too erudite, even with four F.R.S's. joining in the debate. His eye remained fixed on clarity. This edition of the programme evoked some interesting comments in the press reviews. Maurice Richardson wrote in *The Observer*:

'Four FRS's: Sir Harold Spencer Jones: Sir Alexander Todd: Professor H.S.W.Massey: Professor P.B.Medawar; Astronomer, Biochemist, Physicist, Biologist, with Jeremy Thorpe as an efficient chairman, they proceeded to give you the most exciting half hour in the history of Television. Viewers questions about the nature of matter and life... some of them of the naive, urgent kind that one always wants to ask oneself... had been carefully picked so that we were taken in an orderly spiral progress from the microscopic to the macroscopic, from the electron to the nebula, from the inorganic to the organic. There was a film through an electron microscope, of chromosome division in a living cell: a demonstration of a model of the immensely complex molecule of nucleic acid, which seems to be the basis of life. We finished up with the spiral nebulae and a nibble at the continuous creation hypothesis. This was a very crowded half hour, almost too stimulating at bed-time for anyone who likes to indulge in science-fictional fantasies.'

Despite receiving a friendly notice,

'Directed by Brian Taylor, who is clever enough to let us feel there is no directing.'

and a morning summons, to the office of the senior Deputy Controller, Cecil Lewis, who told me he thought it was the most entertaining factual programme the company had transmitted so far, it was somewhat of a surprise to find myself in his office again, some two hours later. He was standing by the window, staring into the distance,

"Oh Brian," he mumbled, "about your science programme, last night. Roland Gillett (the Programme Controller) saw it and said it was the most boring piffle he'd ever seen in his life. If you do it again, he'll throw you, Jeremy Thorpe and your scientists out of the window."

"From which floor?" I said, and left quickly.

I learned later that Lew Grade, who was in charge of the ATV transmissions each weekend in London and the new Birmingham station, due to open the following Spring, was watching the programme to assess if he might use it for networking to the regions. He hated the whole concept, asserting that Jeremy Thorpe gave it too much of an up-market, London based appeal, and accordingly told Gillett. A few months later, when the Midlands came on the air, our programme received the chop and *The Statesman* noted:

'*The Scientist Replies,*... one of the programmes recently cited by Sir Robert Fraser, the Director General of the Independent Television Network, in a somewhat sophisticated argument for the high cultural value of ITV,... is the latest victim of this euthanasia,... which buries all.'

However, we were able to have the last laugh on the final programme. Professor Wynn Jones made sure we would be remembered. Dramatically, he blew us off the viewers' screens with an explosion that shattered the sound system at Wembley Studios, from where the programmes were broadcast, and had everyone telephoning anxiously to see if we had survived.

For Jeremy the adventure into science had been an astonishing triumph. Even more so when, as if on cue, the BBC poached the idea and presented their own *Question of Science*, but without him, as Chairman. It was a pedestrian effort lacking originality and the rippling, fast thinking wit that suffused ours. The press were not slow in reaching their opinion, calling it,

> 'plodding earnestness, missing the touch of elegance brought by Jeremy Thorpe.'

As a practising barrister he had shown no distress in mastering his brief and during the next few months, when I became the studio director for the news magazine programme *This Week*, I arranged for him to interrogate many of the politicians we interviewed, including Hugh Gaitskill, Joe Grimmond, Ian McCleod and Richard Crossman. In front of them he was able to show his skill at cross examination. His own political career was also on the ascendant, and he convincingly won a parliamentary seat and followed his father and grandfather into the House of Commons.

We retained our links. My wife and I visited his home, where he lived with his mother before marrying his first wife Caroline, killed so tragically in a car crash a short time later. He enjoyed the opera and the ballet and was an accomplished violinist, so we talked about playing trios and quartets together, if our careers would ever allow us the time.

Naturally, I watched with interest, his spectacular progress as a politician over the years. I am not sure that when I first met him, he was merely flirting with television because he found it stimulating and different, but I have often pondered how he might have developed as a media personality rather than as a party leader. He had a distinctive style of his own. A much sharper cutting edge than either Robin Day or David Frost. And his special characteristic of exuding Britishness, might well have seen him reach dizzying heights in the personality stakes, if he had tried an assault on the American networks. On the other hand, should he have followed the legal route he had initially planned, he might have, through his grasp of court procedure and the bounds of justice, gained very rich rewards.

He frequently left me silent in admiration, as he whisked around the sombre shadows of the High Court, after we had finished a programme briefing or an interview in Television House. The studios in Kingsway were a stone's throw, through the back alleys, into the rear entrances of the Courts, and his expert knowledge knew just the right one to dive into. Inside he would hurry me from session to session, summarising each trial, and nodding a pleasant, "Good day, how are you?", to the ushers who would allow us to slip in and out. Then he would recount some outrageous piece of gossip about the Judge or the Counsel in each case. "Don't ever come up before him in the afternoon for judgement," he would whisper about one learned gentleman. "Pissed as a fart, after lunch." And he would joke about another, "Can't keep his hands off the girls, that one. Make sure when you go before him, you have lots of pretties in the witness box. He'll believe anything they say."

Yet despite his familiarity with the inner rules of the law, his later misfortunes showed he, too, could become a victim of their operation. I had never any sign to suspect that fate would treat him as it did. During the time we worked together no suspicions arose in my mind, for he certainly made no advances toward me, and the accusations in the Old Bailey trial of 1979 did not seem to match the conclusions I had drawn earlier.

In the aftermath of the prosecution, with the shot dogs and conspiracies laid to rest, by a strange turn of fortune, Lord Grade suggested that Jeremy should front a Television programme from Birmingham. It was as though his lordship was attempting to offer compensation for his earlier remiss in chasing *The Scientist Replies* off the air. But it was too late to recapture the old magic and Jeremy declined. The early onset of Parkinson's disease has slowed him down considerably, but maybe the bitter shocks he endured were just one step too far. Certainly there is no denying that the seventies were strange days.

It is still not plain what forces were abroad which ventured to discredit so many politicians and public figures. Peter Hain, Harold Wilson, Edward Heath and Ted Short, all suffered one way or another, while Guildford Fours, Birmingham Sixes and the rest must cause the same concern as we earlier viewed the smears of the spy masters, and the McCarthy era in the United States.

Perhaps we expect too much of the keepers of the Law. The benevolence we used to treasure in our friendly neighbourhood policeman, seems lost in combating a welter of violence and corruption. Though always justice must be seen to be done if it is not to end in a festering hate. When it is a weapon of revenge, or used as a rough balance to sort out greed and power, then its purpose disappears. I reckoned this aspect the most alarming when once I helped to clear the slurs hanging over my friend Benn Toff caught in a chain of circumstance not dissimilar to that, which almost completely engulfed Jeremy Thorpe.

One evening, Benn telephoned. He asked to see me straightaway as he was in serious trouble. When he arrived at my home he told a horrific story. Three hours before, he had left the Royal Festival Hall when the ballet performance was under way, to go the short distance to Southampton Row, where he lived with his elderly father, who was unwell. He walked towards the bus stop at Waterloo Station, but wanting a pee turned into the Gents loo for relief. There seemed to be no-one else around, yet as he stood at a urinal, someone came out from the cubicle behind him and someone else walked down the stairs from the street. He took a short while to finish, perhaps a few seconds longer for reasons that will appear later, and then turned to zip his flies and rinse his hands. As he did so, one of the men came up to him, flashed a Warrant Card, and declared Benn under arrest. Benn stood flabbergasted, and as they made their way to the pavement above, demanded an explanation. They hustled him to the kerb, stopped a taxi and gave directions to Bow Street Police Station. Ignoring his protestations, they commented he would hear all, shortly.

In front of the Duty Sergeant they charged him with importuning and indecent exposure, but he had the presence of mind to make a telephone call and contact the Festival Ballet solicitor, Victor Mishcon, later Lord Mishcon, a doughty fighter on behalf of the Arts and the Theatre. Mishcon reacted quickly, so that within an hour Benn was released and the charge adjourned.

It was a shattering experience. The whole episode seemed ludicrous, but I could see Benn was on the point of breakdown, worried how the news might affect the health of his father. The sheer amount of fabrication and injustice was crippling, so I decided to call our Doctor friend, John Allison, for support. Benn told me he had recently been under medical treatment, and when John arrived we listened to the full story and how the events had unfolded. What was disturbing was that on arrival at Bow Street, one of the policemen had said to Benn,

"Are you one of those Ballet boys, then? We saw you at the stage door, so you must be."

Anyone less like a dancer was 16 stone Benn,... hardly a fairy to float on a wire.

John was helpful and precise. Benn had, in fact, been consulting him about a bladder problem. It would be perfectly normal, given the circumstances, for him to stand a long time urinating, and any police evidence on this looked discredited. The real crux of such a charge, however, depended on the justices and their inclinations to support the police evidence, come what may, as a means of preserving the law. This needed countering and rebutting, without directly suggesting the police were incompetent.

At this stage I left the technical side in the hands of the solicitors and the medical advisers, yet providing Benn with personal back-up, so that in court he would appear relaxed and confident. Mishcon carried out his role in fine style. He used Dr Allison's diagnosis and treatment records to telling effect when cross examining the two policemen, leaving them suspended, in a sea of uncertainty, about the real reasons for Benn's delayed pee. Their primary impressions now took on a different hue. Benn performed well in the witness box and it was soon apparent that his version of events claimed serious attention, as the prosecution resorted to innuendo and doubtful conclusions. The magistrates dismissed the charges and the only nag remaining was what might have resulted had expert guidance been unavailable. Unfortunately, Benn's own personal pressures did not end there. As he went into the defendants room to collect his coat, the two policemen approached him, friendly and jovially,

"We'd like to take our wives to the ballet one evening. They've always wanted to try it. Can you get us tickets? There was no offence meant against you, Benn. You were fair game that night. And when we are out on a queer bashing round, we have to charge someone. Otherwise it wouldn't look good for us, would it?"

As far as possible, Benn hid the incident from his father, but when the old man died a short while afterwards, he wondered if his life was shortened by what he might have heard casually or read in the press. The stress on Benn, also, had its long term effects. From then on his health began a slow decline and he was never quite the same bright open fellow he had been. Perhaps he was as stunned as I was, realising that institutions previously upheld for their infallibility, had proved so unsteady when challenged. Faith we held from infancy lay undermined, with our trust betrayed. Such is the frailty of the human state. Our ability to combat the abuse of such power is made ever weaker as greed and jealousy establish their bid for supremacy. Thus our relationships are undermined and our faith impaired. Our only defence rests in our hearts, and in constant determination to fight for what we believe is right and just.

NINETEEN

COOL FOR CATS

WHEN *THE SCIENTIST REPLIES* came off the air I was in demand to direct other programmes, so that in a short time I was looking after four or five major transmissions a week. My Production Assistant, Ann Stead, had to cope with the administrative side of shooting scripts, contracts, requisition of facilities and rehearsal space, while I spent every spare moment, in conferences with casting directors, set designers, wardrobe ladies, lighting supervisors and the other paraphernalia of presentation. It was a busy period and our fingers were in a multiple of pies.

The provocative current affairs programme *This Week* had only recently made its debut under the ex-BBC producing team of Caryl Doncaster and Peter Hunt, and sought a studio director. Caryl enlisted me to control the live interviews and discussions from the studio, which in their own way set new standards in news reporting. For one thing they attracted an untapped seam of youthful talent: young men who had found it almost impossible to break down the nepotistic systems of recruitment into the BBC. On the weekly programme we introduced Daniel Farson, Michael Ingrams, and Desmond Wilcox, all later to become television personalities in their own right, as well as Cyril Bennet, Ian Fordyce and Elkan Allan who rose to high appointments in the industry. It was part of the fresh winds of change that commercial television was breathing into previously 'closed shop' areas of entertainment.

At the same time, *Cavalcade of Sport*, a one hour weekly challenge to the BBC's *Sports Night*, acquired my services for overall presentation and direction. Ken Johnstone (a former newspaper man) was the Head of Sport, and with Kent Walton (an actor turned radio commentator) booked the various sporting items for transmission. Each Tuesday I wrote the narratives to previously filmed sports stories; Kent recorded them in the news studios of ITN, and then later in the day we set up the linking arrangements to bring the live sports action into the running order of the show at 8 p.m. It sometimes produced a heap of headaches, when either foul weather, or bad luck, interfered with the relays from the venues around the country.

Another programme in my schedule was *Kingsway Corner*. We started with one programme a week, but it proved so popular with the viewers, because of its 'off the cuff' format, that it became a daily feature. Stephen McCormack had originated the idea and we sited our cameras on the pavements outside Television House in Kingsway, with a team of interviewers including David Jacobs, Muriel Young, John Witty and Kent Walton, who stopped passers by to talk to them.

In a way it was an extension of radio's *In Town Tonight*, except it used cameras to introduce people from the streets of London; a natural sort of actuality television. We realised that although the British may have a reputation for reticence, place a camera and a few technicians on the roadside, and within seconds, someone stops to see what is happening. Others join in and try to peer over the shoulders of those in front, and as the crowd increases on every side, so does the cast. Should things not run smoothly, or rain interfere, we had a stand-by studio on tap, a few feet away, in Television House, where we chatted to celebrities who were working in the area. There were always actors and actresses from the theatres around the Aldwych eager to appear, and together with visiting overseas stars in the Savoy Hotel close by, and a Q.C. or two from the Law Courts, we kept a lively programme bubbling along. We set up our control room at the front of the building, and I had an easy task mixing between the pictures of the visitors and the passers-by. The half hour became a feast of informal television as the stories unwound. Something the media creates, so effortlessly and effectively, like no other form of entertainment.

Of course, there were transmissions when things did not go so well and retaining a picture on air could sometimes be nerve racking. While it was never difficult to create a second of uncertainty (if needed to emphasise a particular dramatic point, or, what is more important, to ensure the audience stayed on through the commercial breaks) it was the unexpected mini disaster that was the trickiest to handle. *The Scientist Replies* never presented such a problem, for a very competent Jeremy Thorpe covered up the duff laboratory experiment or a wrong piece of film. But it was totally different when a whole line of reasoning fell apart on the turn of a single factor.

In *This Week* the volatility of politicians, investigative journalists and public relations consultants was often a nightmare. One evening as we were airing some political party hobbyhorse, I cued the Floor Manager to alert the Labour M.P., George Brown, that he was next on camera. We found him in the Hospitality Room, fast asleep, and in no fit state to appear. He seemed to have accepted our hospitality at its face value. The presenter, Michael Westmore, was already making the initial introductions, so I rang the phone on the desk beside him and whispered,

"Pretend you have got George Brown on the line."

Michael was right on the ball, and delivered a wonderful solo performance. He asked a whole sequence of pointed questions, summarising a typical politician's evasion to each one, without us either seeing or hearing the other person. Afterwards, nobody seemed aware of any inconsistency. It merely proved our theories that Honourable Members rarely have anything important to say, apart from party claptrap, while confirming their ability to perform as circus contortionists when they require a convenient face saver. For us the experience proved a useful standby procedure in future transmissions.

Another setback occurred on a sports programme, when we interviewed the young boxer Peter Waterman. He was already showing championship potential and we organised a ten minute spot for him to talk about a forthcoming fight. As the interview consisted of a pre-arranged set of questions from Ken Johnstone, we had opted to write out the answers on the Autocue machine. This would allow Peter to speak directly to the lens of the camera, and read off the text, avoiding hesitancies and any loss of words. At that time, sporting heroes often lacked the public relations techniques they have developed in recent years, since financial rewards have become more dependant on their screen personality, and in this case, we had noted that the fighter was somewhat more assured in the ring than in the studio. With the interview prompting system ready and a rehearsal showing that Peter could handle the situation quite adequately, we counted the seconds down to the 'on air' signal with confidence. Unfortunately, as we mixed into the studio setting and Ken Johnstone began his introduction, the Autocue mechanism took on a life of its own and spilled out the rolls of written answers across the studio floor. Ken flinched visibly as though hit by a right hook, and for a long moment seemed prepared to throw in the towel. Then he winked at Peter and started to ask some straightforward questions, requiring a simple 'Yes' or 'No' answer. The operator gathered up the loose paper, rewound it, and tried to catch up with the interview, but things settled down and, with nine minutes gone, I ordered the wind up procedure. We passed professionally into the closing remarks, ran the final title routine, and left the credits to tick over slowly, using up any spare seconds.

No-one outside the studio was aware of the problem or queried the obvious change of pace. Strangely, the station duty announcer, tucked away in the presentation suite at the top of the building, remarked to us, over the intercom he reckoned we had brought some real tension into the programme, 'rather like Waterman goes through when he enters the ring'. Little did he know!

Peter won his contest the following week with far less concern than we had displayed in the studio and afterwards we discarded the theory of trying to pre-empt the results.

Prompting equipment was not the only machinery that could bewilderingly fail in its task. Anything functioning normally during rehearsal and even into the final check out, half an hour before transmission, could mysteriously fizzle out the moment we started countdown. As the Production Assistant called the seconds from her seat in the control gallery,

"Ten, nine, eight, seven,..."

so the spell was broken.

One night it was not an isolated piece of delicate electronic wizardry that went on the blink. The complete studio surrendered, plunging us into darkness, and the normally infallible intercommunication system played dead. As the emergency lighting flickered into life, the five seconds we had before we were due on the network were of no help. Cast and musicians, floor crews and studio staff could only hang on, looking glum. A message eventually reached us to close down, as a serious mains' fault had severed the local electricity supply. I had to tell the artists that pay outs depended on a completed transmission and company contracts were void. Only a small sum, for the rehearsal period, became due, with the major payment forfeit. However, on my protestations, the paymasters rescinded this earlier ruling and offered a double reward, so that not only the artists secured full amends, but some weeks later we successfully re-produced the programme on air for an extra fee.

Yet, there was never any doubt that stress and anxiety represented part of the deal when the 'on air' signal flashed. It was no idle remark that matched a director's survival with the number of missions he might have weathered in a wartime bomber squadron. For it seemed the control room was a cockpit of uncertainty every second the pictures flickered forth. When in later years the names of colleagues appeared amongst 'the fallen', we all wondered what pressures and mischance, engendered by the failure of cameras and microphones, or the human frailties of artists and technicians, had eventually taken their toll. Healthy bodies bore a terrible beating. Small wonder the Insurance companies were loath to cover the risk.

Sometimes, though, the qualms could be fun. Planning a *faux pas*, as part of a programme to keep the audience on its toes, brought a fund of suggestions from the technical boffins. When we first introduced the sports programmes, a ball aimed directly at the camera lens was often persuading enough to compel some viewers to duck, if they were watching at a certain angle. But as sophistication replaced the innocence, tricks had to be more elaborately executed. One of the most popular items we presented was Professional Wrestling. A muscle testing contest between a 'Giant Mountainsides' and an 'Ugly Bear' had a peculiar ability to attract a large audience, and we created a regular spot in our weekly *Cavalcade of Sport* to meet the demand. We all reserved an opinion about its validity. Nevertheless, we refused Kent Walton's challenge, as he announced from the ringside, "If it is a fix, I'll arrange for you to have three rounds with whichever wrestler you'd like to choose."

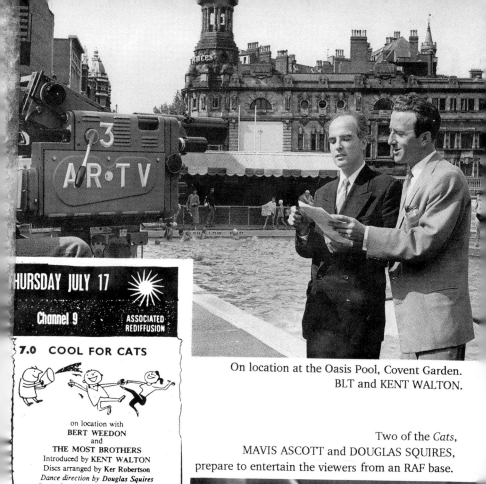

On location at the Oasis Pool, Covent Garden.
BLT and KENT WALTON.

Two of the *Cats*,
MAVIS ASCOTT and DOUGLAS SQUIRES,
prepare to entertain the viewers from an RAF base.

The *Cats* girls, UNA STUBBS, BETTY LAINE, BARBARA FERRIS and MAVIS TRAILL
stand ready with their dancing partners.

MAVIS TRAILL attracts the passing crowd outside the *Daily Sketch* offices in Central Lond

DOUGLAS SQUIRES and PAULINE INNES start out on another edition of *Cool for Cats*.

BLT and AGATHA CHRISTIE on the set of *The Spider's Web*.

STEWART GRANGER, CYRIL FRANKEL and BLT discuss the *Trygon Factor*.

Transforming the **Candlelight Room** at the May Fair Hotel.

The May Fair Theatre.

EDWARD J. DANZIGER.

HARRY DANZIGER and Sir RALPH RICHARDSON.

Sir RALPH RICHARDSON in *Six Characters in Search of an Author*.

WILLIAM BALL.

NORMA and BLT.

Despite his faith, I persuaded Kent to talk to the promoters about a promotional gimmick for the programme, which I hoped would increase the audience. The strategy was for the 15 minute visit to begin with one of the wrestlers thrown from the ring by his opponent, to put an early finish to that contest. Perhaps it might appear we were caught unawares at the very moment of a high spot and leave those at home in front of their screens, asking for more, in traditional show bizz fashion.

That Tuesday evening as the seconds ticked away to 8 p.m., we started the count down, ran our opening titles, faded in the introductory remarks by Ken Johnstone from the studio, and warned the wrestling venue we were ready to mix to them. Kent Walton immediately took up the commentary, but as the picture on the screen focused on the action, we saw the huge bulk of 'Judo Al' holding his 18 stone opponent high above his head and then whirling him around like a distorted propeller. After a gigantic heave, the mass of flesh flew out of the ring, directly towards the camera where Kent was watching and speaking. In a flurry of arms and legs everything collapsed: equipment, furnishings, canvas and Kent tumbled to the floor. We could hear only a strangled whimper,

"I think we had better return to the studio, while we sort this lot out."

On standby for a quick exit (not necessarily so mischievously achieved) Ken Johnstone waited to start a film report about Mrs Topham and the Grand National, and without loss of pace we carried on smoothly. Later, we even chanced another visit to the ringside when a more sober contest was in progress.

The viewers seemed to appreciate the entertainment and our mail was full of congratulatory messages at catching such a peak incident as it happened. Never did I question the authenticity of those professionals again. Neither were we able to repeat the feat by capturing a goal at a football match when we prayed it would occur. Still the trend caught on, and at various times our reward was very unusual, as the lens pointed towards the subject at exactly the split second something dramatic occurred. A really first class cameraman developed a unique sensitivity in capturing the precise moment, so that you could say of some of them they never wasted a shot. The best would always have a nose for a topical story as well. Bill McConville, an ace from the movies if ever there was one, had learned his skills on the war time Pathé Newsreels supplying a twice weekly edition to hundreds of cinemas. For us he recorded the most memorable incident during an item in our sports coverage entitled *Where are they now?*

In 1956, he rediscovered a superstar of English cricket, Eddie Paynter. Eddie was the man who saved the Ashes in Australia during the Body-Line tour of the thirties. He rose from his sick bed to knock a century, as the wickets were falling fast around him and England were on the point of collapse. After he returned home to a hero's welcome and national acclaim, it seemed impossible ever to forget Eddie. Scarcely twenty years later, he was working as a labourer in a builders' yard in Lancashire. McConville found him playing cricket during his lunch hour with a sawn off plank as a bat, a chalked up wicket on the wall, and a half brick for a ball. It made the biggest emotional moment any of us had witnessed on the programme.

Much of the excitement that came from this work was because, with the arrival of commercial television, the whole field of broadcasting became subjected to a breath of fresh air. New people brought new ideas. Sophisticated equipment came on stream to satisfy higher standards and for a while the shake up had stimulating results. It was a period when personal initiative was unleashed, away from the bureaucratic rigidity of BBC officialdom, awarding imaginative innovation a free reign. Dick Lester took the Goons from radio and let them rip in front of the cameras, and what a riot of comedy and humour that revealed. There was *Sunday Night at the Palladium* to offer a blood transfusion to the traditional variety show. *Coronation Street* and *Emergency Ward 10*, institutions in their own right, and *This Week*, and *World in Action*, triumphs of screen journalism; just to name the barest few.

Then, as the Independent network moved into every region of the United Kingdom, more and more viewers became attracted to it, and, in turn, more and more programmes appeared on the screen. It was the audience John Grierson dreamed about in the thirties but never quite succeeded in finding. Here it was at last, the biggest communications break through since the invention of the printing press. Fortunately, those of us in at the beginning, like Denis Forman and Robert Fraser, felt our main task was to prevent its misdirection, and fought against its use as a weapon of government. There was no way it must ape the censorship restrictions it tolerated in the totalitarian countries of the Eastern Bloc. We had the intrinsic good sense of the British viewer to support us, winning a freedom, reasonably preserved intact today. We determined, also, to prevent the malaise which affected the feature film industry so disastrously, from paralysing the new baby. We strove to resist a mentality demanding excessive large crews and rigid demarcation, where it was custom for a one man job to immobilise two or three people.

At the older film studios everything was doubled up: three assistants and a runner to help a director, hoards of property men, carpenters and painters when the art designer wanted to re-arrange the furniture on a set; tasks that anywhere else were the work of one or two. A cameraman forbidden to adjust an electric lamp, illuminating the subject he was photographing, without calling an electrician and a rigger. So it multiplied. This, unfortunately, was the sickness that had plagued British industry for so long, permitting outdated working conditions and practises to remain in place. It was also the perennial reaction to the dreaded word 'change' by those afraid of their own shadows. It could creep up unawares.

On one occasion Stephen McCormack and I had to fight very hard to keep our resolutions about a 'new order of working' in television, well and truly alive. When we decided to place our cameras on the street, outside the studio walls, it raised a number of eyebrows.

"Don't know what the boys in Racks will say about this, old man. It could upset the whole basis of picture contrast. And the image and sound will be terrible."

This, after we had only been on the air for a few months! But we bullied them to test it, and their resolution was weak. For surely, our knees were browner than theirs!

Of course, we were right and nothing went amiss, as the industry outgrew its chrysalis stage despite the setbacks. Now it expands faster than any other twentieth century invention, its tentacles stretching into every corner of the globe, embracing colour transmissions, satellites and computerisation; a revolution that upholds the space age. The programmes I directed (some 200 in the first twelve months at Associated Rediffusion) were adding to my own expertise, but like so many operations that start out to initiate something no-one else has tried, the financial upsets can prove a messy affair. Commercial Television, at its commencement, was prone to these same business problems, overspending, resulting in a cash squeeze, and cut backs at the first sign of a loss in revenue. Crises developed quickly and unexpectedly. One week, when redundancies looked imminent, I appeared before the Head of Production (at this time, John McMillan, replacing the former Head, Gillett, who had disappeared in a previous upset). He told me I was doing a good job and despite the rumours of sackings, I remained secure with my position 'rock steady'. The next week he called me again to say I was out. I merely asked,

"How steady is your rock, John?"

Within days of this severance I was back in the studios, working for Norman Macqueen's company, as a line producer and writer on the advertising magazine *Mr. Marvel,* with Hugh David and Muriel Young. The programme attempted to link science, directly to ranges of advertisers' products, twisting an item on Faraday and elementary electricity to highlight a particular brand of light bulb or electric kettle. It was not altogether a success with its conflicting purposes. In one programme after a Skin Consultant stated it was not possible to grow hair on a bald head, minutes later we were screening a commercial for Silvikrin Hair Restorer.

Fortunately, I was asked to work on a free lance basis for the BBC, A.T.V., and Associated Rediffusion and when Norman had a contract from A.B.C. Television in the United States, to film items for their programme *You Asked For It*, I used Kent Walton as the European presenter. We filmed David Berglas, the magician, performing his tricks under water with diving equipment and submarine cameras; a series of continental circus acts that took a camera up on the trapeze and the high wire and a particularly cunning deployment of sound in St. Paul's Cathedral. For this we recorded the harmonies of the choir and organ from the Whispering Gallery during the Lenten services, and filmed the strange effect of the music travelling around the Dome. After transmission in America on Easter Sunday, it brought a subsequent flood of enquiries from overseas visitors directed at the Cathedral staff, which they had to answer for years afterwards.

As a result of this I became very interested in the latest

developments of television cameras and sound equipment, and Associated Rediffusion contracted me to head their demonstration unit at the Radio and Television Exhibition at Olympia in 1957. This, in turn, brought an offer for me to present one of the company's pre-Christmas programmes, alongside another very talented director, Joan Kemp-Welch.

Earlier that summer Joan rescued a programme called *Cool for Cats* from the axe. Primarily it was a 'pop' records show for children, but Joan, with the help of the Daily Sketch music writer, Ker Robertson, reorganised and developed it into a lively and up beat production that quickly outgrew its afternoon spot, and moved into peak viewing time. The company decided to expand it further, and I joined in to experiment with new equipment and techniques to back up the regular dance team, 'The Cats'. It was a golden opportunity for me, but displayed a considerable risk for Associated Rediffusion, who by their support opted out of the old fashioned static formats for light entertainment.

All aspects, regarded as sacrosanct in the television manuals came under scrutiny and we ventured into uncharted waters. One of the conventions then, maintained that we fashion the screen pictures, in dull dreary greys (it was the age of black and white) so as not to upset the contrast controls on viewers' sets at home. Yet our research showed that transmissions and television receivers could cope with stark tones, and the only lacking ingredient was in the change itself. Another question posed concerned the inter relation between filmed inserts and live camera shots. Until we tried it and proved it could work, without any noticeable deterioration in picture quality, few producers had bothered to experiment with the possibilities. Split screens, overlays, superimpositions and hand held cameras, also stayed under used facilities, a situation scarcely realisable in the world of computer graphics and fibre optics of today. Yet, at that time, our adoption of them became regarded almost as sheer innovation. Perhaps without the example of *Cool*, the developments we now take for granted might have taken that much longer to arrive on the screen.

We worked as a team in preparing the programmes. First, Ker Robertson selected ten or eleven discs from each week's releases, which would probably reach the Top Twenty either because of their musical value or a distinctive performance. Next, we edited the music tracks to a manageable length of about 2½ minutes, and reached a decision on their visual treatment. Some were for Dance interpretation, or a Mime sequence, others for illustration by cartoon, still picture or film, and one or two for personal appearances by the recording artistes. As our dancers were very popular with the viewers, a great deal depended on the choreographers. On the early programmes we used Douglas Squires, a brilliant young man who had not only an attractive screen personality, but brought a new concept to dance on television. Later Denys Palmer followed on. He was an ex-soloist from the International Ballet, and imported a stock of breathtaking steps and choreographic patterns from classical traditions.

We tried always to supplement the chamber style ballets with the gadgetry of the studios: back projection, unusual camera lenses, electronic tricks, everything we could harness to reveal the immense range of effects we had at our beck and call.

Often, we arranged a consistent theme through each programme. The set designers, Roy Stannard, Timothy O'Brien and Sylva Nadolny would build a Cowboy shanty town from the Wild West, or re-produce a riverboat on the Mississippi, so that the selected discs could feature Country and Western melodies and the jumping French Quarter jazz of New Orleans. On all these occasions our costume designer, Sheila Jackson, created a distinctive wardrobe to dress the artistes and the guests.

My special delight was to encourage the use of the outdoor locations around us, exploiting the huge Stadium and old 1924 Empire Exhibition grounds on the back lot of the studios in Wembley; or opening up the doors onto Kingsway and the Strand. For a romantic treat we visited the roof tops of Television House with its view of Tower Bridge and St. Paul's, transforming the City of London into a living backcloth. Then, as the moon rose above the glittering street lights, the *Cool* dancers waltzed and pirouetted to the themes of *My Fair Lady*, and mimed the words, 'I could have danced all night.'

To transfer the decor away from the confines of studio lighting was a novel challenge. Once the dancers had adjusted to the uneven floor surfaces and the crews had become reconciled to the extra space, we convinced all the faint hearts that performing in the open air was as controllable as being within the studio walls.

COOL FOR CATS

The imperturbable Kent Walton made the ideal anchor man. With him aboard to supply the announcements and the showtime gossip, we quickly rose even higher in the viewer ratings. We were also attracting some interesting comment from the press. *The News of the World* said,

> '... ITV's *Cool for Cats*, the programme which regularly uses the electronic tricks of television as they should be used more often.'

and the *Daily Mirror's* critic highlighted,

> '*Cool for Cats*, my pick for ITV's best series of the year.'

When the summer arrived and Joan Kemp-Welch (who had alternated with me on the three programmes a week schedule we maintained that winter season) left to produce a large Gala show of light entertainment, I decided I would spread my documentary roots further into song and dance. I had long harboured a deep affection for the M.G.M. musical *On the Town*, based on a ballet by Jerome Robbins, with a score by Leonard Bernstein. The story of three U.S.Navy sailors in New York on a day's shore leave, created a pulsating fantasy around the skyscrapers of Manhattan, while the music, movement and storyline met in natural unity. It seemed to me that a similar approach in *Cool*, permitting us to perform the complete half hour on location, as distinct from the odd sequence we had transmitted previously, would enhance our pictures. It would also provide an overall purpose for the dance themes in the programme. Undoubtedly, the dancers would miss the sprung floors of the studio and the theatricality of the presentations, but by exchanging that for the hard pavements and the concrete paths of the city streets, we would enlarge the dramatic canvas in an exciting way.

Of course, it meant saying good-bye to painted cycloramas and scenic flats that dropped in behind the artists to alter the background. Now they must relocate to the setting, often quite a distance away. And if the heavens should open,... well, there was always an umbrella to keep them singing in the rain.

For our first Remote Telecast (as we named such events) we were not to venture too far from our home base, but just across the Thames to the Royal Festival Hall. It was a dream of a location. The grand sweep of architecture that borders the river, with Big Ben and the Houses of Parliament on one side to Somerset House and the Savoy on the other, made up the panorama of Westminster, which even Hollywood was unable to match. One way or another we determined to feature the unique skyline and as the rehearsals started and the music thundered through the exterior speakers, a large crowd gathered to watch the proceedings. It all seemed very natural, adding a realism to the event, that would be impossible to duplicate in the studio.

The principal difficulty for the cast was, as we expected, negotiating the distances between one set piece and the next. Kent solved his problems by borrowing a bicycle and riding, after each announcement, to a different viewpoint alongside the water's edge. Our audience looked on mesmerised by such rapid changes as we switched from one huge block of buildings to another. Yet the superb back-up facilities we had within the Royal Festival Hall, from dressing rooms to make-up and wardrobe, boosted our confidence in the ultimate result. The show ran perfectly and we gained an unscripted bonus, adding to the visual impact of the occasion. A group of spectators, who had gazed idly at the performers during the afternoon, suddenly joined the dancers and stepped liltingly in rhythm to the music. The cameramen seized on the diversion, and while the mobile crane platforms, with their cameras swept upwards, they captured a landscape of dancing men and women, overlooked by Big Ben, towering in silhouette against the evening sun. When we closed down and the programme ended, we felt we had shared a truly wonderful experience together. The telephone in the control scanner buzzed busily with congratulatory messages, and we all sat back to savour the success.

During the summer months we went on location every week. We took the programme to the RAF Base at Odiham, where Kent Walton renewed wartime friendships with members of his old Bomber Squadron, to the Battersea Pleasure Gardens, Chessington Zoo, the Soho Fair and to a Women's Royal Army Corps camp in Richmond Park. At the offices of the *Daily Sketch* newspaper, the dancers performed their routines around the journalists working at their typewriters and beside the monster printing presses, producing the first editions of the paper. It did not stop us gaining a rave revue in the columns.

Sometimes it was not all plain sailing. The evening we chose to transmit from the open air Oasis Swimming Pool, in the centre of London, we faced a serious crowd problem. The dancing went well enough, and routines on the diving boards and in the shallow end looked good, but the moment we introduced the actor-singer, Harry Belafonte, the cast and cameras almost fell into the water, pushed by the weight of fans pressing to touch their film star idol. Fortunately, the technicians held their ground as they struggled to cover the interview, and we succeeded in relaying the pictures. It was their sheer resolution that saved us.

On another occasion, by the time we transmitted the programme from Chessington Zoo, it was late in the summer and the evening light at 7.30 p.m. was deteriorating rapidly. That particular day it seemed to fail even faster and we noticed the cameras were not coping with the reduced light levels. But our crew contained a real veteran of a lighting director, Bryan Love. I had first met him years before when he was touring with Festival Ballet, where he had developed an uncanny ability to sense when things were going wrong. Grabbing a couple of assistants he moved a large, heavy 10 KW arc lamp, connected it into the mains supply and wheeled it around from one shooting point to another. Behind him trailed hundreds of feet of cable and a team of electricians. Somehow the extra boost of power kept our pictures viewable and anxieties in check, so that we produced a corporate sigh of relief when the end caption filled the screen.

With the increasing popularity of the show, we began to enlarge the programmes into short story situations. We arranged the recorded numbers to form a continuous link between characters and action, as in a West End musical comedy. Our aim was to construct a format for television, which would allow us to introduce song and dance in a natural flowing way, rather than just through the choreographed movements of the artists. Backing up the dance captains, we had a strong team of people prepared to experiment and try out these new ideas. There was Eric Dodson and Tony Bateman turning their theatrical acting techniques into mime and humour. Desmond Henessey, a talented animator, whose cartoons we used in unusual decorative ways. Charlie Squires, the film editor, who with extraordinary craftsmanship, made sequences of film jump smartly to the most complicated musical rhythms. And supporting the whole caboodle, with his writing and propaganda, the Daily Sketch's Ker Robertson.

It was an overall co-operative effort, determined by a schedule of three programmes a week, while at the same time seeking to retain originality and spontaneity. The sheer output of work left everyone gasping. We were amused to hear that, when the U.S.Networks approached the company's marketing division for transmission rights, they pulled out of a deal because our rapid turnover of programme material would jeopardise the American entertainment union contracts. In fact we would have required a huge extra input of staff and technicians to guarantee the observation of their rules.

For Joan Kemp-Welch and me, plus our versatile group of personnel, it was all very gratifying, especially when one considers that before *Cool for Cats*, pop videos were an unknown quantity. No-one then had considered the potential of such a presentation. Not only was the facility to record pictures on magnetic tape still in its infancy, but popular dance on television generally consisted of a line of chorus girls, and recording artists sang their lyrics straight to the camera.

Even in the broader fields of dance, like classical and modern ballet, the progress had been slow. BBC producer, Christian Simpson, with choreographer Celia Franca and a small number of others, had tried to be more adventurous in the presentation of dance drama for television. It suffered the same difficulties filmed ballet emphasised: the emotional content could not bridge the gap between screen and viewer.

Although the television ballet productions were transmitted live, somehow they lacked the feeling of being alive. They missed the very essence of the union between a stage artist and the audience in the theatre. Many dance films had proved unsatisfactory in this respect too, when attempting to make a straight transfer from one art form to another. Gene Kelly's *Invitation to the Dance* and the ballet sequences of *Red Shoes* had both failed to make this contact, and our success was in breaking this deadlock. The solution was to rely much more on personalities, as distinct from the display of large ensembles. We concentrated on just six dancers, three matched couples, making the small screen appear much less overcrowded. The choreography was neat and tidy, ensuring an emphasis on the steps rather than on grand theatrical gestures, and the attention of the viewer veered towards the general pattern, away from rapid changes and disturbing close ups.

Although the dancers varied on each programme, dependant on their commitments, we retained a small nucleus of seven couples, encouraging the audience to recognise their favourites. So it was we told the stories around the personalities of the dancers. Una Stubbs, Barbara Ferris, Mavis Trail, Mavis Ascott, Betty Laine, Roy Allan and Robin Hunter; personalities who, in later years, achieved success in theatre, film and television. Sometimes we engaged an artist for a series of cameo parts. Ronnie Corbett and Patsy Rowlands were able to obtain some of their early experience in this way, and we introduced a number of ballet artists into the team for added strength to the line up. John Gilpin, Louis Godfrey, Noël Rossana, Monica Leigh and my wife, Mary Munro, appeared with permission of the Festival Ballet administrators.

This could make for some interesting side effects. On the occasion we closed down the transmission at Chessington Zoo at 7.30 p.m., I had to send Mary hot foot from jiving in a sizzling jazz finale to Sadler's Wells Theatre. She was appearing there as a guest artist for the Ballet Rambert at 8, dancing a highly serious dramatic role in Anthony Tudor's ballet *Dark Elegies*, to the distinctly sobering music of Mahler's *Das Kindertoten Lieder*. She stepped from the taxi, in her make up and costume, directly into the performance on stage, and not a soul was aware of the transformation.

There was, however, another great contribution to the programmes: the live appearance of recording artists. We introduced the Everly Brothers, Shirley Bassey, Petula Clark, Alma Cogan, Bert Weedon, Eddie Calvert, Frankie Vaughan and Lonnie Donnegan, amongst a welter of great performers from both sides of the Atlantic. The list was like a billing for the Royal Command Performance and with the increased success of the programme, disc stars looked to an early debut on *Cool* as a guide to eventual sales. The record companies too, realised the potential of the huge audiences we were introducing to popular music, and quickly stepped up their own publicity campaigns to take advantage of the interest we had created. Soon they were asking us to help them produce their pop videos.

Naturally, this climate of achievement persuaded the programme planners to search for a similar format for other presentations, so that Joan and I coaxed them to chance another proposal. It was an extension into musical drama based firmly on a Hollywood formula. In the *Rush Hour* series, we employed many of the team we had nurtured so far. Both Douglas Squires, later to organise a unique Television dance group, *The Younger Generation*, and Denys Palmer, played a large part in the choreographic arrangements, and some of the *Cool* dancers extended their roles to embrace singing and acting in the versatile way we expect of Broadway artists and the performers in West End musicals of today. The general musical side was supervised by Steve Race, as conductor and orchestrator, who brought a wealth of understanding to each production, but our prime talent was the writer, Hazel Adair, who went on to create *Crossroads* and *Compact*. She had a knack of turning a few stumbling thoughts into brilliant words and scenarios. Once we had sketched out a story outline in a morning conference, she would have the completed shooting script ready by early afternoon. And one week we were very grateful for this expertise.

On a Monday morning, as the five days rehearsal period began, the leading lady fell ill and we had to abandon the script. Brilliantly capitalising on the incident, and using the background of *42nd Street* and *A Star is Born*, Hazel wrote immediately a behind the scenes story, which pre-dated by many years the theme of the Shirley Maclean film, *The Turning Point*. All the elements that formed part of putting on a show were in it. The heartaches and the personal anguish. The rehearsals and the opening night. A combination of sweat and emotion. We devised a tear jerker featuring the rise of the lowly production assistant to stardom. It caught everyone's imagination and Millicent Martin, Maggie Fitzgibbon, Peter Gilmore and John Hewer performed magnificently in the leading roles, so that as the end titles faded all that was missing was the fall of the curtain and the cheers.

In real terms television is often just as dramatic. Careers progress, or spoil, overnight. Reputations become enhanced, or ruined. But despite the glitz and the external glamour there is a remorseless machine, trundling and grinding onwards, demanding more and more in its hunger for fresh ideas, fresh stories, fresh programmes. Once, not so long ago, there was merely one lone BBC station. Sixty years later, as the cables, the satellites and the optics open up network upon network, the sky seems insatiable. To be part of that, another sixty years hence, could proclaim an orgiastic awakening of the mind.

TWENTY

EDWARD J. & HARRY LEE DANZIGER

EARLY IN 1959, after eighteen months of *Cool for Cats*, I began to look around for alternative sectors to work in. Norman Marshall, head of Drama at Associated Rediffusion and with an impeccable record in theatre, had spoken to me about directing a straight play for the company and I fancied the dual role of writer/director. Denis Forman at Granada Television, also approached me to direct programmes in Manchester, but another intriguing possibility was available. At a ballet party Mary gave before we married, I met a very unusual American film producer, Harry Danziger. He was the younger of two brothers, who had arrived in London during the early fifties and set about outlawing all the weary shibboleths and restricted practices that inhibited film making in Britain.

Harry and Eddie totally rejected the rigid rule on these shores, which dictated a maximum of four minutes screen time each day in the studios. It was not for them. Inside a week of hiring their own production unit they upset the established applecart and were topping eleven and twelve minutes a day, without a murmur of dissent from anyone. By 1959, with one highly successful venture under their belts, they prepared for further victories when they turned their attention towards the archaic practices in the Hotel and Theatre business.

Harry was a devoted balletomane and when we met we immediately began to stretch each other's enthusiasms. He had received a musical upbringing in New York, becoming an accomplished violinist and orchestral conductor, so that at music

318

recording sessions for his films, he often pushed the resident director aside and proceeded to whip up the musicians into performing some very revealing interpretations of the score. I met his elder brother, Eddie, sometime later. He was a smallish figure of a man, with glasses, and there was no mistaking his intellectual capacity and mesmeric driving force; useful accomplishments in his earlier days as a lawyer. Both brothers had visited pre-war Europe with their father and became intrigued enough to want to explore it in a more leisurely manner. A wish granted sooner than they anticipated. Harry found himself commanding a tank squadron in North Africa and Italy, where he won the Medal for Valour, and Eddie prepared for D-Day in London as Head of the Legal Section to U.S. Army Headquarters. At Nuremburg, in 1945, he was one of the prosecuting counsel in the War Crimes Trials.

On demobilisation they settled again in New York to engage in a frenzy of local movie and theatre production. However, recalling a war time nostalgia for London, they returned with a package of half hour film scripts for a television show featuring a Private Eye attached to Scotland Yard. Out of this grew a popular series, some 150 episodes in all, about a one arm detective, Mark Saber, played by ex-BBC news reader Donald Gray. The idea of a disabled policeman was a new departure then for television drama, but over the years it has set the trend for a score of wheel chaired lawyers and crutch supported lawman. This, plus the stiff upper lipped British gentleman, the plummy accents and the London fog caught the imagination of the American viewing audience. By the time I met them they had scripted another four or five diverse series for production in Europe, as well as some thirty feature films, already pre-sold to distributors in the United States.

Working in Britain they had quickly decided it was more advantageous to own their film making facilities rather than rely on the variable factors associated with hiring studio space. So they purchased a large abandoned shadow factory, last used to produce aircraft engines for the wartime R.A.F. It stood close by a vast reservoir at Elstree, on the outskirts of London, and they turned the old workshops into five sound proofed studios, with cutting rooms, recording suites and all the back up of a fully fledged Hollywood movie plant. Within its gates was enough space to provide two separate production lines, so that both the television series and the cinema features could operate, side by side, and hundreds of artists and technicians work there every day. Heading its senior management staff were a shrewd Irish accountant, Bob Faloon, and two first rate Art Directors, Eric Blakemore and Don Ashton who saw to the everyday organisation of the shooting programme. But here was the rub. The Danziger brothers now required this small team for another enterprise they were hatching, the refurbishment and re-organisation of a chain of hotels and restaurants, on the point of take over.

The Gordon Hotels group had two flagship hotels in London, the May Fair and the Grosvenor, both desperately in need of a thorough revamp. There were others in Southern England, Monte Carlo and the Bahamas, all suffering from the lack of a co-ordinated policy. It was a company ripe for a managerial shake-up. Eddie and Harry had a problem. They needed urgently someone in charge of their film operations at Elstree to relieve them of the pressure of shooting an enormous schedule of pictures. Then, they could concentrate on the revival of a declining asset.

After Mary and I married in 1955, Harry and his wife, Angela, met us frequently at the ballet and joined us later to eat. Often he asked about my work and we discussed the contracts he was signing with Associated Rediffusion for the British rights of another television series. As the shooting date grew closer, he asked for help. Would a return to the film industry interest me? The following Friday I directed a final programme of *Cool for Cats*, and the Monday morning afterwards was on my way to the New Elstree Studios to start work as Productions Supervisor.

I was now in charge of a factory for mass producing movies, with the creative talents of a regiment of writers, actors, designers and technical staff at my disposal to make it happen. Only by using industrial production methods could we ever hope to achieve satisfactory results, and one great advantage of working with the Danzigers was their simple philosophy about film making. Keep to the delivery dates and the artistic control is entirely yours to balance any overspend on one project with an underspend on another. Their concept of a continuous flow of movies, geared to an agreed script, copied the Hollywood formula. It was dependant on 'up front' cash, to commission writers well ahead of the time their stories were in front of the cameras. In Britain this was where the bottlenecks had constantly occurred and why films at the major studios of Pinewood and Shepperton seemed destined to be on a stop-start basis. It was essential to iron out the snags before the cameras rolled, instead of later in the middle of production with all the complications of extra expenditure. This was the theory and the aim. They had done their part by financing a library of approved scripts. It was only necessary to make the system work by employing staff prepared to adapt to unaccustomed conditions. This we achieved by a careful selection of the production team, despite the rigidity of union rules and outdated notions, which had so often stopped other producers in their tracks. Bob Faloon was the lynch pin in this process. His knowledge of budgeting and cost control, gathered from long experience with Rank, Korda and Associated British Pictures, guided me in the selection of the key personnel, prepared to outlaw destructive trade practices and progress the programme in the fastest and most economic way.

My own familiarity with rapid turn around, so necessary in the television studio, was invaluable, as our completion deadlines gave us just two and a half days shooting time for each episode in the series and ten days for our features. Up to then, five days was the reckoned scheduling for a half hour production in the studio, and a month on a small feature. With the first series, *Man from Interpol*, we hit the button with the opening story. Two and a half days on the floor, three weeks to wrap up with titles, music, effects and a show copy. From that moment on, we delivered two episodes a week.

I suppose it was the deftness of sticking to delivery dates and budgets which made the Danzigers so much of a contrast to other film makers in London. The history of British film production stands littered with the failures of the most brilliant screen impresarios. The magic of the multi-national film empires of America is a hard taskmaster to imitate, and sadly the saga of the disasters so many of our home grown companies have faced, from too close a reliance on Hollywood, makes sorry reading. The big names are all there. Korda, Balcon, Rank, British Lion, Goldcrest, one after another, with the lesser lights fitted in between, and always the same dismal result,.... flops. Plus the disillusionment of the backers and an unemployed workforce back at home. There have, of course, been the few singular exceptions from the days of

Charles Laughton in *Henry VIII* to *Chariots of Fire* and *The Crying Game*, but generally the bottom line is red, written off to experience.

The New Elstree Studios defied this pattern, and although the product did not pretend to win any Oscars, neither did it owe a penny to the banks nor fail to pay its staff. The discipline the Danzigers brought meant survival in a jungle fraught with pseudo artistic consciences and bloated personal egos. I soon realised that the philosophers of the creative image of film making were a menace, particularly when they opted out of any financial responsibility. Should you value the future of the industry, then beware the false Messiahs, who proclaim their own integrity above all else. Limiting factors of budgets and schedules require as great a creative principle to fulfil, as the licensing of artistic freedom. This must apply to everything, whether it be the actor employed to play the leading role, or the cameraman to frame the picture. Professionalism is the sole criterion and the prime requirement to a proper and fair reward.

Too often during my working life in film, television and theatre I have witnessed the irresponsibility that tries to recruit artistic integrity as an ally. Grounds that generally are nothing more than the results of a petty whim. On one occasion, during an overnight shoot, not connected to the Danzigers, I bore witness to a costly production fiasco. Overtime payments and extra facilities were creating chaos with the budget, and then the Internationally famous film director demanded that red roses, part of the background decoration on the set, be changed to yellow ones.

"I can't possibly work with that colour rose. They must be replaced before I shoot a frame."

Some unfortunate assistant was despatched to Covent Garden flower market to rectify the remiss, although it meant a three hour delay. It was scarcely important in the black and white movie he was making and barely warrants a mention except as an attitude of mind I totally condemn. Thereby hangs the spectre that haunts the under-employed industry of cinema in this country today.

Yet, however much the critics carped, the Danziger movies were always entertainment. That some were lowly in content does not detract from the achievement. For a decade, they provided uninterrupted production runs and continuous employment. They dismissed the nagging worry constantly confronting the free lance employees of an industry noted for short working periods and a perpetual uncertainty of jobs. Deplorably, the reckless actions of a variety of 'Sammy Glick' movie producers have injured far too many talented people. Their aspirations to earn a fortune at the expense of everyone else, has plagued the industry since the days the lantern slide replaced the moving picture. Attitude and personal example must be the key. If the 'guys at the top' do not care how they spend the money, how can anyone else share the responsibility? Eddie Danziger made it very clear where he stood. A carping Union official was granted a swift rejoinder when he dared suggest,

"Mr. Danziger, if you give the crew the extra payments they want, at least it will make them happy."

"Happy? Why should they be happy? I give them a steady job, what more can they want?"

When finance was thin, Eddie and Harry scrimped and saved. Once in New York, when we received a dismal reception to our hopes of raising extra cash, Eddie inveigled a way of making his long distance telephone calls from the offices of the offending film distributors, and, by tipping the post boy, delivered a sackful of overseas mail through the company's private network. That way we salvaged enough to pay for the deposit on the film stock and the production went ahead. A case of making dollars and sense! He reckoned that London was a lucky place for him from the moment he stepped out on the pavements, the morning of his arrival in the fifties, and picked up a ten shilling note lying there. It provided a good omen and Bob Faloon summed it up,

"We will never be millionaires until we learn to use our discarded envelopes for the next memo, and the end of the cigarette packet for an *aide mémoire*."

You knew you had a problem the moment you saw Eddie reach for a screwed-up clipping in his top pocket and you received the nod to sort it out. Yet, from my first days at Elstree I realised the relationship was going to be an interesting one.

Almost on the day I joined them they pitched me into completing a wild adventure story, shot in Cuba during the Revolution, featuring Errol Flynn. An army friend of Harry's, Victor

Pahlen, had sailed around the island with Flynn, recording the conquests and rise to power of Castro, and had thousands of feet of historic film coverage. The two of them were in their element interviewing the freedom fighters and talking to Fidel in the battle lines at the take-over of Havana. However, the subject matter could hardly avoid an anti-U.S. slant.

I had to try to bring some balance into the narration and smooth over the obvious bitter defeat of the Americans. But after I had cut round some of the sequences and added a commentary, Victor rushed off to the Film Festivals with his treasure. It was certainly a hit in Eastern European countries and, although it involved the Danzigers only indirectly, their stock soared amongst the small group of McCarthy witch hunt veterans resident in London. In a further spin off, the Danzigers and Flynn jointly held the title, *Bay of Pigs*, specially registered for film rights. Unfortunately, we were never able to find the key that might turn it into a tale of political conspiracy and pre-empt the Vietnamese debacle.

Just before the main studio work for the first series *Man from Interpol* commenced, I set off on an overseas location shoot for back projection plates and linking material. The leading man was Richard Wyler, a British actor, who had been in Hollywood and starred in several Westerns. He had a relaxed and rugged pre-James Bond look and seemed the type of character who would rove around the capital cities sorting out International criminals. I filmed him in Rome, Paris, Amsterdam, Brussels, Berlin and Vienna to validate the overseas settings we were building at Elstree. As one of the American sponsors was Pan Am, we flew freely around in sparkling brand new 707's. We had a feeling though, that we might be the guinea pigs for the tourists who only remember the day of the week, from where they are. As we journeyed from the concrete apron of one airport terminal to the next, I shouted 'Action' to the cameras and Wyler stepped forward from the aircraft silhouetted against a different control tower and a distinctive national flag. In fourteen days we collected every conceivable covering shot of police headquarters and historical landmark in Europe, for the 39 episodes we produced in the studios.

After that series we went straight into another 39 episodes of *The Cheaters*, this time about an Insurance claims investigator, played by the craggy John Ireland, and no sooner had we completed that, than Dermot Walsh became *Richard the Lionheart*, supported by jousting Knights in armour, courtly love and the Infidel Saracens. The variety, at least, was extraordinary, while the logistics that sustained us, week by week and month by month, hardly allowed a few hours respite to the five large studios, the seven outside settings on the nearby lot, or the reservoir beside it, where we filmed our sea and water sequences.

The art department was a hive of industry as the drawing boards unveiled design and detail for a thousand settings the construction workshops turned into reproduction. No part of the world escaped the techniques of the fantasies we unfolded in fibreglass, timber and paint. Because I felt the television designers had something to offer in fast turn-a-rounds, I recruited Peter Mullins from Granada Television and Roy Stannard who had worked with me on 'Cool for Cats', as Art Directors, and graphics wizard Desmond Henessey, another treasure from Rediffusion, to animate all our title sequences. Our extra good fortune in overcoming Film Union objections to Yvonne Blake, meant that an old ballet friend, who was a brilliant costume designer at Bermans, the Costumiers, was able to bring her expert knowledge of period styles and furnishings, to the wardrobe of the Crusaders. I felt especially pleased when later she won an Hollywood Oscar for her costume designs in the movie *Nicholas and Alexandra*.

To service the casting for both feature films and the television series, required a repertory company of artistes, almost permanently on call. Often an actor, after completing a role in *The Cheaters* or *Richard the Lionheart*, would find himself filming a scene for the features unit, bearing no relation either in costume, make-up or dialogue, to the character he acted half an hour before. We might easily have used the list of performers as an index to the casting directory *Spotlight*, because it read like a roll call of the theatrical profession.

Many of the stars of today started their careers in a one line assignment at New Elstree Studios. In a week, we might have a turn over of 250 artistes, 1000 crowd personnel and a platoon of stunt men, doubles, stand-ins and back-ups, although once a series was in production, the main five or six characters and twenty or thirty alternating minor parts would remain constant. The features we produced on the other stages, also had a complete switch of cast and senior crew at each ten day changeover. Sandwiched between the regular productions were also other less routine projects. The intriguing Agatha Christie spent a lot of time at the studio, helping us to film her thriller, *The Spider's Webb,* with Glynis Johns, John Justin and Cicely Courtneidge. On another occasion we nursed a fledgling 12 year old Denis Waterman, through his first major part in *Night Train to Inverness* with Norman Wooland and Jane Hylton. In that production the talented Anton Rodgers also made one of his first screen appearances. Later we attempted a skin movie, in the days when the slightest departure from the Code of strict purity might saddle you with a picture no-one could show. But our story of a Nudist Camp shot in the open air at Brickett Wood, near the studios, was of innocent naivety with song and dance. Apart from the cultural shock our film crew suffered as they watched a horde of naked bodies dive into the swimming pool, and the unfortunate remarks of the First Assistant Director when we were ready to shoot the introductory sequence on the large grassed games area in front of the clubhouse,

"Alright everybody, the camera's turning. Play with your balls."

We succeeded in bringing the picture to completion before the English weather closed in on us. It earned no more than a Censor's rating of a 'U' Certificate: suitable for all ages.

It was inevitable that some projects were more memorable than others and personal experiences, from the past, often represented part of the appeal. One story that came my way, written by Brian Clemens creator of *The Avengers*, was almost a repeat of my war time encounters in Germany. Featuring Cyril Shaps, subsequently a star at the Royal National Theatre, and Francis Matthews, *The Pursuers* showed the conflicts arising between survivors from the Concentration Camps and the ex-Nazi guards they sought to kill in revenge.

I returned to Berlin and Hamburg to trace old newsreel material for inclusion in the film and it became, for me, a nostalgic voyage. In East Berlin, a short while before its isolation behind the Wall, I felt strangely under threat. The politics of East and West were on parade as I watched the film archive footage of ghastly murder at Auschwitz and the pre-war glories of Hitler's Reich. Outside the city was awash with intrigue, and the corrupt spirit that pervaded the atmosphere when I was there with the Desert Rats, was even more apparent and claustrophobic. It was this smell of rottenness that John le Carre so skilfully revealed in his novels. Our film, too, caught the decadence and fear of it all, especially through Shaps' brilliant interpretation of a fugitive Nazi death camp commander. Perhaps his own Jewish roots gave him a particular purpose in setting the record straight.

Yet, without doubt, the real challenge in this multiplicity of film making, was the variation of historical background we considered for each production, especially its relationship to our programme as a whole. One month we would be up to our knees in mud reproducing the battlefields of Europe in war time dramas; the next, we would be away to the nearby sandpit 'Desert', with dust spilling from our boots, as Richard fought the Crusades, married his Berengaria, and his knights chased Saladin from sandhill to sandhill. Then, irresistibly, we took a stroll down the Rue Morgue, into the re-built streets of 19th century Paris, ready to film the macabre classics of Edgar Allan Poe. Horrific special effects and flickering gaslight brought a chilling quality to a version of *Tell Tale Heart*, which starred Adrienne Corrie and Laurence Payne, enriched by a symphonic jazz score from Bill Le Sage and Tony Crombie. It was a strong piece of cinema entertainment. Harry Danziger suggested for this one that we create a pre-film trailer, a throw back to the days when audiences wallowed in nervous thrills from their double seats, in the dark of the auditorium.

"Beware, when you hear this sound,... should you
be weak of heart, close your eyes and don't open
them again until it stops."

And as the severed heart of Poe's story pulsed its bloody way across the floor of the house in Rue Morgue, the music bleated out a howling screech on the saxophones, of such a piteous nature, only the strongest could refrain from screwing their eyes up tight and clinging to their neighbour.

... Or so we liked to think.

However to spend the rest of my working life in the intense heat of the studio floor, and the furnace of distribution deals, tracing the movement of time by the thousands of feet of film negative delivered to the processing laboratories, was not something I could settle for permanently, whatever the sense of achievement it evoked.

But with the Danzigers in charge it was not likely to happen for too long. Almost every day when I saw them, either Eddie or Harry would be pursuing a new idea. Their interests ranged over a wide field of enterprises. Disposable cameras to multi-track recorders, factory produced housing to holiday cruise ships, credit card schemes to car delivery transporters. If the risk involved a change in present practice then it was a matter for consideration. Part of the American attitude of 'get up and go', which fascinated many of us during the 'you've never had it so good' days of Harold MacMillan.

Nevertheless, they balanced this broad philosophy alongside family life and its commitments: we all had families to cope with at various stages of development. My first daughter, Melanie, had been born shortly before I went into the control gallery to direct a *Cool for Cats* programme in April 1958, so that Kent Walton surprised me by announcing her arrival during the transmission. A little later, when I was at New Elstree studios, Celia appeared in 1960 and Stephen in 1962. Harry and Angela Danziger had two young sons, Nick and Richard, Eddie and Gigi two slightly older ones, Danny and Jimmy, so there was solid framework to the image we displayed to our colleagues. For the brothers, this was an important consideration.

They were part of a large family group in New York, who visited the studios when they were, in London, on holiday. One brother-in-law, Walter Lowendhal, joined me at Elstree to develop large screen colour television, which we hoped to employ on close-circuit links between selected cinemas and the horserace tracks. Unfortunately the plan was a little premature for the racing and betting fraternity, who preferred to ignore the large potential audience of punters we reckoned on attracting. In our view, there was a clientele available from the unexpected numbers prepared to play bingo and visit the gaming tables, which had become such a feature of leisure pursuits in the sixties. By introducing racing to them on a large television screen, might both increase the profitability of the race tracks and improve the attendance figures at the cinemas. The movies were in the doldrums as they tried desperately to compete with the small screen and with a promise of colour television only months ahead, attendance figures needed a boost. However, although we had detailed discussions with the Duke of Norfolk and his supporters on the Horse Racing Betting

Board and in the racecourse community, the opposition was too strong and what might have been a valuable blood transfusion to two failing industries remained untested.

It was this spirit of adventure that I liked about the Danzigers. When I first considered a move to them, Ker Robertson, through his financial contacts on the Daily Sketch, obtained a run down on what Throgmorton Street thought of the Brothers' chances. Their film successes were noted, and the City seemed prepared to watch, with interest, anything further they undertook, particularly as they appeared high calibre managers. Their peculiar skill was in the way they backed each other's ideas. Harry's imaginative flair found support in the legal solidity of Eddie. This made it difficult for outsiders to distinguish them apart. On the telephone one brother seemed instinctively to pick up from the other, at the exact point a previous conversation ended, so that in negotiation you never quite recognised who you were talking to. It could be a hair raising experience for anyone attempting to oppose them and led to instant capitulation against overwhelming odds. Long faced losers, after such a telephone encounter, would complain,

"Was that Eddie or Harry I just talked to?"

Bureaucratic mismanagement was mincemeat to them. They had no truck with mindless obstruction at whatever level if time consuming procedures became part of a delaying process. Ministry officials, planning officers and valuation advisors needed cast iron reasons in any dithering or put-off. They gave no quarter and in Brooklyn street fighting mood, delivered as good as they got, with added interest.

This style was apparent in their approach to a tricky financial scandal of the fifties. It was part of the reason I was working at the studios and I watched their progress with close attention. The Gordon Hotels Group was a respected Public Company with interests in the heart of London and in various countries of the world. Sheltered by a register of rather elderly, out of town, stockholders, who seldom visited the annual general meetings, its management was doddery and inefficient, wholly incapable of monitoring suspect and conspiratorial dealings committed by its senior executives. Into this stew the Danzigers launched a take-over bid, designed at letting daylight into the affairs of the Managing Director, Leslie Jackson, and his henchmen. Backed by ex-Naval Commander, Lord Roger Keyes, and a group of practised lawyers and accountants they carried out a buying coup that put them in charge of the business and dismissed the offenders. Then they set about rectifying some of the financial damage the company had suffered through negligence in the previous years. Jackson went to prison and his followers routed, but they left a nest of administrative delayed action bombs, which only with the greatest skill, the Danzigers diffused.

Another factor was the treatment of Eddie and Harry by the traditional established hoteliers. Upsets in ownership in London's West End had been few and far between. The old order flourished and new boys promising a revolution by importing American practices found themselves scorned as interlopers. The Danzigers treated such murmurings with a fair amount of humour,

"What more understanding do you need, than the fact you have stayed in every important hotel in the world," they replied in retaliation. "Half the guys who are quibbling have never been across the English Channel and their Italian waiters have forgotten how to speak Italian."

That was that, except they defined their policy to us as,

"We are going to make these hotels everything being an innkeeper should be about. The best accommodation, the best food, the best hospitality and the best entertainment anywhere."

It was a proud goal and from the way they proceeded it seemed a pretty fair proposition. Taking all the factors into consideration it was a huge undertaking. Apart from the plus of the site, in the centre of Mayfair, their flagship hotel was an old fashioned, out-dated building, without air conditioning or fast lifts. It contained dismal corridors of bedrooms, not a single one sporting its own bathroom or toilet, and kitchens suffering from a surfeit of dilapidation and old equipment. In turn, these were meant to serve tatty hospitality facilities which emitted such an air of dowdiness, that they infected the staff with the same characteristics.

It was a question of scooping out the centre of the six storey structure and replacing everything with new fixtures and fittings to breathe a sense of luxury and comfort at every level. But there was one major hurdle: how to achieve this without closing down and losing all the customers?

I suppose the years of improvisation that the selected design team had shared in the film studios contributed to the formula. One way or another, restaurants, bars, bedrooms and kitchens underwent a sea change, so that the May Fair began to take on the mantel of the capital's most splendid hotel and guests arrived from all over the world to enjoy the refurbished premises, even while the work remained uncompleted. As the public areas returned to use, I organised the light entertainment which the restaurants provided. In pre-war days, no London hotel worth its salt was without its own exclusive dance band, so that Carol Gibbons played at The Savoy, Sydney Lipton at Grosvenor House, Jack Jackson at the Dorchester and Harry Roy at the May Fair.

Harry Roy's Band was one of the first I had ever seen when he opened the rebuilt Coventry Hippodrome in 1937. I remember being knocked for six at the appearance of his beautiful film star wife, Princess Pearl, whom Harry introduced on stage. The throb of his music, the brilliance of the lighting and the enormous space of the new theatre auditorium had brought my theatre visits bang up to date. Now, nearly 25 years later, he was playing again in the Candlelight Room at the May Fair, a restaurant specialising in dining and dancing. He had reduced the orchestra to six players, yet still coaxed a swinging tempo from his clarinet and stirred the couples to step out to *Tiger Rag*.

Times, however, demanded something a little rougher and more colourful, so on a hunch, I arranged for a recently arrived group from the Caribbean to perform as the relief band, and Bosco Holder and his West Indian drummers calypsoed into the hearts of the diners. Harry Danziger became an immediate fan and coined a title for the group, 'The Pinkertons', which was clever enough to let you believe you ought to know them. Their repertoire was all spectacle, from fire eating to Wellington Boot dances, and racy songs to home made instruments, expressing the immense energies of Caribbean folklore. The show was surprisingly popular, so that the restaurant filled each night and the performances continued month after month with only the minimum of alteration. Harry Roy did not welcome the intrusion of another band, but he played on and somehow the sounds of the past, like the Hotel itself, became melded into those of the future.

Very quickly other developments in the hotel took shape. Complementing the menus of the Candlelight Room and Le

Chateaubriand grill, was a brand new Polynesian Restaurant, The Beachcomber, with a huge waterfall and live crocodiles, cavorting in a thunderstorm of tropical rain, to add to the decor of palm trees and bamboo. It pre-dated the Hilton's Trader Vic by a long margin and its Pacific islands food and rum cocktails were an instant hit amongst young lovers and older gourmets. To underline our debts to a film heritage we built a luxurious small cinema, with super high-fi sound and projection equipment, serving drinks and snacks to an audience of 60, seated in plushy armchairs. It soon became a favourite meeting place for the hotel guests when relaxing away from the re-vamped bedrooms and suites on the floors above.

Maintaining these new venues with entertainment kept me very busy. I hired a group of musicians from the Friendly Isles, appropriately named the Paradise Islanders, who with Hawaiian guitars and grass skirts brought their rhythms to The Beachcomber. Then using some former *Cool for Cats* dancers under the direction of Denys Palmer, I produced a late evening cabaret, *Parisian Nights*, in the Candlelight Room. These presentations began to stretch the back-up facilities in the hotel to the limit, while the demands on lighting and sound systems, the storage of settings and properties, as well as dressing room space, increased by the week. Our ambitions were soaring and as we broadened the canvas of entertainment to include other orchestras and groups along with Harry Roy, the May Fair became a major employer of artists and musicians and a cramped one too. For star monthly engagements we had Ray Ellington and his Band and then the Temperance Seven, while I had personal memories richly renewed when Johnny Gray (who marked his debut with the saxophone back to Billy Monk at the GEC Ballroom in Coventry) played with his swing group and a bevy of solo singers.

Just then, an air of uncertainty suffused this form of musical presentation. In retrospect, Britain awaited the arrival of the Beatles and the Rolling Stones to sweep away the sentimental cobwebs of Music Hall for ever. Part of the mood developed from the large stay at home audiences viewing television, and losing touch with the historical tradition of theatre going. The early post war years had heralded a revival in variety shows, just as they had done in all the arts, with drama, opera and ballet consolidating their popularity of the period 1939-45.

In this the support of the Arts Council had been vital to establish permanent state theatre companies, but the catalyst it had released in commercial show business was fading fast. This coupled with the closure of theatre buildings throughout the country, soon had developers converting valuable sites into even more profitable investments. Maybe it was time to start something new? Perhaps a more comprehensive formula could evolve with the right opportunity? After all, the old theatres that stood empty were hardly a serious loss, in terms of modern requirements. They needed an expensive update with air conditioning and better sight lines, so that every seat occupant could see what was happening on stage, while the facilities behind the curtain were a dismal hangover from the Victorian era. Might therefore the experience we had gained from the success of the comfortable small cinema in the May Fair, provide us with the key to opening a new style theatre?

I suppose we were wrong to believe that others could share our enthusiasms for the idea. The large cinema circuits, who provided the bulk of leisure premises, had no cause to complain of their status or do much to improve their facilities. The tightly controlled policies that permitted their almost exclusive rights to show films, protected them well enough, and similarly West End theatre owners, unlike their colleagues in the provinces, still held a monopoly position. This they neatly protected from usurpers in a series of closed agreements with ticket agencies, artists' representatives and programme advertisers, so that it was almost impossible for any rival newcomer to survive. The challenge from more up to date buildings, with the construction of the National Theatre and multi-purpose halls, was still a distant threat; but even allowing for the lethargy of the established impresarios, our proposal for a theatre in a hotel received a cool hearing.

At the height of the arguments designed to warn us not to waste our time, I was fortunate to have my musings jolted by a trip to the United States. Casting for the next television series required conferences with the American sponsor and I became exposed, for the first time, to the razz-a-matazz of Broadway. Just two hours after stepping from the flight I met it all head on. It was a young man's dream, or, more correctly, it seemed that the hours of misguided youth I had spent watching the movies, were there for real. Off I went to Radio City Music Hall. Serried tier on serried tier of balconies, stretching up to the top of the roof: an audience of seven thousand spellbound souls gazing at the best value in town,... a two hour Hollywood filmed musical, plus live on stage, a classical ballet company, a choir, an orchestra, trapeze artists and comics, topped with a heart stopping finale: the finest high steppers in show bizz, a chorus line of forty-six Rockettes.

Small wonder that my favourite movie *On the Town* had said it was just like this. In my ten day stay I watched 22 theatre presentations, walked around 10 art galleries, climbed the steps to 15 museums, and discovered eating at the Automat, with eggs that were Sunny Side Up. I needed no further convincing what to do next. A brand new theatre must be the answer.

Fortunately Harry and Eddie Danziger's strength lay in their handling of this sort of situation. Untried, but practical ideas, which might challenge orthodox thinking, gave a simple guarantee to raise their interest. They each had notions enough to occupy the attention of a team of production men, yet should you have a project that fitted into their routine, they would back it, and you, right to the hilt. Nevertheless, as hot as they considered the concept of a new theatre to be, until we wrapped up the current television series and delivered it to the networks, everything else must wait on the back burner. That season *Richard the Lionheart* was shooting at the studios and we were already in negotiation over the next series, *Ali Baba and the Forty Thieves*, so we could only contemplate one side line possibility as theatre managers, Summer Stock Theatre. We thought of using the large ballroom in the hotel, under-booked during the summer months, as a temporary 'theatre in the round'. Here we could present potted versions of the old musical comedies of Cole Porter, Gershwin and Irving Berlin. But on reflection, the format did not seem ambitious enough for London and we decided to wait for a more convenient excuse.

It occurred in an unexpected way, the moment the auditors revealed their yearly financial report. It showed the costs of operating the Candlelight Room restaurant with a cabaret could be more financially successful if we gave each of our clients a pound note to stay away. Of course, this was not the sole arbiter. Such activities always appear costly if examined in isolation. After all, we were seeking to provide a comprehensive selection of entertainment and allow other high profit generating alternatives to provide the extra boost to revenue, offsetting the losses. Still, the costings were salutary and might emphasise a more sensible approach to possibly richer pickings in another field.

Later that summer, we coupled this information to indications our *Ali Baba* series might run into difficulties. Associated Rediffusion were uncertain about their commitment to the UK rights. They had recently transmitted a musical extravaganza built around the story of *A Thousand and One Nights*, which had proved an expensive flop. As our stories covered a similar topic, they waxed cool on the question of signing a contract. Eddie Danziger tried to switch sponsorship, but the mix did not work. The option was either to back it ourselves, or delay it. There was another worrying factor. Colour television was taking over fast: we planned to shoot in Black and White and must resolve a financial shortfall to justify the extra costs of colour negative. Our feature productions, too, were at a standstill. One of the periodic hiccups with distributors, who were belatedly blaming television for the loss of their audiences in the cinemas, forced a gap in the production line. By the end of September the pattern was clear. Shooting ended. My hard routine of early morning alarm clock awakenings to urge me to the studios for 7.30 (far too reminiscent of army reveilles) was temporarily suspended. A breathing space was imminent and with it a chance to examine the theatre project in detail.

TWENTY ONE

THE MAY FAIR THEATRE

I T IS SURPRISING how quickly one pattern of life style is
replaced by another. In a matter of days a completely different
focus emerged as I passed from driving each early morning
against the commuter traffic towards the outskirts of London, to
joining in the 9 a.m. rush into the centre of town. The first day I
viewed the final camera rushes from the studio at the May Fair
cinema and then took an hour or so climbing over the flat rooftops
of the hotel with the group's resident architect, George Beech. He
had previously worked on the conversion of the studios at Elstree,
and was used to the fancies of the Danzigers, so, in a short time, we
reached a decision. We could build a theatre within the hotel, if we
took over the floor space of the Candlelight Room together with its
underground kitchens and storage space. It was a simple enough
notion. The restaurant would form the auditorium; the basement
plus a dozen bedrooms from the main building above, would provide
the stage and the fly tower. Maybe it was a cheeky plan, sure to
cause raised eyebrows on the hotel management side, who would
regard the sacrifice of any rentable suites, as sacrilege. Yet, I felt
sure that Eddie and Harry would approve the enterprise. However,
George and I agreed to say nothing to anyone until we had studied
the detail a little closer, especially as we realised the officials at the
licensing authorities could give us a bumpy ride.

The opportunity to broach the idea and test its fallibility
occurred the following day. The Danzigers wanted me to screen
one of the latest show prints before delivery to the distributors,
and I arranged for viewing at Humphries Film Laboratories in
Whitfield Street. The three of us walked back to the hotel
afterwards. They soon asked,

"How are you getting along with the potted musicals project? Now that you are away from the studio commitment, are you ready to set it up?"

"Well, it's interesting you should mention that, but,..."

Ten minutes later, they queried,

"How practical is all this?"

"George Beech seems to believe it is."

"Right. We'll do it."

We were on our way.

That same day I ran through the financial implications with Bob Faloon, checked publicity and advertising schedules with Stuart Allan, the PR man at the May Fair, and called in our construction manager to earmark the necessary personnel. George Best had been in charge of the set building and fabrications at the studios and I knew that if he promised a date for completion he would stick to it. At Gordon Hotels he controlled the maintenance crews for the group and would be a lynch pin in any structural alterations.

When the news of the proposals leaked out, there was considerable agitation from the staff involved. Closing a restaurant meant a large reorganisation, but as we had already decided to open a new restaurant to replace the Candlelight Room, the personnel would have a minimum of upset. Harry Danziger wanted to open a Parisian type bistro to follow up the success of our French Cabaret and the already French biased menus that emerged from the head chef, Calderoni. So we contracted the theatre and film designer Roger Furse, who had fashioned the sets for Laurence Olivier's *Hamlet* and *Henry V*. He had spent his student days in Paris and we asked him to create a Boulevard Café in one of the old hotel lounges. The space looked neglected, considering the changes the building had undergone during previous months, so Furse had a free hand to work his magic. This he did by painting the skyline of Mont Martre and St Germaine on a large panoramic backcloth. Lighting it with a formidable battery of motorised spotlamps and colour changers, he produced morning sunshine, a sunset, and a purple dusk at the touch of a switch, so that the tables and umbrellas, on the Parisian style pavements, reflected a spectroscope of day and evening shadows. It looked like a lot of fun, even before we introduced the smells of Gauloises and garlic.

For some, of course, it was a disastrous break up of something they had treasured for an era. I knew that my task of telling Harry Roy about the plans was not going to be easy. Thirty years' association with the hotel had been a long time for Harry to serve, and he had devoted the major part of his professional life to entertaining many people there. Few items in the social whirl had missed his scrutiny. He had led the dancing of the Flappers and Charlestonites, serenaded the romances of the Windsors, the Sweenies and the Mountbattens, and made the Nightingale sing just round the corner in Berkeley Square, as the bombs of the blitz amplified his accompaniments to *We'll meet again* and *Room five hundred and four*. Now the twisting of Chubby Checker, and the bubbling revolution of sound that the Beatles were hatching, was putting Harry's suave music away for ever, and at the May Fair we were a tip of this change.

The farewell was very difficult. Harry did not take the matter lightly and could not understand the need for a theatre in the hotel, but I arranged a handsome pay off as gracefully as I could. When he died a few years later, the big swing over to the new star disc personalities had left Harry almost forgotten, although still the sounds of his Tiger Rag jingle out for the wrinklies to remember.

In a way it was the same when Roger Furse and I examined the fabrics and the furnishings of the lounge we were re-cycling. The materials, after over forty years hard wear, dusty and stained as they were, still displayed a magnificent testimonial to the nostalgia they represented. While we were discussing this on the day before the construction teams arrived to tear it apart, the oldest habitual visitor made his morning appearance. An elderly man, probably well past eighty, always arrived promptly twice a week at 11 a.m. to meet two lady friends. Dressed immaculately in a dark grey, double breasted suit, winged collar and cravat with a red rose in his buttonhole, he might have stepped straight from the Adelphi. Then, as the ladies approached, he stood up tall to greet them. They were of a similar mould. Their pearls and discreet gold bangles set off the formality of their carefully tailored skirts and blouses, topped by smartly coiffured greying wavy hair.

Even in Belgravia and Mayfair this lifestyle was fast disappearing. They sipped their tea and chatted away and we marvelled at a page of history that had been part of the reason for opening the Hotel in the first place. When the old man removed his gold hunter watch from his waistcoat pocket to check the time, I felt the moment had come to tell them about the future we were preparing for their long standing rendezvous. I suggested they may like to try our American Coffee House, off the main foyer, instead. Politely, I was dismissed,

"Perhaps we might call in from time to time, but your Boulevards and your theatres are not really for us. They are not part of the May Fair we would care to remember."

So I bowed to the inevitable, smiled my 'Good-byes' and muttered to myself,... 'Well, maybe it was before your day, but when Will Shakespeare was around all good inn keepers kept a theatre company in the courtyard!'

Work was under way next day. The Boulevard de Paris quickly took shape and soon we swopped Harry Roy for French accordions, and the Roast Beef and Shoulder of Lamb for cassoulets and Coq au Vin. The entire waiter crew under old timer Maitre Gunzi left the routine of romantic cabaret dinners in the Candlelight Room for the daily parade of the fashion models around the business lunchers. Meanwhile the pneumatic drills tore apart the guts of their former service quarters.

At first, the licensing authorities listened politely to our plans. It was as if they had heard it often enough before, but found, in practice, nothing ever happened. I suppose their experience during the early post war years had hardly been encouraging. Brand new theatres were not the flavour of the month. Developers, with sites available, produced office blocks rather than unprofitable auditoriums. Where old theatres stood closed for lack of a live production, cinema shows took over, and the Coliseum, the Saville and the Cambridge theatres had already succumbed. The Prince Charles, the only new West End theatre to open in the early sixties, had arrived in a blaze of publicity with a programme of live presentations. Sadly, it rapidly sought planning permission to revert to the more secure earning powers of the silver screen.

There had already been an even greater cause of concern. Some theatres, in particular the architectural jewel the St James, despite a determined campaign by the acting profession led by the Oliviers, lay demolished, and the Stoll, the Gaiety and the Lyceum had for various reasons, also ceased to exist. The pressure of further losses was evident in every part of the country as the Music Hall gave way to Bingo. So the reaction to our proposal was hardly unexpected when it drew a standard response,

"Why don't you come clean with us and say you want another cinema in the May Fair?"

However, George Beech and I determined to press our case, and we called in George Barden, a retired structural engineer, who as a young graduate worked on the design of the original steel framework. He knew about intricate loading and weight considerations from his earlier calculations, and when we outlined a plan to defeat the sceptics who fancied we were building a cinema, he produced a formula, not only ideal for our purposes, but one that would form a permanent obstruction to any future attempts to alter its prime use as a live theatre. He carefully positioned a new main steel beam, in such a way, as it would not interfere with the view of the audience, but would make it impossible to set up a projector for either back or front cinema projection without tearing the building completely apart. When we saw the metal girder arrive from the rolling mills in Scotland, we gauged only complete demolition of the rest of the May Fair would ever negate the situation.

Our final presentation of the construction details to the planning authority, with an elaborate set of safety devices to satisfy the Fire, the Health and the Police regulations, brought acceptance of our solutions without a major fuss. Apart from small alterations we reckoned we would achieve our aims. Of course, nothing is totally straightforward, and we underwent a week of anxiety when the Transport authority and the Metropolitan Police queried the plans on traffic grounds. The hotel's parking limits were set up 40 years previously and a nearby hotel management, at the instigation of some out-gunned supporters of the former crooked Leonard Jackson regime, brought pressure on the council officers to ban the theatre. They claimed that local parking conditions would improve if there was no theatre building. However, simple logistics emphasised that theatre visitors would arrive outside normal business hours, and the opposition was nonsense.

Yet, these administrative knee jerks were not our real cause for concern, as we put in hand the ordering of the necessary materials. It was here we met our major headaches. The fact that since the days of the massive boom for cinema buildings in the thirties, when every High Street boasted a new Gaumont Palace and an Odeon, there was little demand to produce equipment for theatres. The expertise was simply not around any more. Apart from restoring buildings after the bombings, and a few new ones like the Belgrade in Coventry, the Playhouse in Nottingham and Bernard Miles' Mermaid, the only active construction was a handful of concert halls, sponsored by local authorities.

It was therefore essential to look towards Europe for examples. In France, Germany, and Holland the tide of rebuilding, once the battlefields disappeared, had favoured a rapid return to full use of all the damaged theatres. In Germany particularly, the priorities had placed such work ahead of the need to provide living spaces. While Hamburg, Berlin and the bomb blasted cities of the Ruhr had new opera houses up and running, almost before the streets were free of debris. I went with George Beech to look. We returned inspired by fresh thinking on seating, staging, air conditioning and decor, and full of admiration for the way the Europeans were approaching their cultural heritage.

As a result we decided to attempt a novel approach of our own. Both George and I had acquired a fair amount of new skills when we had worked in the recently built television studios around London, during the development period of commercial television. The flexibility of the production facilities was unique, whether it was because of the mobility of the lighting rigs that permitted a rapid change of settings or the large amount of clear space the floor plans provided. It was these excellent working conditions we wanted to duplicate, and consequently we chose a flat floor area in the main theatre, rather than a sloping floor with raked stalls. Our seating would rest on top of this, yet instead of remaining permanently fixed, would fit onto a stepped metal framework. Not only would it give impeccable sight lines, but would allow free movement of the seating to suit the production, whether for proscenium arch, apron or in the round staging.

Benn Toff, of Festival Ballet, was a knowledgeable help in these technical deliberations. Because of his experience with the stagings at the Royal Festival Hall, with no rigid safety curtain fitted, I was able to pre-empt the doubts of the licensing officers in foregoing one at the May Fair. We marked our drawings accordingly, by proposing that all scenery and settings would consist of inherently fire proof material, which although calculated to be more expensive than the traditional scenic cloth and soft timber, would extend our design potential. It would also fully satisfy the standards for public safety. Benn similarly contributed to our bid for audience comfort by introducing us to some contemporary seats for concert halls. We modified these with some ideas we had noted in Germany, and produced what was certainly the most luxurious seating available. Similarly, with lighting, stage equipment and sound amplification, we were determined to use the most advanced systems we could lay our hands on.

While the building work proceeded some of the other rehabilitation projects in the hotel were completed, and we began to appreciate the possibilities of the integration of the various enterprises forming such a centre of entertainment. The final phase became a public relations exercise directed towards guaranteeing this concept. We wanted to ensure the advertising and the presentation had a common goal and one of the prime factors in this was the treatment of the theatre programmes. The Danzigers insisted we took a lesson from Broadway's free programmes, a distinct plus to New York theatre going. The miserable offerings that were sold in the London theatres were no credit to anyone, but as we had already learned, the monopoly powers wielded in the West End were too difficult to challenge. Now with management in our control, the strangle hold was broken. Stuart Allan edited a convincing programme mock-up we decided to back, full of interesting articles, photographs, show business news and details of the current production, which would provide both a magazine and a guide to the play, without charge, to every ticket holder. So we progressed and as we were getting close to fulfilment of our production plans, concentrated on starting off some fresh rumours in the theatre world.

Suddenly it all fitted into place. Eddie Danziger had been in New York during the Spring of 1963, where he met a young theatre director, William Ball, who had directed an outstanding off-Broadway success of Pirandello's *Six Characters in Search of an Author*. When he saw the play Eddie reckoned it would make an ideal vehicle for Sir Ralph Richardson in London and on his return Eddie, Harry and I went along to talk to this remarkable actor, at his Hampstead home.

Richardson spread a wonderful air of well being and relaxation around him and enthused at the idea, especially as it meant he would be in an opening production at a new theatre. He was proud of his record of involvement in a score of new theatres, as well as his appearance with the Lilian Baylis' company at the Old Vic inauguration in 1930. It was this that marked such a great renaissance in English theatre and became part of a Golden Age, when the Oliviers, Gielgud, Guinness, Ashcroft and Schofield built the solid foundations of the future National Theatre. He welcomed the opportunity to work with a young director, like Ball, having heard reports of the American's sense of occasion and imaginative dramatic insights. Yet, most of all he relished the chance to take part in another 'First'.

With Richardson's agreement to appear, we contracted Ball to direct the opening play at the May Fair Theatre. When he arrived some five weeks before our deadline, he went into total panic at the sight of the unfinished building. He was obviously expecting to see a glistening new theatre, ready and prepared for his entrance, and the shock took his breath away. He had enough left, however, to threaten an immediate return to New York. However, after I had introduced him to the construction manager (the unflappable George Best, who, on far tighter schedules had never let us down) and I went on to show him some of the latest technology we were using and explain our aims, he became quite enthusiastic and ready to start casting. I had brought Betty Kellond from the studio to organise this and very soon Ball was joining in with our other ex-film people, amongst them Yvonne Blake to design the costumes, Jack Sullivan and Barry Copeland to install the lighting and sound equipment, and a large crew of plasterers, carpenters and painters, who brought order to the birth of our dream. We allowed nothing to interfere with our efforts to make the venture a success.

There was no avoiding the tight schedule we had set and I reckoned that an unexpected slip up would spell disaster. We had to trust that the suppliers would deliver the goods, although we felt that theatre traditions ran deep enough for it to be alright on the night. It was a good omen when Strand Electric arrived with the latest electronic dimmers and control boards for their engineers to install into our control room, the day before they had said was the earliest possible moment they could deliver. That was followed by Hall Stage Equipment organising special cranes on a Sunday, to hoist their elaborate machinery over the rooftops and into the fly tower of the theatre in the centre of the hotel complex. Not one guest complained.

Of course there were upsets. The ducting system caught fire, set alight by sparks from the welders' torches, and the Fire Brigade arrived to sort it out. Then a flood of water deluged the false roof in a mighty rain storm, so that we had to paint the ceiling decorations afresh. However, although the first dress rehearsal was accompanied by an orchestra of hammering and drilling, Ralph Richardson consoled us by relating that the Old Vic opening was far more dramatic. Lilian Baylis, the driving force behind the whole venture, had missed the final rehearsal. She lay in hospital, badly injured in a taxi crash. "Anyway," he said, "this is what making history is all about,... the unexpected."

Nevertheless, it provided little consolation to Harry Danziger and myself as we pondered on temperaments and last minute nerves from the director and his assistants, who delivered 'final-final' ultimatums about one thing and then another. I discovered Harry Danziger dodging behind the ventilation chimneys on the roof as I bolted for a similar hide out to escape the retributions that would fall on all our heads if the sound system failed again. It seemed to cause no end of amusement to Ralph and his leading lady, the calm and purposeful actress, Barbara Jefford. They smiled and waved to us through their dressing room windows, as we skulked in the afternoon sunshine to avoid the thunder clouds inside.

Despite the apparent divergence of effort between the remaining construction detailing and the finishing touches the production of the play demanded, the cast seemed to remain splendidly aloof from the dramas unfolding around them. Their many exposures to similar trials at dress rehearsals, probably confirmed their immunity to such frivolities. Megs Jenkins, Ellen Pollock, Mary Yeomans and Eric Dodson sat back on their theatrical upbringing, and relaxed in brave humour.

If anyone should have received our sympathy it was Eric. Although I had prompted Ball to audition him, he was entirely the director's choice along with Eric's wife, the actress Pearl Dadsworth, for parts in the Acting Company group of the play's characters. It was an unusual event for them. Despite the many performances they had given in individual productions, they had not acted together in a play, since their days in provincial rep after the war, when Eric had returned from flying bombers in the R.A.F., and before they married. But often, real life can be more surprising than the playwright can conjure up, as well as fatally more tragic. Two weeks before our opening night Pearl became seriously ill, entered hospital and died seventy-two hours later. Just before she died she told Eric it was her wish that he keep working, and the progress of the production became a symbol of mourning for the loss of our colleague. Later during the run of the play, Eric took over the role of the father from Ralph Richardson and, for us, his loyalty to the spirit of theatre was a touching tribute to what it was all about.

Then, quite surprisingly, everything was ready. The hammering ceased, the cleaners were out of the way and the paint was touch dry. On stage the last instructions to the cast, the readjustment to the spotlights' focus and a general tidy up of the setting had begun and for a moment the tension slackened.

The time had now arrived for a very special engagement I had with my father-in-law. Bill Munro worked at St James' Palace, where he was the assistant to the Lord Chamberlain and in charge of Theatre Licensing. Since leaving the Regular Army, after thirty five years service, his say so governed the operations of London theatres as places of public entertainment. An Act of Parliament ruled that all theatre presentations faced censorship by the Lord Chamberlain, acting on behalf of the monarch, if they were judged inappropriate. There were no such difficulties with our Pirandello play, but because we planned to open a new theatre, the various safety regulations became the legal responsibility of a licensee, again under the authority of the Monarch. I was the nominee.

Almost with Army courts martial correctness, Bill lined me up behind him, and we marched into the presence of Lord Cobbold. I sensed he thought he was getting his own back, as he whispered under his breath, 'Halt. Right turn. Keep your eyes to the front,' for all the raggings I had given him about his favourite regiment, the Royal Sussex. But the Lord Chamberlain played his part too. Looking straight at me as if he was about to pronounce sentence of life imprisonment, he said,

"Well, Major, what do you know about this young man and was he fit to marry your daughter?"

I suppose that broke the ice as he added,

"I gather you two know each other?"

For all the dignified informality, I did not fancy crossing swords about anything, and accepted the Royal Warrant, a glass of sherry and the good wishes for success, with all the grace I could muster. A cell, in the underground darkness of that Palace for disobeying the rules, was the last thing I wanted!

That evening the 17th June 1963 (twenty years to the day I had joined the Army) I hovered in the foyer with Harry Danziger awaiting the arrival of the first members of the audience. We felt sure we were about to witness a rather special night. Harry was standing in for Eddie, who was in the United States and we decided to move around to see if all was well. Backstage there was quiet and confidence. The artists prepared their make up in the dressing rooms, which until a few days previously was hotel accommodation, with room service still on call at the touch of the bell, and the wardrobe ladies gave the costumes a last smoothing with a hot iron.

The technical staff were under the management of Joe James, who I knew previously as the Stage Director at Festival Ballet. He had joined us at the suggestion of Benn Toff and was, a little nervously, calling for the final check out on the equipment, but in front of the setting the main auditorium looked like a glistening diamond. The sheen from the blue silk covered walls sent shimmers of light towards the huge smoked mirrored control gallery and onto the gold plating of the decorative metal rails lining the side balconies. Above the foyer steps leading down to the main theatre doors, an internally illuminated stained glass sculpture, created by John Piper, turned slowly on its axis, and at the entrance the ushers handed out the free programmes as the audience surged forward to their red upholstered seats.

Then it was curtain up and Ralph Richardson's appearance met with warm applause. The performance was under way and the theatre operational. For some of us, though, it was not quite plain sailing. Ten minutes into the first act and I realised the theatre seemed much warmer than I had expected from our earlier testing of the air conditioning, and a cool flow of fresh air did not appear to be seeping through from the grills beneath each seat. I decided to investigate and slipped away through a side door. Harry Danziger had the same idea and we went off to locate the plant controlling engineer. His office was shut and he had departed for the evening, leaving only the general duties' man on call. We explained the problem to him, but as he was a stand-in relief he was not familiar with the new theatre system. However, he showed us the control panels, and though all looked in order, things were far from well. The theatre was growing hotter by the minute.

Phone calls to the main ventilation contractor failed to help and Harry and I, decided we must commence some emergency ventilation system of our own. He stood at one set of doors, out of sight, while I stood at another, opposite, behind a curtain. Then by alternatively opening one side and closing the other, we brought some air movement through the theatre auditorium, from the cooler atmosphere of the foyers. It worked just sufficiently for us to reach the interval, when we opened every door, front and back stage, and succeeded in reducing the temperature.

The last act was well under way, before the engineer finally came rushing back. He had forgotten the timing clocks for the cooling plant, set up for the previous week's rehearsals, automatically switched the circuit out at 7 p.m. It was not the best news Harry Danziger and I listened to, for we had reached a state of utter exhaustion as we opened and closed the doors while pretending that nothing was amiss.

Without question, the grip of the play saved us. It held the audience captive and they forgave everything. Ralph Richardson and the cast acknowledged curtain call after curtain call as the Bravos echoed for the first time around the auditorium and the triumph was real. When the audience finally went home, we held a champagne celebration for the artists, the press and our guests. London may have had larger opening nights, but on very few occasions in the post war years had there been a more adventurous one. Even the press were a little bewitched by the way we had preserved the secret of a new theatre almost to the day of our opening presentation, and the burst of publicity it received for its daring was enough to guarantee a full house for months. The newspaper coverage was something to remember,

'Pirandello shows off a new theatre's resources,'

ran *The Times*.

'Gorgeous, classical and amusing,'

headlined the *Daily Sketch*,

> '...in a luxury theatre, plush seats without a creak,
> and a great fat programme, free of charge, that
> shames every penny-pinching theatre in London.'

So Fleet Street welcomed the event. Herbert Kretzmer commented in the *Daily Express*,

> 'The May Fair is a new intimate theatre built into
> and under Westminster's May Fair Hotel. The
> Danziger Brothers, who control the place, are to be
> congratulated on as a dashing a piece of enterprise
> as London has seen in many a year. The capture of
> Sir Ralph Richardson as the star of the theatre's
> baptismal production, is an example of initiative
> that should make others look guiltily to their rusted
> laurels.'

It took quite a while for the excitement of that opening to wear off, and as we settled into a long run it was a new experience for me. Over the years, after a succession of films and television shows, I had become somewhat resentful of all the efforts that we had devoted to a production disappear with the list of end credit titles on the screen. Sometimes these days, even these are ruthlessly truncated. At least the tension and reward remain in the theatre, as each fresh audience appears anxious and unconquered, all attentive, to be won anew. This, added to watching a great artist of Richardson's calibre, respond to the subtle differences in interpretation that every audience demands, is something to treasure. A couple of months later he left the cast to pursue a film commitment and we introduced Stephen Murray and Michael Gough into the play, and as the season continued Eric Dodson took over the leading role when Madalena Nicol, Robin Phillips and Olaf Pooley joined the cast.

When Bill Ball returned to New York, I directed the rehearsals for the changes of cast. The philosophical content of Pirandello's words in his attempt to discover truth, became a valid starting point for me to start working with each new group of actors. Indeed it surprised us how much the pattern of the play influenced our daily lives. It certainly had unusual repercussions amongst the normally staid and conservative members of the hotel staff.

They began to centre their working day around the arrival of the audience at the theatre each evening, instead of as before, when focusing it on the departure of the hotel guests at twelve noon. Now the doormen escorted visitors to the box office in place of the main reception desk, and waiters and barmen talked show business gossip rather than the warmth of the bath water or the comfort of the bedrooms. I noticed that even the General Manager mentioned the play and the players, ahead of recommending the chef's dish of the day. And then I really knew that we had completed the circle and that private enterprise could adapt to our latest innovation, just as it had to each of the other changes.

One matinee day, Barbara Jefford arrived early for the performance, to discover a young man fast asleep on the large divan in her room. As she entered he woke up and yelled,

"My God, what's going on?"

Barbara did not wait to hear his story and rushed off for the stage manager. When I heard about it, things were already on the verge of a half cocked riot. The artist's union, Equity, were on alert and they called me to explain the management lapse. It took a little time to resolve but was far more amusing than it first appeared. I discovered a night reception clerk had found a way to line his pocket, on the side. By letting accommodation to late guest arrivals at a reduced rate, and without an official registration, he shunted them into the stage company's dressing rooms (as luxurious as any suite in the hotel) after the actors had vacated them at the close of their evening's work. The crux of his personal initiative was to select only those guests who would depart early, allowing him to see them cleanly off the premises before anyone else realised the deceit. Unfortunately, that day of the matinee he failed to remember one of his temporary overnight boarders was still asleep in a star dressing room.

So a fresh chapter commenced. Our mixture of show business and inn-keeping was likely to provide, at least for a while, a great deal of pleasure and enjoyment to a large number of people, who might through it discover something exclusively special within themselves. For those of us sharing the experiment, it had developed a lively cosmos of uncharted possibilities, a cosmos which embraced what is probably the most exciting creative art form a group of people could undertake together: theatre performance before a live audience. It is that which satisfied us above all else and was part of my own personal quest for fulfilment. That was why the journey had been so rewarding. To do that, occasionally, in life, was an aim I had always cherished, for whatever the past and the future may release in oneself, the most precious souvenirs are those that leave the most loving memories.

TWENTY TWO

FORTY YEARS ON

THERE WAS ALWAYS something very ominous about a fortieth year, whether because it was the one we sang about at school, when it looked so far away, or because it heralded the decade that had a chilling ring about it for the men on my mother's side of the family. To be more precise, it was the forty second birthday when so many of them called it quits or as my mother preferred, passed on, as though summoned to perform some other duty.

Whatever it was, it had happened with a dull regularity to two great uncles, a great grandfather, sundry distant cousins and my favourite Uncle Jim. He had survived everything World War One had hurled at him, but come that fatal number during the crazy days of peace and he was off to join his old comrades at the setting of the sun. It worried me in a niggling sort of way. Distinctly more so as a young man, when an Indian palmist read my future and I speculated on the implications of his prophecy that I should prepare myself for a substantial loss around the fortieth year. Could it be my life on the line?

My father's contribution, while I was learning to read and write, was to instil in me a fascination with numbers. His musical groundwork of scales, notes and octaves seemed pure witchcraft. I found the seven times table particularly intriguing, and there was no mistaking the attraction of 42 and 49, with a distinctive seven times six, and seven times seven. What years but those could offer more significance in a mid-term crisis?

Looking at my friends there was no denying the problems that confronted them as they endured that pivotal phase. They were knee deep in a mish-mash of divorces, re-marriages, growing families, change of jobs and financial upheavals. The omens appeared somewhat mixed for me.

At forty I was enjoying a particularly productive run. I had opened a new theatre, shared in the success of a West End play, and with children maturing at home the future looked rosy. Then came forty-one: the forty second year and the wind changed. All too casually it was a different game. First, the replacement for the excellent play, *Six Characters in Search of an Author*, dissolved into an embarrassing flop. We opted for a musical suggested by William Ball, who then left us high and dry a few days before rehearsals were due to start, with artists and sets contracted and an opening date already on the posters. His eccentricity in not even offering a 'by your leave', was as mysterious as his obscure death in Hollywood years later.

Too late, it meant the treadmill was grinding forward and there was no choice but to steam ahead and present a middle of the road song and dance version of Sheridan's *The Rivals*, adapted and scored by two young off-Broadway writers, Bruce Geller and Jacques Urbont. At least the casting was impeccable with James Fox, Ronnie Barker, Peter Gilmore and Annie Ross. And although we hired a replacement director, the accomplished Duggie Squires, with Alan Barrett as designer, it developed into one long headache of not being quite right or good enough.

We shrugged that off on the basis of 'some you win, some you lose', but as we announced the close down two weeks after opening night, there was a lot of backstage sadness and regret. Unfortunately, it proved a double whammy. The same week we opened to a critical fiasco, Eddie and Harry Danziger sold their hotel interests to Maxwell Joseph, of the Grand Metropolitan Hotels. The era was ending, fast.

It was not as if I had nothing to do. A holiday in Spain with the family was the break I longed for over the last couple of years, except that it, too, ended in disruption. The moment we returned, Mary went to hospital, for a nasty internal operation, and required careful nursing. Was I on the verge of confirming my Indian mystic's warning at forty-two?

As she recovered, I tried to dismiss the negative thoughts. If family history was anything to go by, it was me for the chop. However, the reaper of souls was kind in the past, given the myriad opportunities of the war, and the infant mortality rates of the twenties and early thirties. Children of those days had more at stake than a mere dose of diphtheria, scarlet fever or pneumonia, and classrooms could show a swath of empty desks after epidemics of flu, meningitis or polio.

A young lad, Alan Stone, had shared a school bench with me right from infant days. Then one morning he was absent, dead the next. A killer disease struck him low and a class of eight year olds learned of tragedy at first hand. From then on, the stark fact we were not immortal played its part in how we looked at the living.

The loss of friends or relatives always produced its after effects. It was impossible to ignore the break up of families and households, and the forced sale of belongings. I watched the pattern unwind when my twin cousins lost their 42 year old dad. They swapped the security of their respectable middle class home, for the stress of single parent stewardship, at the age of twelve. The whole burden fell on their mother.

Today the hardship, if not the sorrow, is partly mitigated by the provision of a modicum of State aid. Yet, when families suffer the premature loss of a breadwinner, it is a bitter shock, whatever the support system. My daughter Melanie received an early lesson in this school when her close childhood friend, Susanna, lost her father, Nick Tomalin in the Yom Kippur War. A neighbour and friend of ours, he died in a bizarre incident, also at the age of 42. Such a twist of destiny, which demanded his death on someone else's distant battlefield, makes the timing and the tragedy that much more startling.

It is these parental deaths that are unlike any other. When they occur, they are likely to catch us by surprise, presenting a striking alteration to how we regard ourselves and how we think of others. While parents go about their daily business, there can be a cosy sense of self security. Their presence, during our adult lives, with its continuing inbuilt feeling of safety hanging on from our childhood days, acts as a buffer. It grants us an emotional back stop, an excuse for our own worst excesses. Should things go wrong, the strength of their support and loyalty is often strong enough to provide the confidence to carry on. Only when they are no longer there are our birth roots fully exposed.

After I left home, like many of my friends, I rarely needed my parents' counsel or help. Indeed, the strangeness of my lifestyle might well have proved beyond their natural understanding. Allowing for the odd mishap in family relationships, the majority of my generation enjoyed this understanding with their mother and father. The hardest path to tread is where that experience is missing because of premature death. However, my parents spared me that trauma, as they were around to see me through to the stage I became established in my own family circle. But, whenever such a loss occurs, it is a time for heart searching. What is dramatic and undesired at twelve is no less chilling and lonely at forty.

In the months after I left the May Fair Theatre my job became much less definitive. The Danzigers wanted me to continue with them and I worked in a consultancy role planning theatres, cinemas and restaurants in ventures they were examining. They purchased control of a group of fifty cinemas in the Home Counties to refurbish them, while they sought planning permission for a large hotel, with its own theatre, in Kensington, as well as similar ones in Paris and New York. Yet, as I began plotting multi-screen conversions in city centres with Peter King (Harry Danziger's brother-in-law, and later the founder of the news magazine, Screen International, who worked then with his elderly father, Sam King at Shipman and King Cinemas) I also became involved in the production of a major feature film *The Trygon Factor*, starring Stewart Granger and Susan Hampshire.

I persuaded the financiers to contract my old army soul mate Cyril Frankel to direct, despite their preference for some lesser talent, and we set about improving an Edgar Wallace detective story by calling in another friend, Kingsley Amis, to re-write the script. With the Canadian painter, Stephen Andrews, as adviser on sets and costumes and Robert Morley, James Robertson Justice and Cathleen Nesbitt playing character parts, we moved into the film studios at Shepperton on an eight weeks' summer shooting schedule.

Unfortunately, there was a rude interruption to this peaceful sequence, and shadows that had threatened for some time, took their toll. My father, suffering an almost insignificant illness, suddenly died, shortly after I had visited him one Sunday. Just four hours since saying good-bye and arranging to see him the following Saturday, I was back on the Motorway to gaze at his dead body in hospital at Coventry.

The mourning was substantially different to any I had experienced before. Comrades I had lost during the war and close friends since, generated a distinct sense of sadness, yet it was as if the relationship had already prepared you for its demise. Their end was already a part of the association from the moment the initial contact was formed. Whatever pain there was seemed diminished by the mourning. On the other hand the death of a parent had the deeper responsibilities of blood ties. In one sweeping gesture, you were head of a family, the top branch of a tree, and with no-one left to pull you up beside them. It is the inevitable unending pattern, as the old generation gives pride of place to the succeeding younger one. It comes to us all. To you. To me. To our children. To their children. And free choice flies out of the window.

As I ferried my father's personal effects, his trousers, jacket, shirt and shoes, back to my mother at home from his hospital room, I looked at them on the front seat of my Ford Corsair. They were creased and abandoned and I felt frozen in an acute point of loneliness. It was the unimportant that began to matter. The small memories that jogged their way before me. His death at 77, a triumph for our obsession with numbers and the seven times table. Seven years of retirement after seven times eight (56) years of industrial torment, forging the weapons of hate in the armaments' factories that employed him. For that, he never forgave himself, although had he cared to look at a balance sheet, his music might have compensated the guilt.

When I handed the clothes to my mother, she placed them on one side and murmured, "The poor lad, the poor lad," as though for a moment she was young again and mourning for the whole of that rapidly fading epoch she represented.

A few days later at the Canley Crematorium, one of his oldest work mates, Ike Riley, looked up at the chapel building, while we stood outside after the short service.

"There goes George," he said as a puff of smoke shot from the chimney, "Dead on cue, and in front of us all."

My mother was loath to stay around. For her there was no longer joy or purpose in living. She was not inclined to forget her companion of fifty wedded years. In less than twelve months she succumbed and the house I had been born in stood empty and remote, as it ceased to represent the headquarters of the family.

355

After I returned to my wife and children in London, the framework of our lives rested on new foundations. The fruit on the tree had become the tree itself. The metamorphosis emerged complete, although nothing had changed the exterior it was the inner relationship that had surfaced, on unfamiliar ground. The eye may view things as they had been before; but the mind, recording an attitude towards them, remained substantially altered. A subtlety perhaps, but a vital realisation. Only as other events fitted into the long term perspective and a different pattern appeared in what was important and worth while, did I understand the remarkable significance of the cycle of human life. My parents' days were over, mine were possibly half way through, the two sections together, marking the whole physical span, from birth to death; my earliest memories of them starting at the years I yet had to travel. It was an example of our interdependence on one another and evidence of eternal survival through the spirit that transfers itself, from mothers and fathers, to sons and daughters.

So with this in mind, perhaps the moment has arrived for a pause. A chance to stop looking backward and a return to looking forward, ominously restated in the words of the song, 'Forty years on,...'

INDEX

A

Ackland, Rodney 253
Adair, Hazel 284, 291, 316
Adams, Bill 64
Adams, Phyllis 64
Alexander, Donald 249
Alf of the Golden Cross 135
Ali Baba and the Forty Thieves 334
All Quiet on the Western Front 26
Allan, Elkan 300
Allan, Roy 315
Allan, Stuart 337, 342
Allison, John Dr 276, 280, 298
Allison, Susan 276
Ambrose, Kay 233
Amis, Kingsley 354
An Inspector Calls 237
Anderson, Max 249
Andrews, Stephen 354
Anstey, Edgar 258, 266
Arabesque 231
Arletty 252
Armstrong, Thomas Sir 71
Arova, Sonia 274
ARP Post 404C 123, 128, 135,
   187
Ascott, Mavis 315
Ashton, Don 320
Ashton, Frederick 272, 275
Associated-Rediffusion 287, 307,
   309, 318, 320, 335
Atkinson, F.S. 47, 92

Atlas, Charles 161
Auden, W.H. 266
Australian Film Board 261

B

Baillie Stewart, Lieut 202
Balcon, Michael Sir 256, 259, 321
Ball, William 342, 349, 352
Balls the Butchers 127
Bantock, Granville Sir 19, 64
Barden, George 340
Barker, Ronnie 352
Barnard, Betty 247
Baronova, Irina 270
Barrett, Alan 352
Barry, Iris 253
Bartlemas Fair 231
Bassey, Shirley 315
Bateman, Tony 313
Baxter, John 259
Bay of Pigs 324
Baylis, Lilian 343
BBC Television 264, 295
Beaumont, Cyril 278
Beaumont, Mr & Mrs 74
Bee, 'Orpheus' 72
Beech, George 336, 340
Beecham, Thomas Sir 236
Belafonte, Harry 313
Belsen 194, 197, 206
Benn, Sgt (RAEC) 186, 191
Bennet, Cyril 300
Bennett, Jill 256

Berglas, David 308
Berlin Philharmonic Orchestra 221, 232, 263
Berry, Herbert 30
Berry, Lily 30
Berry, Ruby 26, 30
Best, George 337, 343
Bignall, George 9
Bishop, Nevil 145
Blackburn, Mrs (Landlady) 148
Blackett, P.M.S. Prof 292
Bladen, Mr (Church Caretaker) 113
Blake, Yvonne 325, 343
Blakemore, Eric 320
Bohnen, Michael 221
Boisseau, David 291
Bond, Bessie 256
Boomerang 246
Booth, Webster 79
Bowen, Elizabeth 253
Brabner, Jack 7, 19
Brabner, Mercy 3, 7, 19, 22
Braunsweg, Julian Dr 270
Braunsweg, Vera 271
Brave Don't Cry, The 267
Briansky, Oleg 272
Brickwood, Mickey 125
Brickwood, Mr & Mrs 125
Brickwood, Peggy 125
Bright, 'Buggy' 93, 135, 153
Brinson, Peter 260, 263, 279
British Film Institute 253
Britten, Benjamin 266
Brown, George M.P. 302
Brownrigg, T.M. Capt. 97, 287
Bruce, Rev 68
Budbrooke Barracks Warwick 139, 165
Bullard, Edward Sir 292
Bullet in the Ballet 270
Burroughs, Amy (Howarth) 5, 40, 61, 63, 76, 269
Burroughs, George 5, 40, 61
Burroughs, Len 26, 40, 46, 76, 103, 241, 269
Burton, A.A.C. 46, 84, 93, 95, 103, 111, 121, 132, 138
Butters, Fred Major 228, 236
Butters, Patricia 236

C

Calderoni, Chef 337
Call Northside 777 246
Callas, Maria 274
Calvert, Eddie 315
Cameron, Ken 249
Campion, Midwife 33
Carter, Jack 278
Carter, Peter 212
Cartwright Mr (caretaker) 32
Casson, Lewis Sir 208
Castle, Frank Sgt (RAEC) 186, 191
Castro, Fidel 324
Cavalcade of Sport 300, 304
Cavalcanti, Alberto 266
Celibidache, Sergiu 222, 225, 232, 263
Central Office of Information 248, 260, 264
Charles, Nellie (Brabner) 7, 20
Charnley, Michael 272
Chauviré, Yvette 272, 274
Cheaters, The 324
Chopin, Adele 10
Christie, Agatha 326
Christie, John Sir 237
Circus Barum 232
City Speaks, The 264
Clark, Petula 315
Clarke, Harry 23
Clarke, Herbert 18
Clemens, Brian 326

Clements, John 246
Cloake, Anne 231
Clore, Leon 249
Cobbold, Lord 345
Cogan, Alma 315
Coke, Cyril 291
Cole, Sid 253
Confessional 231
Conquest of Everest 261
Cons, George J. 164, 247
Cool for Cats 309, 318, 320, 328
Copeland, Barry 343
Corbett, Ronnie 315
Cornes, James Rev 68, 122
Coronation Street 306
Coronation, The 261
Corrie, Adrienne 327
Cotton, Billy 230
Courtneidge, Cicely 326
Cox, Bryan 112, 118, 127
Cramner, Philip 209
Cranko, John 278
Crombie, Tony 327
Crossley Brothers 21
Crossman, Richard M.P. 51, 295
Crown Film Unit 248, 249, 252, 257
Cuevas, Marquis de 270
Cunard, Lady 237
Cyrano 237

D

Dadsworth, Pearl 344
Dance and Dancers 278
Dancing Times, The 278
Dand, Charles 249
Danilova, Alexandra 272, 274, 279
Danziger, Angela 320, 328
Danziger, Danny 328
Danziger, Edward J. 318, 321, 323, 328, 334, 336, 342, 352, 354
Danziger, Gigi 328
Danziger, Harry Lee 318, 321, 327, 331, 334, 336, 342, 344, 346, 352, 354
Danziger, Jimmy 328
Danziger, Nick 328
Danziger, Richard 328
Dark Elegies 315
David, Hugh 308
Davidson, Jimmy 249
Davies, John Rev 59
Davis, Mr & Mrs 129
Day, Robin 295
Dean, Arthur (Warden) 163, *247*
Delfont, Bernard Lord 237
Dench, Judi Dame 252
Desert Rats, The 211, 219, 228, 327
Desert Victory 246, 257
Deutsches Opera Berlin 221
Devil on Horseback 267
Diary for Timothy 264
Dodson, Eric 313, 344, 348
Dolin, Anton Sir 162, 256, 269, 274
Doncaster, Caryl 300
Donnegan, Lonnie 315
Drifters 249, 256, 264, 265, 266
Dugdale, Nigel Col 279
Dumbleton, C.W. 51
Dupenois, Charles 108, 111, 132, 135, 153
Dupenois, George 91, 132, 199
Dymes, Dorothy M.E. 164

E

E.O.C.Howells Ltd. 69
Ellington, Ray 332
Elton, Arthur Sir 258, 260, 264
Elton, Margaret Ann Lady 266
Emergency Ward 10 306

Esmeralda, Ana 270
Evans, Edith Dame 252
Everly Brothers 315
Explorers of the Depths 256

F

Fall, Dolly 33
Fall, Fred (P.C.80) 58, 107, 202
Fall, Rosemary 26, 29, 35, 202
Faloon, Robert J. 320, 321, 323, 337
Farquharson, J.S. Dr 292
Farson, Daniel 300
Ferris, Barbara 315
Festival Ballet 272, 290, 313, 315
Festival of Britain 250, 272
Fields, Gracie 104
Film Centre 260, 279
Finch, Peter 262
Finch, Tamara 262
Fires were Started 246
Fitzgibbon, Maggie 316
Flaherty, Robert 253, 259
Flynn, Errol 323
Fonda, Jane 162
Fonteyn, Margot 162, 210, 275
Fordyce, Ian 300
Foreman, Mrs (ARP Warden) 126
Forman, Denis Sir 248, 306, 318
Forty Second Street 279, 316
Foulger, Joan 133
Fox, James 352
Franca, Celia 223, 236, 241, 314
Frankel, Cyril 225, 229, 244, 256, 259, 262, 271, 280, 354
Frankel, Denis 236
Frankel, Gerald 236, 237
Fraser, I.W. 93
Fraser, Robert Sir 248, 258, 294, 306
Frost, David 295
Frostick, Michael 233, 238, 274,
276, 279
Furminger, Grace 123
Furminger, Harold 35, 46, 51, 59, 78, 84, 90, 98, 108, 120, 123, 153, 199, 219, 229
Furse, Roger 337

G

G.P.O. Film Unit 247, 252, 264
Gabb, Lieut Col 180
Gaitskill, Hugh 295
Gardiner, Vic 288
Gatherum the Chemist 127
Gebhardt, Ferry 232
Geller, Bruce 352
Gentlemen's Agreement 246
Gibbons, Carol 331
Gilbert, Frank 199
Gillett, Roland 294, 308
Gilmore, Peter 284, 316, 352
Gilmour, Sally 223, 231, 236, 274
Gilpin, John 256, 272, 282, 315
Gingold, Hermione 237
Giselle 271, 274
Glaiman, Mauricio 15
Gloster, John 241
Glover, Stanley 89
Godfrey, Louis 315
Goldthorp, A. 78, 192
Goodman, Lieut (Worcs) 183
Gopal, Ram 270
Gordon, Brigadier 211
Gordon Hotels Group 329
Gore, W.R.T. 153
Gore, Walter 223, 231, 236, 277
Gough, Michael 348
Grade, Lew Lord 294, 296
Grainger, Phillis 64
Granger, Stewart 354
Granville Theatre Fulham 291
Gray, Donald 319
Gray, Johnny 332

Green, Harry 41
Green, Joyce 156
Gregson-Ellis, Maj Gen 232
Grierson, John 245, 252, 258, 260, 306
Grierson, Margaret 259
Grimmond, Joe 295
Group 3 Films 259, 262, 267
Guinness, Alec 237
Gunner, Lieut Col 189, 192
Gunzi, Maitre 339
Gvsosky, Tatiana 222

H

Hackford, Jo Mrs 264
Hall, Harry 65, 73
Hall, Percy Dr 73
Hamilton, John 288
Hamilton Smith, Janet 70
Hammett, Marjorie 102, 119
Hampshire, Susan 354
Hardy, Forsyth 249
Hardy, L.T.N. 93, 111
Hartog, Howard 209
Harvey, Trevor 209, 232
Hawes, Stanley 261
Hay Fever 235
Haydock, Beryl 15, 29, 35, 64, 101, 131, 175, 353
Headquarters 5 Division 228
Hearn, Lydia (Munro) 9, 15
Heart of Britain 257
Helpman, Robert 210
Hemmings Hairdressers 127
Hendricksen, Elvi 232
Henessey, Desmond 313, 325
Henri, Langlois 253
Hermann, Theo 209
Hewer, John 316
Hewitt, Bernard 6, 26, 35, 113, 133, 184
Hewitt, Betty 184

Hewitt, Nelly 6, 18, 113, 122
Hewitt, William 6, 18, 113, 122
Hickman, Gladys 247
Hinton, Paula 274
Hobbs, L.J. 47, 93, 111
Hoch, Johann 112
Holbeche, Gerald Rev 113, 118
Holder, Bosco 331
Hollows, Ernest 161
Hollows, Fred 23, 29, 104, 161
Hollows, Ruby 23, 29, 63, 104
Hollows, Willie 161
Holmes, Jack 258, 266
Holt, Joyce 164
Hooten, Florrie 32
Hore-Belisha, Leslie 167
Housing Problems 264, 266
Howard, W.H. 93
Howells, Evan Lieut. 69, 116
Hughes, Noel (Josh) 89, 90, 94, 95
Humphrey, C.A.B. 153
Humphries Film Labs 336
Hunt, Peter 300
Hunter, Robin 315
Hurok, Sol 276, 279
Hylton, Jack 237
Hylton, Jane 326

I

In Town Tonight 301
Industrial Britain 254
Ingrams, Michael 300
Invitation to the Dance 314
Ireland, John 324
Isherwood, Christopher 223

J

Jackson, George 63
Jackson, Gladys 63
Jackson, Jack 331
Jackson, Joan 63

Jackson, Leslie 329, 340
Jackson, Sheila 310
Jacobs, David 301
James, Joe 346
James, Miss (teacher) 35
Jazz Singer, The 265
Jebb, Kit 256
Jefford, Barbara 344, 349
Jenkins, Megs 344
Jennings, Humphrey 249, 257
Jerboa Theatre, Berlin 231
John, Evan 209
Johns, Glynis 326
Johnson, Al 265
Johnson, H.B. Rev 68, 100, 113
Johnstone, Ken 300, 302
Jones, Miss (teacher) 32, 101
Jones, Wynn Prof 292, 295
Jones, Zoe 15
Joos, Kurt 236
Joseph, Maxwell Sir 352
Journey's End 26
Justice, James Robertson 354
Justin, John 326

K

Kaye, M. Dr 164
Keith, Jens 222
Kellond, Betty 343
Kemp-Welch, Joan 291, 309, 311, 314, 316
Kendall, Henry 237
Keyes, Roger Lord 330
King, Peter 354
King, Sam 354
Kingsland, L.W. 77, 90, 92
Kingsway Corner 301
Krassovska, Natalie 274
Kraus, Gertrud 231
Kretzmer, Herbert 348

L

Laine, Betty 315
Langstone, Margaret 133
Larkin, Philip 85–91, 241
Larkin, Sydney 85, 91
Lawson, Eric 209
Le Petit Club Francais 252
Le Sage, Bill 327
Leacock, Philip 249
Legg, Stuart 249, 256, 258, 260
Leigh, Marion 256
Leigh, Monica 315
Les Sylphides 269
Leslie, Clem Sir 249, 251
Lester, Dick 291, 306
Lewis, Cecil 294
Lewis, M.M. Dr 164
Lewis, Richard 65
Lewis, Roy 46, 67, 73, 86, 101
Lewis, Wilfred 67, 76, 81, 160
Lichine, David 272
Liddiard, F.J. 78, 92
Life and Death of Lola Montez 278
Lipton, Sydney 331
London Can Take It 264
Lord Haw-Haw 118
Lough, Ernest 74
Louisiana Story 254
Love, Bryan 313
Lowe, Joy 122
Lowe, W.B.J. 122, 126
Lowendhal, Walter 328
Ludwig, Walter 209
Lynn, Gillian 223

M

MacDonald, Ramsey 29
Mackerras, Charles Sir 261
Mackie, Philip 248
Macqueen, Norman 291, 308
Maddison, John 249–259
Major, Blyth 79

Make Me an Offer 262
Man from Interpol 321, 324
Man of Africa 259, 267
Man of Aran 254
Mankowitz, Wolf 262
Mann, Tom 51
March of Time, The 246, 249
Marchand, Collette 274
Mark Saber 319
Markova, Alicia Dame 62, 162, 269, 274
Marshall, Norman 318
Martin, Millicent 284, 316
Massey, H.S.W. Prof 292
Massine, Leonide 162, 236, 270, 272
Matthews, Francis 326
Mattocks, J. 92
May Fair Hotel London 320, 330, 336
May Fair Theatre London 343, 352, 354
Maycock, Alistair 13
Maycock, Mr & Mrs 133
McCleod, Ian 295
McConville, Bill 306
McCormack, Stephen 266, 268, 287, 291, 301, 307
McGowran, Alice 65, 73
McGowran Quartette 65
McMillan, John 308
McNicoll, Niven 249
Medawar, Peter Sir 291
Meekhums, Pat (Munro) 9, 15
Memmot, Irene 113, 119
Memmot, Winnie 113, 119
Metcalf, F.H. 47, 76, 89
Metternich, Josef 209
Midland Daily Telegraph 51, 72, 87, 121
Miranda, Carmen 270
Mishcon, Victor Lord 297

Monk, Billy 128, 332
Morley, Robert 354
Morris, Philip Sir 138
Mosley, Oswald Sir 51
Mouilpied, Helen de 248
Mr Marvel 308
Mullen, Barbara 259
Mullins, Peter 325
Munro, Lydia (Bignall) 9
Munro, Mary 8, 15, 229, 275, 290, 315, 318
Munro, Richard 9, 15
Munro, W. E. O. Major 8, 345
Murray, Stephen 348
Museum of Modern Art, New York 253
Myers, Jack 48

N

Nadolny, Sylva 310
National Ballet of Canada 241
National Film Board of Canada 246
Needlers Meats 127
Nesbitt, Cathleen 354
New Elstree Studios 319, 320, 325, 336
New London Film Society 252
Nicol, Madalena 349
Night Mail 246, 266, 267
Night of the Fire 246
Night Train to Inverness 326
Nijinsky, Vaslav 270
Nisbett, Alec 127
Nisbett, Jean 127
Noble, Peter 253
Norfolk, Duke of 328
Norman, Paul 10
Norman, Richard 10
Norman, Stephen 10
Norman, Victoria 10
Norris, Jack 15

Norris, Joyce 15, 29, 35, 64, 101, 131, 175, 284, 353
North Sea 264
Norton Barracks, Worcester 177, 180, 247

O

O'Brien, Timothy 310
Olivier, Laurence Lord 210, 274, 337
On the Town 311, 334
Orrey, Leslie 247
Oswin, Harry 134, 153
Owen, Mr (Swim Instructor) 162
Owens, Jesse 217

P

Pahlen, Victor 323
Palmer, Denys 310, 316, 332
Parkes, Graham 84, 92, 111, 132, 134, 153
Paston Brown, Beryl Dame 164, 247
Pavlova, Anna 62, 270
Payne, Laurence 327
Paynter, Eddie 306
Pears, Frank 57
Penn, Geoffrey 49
Perrotti, Doreen 128
Peter and the Wolf 278
Petrouchka 280
Pett and Pott 266
Phillips, Robin 349
Phipps, H.W. 123, 124, 126
Pike, Magnus 253
Piper, John 346
Plisetskaya, Maya 62
Pollock, Ellen 344
Pooley, Olaf 349
Powell, Dilys 253
Praagh, Peggy van Dame 279
Price, George 43, 47

Price, Hilda 43
Projection of Britain 250
Pursuers, The 326

Q

Question of Science 295
Quirke, James Capt 212

R

Race, Steve 316
Rambert, Marie Dame 162, 231, 236, 269, 271, 274, 280
Ravensdale, Baroness 237
Ravensdale, V.A.J. Capt 173
Rawsthorne, Alan 256
Red Shoes 314
Riabouchinska, Tatiana 272, 274
Richard the Lionheart 325, 334
Richards, R.C. 93, 132, 153
Richardson, Ralph Sir 210, 237, 246, 274, 342, 346
Rider, Bill 92, 153, 172, 199
Riley, Isaac 355
Riley, Peter 134
Roade, Sinclair 260, 264
Robbins, Brian 151, 172
Robertson, Ker (Leslie) 309, 314, 329
Robinson, Eric 154
Robinson, Russell Lieut 183
Rodgers, Anton 326
Roe, H.E.A. (Ernie) 89, 103
Rollins, Donald 64, 70, 81, 120
Romeo and Juliet 165, 274
Ross, A.A. (Angus) 256
Ross, Annie 352
Rossana, Nöel 315
Rotha, Paul 252, 264, 266
Rowlands, Patsy 315
Roy, Harry 331, 338
Royal Festival Hall 273, 280, 341
Royal Philharmonic Orchestra

236
Rush Hour 284, 316
Rushby, Margaret M. 72
Ryan, Pat 289

S

Saberton, Delanoy Rev 41, 47, 49, 77, 80, 167
Sale, A.B. 47
Salt, Clara (Swindells) 29, 63, 131, 353
Salt, George 25
Salt, James 11, 25, 29, 38, 59, 64, 351
Salt, John Thomas 4, 11, 14, 22, 60, 63
Salt, Mary Jane (Langslow) 4, 22, 63, 75, 104
Saville, Philip 291
Sayward, Mr & Mrs 74
Scala Cinema, Charlotte Street 253
Schaeffers, Willi 221
Schonell, F.J. Dr 164, 171
Schulman, Dr 28
Scientist Replies, The 292, 296, 302
Seager, George 260, 263, 279
Seed, Betty (Sister Tutor) 104
Sefton, Lord 176
Shaps, Cyril 326
Shaw, Alex 249
Shearer, Moira 283
Sheldon, Ralph 262
Shell Film Unit 264
Shelton, J.B. 37
Sheppard, H.J. 40, 93, 289
Shepperton Film Studios 354
Shipley, E.B. 40, 48, 93, 111, 144
Shirt, Miss (teacher) 21
Shore, C.B. 78, 92
Shreeve, Ron 84, 87, 103, 111,

132, 135, 153, 199, 210
Siddeley, John (Lord Kenilworth) 18
Sidebotham, Reverend 11, 28
Simpson, Christian 314
Singer, John 175
Six Characters in Search of an Author 342, 352
Slater, P. (Pip) 93, 103, 153
Smith, F.G. (Bish) 90
Smith, Hannah 18, 30, 68, 120
Smith, Miss (Headmistress) 32
Smith, Rueben 18, 30, 120
Song of Ceylon 264, 266, 267
Sopwith, Noreen 278
South Riding 246
Spencer Jones, Harold Sir 292
Spenser, Jeremy 267
Spider's Web, The 326
Spooner, G.W. 148, 210
Sports Night 300
Squires, Charles 314
Squires, Douglas 310, 316, 352
Stables, Eric 76, 86
Staff, Frank 236, 278
Stannard, Roy 310, 325
Stead, Ann 300
Stephenson, Alan 88
Stevenson, Hugh 271
Stoll, Oswald Sir 272
Stoll Theatre 272, 273
Stone, Alan 353
Stopes, Marie Dr 25
Stravinsky, Igor 279
Stringer, John 26, 46, 84, 98, 103, 119, 123, 135
Stringer, Tom 122
Stubbs, Una 315
Sullivan, Jack 343
Sumner, T.C. 78
Sunday Night at the London Palladium 306

Sweetest and Lowest 237

T

Tallents, Stephen Sir 250, 264
Tapp, William 177
Target for Tonight 257
Tattersall, A. 47, 52, 78, 87, 90
Taylor, Arthur 79
Taylor, Ben 7, 18, 19
Taylor, Bertha (Salt) 24, 28, 61, 64, 75, 100
Taylor, Caroline 7, 19, 131
Taylor, Celia M. 10, 328
Taylor, Dan 38, 79
Taylor, Donald (Crown FU) 248
Taylor, Ethel (Salt) 3, 61, 113, 120, 145, 196, 258, 269, 355
Taylor, George Henry 3, 61, 81, 119, 145, 160, 196, 258, 351, 354
Taylor, Jack 7
Taylor, Jack Jnr. 7
Taylor, John 7, 19, 202
Taylor, John (Crown FU) 249, 259
Taylor, John Henry 3, 21, 202
Taylor, Melanie A. 9, 328, 353
Taylor, Nellie (Thompson) 7
Taylor, Norma (Glaiman) 15, 229
Taylor, Sarah Jane (Manifold) 3, 20
Taylor, Stephen J.L. 15, 290, 328
Taylor-Jones, Sid 15
Taylor-Jones, Wylf 15
Tell Tale Heart 327
Terry, Richard Sir 75
Thackray, Catherine 133
Theme and Variations 278
This Week 52, 295, 300, 302, 306
This Wonderful World 253, 268
Thomas, J.Merlin 175
Thomas, Sgt (RAEC) 186, 192, 195
Thomson, Margaret 256
Thorndike, Sybil Dame 208
Thorpe, Caroline 295
Thorpe, Jeremy 292, 302
Timms, Alf 34
Todd, Alexander Sir 292
Toff, Benn 48, 216, 229, 270, 279, 297, 341
Tolemache, Bentley 166
Tomalin, Nicholas 117, 353
Tomalin, Susanna 353
Toumanova, Tamara 274, 279
Townsend, Charles 84
Trail, Mavis 315
Trygon Factor 354
Tudor, Anthony 315
Turrell, Jig 289
Tynan, Ken 256

U

Uddo, Chelsea 1, 9
Uddo, Frank 10
Uddo, Giuseppe 9
Uddo, Michael 9
Ulanova, Galina 62, 274
Uncle Harry 235
Urbont, Jacques 352

V

Valois, Ninette de Dame 231, 269
Van Eugen, Nora 102, 122
Vaughan, Dorothea 253
Vaughan, Frankie 315
Vaughan, Olwen 252
Vickers, Mick 247
Viking Film Studios 291
Volga Boatmen, The 62

W

Walker, Donald 110, 241
Walsh, Dermot 325

Walton, Kent 300, 304, 308, 311, 328
Ward, John 140
Ward, June 127
Warren, Hilary 41, 92
Wass, Capt 180
Waterman, Denis 326
Waterman, Peter 302
Waters, Barbara 101, 133
Watt, Harry 249
Way Ahead, The 257
Webb, E.A.A. 47, 50, 53, 78, 90
Weedon, Bert 315
Weissmuller, Johnnie 161
Western Approaches 257
Westmore, Michael 288, 302
Wheel, Mr (teacher) 73
White, D.J. 148, 172
White Horse Inn 229
Whitehouse, Grace 128
Whitehouse, Jack 128
Wilcox, Desmond 300
Wild, Eric 278
Wild, Irene 278, 282
Williams, LLoyd 288
Williams, Peter 278
Wilson, Barbara 53
Wilson, Peter 53

Winter Night 277
Winter, Robert 156, 167
Wisdom, Sydney 65
Witty, John 301
Woizikovsky, Leon 270
Wolfit, Donald Sir 76
Wood, Christine 101
Woodward, Mr (Caretaker) 28
Woodward, Sheila 28
Wooland, Norman 326
World in Action 251, 306
World of Plenty 264
Wright, Basil 258, 265
Wright, Belinda 272, 274
Wyatt, Joy 13, 122
Wyler, Richard 324

Y

Yardley, Mary 64
Yates, Michael 288
Yeomans, Mary 344
You Asked For It 308
Young, Muriel 301, 308
Younger Generation, The 316

Z

Zenkel, Prof 215, 229